PRAISE FO _____ ____ ___S'
(THAT WE SHOULD LEARN TO LOVE)
by IAN MOSS
selected from over 300 four star Amazon reviews

"What a wonderful book this is, the antidote to those endless lists of best-60s/70s/80s/all-time-rock/country/guitar-Beatles/Stones/ Queen/Floyd etc. albums you must hear before you go deaf!"

"We all like to believe we are broad minded and willing to give everything a chance, but any music fan has to face up to the fact that they incorporate prejudices and received wisdom into their judgements. This is a series of short chapters on records that are generally considered unhip but are recommended for re-evaluation. You won't agree with it all, but then I guess that is the point... I wish I had thought of writing this."

"More than 100 little reviews from a genuine music lover that covers quite a range from Style Council to David Essex and beyond. Does what a music book should do which is make you want to seek out the actual records."

"Not confined by genre, Ian includes soul, jazz and folk. Look forward to discovering more of these overlooked gems in this magnificent little book. Can we have a sequel please?"

THE ORIGINAL SOUNDTRACK
A LIFE THROUGH A THOUSAND 7" SINGLES
Volume I - 1970-79

IAN KEITH MOSS

EMPIRE PUBLICATIONS

EMPIRE PUBLICATIONS
1 Newton Street, Manchester M1 1HW
© Ian Moss 2022

ISBN: 978-1-909360-95-2

CONTENTS

FOREWORD

As years fly by, it's all too easy to leave friends behind in your wake – often not particularly by design. People change addresses, change habits, change telephone numbers… people change.

As I remember it, I first met Ian in a bar called the Cyprus Tavern on Princess Street in Manchester city centre, when I was a slightly bewildered seventeen-year old. I'd not long been a member of Mark E. Smith's band of art-terrorists known as The Fall. The band had a reputation for being stand-offish, even at this fledgling point. I was part of a holy trinity that rarely cross-pollinated with other members of the public, let alone (God forbid!) members of other bands.

Steve Hanley, Craig Scanlon and I were a shifty and furtive cabal; trust no-one, our unspoken motto. That was until we met an equally odd bunch of lads who collectively were a band called the Hamsters. They contained a drummer, Steve Middlehurst – Steve is no longer with us, but it is fair to say he was one of the most dangerous men I've met in my life; he was reckless and unpredictable… undeniably talented too. The two other Hamsters, Ian and Bob, were much more charming characters, who somehow managed to crack the tough nut that was Steve, Craig and myself. The fact that we considered the Hamsters to be the second-best group in Manchester did no harm at all in defrosting our icy exterior, and before too long we had their band regularly opening up for us.

Our friendship grew, and over the ensuing years it became apparent that Ian was one of a select few people (probably the *only* other person apart from Mark E. Smith) who could introduce me to music, new and old, with an extraordinarily high hit-rate. I thought I didn't like Led Zeppelin – in fact a Zeppelin allegiance was punishable by death within our circles – until one day Ian popped one of his faultless mix-tapes into the car cassette deck as we travelled. He played me 'When the Levee Breaks'; my bigotry went straight out of the car window and lay unloved on the hard-shoulder where, hopefully, it remains to this day. I remember vividly Ian extolling the virtues of a song by

Kevin Ayres called 'Lady Rachel'; I knew Kevin had been a part of the ACNE (Ayres/Cale/Nico/Eno) concerts and subsequent live album. I knew his only "hit", 'After the Show', but I had never really been tempted until my mate once again wiped the scales from my eyes. These are just two of many examples I could give…

Ian loves soul music; he loves reggae and dub; he has erected no walls when it comes to music. Crucially, he also has impeccable taste aligned to a social conscience. If you add to those qualities his eloquence and rampant enthusiasm, you have all the ingredients of a brilliant writer who can not only resurrect long-forgotten memories, but also send you off on a mission to discover some hitherto unknown pleasures… pardon the pun!

Marc Riley

BBC 6 Music DJ, musician in The Fall, Marc Riley and the Creepers, The Shirehorses and creator of 'Harry the Head' for *Oink!*

THE ORIGINAL SOUNDTRACK

VOLUME I - 1970-1979

1970

- The UK lowers the age of majority and voting age from 21 to 18
- The Beatles release their final album - *Let It Be*
- *Midnight Cowboy* wins the best picture award at the Oscars
- The Vietnam War spreads as the US invades Cambodia
- Four Ohio State University students are shot dead by the National Guard while protesting against war in Vietnam
- The Tories win the general election; Ted Heath becomes PM
- The third Isle of White Pop Festival features Jimi Hendrix, The Doors, The Who, Miles Davis and Leonard Cohen; 600,000 people attend
- Three airliners are hijacked and blown up by 'The Popular Front For The Liberation Of Palestine' in what is known as Black September
- Elvis Presley begins his first concert tour since 1958
- The first Glastonbury Festival is held featuring Tyrannosaurus Rex and Stackridge
- Cyclone Bhola kills 500,000 people in East Pakistan (now Bangladesh)
- The first march by The Gay Liberation Front takes place in London
- The North Tower of The World Trade Centre is completed; at 417 metres it is the world's tallest structure
- Joe Frazier becomes world heavyweight boxing champion beating Jimmy Ellis in 5 rounds
- Wilf McGuinness is sacked as manager by Manchester United, Everton win the league and Chelsea beat Leeds to win the FA Cup. Pelé's Brazil win the World Cup in Mexico.

NOTABLE BIRTHS

Beck; Melania Trump; Mariah Carey; River Phoenix; Matt Damon; Uma Thurman; Naomi Campbell; Jeff Magnum; Will Oldham

NOTABLE DEATHS

Jimi Hendrix; Janis Joplin; Baby Huey; Tammi Terrell; Darrell Banks; Slim Harpo; Bertrand Russell; Mark Rothko; Charles De Gaulle; Yukio Mishima; Sonny Liston

NOTABLE FILMS

El Topo; A Man Called Horse; Performance; Catch 22; M★A★S★H'; Zabriskie Point; Five Easy Pieces; Little Big Man

NOTABLE BOOKS

Bury My Heart at Wounded Knee – Dee Brown
The Female Eunuch – Germaine Greer
The Driver's Seat – Muriel Spark
I Know Why The Caged Bird Sings – Maya Angelou
A Pagan Place - Edna O'Brien
A Maze Of Death – Philip K Dick
Ripley Underground – Patricia Highsmith
The Atrocity Exhibition – JG Ballard
The Hand Reared Boy – Brian W Aldiss
Islands In The Stream – Ernest Hemingway

IN MUSIC

It's tempting to see 1970 as the dawning of a new decade and a new musical era but of course change isn't instantaneous; it tends to come slowly and the 70s wouldn't shake off the 60s for quite a while. Still, change was afoot and can be detected in the singles selected to represent this pivotal year.

The utopian hippy dream of peace and love had been unceremoniously trampled into the ground in December 1969 at what was the Rolling Stones attempt to stage an alternative West Coast version of the Woodstock festival at Altamont Speedway, close to San Francisco, where a security team of Hells Angels beat and bullied people throughout the day, including an onstage assault on Marty Balin of The Jefferson Airplane, before moving like a pack of wolves and stabbing to death black teenager Meredith Hunter as the Stones played in fear of their own lives. In truth, whilst the hippy sounds and ethos had been taken up in the UK by musicians, out on the street there was no mass presence of flower children beyond a few affluent, and therefore safe, outposts. The UK, despite rumours to the contrary and the perpetuation of the swinging Britain myth, hadn't moved much beyond post-war depression. Many major cities were filthy, dangerous hell holes and all across the country were harsh brutal neighbourhoods where the wearing of kaftans and love beads would have acted as a target on their wearers' backs. The dominant tribes in the U.K. were the Skinheads, who were a more violent, cut price descendant of the mid 60s Mods and the Greasers or Grebos, scruffy motorbike fixated Hells Angel wannabes whose forefathers had been the Mods enemies, the Rockers. Betwixt these were the long hairs, known as Freaks in the *International Times* reading metropolis, or here, in the grim conformist north, weirdos. There was little social interaction across these boundaries beyond meeting to fight each other and little cross over in musical taste. Lines in the sand were drawn and crossed at risk of ridicule and scorn or becoming isolated and ostracised, lost in a lonely no man's land.

Musical tastes were equally rigid; essentially Skinheads liked Soul and Reggae, a soundtrack to dance and fight to. Because of this affinity to black music this first incarnation of Skinheads, unlike the late 70s revivalists who were card carrying Neo Nazis, are viewed in a misty-eyed, sympathetic light as being anti–racist. This is largely untrue. Although there were some West Indian Skinheads in the gangs their presence was often tolerated only if they were handy with their fists and willing to be the butt of put downs disguised as jokes. It was tokenism rather than true acceptance; the odious sport of 'Paki Bashing' was originated by the original Skins, and as they packed football terraces, the sighting of the rare (in those times) species of black footballers were singled out for vile discriminatory abuse and pro-Enoch Powell sloganeering. Skinheads didn't like drugs or druggies, who they viewed as degenerates, but gallons of Watney's Red Barrel or Tetley's bitter was perfectly fine. Greasers liked Rock music and, as amplifiers got bigger and louder, they liked it even more. Give them a singer spouting puerile sexist tripe and a flashy guitar solo, they could headbang or engage in their bizarre thumbs in the belt loops tango, and they were, in the jargon of the day, 'like pigs in shit'. The Greasers too, incidentally, were every bit as stupidly bigoted and hostile to aliens as their shaven headed counterparts. Greaser recreation was enhanced by barbiturates, Newcastle Brown Ale and meat pies. The long hairs, easy targets for both the aforementioned groups, tended to have a kinder, more open-minded disposition. They read books by Solzhenitsyn and Carlos Castaneda, and dug folk and blues music to a degree, but mostly they were attracted to the burgeoning Progressive Rock scene that had mutated from the psychedelic 60s embers. They were known to sip Blue Nun wine and crème de menthe; their drugs of choice were hashish and LSD.

So much for the audience and onto the music, what, if anything, shaped it? What mutations were being undertaken? Certainly Soul music was noticeably changing and becoming more militant, embracing themes way beyond 'boy meets girl' or 'girl meets boy'. This was predominantly an urban music and America's black urban communities were underprivileged and oppressed. Soul increasingly spoke in terms of black pride and carried a civil rights message in the lyrics that was hard edged and unambiguous. To carry these messages, the music too became harder and funkier; sweet harmonies gave way to chanted choruses. Sly and the Family Stone and Curtis Mayfield led the way in this regard. The war in Vietnam was hugely unpopular amongst all creeds in the USA and singles by Creedence Clearwater Revival and Crosby, Stills, Nash and Young, as well as Motown's Temptations and Edwin Starr, address that concern head on. Reggae too provides a social commentary on conditions in Kingston, Jamaica and the Rasta faith was becoming ingrained into the music which moved away from Ska and Rocksteady towards what we recognise as a Reggae rhythm. DJ culture began to flourish as Toasters or Chanters gave live voiceovers to tracks played by the soundsystems creating a whole new style. There was still room as well for Symarip's blatant cash-in aimed at the British audience with 'Skinhead Moonstomp'.

We find guitar groups getting louder as a result of technology moving forward. In 1964, most guitar records sounded thin and weedy; here, 6 years later, Mott The Hoople, The Move and Black Sabbath are muscular and indeed heavy. These high volume sounds are contrasted by the singer/songwriters who enjoyed a huge surge in popularity due to the confessional nature of the material being written that struck a chord with people by revealing a sensitivity that had previously been unheard. As this style became more sophisticated and adult it moved beyond inane sing-a-longs or over-earnest naive protesting. It ceased to be communal music but something to wallow over in isolation, sat cross-legged in dingy bed-sitting rooms. Neil Young and James Taylor provided this kind of lifestyle soundtrack, illustrated by classic singles of the genre, while 60s teen star Cat Stevens completely reinvents himself as a mystical-sounding troubadour. The icons of the previous decade, including The Beatles, Simon and Garfunkel, Elvis Presley and Jimi Hendrix, provide masterpiece singles as reminders of their greatness, while voices who will shape and dominate the decade to come in the forms of T. Rex, The Carpenters, David Bowie, Status Quo and Bob Marley, are found flexing their musical muscles. The experimentation and unorthodox strangeness of Miles Davis, Captain Beefheart, Frank Zappa and Can is welcome, whilst the proto-punk MC5, Alice Cooper, The Stooges and Hawkwind are represented too, in what was a diverse and exciting opening year of the decade.

MY 1970

I was 12 years old when the year started and in my second year at the local comprehensive school which I detested. I'd gone to a tiny church school as an infant of less than 100 pupils and found the transition to a large school of over 1000 difficult as I was essentially a shy boy. I did not like many of my teachers or their style of teaching; information was hammered into us by rote with no regard to reason or context. Our comprehension was regarded as secondary to our ability to memorise the useless facts with which we were bombarded. I was a reasonably bright child and would raise my arm and ask questions that my teachers clearly found a chore to answer. I became disinterested and consequently my work suffered to the point where I came to be regarded as a problem child and seditious influence on my more malleable classmates. I needed stimulus and that came through football; as a player of good ability I could express myself with a ball at my feet. I also began to attend Manchester United games at Old Trafford and away games that were not too far: Liverpool, Everton, Burnley and Huddersfield were among the first places

I travelled to and through this wandering I began to develop an independent spirit.

Music was my other escape from the humdrum routines. Here I was very much left to my own devices. I was the eldest sibling so did not have music taste filtered down to me. My tastes were not inherited from my family as my parents were of a pre-rock 'n' roll generation and their fondness for Mario Lanza and Doris Day was not something I shared. Our first record player arrived; a turntable inside a little red box with built in speakers and my obsession began in earnest. My favourite aunt lent me some LPs including The Beatles *Oldies but Goldies* and the first Monkees album, which I loved. She asked what I wanted for my birthday; "an LP" I replied. "Who by?" she queried... and I answered "Bob Dylan". What bits of money I scraped together went on records; The Upsetters' 'Return of Django' was one and 'Liquidator' by Harry J. and the Allstars another. I attended my first concert choosing to go alone to fully savour the event; Desmond Decker and the Aces were billed as playing an over-18s event at Hyde Town Hall. Somehow I gained admission and skulked around in the shadows fearful of being challenged about my true age and ejected. After several hours a man in evening suit and bow tie appeared on stage and announced that Desmond Decker was unable to appear but chart act White Plains had been secured as a replacement act. The bulk of the audience were there to munch on chicken-in-a-basket and sip Liebfraumilch and were unconcerned by the announcement. One singer was as good as the next, seemed to be the general consensus. I, on the other hand, was already a more discerning punter and was pretty much heartbroken at what had transpired. I sped off home by Shank's pony without sampling the dubious delights of White Plains.

NOTES ON THE LAYOUT

The entries are laid out as followed:
A-SIDE
B-SIDE
ARTIST
RECORD LABEL
HIGHEST UK CHART POSITION
DOUBLE A SIDES ARE SPLIT WITH A '/'.

100
IN MEMORY OF A FREE
FESTIVAL PART 1
IN MEMORY OF A FREE
FESTIVAL PART 2
DAVID BOWIE
PHILLIPS
DID NOT CHART

In its original form this was a track on Bowie's 1969 album. Now chasing a follow up hit to 'Space Oddity', the record company encouraged him to re-record this song. The song itself celebrates a festival Bowie himself organised and performed at in the Municipal Recreation Ground in Beckenham in 1969 and has a wonderfully sunny vibe to it. This version is a lot more rock-infused than the gentle folk-album version and was notable for debuting new recruits Mick Ronson on guitar and Mick 'Woody' Woodmansey on drums.

99
AIN'T NO MOUNTAIN HIGH
ENOUGH
CAN'T IT WAIT UNTIL
TOMORROW
DIANA ROSS
TAMLA MOTOWN
06

Having left the Supremes at the height of their success, there was a lot at stake career-wise for Diana Ross and much to prove. Her first solo single "Reach Out And Touch Somebody's Hand" barely charted. Motown chief Berry Gordy was against releasing this track as a single with its gospel feel and spoken word passages but radio stations played it anyway and writer/producers Ashford and Simpson finally convinced the boss of its potential and were proved correct in their judgment.

98
INDIANA WANTS ME
LOVES YOUR NAME
R DEAN TAYLOR
RARE EARTH
02 (1971)

This record captivated me as a young boy, so cinematic was its scope and so vivid was its storytelling. Written from the point of view of a man chased down by the police, having murdered another man who has insulted his wife. As the dragnet moves in around him he pens his final goodbyes and, as police sirens wail and a voice over a bullhorn implores him to surrender himself, he steps out, presumably with gun raised, to be shot down and end his torment.

97
SKINHEAD MOONSTOMP
MUST CATCH A TRAIN
SYMARIP
TREASURE ISLE
58 (1980 reissue)

Symarip were a British-based pan-Afro/Caribbean band who sensed the potential in a record that would appeal to the burgeoning skinhead movement. And so, taking the melody of Derrick Herriots "Moon Hop" from 1969 and adding some Sam and Dave-style vocalising, they came up with this mini-classic. Gloriously dumb but irresistibly infectious, big in youth-clubs all over the UK, it finally charted a decade after its release on the wave of 'Two Tone' mania.

96

TOMORROW NIGHT
PLAY THE GAME
ATOMIC ROOSTER
B & C
11

Dark and menacing with a riff of great power, this thrilled me. Ex-Crazy World of Arthur Brown keyboardist, and Atomic Rooster main man Vincent Crane wrote this and I forever kept a watchful eye on his musical activities which took in with the likes of Peter Green and Dexy's Midnight Runners, before his sad death by his own hand in 1989.

95

I WANT TO TAKE YOU HIGHER
STAND
SLY AND THE FAMILY STONE
EPIC
DID NOT CHART

One of the greatest bands of all time, 'Higher' had been a glorious highlight of the Woodstock festival. Taken from 1969 album *Stand* this was up-tempo, hot and funky as hell, featuring a wonderful guitar part from Freddie Stone and vamping organ. This was a sensational single; it was covered spectacularly by Ike and Tina Turner as a competing single in their own signature style, which may explain why neither version charted.

94

LADY D'ARBANVILLE
FILL MY EYES
CAT STEVENS
ISLAND RECORDS
8

Having been successful over several years as a singles artist, Cat Stevens contracted tuberculosis and suffered a collapsed lung. While recuperating he took stock of his position as a musical artist. Not liking the direction he had been pushed into, of being a Carnaby Street-packaged orchestral popster, he threw off the shackles. This was his first single unveiling his new sound of simple acoustic folk with sparse arrangements. It was a beautifully bewitching love song with a dark undercurrent; the 'Lady D'Arbanville' invoked in the song is dead. This was a metaphorical comment on his relationship with model Patti D'Arbanville, a very public ending to their life together.

93

I GOT A THING, YOU GOT A THING, EVERYONE GOT A THING
FISH, CHIPS AND SWEAT
FUNKADELIC
WESTBOUND RECORDS
DID NOT CHART

From the first Funkadelic album, and therefore our introduction to this new form of 'cosmic funk', came this glorious single written by Clarence 'Fuzzy' Haskins, a long time band mate of George Clinton. Here the groove is snail-paced before, at its mid-point, the track kicks and picks up speed. We are at the start of Funkadelic's odyssey into sound here, but already in place are the slinky rhythms and the acid drenched guitars.

92

THUNDERBUCK RAM
YOU ARE ONE OF US
MOTT THE HOOPLE
ISLAND RECORDS
DID NOT CHART

Listening to this single, I'm hurtled backwards into the Manchester that I was discovering with huge excitement as a brand new teenager, walking around the late lamented New Brown Street before it was demolished to create room for the monstrous Arndale Centre, soaking up what passed for a bohemian atmosphere amongst the boutiques and late-hippy hangouts. There always seemed a sense of melancholia in the air and a struggling to make sense of what was going down between idealism, police harassment and the feeling that we were on the cusp of a change. All of that is contained for me in this murky sounding half-dirge penned by Mick Ralphs and produced by the legendary Guy Stevens. It's a scruffy record by a scruffy, down-on-their-luck band. What makes it great is that it is imbued with deep-pained soul and a street-level humanity.

91
SOUL SACRIFICE PART 1
SOUL SACRIFICE PART 2
SANTANA
CBS RECORDS
DID NOT CHART
The only band to play the Woodstock festival without a record to their name, Santana triumphed and this single was their set closer. Displaying their hybrid style of Latin rhythm with jazz-tinged soul, this single breaths fire with scorching solos by Carlos Santana over chattering congas and a superb utilisation of organ.

90
CRASH
DHOOP
FLOWER TRAVELLIN' BAND
WITH TERUMASA HINO
COLUMBIA
DID NOT CHART
Flower Travellin' Band are one of those select few 'important' bands, such as MC5 and the Stooges, who need to be checked out as forerunners of future sounds. Formed in Japan by Yuya Uchida after he returned from a trip to London spent with his friend John Lennon, who had introduced him to the music of Jimi Hendrix and Cream amongst others, this was their first single and it is an incredible piece. It starts with muffled noises that come together to form the main part of the song, a searing piece of riffage and urgent half-screamed vocals; free Jazz expressionist Yuya Uchida joins the fray providing a trumpet solo before the whole thing subsides into a lounge music outro. They don't make them like that anymore but, outside Flower Travellin' Band, they didn't make them like that back in 1970 either.

89
DOWN THE DUSTPIPE
FACE WITHOUT A SOUL
STATUS QUO
PYE RECORDS
12
"Down the dustbin with this one" chirped Radio 1 DJ Tony Blackburn; how wrong he was. This was the pivotal point in Quo's career. It not only put them back in the charts after several years absence but it was also the first time they utilised the 'boogie shuffle' which became their calling card. Featuring harmonica playing roadie Bob Young (he would go on to become a key songwriter for the band) this single was an absolute blast and a new beginning for one of the great British bands.

88
WILD WORLD
BE AWARE
JIMMY CLIFF
ISLAND
8

Sharing the same record label, Jimmy Cliff was played a demo of Wild World, a song by Cat Stevens. He was a lot keener on it than the composer and spoke to him on the telephone to express his admiration for the song. Stevens was delighted and offered the song to Cliff along with his services as producer. Into the studio they went, with Doris Troy providing backing vocals, and cut the track in a baroque Reggae style with Cliff proving to be a superb interpreter of his friend's work. The sentiments of the song provoked the ire of some feminist commentators who thought it displayed a patronising sexist message. Stevens claimed it was in fact a message to himself to wise up and be less naive as his career was rebooted from the ashes of his 60s pop stardom.

87
MEMO FROM TURNER
NATURAL MAGIC
MICK JAGGER
DECCA
32

Mick Jagger's first and only worthwhile solo single was this gem taken from the Donald Cammell film classic *Performance* where Jagger, in the lead role, played Turner, a washed up Rock Star. This song was cut in different versions by the Rolling Stones and Traffic but this single release features, amongst others, Ry Cooper on guitar and Randy Newman on piano, along with a stellar vocal from Jagger that inhabits all the darkness and drama of the song. Special mention must go to Ry Cooder's magnificent 'Natural Magic' which is a superb B-side track.

86
HURRY UP SUNDOWN
MIRROR OF ILLUSION
HAWKWIND
LIBERTY
DID NOT CHART

The first Hawkwind single was this edited version of one of the stand-out tracks from their debut album. For anyone used to the sonic attack incorporated by the band, and for which they are rightly associated, this single with prominent acoustic guitars high in the mix may come as a surprise. Listen closer though and the drums are as propulsive as ever with the bass kept to a minimum so as not to clash. No wailing sax from Nik Turner either but there is effective use of the harmonica. All-in-all this was a highly promising start to a fascinating stellar journey with these space rock desperadoes.

85
PATCHES
SAY IT ONE MORE TIME
CLARENCE CARTER
ATLANTIC
2

Written by General Johnson and Ron Dunbar, but such was the roll they were on, Chairman of the Board felt this was no more than B-side material and it duly appeared on the flip of their 'Everything is Tuesday' single. Legendary producer Rick Hall had a higher regard for the song and persuaded blind blues singer Clarence Carter to imbue the song with such harsh subject matter with real emotion. They cut the single at

Fame studios in Muscle Shoals with a minimalist spare backing, allowing Carter to produce a powerful and heartbreaking vocal that painted a vivid picture of the hardships of poor black sharecroppers in the Deep South.

84
WHOLE LOTTA LOVE
BOOM BOOM
CCS
RAK
13
CCS, or to give them their un-abbreviated title, the Collective Consciousness Society, were a large ensemble led by blues guitarist and vocalist Alexis Korner. This was their debut single and was a bold version of the Willie Dixon written classic, popularised by Led Zeppelin. It sounded remarkable, and delivered a freshness to the material becoming the iconic theme music for the BBCs flagship pop program *Top of the Pops*.

83
RIVERS OF BABYLON
RIVERS OF BABYLON VERSION (BEVERLEY ALL STARS)
THE MELODIANS
SUMMIT
DID NOT CHART
This was a testament to the belief in the Rastafarian faith, written and recorded by Brent Dowe and Trevor McNaughton, based on the biblical psalm 137. The song was banned by the Jamaican government who considered its message inflammatory and subversive. In 1972 it was included on the soundtrack to the hit film *The Harder They Come* and became popular; so popular that in 1978 a completely sanitised version

by German hit makers Boney M topped the charts and it remains one of the top 10 highest-selling singles of all time.

82
ARCHANGELS AND THUNDERBIRDS
EXCERPT FROM SOAP SHOP ROCK
AMON DUUL ii
LIBERTY
DID NOT CHART
Taken from their seminal album *Yeti*, this was a brooding, riff-heavy piece featuring a doomy atmospheric vocal from female singer Renate. Totally un-American sounding, which in 1970 was a pretty revolutionary concept.

81
OHIO
FIND THE COST OF FREEDOM
CROSBY, STILLS, NASH AND YOUNG
ATLANTIC
DID NOT CHART
Written by Neil Young in horror and outrage at the shooting of four peace-protesting students by National Guardsmen at Kent State University and rush released as a piece of reportage. This record pulls no punches; it is straight to the point and completely unambiguous. It works on every level – the central riff is captivating and acts as a clarion call of opposition to the murderous authorities. Neil Young's unadorned lead vocal is raw and vivid while the anguish in David Crosby's voice as he calls out 'How many more?' is so emotional that, half a century on, it is still heart-wrenching.

80
EXUMA, THE OBEAH MAN
YOU DON'T KNOW WHAT'S
GOING ON
EXUMA
MERCURY RECORDS
DID NOT CHART

Exuma was the alias of one MacFarlane Gregory Anthony Mackey, a Bahamian musician whose free-wheeling style could not be pinned down and placed within a single genre. It contained carnival music, African traditional fare, reggae and folk along with much more. This single opens with the sounds of insects and toads croaking before acoustic guitar, drums and whistles enter and Exuma begins his tale which is akin to a ju-ju Bo Diddley, weaving his magic and casting his spells. This is a truly marvellous record.

79
WHEN I'M DEAD AND GONE
LAZY AFTERNOON
McGUINNESS FLINT
CAPITAL
2

Here we have a mandolin-led stomping sing-a-long classic written by band members Gallagher and Lyle who would, later in the decade, enjoy much success after departing McGuinness Flint. The lyric was based around the short life of blues legend Robert Johnson. Despite the subject matter, the song is not at all maudlin but rather a celebration of living life to the full and having no regrets.

78
ALL RIGHT NOW
MOUTHFUL OF GRASS
FREE
ISLAND RECORDS
2

Written largely by 17-year old bass player Andy Fraser, this catapulted Free onto the upper echelons of the singles charts and into national consciousness. It was an air-guitar classic with a memorable chorus and was inescapable as it blasted out of transistor radios. If over-familiarity has now deadened its charms for many people, I'm happy to report that is not the case for me and on hearing the opening chord of this I am jolted and electrified, and as excited now as I was then by this great record.

77
TRAVELIN' BAND/
WHO'LL STOP THE RAIN
CREEDENCE CLEARWATER
REVIVAL
FANTASY
8

Briefly Creedence were undoubtedly the number one rock band on earth, as evidenced here on this magnificent release. 'Travelin' Band' is a Little Richard inspired 'rock & roller' about life as a touring band that seriously kicks up a storm. 'Who'll Stop The Rain' on the other hand is poignant and reflective, alluding at different points to the war in Vietnam and the Woodstock festival.

76
PEACHES EN REGALIA
LITTLE UMBRELLAS
FRANK ZAPPA
BIZARRE
DID NOT CHART

Frank Zappa had recently broken up

his band, The Mothers Of Invention, and this single was a left-turn from that band's satirical style, being an instrumental jazz fusion piece. It is beautifully written and beautifully performed on a variety of brass and woodwind instruments alongside keyboards and the intriguingly named 'octave bass'.

75
THE THRILL IS GONE
YOU'RE MEAN
BB KING
ABC RECORDS
DID NOT CHART
BB King was an exquisite guitar player of great taste with a plaintive, soulful voice, and this recording of the 1950s standard became the definitive version. The song about breaking free from a failing relationship plays out over a generally sparse, jazz-tinged backing and the verses are intercut by King's 'crying' guitar; it's emotional.

74
OCTOBER 26
COLD STONE
PRETTY THINGS
HARVEST RECORDS
DID NOT CHART
Who could not love the Pretty Things? Perennial underdogs who always faced an uphill battle for acceptance, in the 1960s they had been everything The Rolling Stones had pretended to be. In 1969 they had delivered their 'rock opera', *SF Sorrow*, only for it to be ignored in the wake of The Who's opus *Tommy*. Still, they continually made wonderful records and this is a gently psychedelic delight with a twist, perhaps a eulogy to the death of the hippy dream. It is an agonised crawl, wistful and reflective but, as always

with the 'Pretties', carrying an edge of menace too.

73
HELLO HELLO
IF I COULD DO IT ALL OVER AGAIN, I'D DO IT ALL OVER YOU
CARAVAN
DECCA
DID NOT CHART
Mainstays of what became known as the Canterbury scene, a collection of art-bands with jazz leanings who usually were blessed with a spirit of irreverence and anarchy that made them a joy to listen to, this single was plucked off their second album which took its title from this single's B-side, which was in turn a borrowing of a phrase used by Spike Milligan (though Bob Dylan has been suggested as an alternative source). The single earned them an appearance on *Top of the Pops*, which was almost a guarantee of some chart action. Alas, the nation's youth presumably found Caravan's appealing oddness a tad too much for their conservative tastes and the record didn't even graze the lower echelons of the hit parade.

72
THE PRETTIEST STAR
CONVERSATION PIECE
DAVID BOWIE
PHILLIPS
DID NOT CHART
Apparently written for his girlfriend, soon to be wife, Angie and used as part of his proposal to her, this was the follow-up single to his huge selling 'Space Oddity', and despite its obvious commerciality and the presence of soon to be superstar Marc Bolan on guitar, this stab at

success reputedly recorded sales of less than 800. Possibly the rivalry that ensued between Bowie and Bolan was fuelled by the remark made by Bolan's wife June, directly to Bowie, that "Marc's too good for you to be playing on this record". Ouch!

71
WHO DO YOU LOVE
WALKING DOWN THE
HIGHWAY
JUICY LUCY
VERTIGO
14
The word 'rollicking' is defined as 'exuberantly lively and amusing' and it perfectly sums up this high-powered, speedy romp through this Bo Diddley classic. It is hard rocking, bluesy and ballsy, and a defiant spit-in-your-eye statement of pre-punk bad attitude.

70
KNOW WHO YOU ARE
DAPPLE ROSE
SLADE
POLYDOR
DID NOT CHART
Sporting a skinhead that was meant to help them gain a higher profile, but which in truth simply made them mistrusted pariahs, this was taken from the album *Play it Loud*. It was the stand-out track, displaying dynamics ranging from sweetly melodic to all out frontal assault. Slade sounded intense, they sounded like they meant it, they sounded, in short, like the MC5 supplanted from Detroit to Wolverhampton. This should have been the record that broke them into the big time – but it wasn't. The wait continued...

69
WAKE THE TOWN
BIG BOY AND TEACHER
HUGH ROY
DUKE REID
DID NOT CHART
This was U Roy's first Jamaican hit and we still feel its influence half a century later in every utterance of rap spat out from Brooklyn to Brixton. The record was initiated when John Holt attended a sound system dance that U Roy was DJ-ing, demonstrating his talk-over style as he spun the discs. He persuaded Duke Reid to record U Roy talking over some of the Treasure Island label's classic rocksteady rhythms. Wake the Town then introduced the world to the concept of 'toasting' which, as we know, in turn morphed into 'rapping'. That is the background to this record, but most important was the way it sounded which was thrilling and revolutionary with U Roy gleefully letting rip over the groove, it remains a magnificent record.

68
MAMA TOLD ME NOT TO
COME
ROCK 'N' ROLL WIDOW
THREE DOG NIGHT
DUNHILL
42
This was a typically humorous and superbly written song from the pen of Randy Newman, composed for ex-Animals front-man Eric Burdon's first solo album in 1966. In 1970, Newman included his own version on his album *12 Songs*, in an R&B style. Three Dog Night took the song and introduced the funk element into their recording. Also, singer Cory Wells approached the song in a theatrical way, performing certain

lines in an exaggerated, astonished fashion as he recounts the tale of a straight-laced youth at a party where, to his horror, marijuana and whiskey are prevalent. He is uncomfortable in the extreme, hence "Mama told me not to come, that ain't the way to have fun, son".

67
NEANDERTHAL MAN
YOU DIDN'T LIKE IT BECAUSE YOU DIDN'T THINK OF IT
HOTLEGS
PHILLIPS RECORDS
2

Ex-Mindbender Eric Stewart, hit writer Graham Gouldman and Dakota's road manager Peter Tattersall put their money together and, in 1969, purchased a recording studio in Stockport that they named Strawberry. Gouldman's long-time friends Lol Creme and Kevin Godley were invited into the fold as partners and musical collaborators. Neanderthal Man was created by the trio of Stewart, Godley and Creme (Gouldman was in the USA) as they dabbled with the possibilities offered by newly installed studio equipment. The song was a conceptually brilliant piece and great fun, with a chanted chorus, simple acoustic guitar and loud rumbling drums. It was a huge hit. They tried other novelty singles and thankfully, in view of how it may have affected their trajectory, none of them became hits. The musicians licked their wounds, re-thought their strategy and returned as 10cc.

66
COME AWAY MELINDA
UNIDENTIFIED FLYING OBJECT
UFO
BEACON
DID NOT CHART

Before becoming a horrible, stodgy, heavy rock band, UFO had been a much more interesting, though far more unsuccessful proposition, playing psych-inflected space rock. This came from their first album, *UFO 1*. It is an anti-war song, originally recorded by Harry Belafonte. Here it is taken as a stumbling blues with an overwrought vocal reflecting the song content before improbably lurching into an extended guitar workout and finally the sound of gunshots; wonderful stuff.

65
NO MATTER WHAT
BETTER DAYS
BADFINGER
APPLE
5

The Paul McCartney written 'Come and Get It' (probably the best unreleased Beatles song) had propelled Badfinger into the charts all over the world in 1969. A gift like that can prove to be a poisoned chalice unless you have the talent to follow it up. Badfinger, thankfully, had songwriting ability in spades as well as superb musicality and harmonies. 'No Matter What' is a glorious pop record that glistens and shimmers. It showcased the band superbly and set the template for the likes of Cheap Trick, the Raspberries and Big Star.

64
BUTTERFLY DANCE
"PUIS-JE"
KEVIN AYRES
HARVEST
DID NOT CHART

Kevin Ayres was someone I followed avidly throughout the 70s and his music still means much to me. Here he is backed by his fabulously inventive band of the period The Whole World including, on bass, 17-year old future superstar Mike Oldfield. There are more ideas thrown into this quite magical four minutes than many acts conjure in a career. As if to show both his versatility and the extent of his talent, Ayres places a beautiful French-language version of his languid melodic gem 'May I' on the flip-side of this exquisite 7-inches of aural pleasure.

63
IF NOT FOR YOU
NEW MORNING
BOB DYLAN
CBS
DID NOT CHART

This, though quite slight and without the intricate word play its author is famed for, is a beautiful love song with a lilting, engaging melody that bewilderingly did little sales business in this form. It was, a year later, a hit for Olivia Newton-John and appeared on George Harrison's huge album success *All Things Must Pass*, Harrison having played on the original recording of the song with Dylan. Dylan apparently liked the song well enough as it was frequently played in live performances.

62
BY THE LIGHT OF THE
MAGICAL MOON
FIND A LITTLE WOOD
TYRANNOSAURUS REX
REGAL ZONOPHONE
DID NOT CHART

Marc Bolan's Tyrannosaurus Rex years were characterised by their gossamer thin tales of mystical enchantment; quite magical in their own way but with a very limited appeal. The question for Bolan, I suppose, was whether to stay within the comfort of his cult status or go for the stardom which this ambitious ex-Mod had patently always craved. This was a turning point, taken from the fourth album *A Beard of Stars*, where the troublesome Steve Took was replaced by the prettier and more malleable Micky Finn as Marc's bongo bashing foil. Electric guitars replaced the gently plucked acoustics of yore. Lyrics, though still bafflingly obscure, became shortened and much less verbose. This single then shows Marc at the half-way stage in his transformation from Tolkienesque troubadour to Electric Warrior. It is not quite there, but greatness is only a heartbeat away.

61
SUPERBAD PARTS 1 & 2
SUPERBAD PART 3
JAMES BROWN
KING
DID NOT CHART

The self-styled Soul Brother Number 1 had a tumultuous time of it in 1970, losing the majority of his band, the Famous Flames, and replacing them with members of an unknown act called the Pacemakers, including bass genius 'Bootsy' Collins and his guitar playing brother 'Catfish'. If anything these changes freshened things up and musically James Brown in 1970 was as relevant as ever. 'Superbad' is lithe, supple funk of the highest order, celebratory in mood and in JBs vocal exhortations and squeals, with a lovely nod to John Coltrane thrown in for good measure amongst one of the numerous, quite magnificent, horn breaks.

60
WE GOTTA GET YOU A
WOMAN
BABY LET'S SWING/THE LAST
THING YOU SAID/DON'T TIE
MY HANDS
TODD RUNDGREN
BEARSVILLE
DID NOT CHART

Some might choose to criticise Rundgren's depiction of women; others may choose to interpret the song as a glorification of them; you decide. What no-one could deny was this was a ridiculously infectious concoction of superb musicality and displayed a heart-warming concern for the plight of another.

59
BLACK NIGHT
SPEED KING
DEEP PURPLE
HARVEST
2

Deep Purple were a deeply silly and pretentious band. Their 'Concerto for Group and Orchestra' for instance, was an absolute nonsense and barely listened to without inducing a coma brought on by boredom. They pulled in separate directions and the individual members, by all accounts, hated each other. And yet, when they settled down to do something simple (even if they thought it beneath

them) they came up with some spectacular results. This stand-alone single is evidence of that. A brutal riff, nonsense lyrics that are screamed hysterically, a guitar solo followed by a high-powered organ interlude – great fun and perfect for the long-hairs to 'freak out' to. Bingo! It was a classic of the age.

58
SOUL SHAKEDOWN PARTY
VERSION
THE WAILERS
TROJAN
DID NOT CHART

The Wailers were at the height of their considerable powers during this period, though not all in the garden was rosy. Cracks were appearing between the three friends and partners, and their relationship with producer Leslie Kong was rapidly souring – Bunny Wailer going as far as to place a curse upon him. You wouldn't know that though from listening to this glorious slice of vinyl which transports you to a carefree and happening party, where life is lived in fine style and celebrated accordingly.

57
MALNUTRITION
SEVEN DAY LOVER
JAMES FOUNTAIN
PEACH TREE
DID NOT CHART

I know next to nothing about James Fountain, the gritty-voiced singer on this record. He released a few singles between 1969 and 1971 that did little in terms of sales. This was written, produced and released by William Bell (of 'You Don't Miss Your Water' and 'Private Number' fame) on his tiny Peach Tree label in Atlanta, Georgia and presumably sold next to no copies. The A-side, in truth, is no more than fair but on the B-side there was magic; a wonderful piano-led dancer that James Fountain's vocal bestrides magisterially. A single copy found its way into the clutches of Northern Soul DJ Ian Levine and it became so highly desirable that the next copy that appeared sold for a whopping £500 in 1975. Re-issued several times after that, allowing we mortals with shallower pockets to own a copy, this is Northern Soul gold.

56
APEMAN
RATS
THE KINKS
PYE
5
The pen of Raymond Douglas Davies scribbled gem upon gem in the 1960s, and in the early 70s the run continued unabated. This cry for sanity from the midst of the increasingly industrialised and mechanical urban landscape was as humorous as it was pointed and sharply observed. Never has swinging between trees in the jungle sounded quite so appealing, and what a glorious release from the mundane it was, to bellow along to the chorus and proudly proclaim "I am an Apeman". Brother Dave wrote the singles flip, Rats, which is an incendiary guitar tear up with a vocal displaying contempt for music-biz movers and shakers of low moral substance. It is wonderful and required listening too.

55
IF THERE'S A HELL BELOW WE'RE ALL GONNA GO
THE MAKINGS OF YOU
CURTIS MAYFIELD
BUDDAH
DID NOT CHART
One of the most frighteningly apocalyptic records I've ever heard; I still remember being absolutely stunned hearing this for the first time. Distorted guitars and bass, echoing vocals and then a scream open up the record before a mix of strings, wah-wah guitar and heavy fuzz-bass take us into the song proper that rides on a rhythm of Latin percussion. Curtis described it as "a warning regarding the state of race-relations and the tempest growing within America's inner cities". He pulled no punches here in what was highly experimental, complex music that was the aural equivalent of a coming storm.

54
I'M WITH YOU
ROBERT MONTGOMERY
LOVE
ELEKTRA
DID NOT CHART
Love were largely written off after the break-up of the original band, which seems ludicrous considering the undisputed talent of Arthur Lee who remained *in situ*. The new band were a harder rocking outfit than the first incarnation, but this glorious single harks back to the celebrated sound of yore. Flamenco-style guitar opens proceedings; Lee's vocals are as cool and assured as ever. The song is slippery, it changes shape constantly but never loses its momentum; it is spellbinding. And on the other side of the record there was no decline in quality; "Robert Montgomery"

being one of the finest tracks ever recorded by this iconic outfit.

53
HAD ME A REAL GOOD TIME
REAR WHEEL SKID
THE FACES
WARNER BROTHERS
DID NOT CHART

The Small Faces lost singer/guitarist Steve Marriott in 1969. His replacements came in the form of Jeff Beck Group refugees Ronnie Wood and Rod Stewart. The chemistry between them was there from the off and they were hugely charismatic, playing a music that linked the good-time spirit of the music hall with a potent brew of swaggering blues and rock & roll. They should have been irresistible... but they weren't. In fact, they were barely visible to the public at large. This single, a scorcher, a raver, a mover, was superb. It displayed all the bands rakish 'don't give a monkeys' charm. The music lurched wonderfully, propelled by alcohol fumes, and Rod Stewart rasped cheerfully and defiantly. I was hooked.

52
THE STEALER
LYING IN THE SUNSHINE
FREE
ISLAND
DID NOT CHART

Following the mega-success of 'Alright Now' and its attendant album, Free were quickly back in the studio to record *Highway*, a brand new album that would surely consolidate their position. They produced a much more reflective piece of work and it sold poorly. The single though, would prove to be a winner, they must have imagined. Going against the record company's wishes, the band insisted on issuing 'The Stealer' which was the albums killer track. It absolutely rocked and went down extremely well when played live. It was catchy and memorable, perfect pop/rock in fact, that simply couldn't fail... It bombed, disappeared without trace. The pressure on the extremely young group began to tell. It was the beginning of the end of their story.

51
STILL WATER (LOVE)
STILL WATER (PEACE)
THE FOUR TOPS
TAMLA MOTOWN
10

After a period in the doldrums, the Four Tops returned to sparkling form with this song written for them by Smokey Robinson and Frank Wilson, and featuring a beautiful guitar part played by Marv Tarplin of the Miracles. This song was a world away from the bold and boisterous hits the Tops had enjoyed in the 1960s; it was slow and gentle, almost hymn-like, and the lead vocal from Levi Stubbs was an aching masterclass in singing simply, but phrasing the words to their best advantage. This was elegance and class epitomised.

50
IN THE SUMMERTIME
MIGHTY MAN
MUNGO JERRY
DAWN
1

Out of the blue came this single which became the sound of the summer. This good-time anthem was inescapable. It was utterly contagious and the fact that it came from a hippy jugband named after a poem by TS Eliot didn't seem in the least peculiar.

Briefly, Mungo Jerry-mania was on us and in 1970 nobody questioned whether the lyrics were politically correct or not. They weren't meant to be offensive and nobody took offence; they captured the carefree attitude of the time, although in the here-and-now they are a trifle anachronistic.

49
SOLDIER
ECCENTRIC MAN
GROUNDHOGS
LIBERTY
DID NOT CHART

Set in the trenches with certain death imminent, the soldier is being told to look on his foes 'not as men but as enemies of the King' and warned that to desert will mean death by firing squad. Groundhogs pulled no punches and were one of the truly essential acts to listen to and see perform. They could be fabulously intense players of hard, fast, dense rhythmic music but 'Soldier' displayed a more nuanced side of the band.

48
APACHE DROPOUT
FREEDOM
EDGAR BROUGHTON BAND
HARVEST
33

This inspired combination of the Shadows 'Apache' and Captain Beefheart's 'Dropout Boogie' put these Black Country freaks into the hit parade for the second time in 1970 (following 'Out Demons Out' which reached number 39). Sadly, that was as good as it ever got for the Broughtons in terms of chart success. It did, though, turn me into a lifelong fan.

47
EXPRESS YOURSELF
LIVING ON BORROWED TIME
CHARLES WRIGHT AND
THE WATTS 103RD STREET
RHYTHM BAND
WARNER BROTHERS
12

Sassy strutting funk of the highest order, an uplifting urging of social empowerment, sung with nonchalant ease over a guitar groove and an exceptional horn arrangement, make this an undeniably joyous experience for one's ears. There was a coolness about how loose limbed this felt, and its relative restraint, which made it hypnotic and added a touch of gravitas to its message that reflected the growing move towards black pride.

46
IN MY CHAIR
GERDUNDULA
STATUS QUO
PYE
21

After a few years absence from their psychedelic period hits, Quo re-emerged in 1970 with Down the Dustpipe, an outside written blues shuffle; it was a fine record. This was the follow-up and was even better. Written by Francis Rossi and Bob Young, it was again blues-based but contained a killer guitar hook so hypnotic that I've never shaken it out of my head. It contains an absolute genius B-side too. In 1971, Quo would be the first band of many thousands I would see play live. They were, of course, magnificent.

45
IN A BROKEN DREAM
DOIN' FINE
PYTHON LEE JACKSON
YOUNGBLOOD
3 (*charted on re-release 1972*)

Python Lee Jackson were an Australian group who turned up in the U.K. seeking fame and fortune. They began to record an album but struggled with the vocals on what was easily their best number. The pre-fame Rod Stewart was hired for the price of some carpeting for his car and delivered a scorching vocal for them. The guitar-line soared and was full of fire; all-in-all they had created a mini masterpiece. It predictably sank like a stone, and equally predictable became one after Maggie May had made Rod Stewart a star.

44
SMALL AXE
DOWN THE ROAD
THE WAILERS
UPSETTER
DID NOT CHART .

The Wailers released fourteen singles in 1970 alone. This was perhaps the best; written by Bob Marley and producer Lee Perry, who filled the track with a sense of mighty dread, this took seditious aim at the twin powers of the Jamaican recording industry, Duke Reid and Coxone Dodd. They were the 'big tree' and the musicians were the 'small axe' which was being sharpened to cut them down.

43
I CAN'T GET NEXT TO YOU
RIDE SALLY RIDE
AL GREEN
HI
DID NOT CHART

Al Green, who would go on to be one of the most significant figures of 70s music, was two years into his tenure with producer Willie Mitchell, as important to Green as George Martin had been to the Beatles. Nothing had quite clicked with the public when they took this up-tempo Temptations hit and turned it on its head. They slowed it right down and dispensed with the harmonies, instead letting Green's sensational voice do all the work in tremendous fashion, as he wound up the tension of the piece in a pleading, passionate performance of gospel-tinged soul. The UK public ignored it, but Green had an American hit to ignite his career.

42
THE WEAVER'S ANSWER
STRANGE BAND/HUNG UP
DOWN
FAMILY
REPRISE
11

Family were a band who couldn't be pigeon-holed. Their music contained elements of jazz, rock & roll and psychedelia... with a psychotic edge to it. They also had Roger Chapman on vocals, a man who frequently sounded as if he gargled broken glass and had a demented stage presence. I loved them and was awed by their music. This single wrapped all they were into a perfect package that still retains its wow factor.

41
THE HUNTER
BOLD SOUL SISTER
IKE AND TINA TURNER
HARVEST
DID NOT CHART

Here is where to look if you need some dirty, funky blues in your life. Ike and Tina at the peak of their powers covering Albert King's dangerous sounding blues, with the renowned guitar slinger guesting to fine effect, playing notes that sound like shards of glass splintering around you. Meanwhile, Tina delivers one of her most devastating performances, totally in control of the song with her power turned to maximum whilst challenging the assumed gender roles of hunter and hunted.

40
SHAKIN' STREET
THE AMERICAN RUSE
MC5
ATLANTIC
DID NOT CHART

More noted for their revolutionary zeal and twin lead-guitar attack than having a pop music sensibility, this is a fairly untypical MC5 song culled from their second album *Back in the USA*. Here the song has a simple utopian message; namely that 'the kids should be able to come together, under the umbrella of rock 'n' roll, and be allowed to do their thing'. Lead vocalist Rob Tyner hands the microphone over to guitarist Fred 'Sonic' Smith, whose untutored voice is perfect for this song, which is closer in style to the chiming sound of The Byrds than the out-there, free-expression of Sun Ra.

39
BALL OF CONFUSION (THAT'S WHAT THE WORLD IS TODAY)
IT'S SUMMER
THE TEMPTATIONS
TAMLA MOTOWN
7

From the pen of Barrett Strong and producer Norman Whitfield came this slice of powerful social commentary. Strongly influenced, soundwise, by the likes of Sly and the Family Stone and Jimi Hendrix, this was a most un-Motown record. The lyric attacks the war in Vietnam and President Richard Nixon, and also addresses a multitude of the issues of the day, suggesting the world is in chaos, but everyone would sooner ignore the problems – "and the band plays on" is a repeated phrase to illustrate the point. The Temptations weave the lyrics between the five vocalists, which adds to the feeling of the world in chaos.

38
RAG MAMA RAG
THE UNFAITHFUL SERVANT
THE BAND
CAPITOL RECORDS
16

The Band were capable of grace and beauty in their music, but this song benefits from the ramshackle nature of the performance. As a song it amounts to almost nothing, and yet the atmosphere it creates helps paint a bawdy, raucous night in some saloon of ill repute. It is a boozy, bruised ragtime, bashed out on fiddle and upright piano and sung with perplexed wonderment by Levon Helm, throwing himself into the role of ill-treated beau.

37
GIVE ME JUST A LITTLE MORE TIME
SINCE THE DAYS OF PIGTAILS AND FAIRYTALES
CHAIRMAN OF THE BOARD
INVICTUS
3

The writing trio of Holland, Dozier & Holland quit Motown in dispute over pay-packets they felt were not adequate reward for the amazing string of hits they provided the label. They set up their own company, put together their flagship act, Chairman of the Board, for whom they wrote and produced this debut single, along with Ron Dunbar using the pseudonym Edythe Wayne, due to a pending lawsuit from Motown. They cheekily, albeit wisely, recruited Motown's uncredited musicians the Funk Brothers, who shared their grievance about pay. They served up a typically tight-as-a-nut track for Chairman of the Board to sing over, and lead vocalist General Johnson produced an electrifying performance, full of twitches and hiccups, squeals and yelps, that conspired to make this one of the most exciting records heard in a long time.

36
WAR
HE WHO PICKS A ROSE
EDWIN STARR
TAMLA MOTOWN
3

Penned by Norman Whitfield and Barrett Strong, and recorded by the Temptations for their *Psychedelic Shack* album, demand grew for a single release, but Motown and their biggest selling artists, the Temptations, feared that such a controversial anti-war song in the time of the Vietnam War might prove damaging to their career. Whitfield made entreaties to label boss Berry Gordy, who refused to release the Temptations track, but agreed one of the label's lesser artists could re-record the song as a single; enter Edwin Starr. Edwin had been the biggest act on Ric-Tic Records, a Detroit label Motown had purchased in 1968 to kill off competition. At Motown he found he was fed the song-writing scraps and consequently his career was compromised. He jumped at the chance to record 'War' and so Whitfield built a bigger, louder, more dramatic monster of a track to suit Starr's 'James Brown' type voice. Starr seized the moment and let rip, pouring his heart into the track. This ended up more than a pop single; it became a statement and a cry for peace.

35
(THEY LONG TO BE) CLOSE TO YOU
I KEPT ON LOVING YOU
THE CARPENTERS
A&M
6

The brother and sister duo were never going to be considered cool. They were outwardly wholesome and aspired to make sweet, but sophisticated, pop records; they achieved that beyond anyone's wildest dreams. Piano-playing brother, it turned out, was a musical genius and a brilliant arranger. Drumming-sister Karen, meanwhile, had a one-in-ten-million voice that floored everyone who heard her. On record she sounds as if she is in the room with the listener, such was the intimacy of her performance. All they needed was the right song; Burt Bacharach provided this. It was their breakout hit, with many more to follow.

34
BIG WHITE CLOUD
GIDEON'S BIBLE
JOHN CALE
COLUMBIA
DID NOT CHART

After being sacked from the Velvet Underground, John Cale took his time launching his solo career with the low-key album *Vintage Violence*; the centrepiece was this single. Big White Cloud was a meditative piece of dream pop; strings float like clouds over a country-style backing and Cale becomes one with the sea, the sky and the earth. Bonkers, yes, but gorgeous and unique too.

33
THE SEEKER
HERE FOR MORE
THE WHO
TRACK RECORDS
19

Pete Townshend gets all metaphysical and philosophical on this one-off single that was the Who's first release after *Tommy*, their mega-selling 'rock opera'. It's powered along in typical swashbuckling Who-style, bolstered further by a rolling piano part, courtesy of Nicky Hopkins, and soaring backing vocals. The song is about the endless search for an answer to the question "what does life mean?" - Bob Dylan, the Beatles and LSD guru Timothy Leary are all name-checked and found wanting in this quest for the eternal truth. The conclusion is that the only answer is, "we live to die". Not your usual pop-chart type of song, but still a quite glorious racket, and that is definitely part of the charm of The Who.

32
CAT FOOD
GROON
KING CRIMSON
ISLAND
DID NOT CHART

This anti-consumerist single paints a nightmare vision of the way we live and the horror of the convenience food we are tempted by. It features a fabulous avant-garde piano part by Keith Tippett, and unusual time signatures. Amazingly the band were, for the first and last time, invited to perform on *Top of the Pops*, where they mimed atrociously and the puzzled audience attempted to sway along to the track and failed dismally; an audience utterly defeated and quite horrified by these strange people and their strange music.

31
FIRE AND RAIN
SUNNY SKIES
JAMES TAYLOR
WARNER BROTHERS
42

A few years later, the music of James Taylor was so comfortably smug and bland, that single-handedly he was reason enough for Punk to happen. It may be, though, that he had been through some rough times due to depression and addiction to hard drugs, and in his early career he had moments of brilliance and created songs that touched the soul. It is also worth noting that his voice was extraordinary, as sweet as honey but with real strength to it. Fire and Rain is a magnificent single, a brilliant song full of pain, touching on the suicide of his childhood friend Suzanne whilst he was in London recording his first album. It is unflinching and cloaked in sadness. Incidentally, the pianist on the session was Carole King, who was inspired to write 'You've Got a Friend' in answer to James Taylor's line "I could not find a friend".

30
SOUL DESERT
SHE BRINGS THE RAIN
THE CAN
LIBERTY
DID NOT CHART
Can, or The Can as they are known here, were one of the most forward-thinking musical combos of the late 20th century. They combined elements of the avant-edge of classical music, tribal beats, space rock, reggae and whatever else took their fancy. Based in their castle/studio in Cologne, here they are fronted by their original American singer, Malcolm Mooney. Both sides of this single, originally for German fan club members, are totally mesmerising; stunning in fact, and they retain their contemporary feel a half-century later.

29
I'M EIGHTEEN
BODY (IS IT MY BODY?)
ALICE COOPER
WARNER BROTHERS
DID NOT CHART
The Alice Cooper group had recorded two madcap, entertaining but unfocused albums for Frank Zappa's Bizarre label, before landing at Warner Brothers. Here, the seemingly impossible task of refining the bands ideas and making them a commercial entity fell to rookie producer Bob Ezrin. It is to his eternal credit that he recognised the talent within the band and encouraged them to follow their ideas to fruition. This was the first single of the liaison.

It is a kind of American update of 'My Generation', replacing the wired, speedy angst of that song with a belligerence, bordering on dumb insolence, very much punk before Punk. It is of little surprise that, as John Lydon auditioned to join the Sex Pistols by miming to a record on the 'Sex' shop jukebox, this was the chosen track.

28
THANK YOU (FALETTINME BE MICE ELF AGIN)/
EVERYBODY IS A STAR
SLY AND THE FAMILY STONE
DIRECTION
DID NOT CHART
These tracks were recorded as part of what was to be a new album that never materialised, which was a shame as they signalled a significant change in style for the band; ending the first phase as an uplifting, up-tempo dance act and moving towards a looser, slower grooved, darker music that aimed as much for the head as the feet. 'Thank You' is a sinuous, moving, nursery-rhyme funk piece… and we all know nursery rhymes hide dark significance. 'Everybody is a Star' is the opposite; a call to recognise that each individual has the potential to be special.

27
THE LOVE YOU SAVE
I FOUND THAT GIRL
JACKSON 5
TAMLA MOTOWN
7
Late in 1969, the Jackson 5 exploded onto the world stage with their first major release 'I Want You Back' and there was no stopping them from that moment. This was their fourth hit in a row, all powered by

pre-teen Michael Jackson who was clearly a force of nature. Neither the constraints of vinyl, or even a TV screen, seemed able to contain his exuberance and raw talent. This was another up-tempo number with Jermaine Jackson doubling up on the lead vocals and Marlon, Tito and Jackie lifting the chorus to a crescendo. They cry in unison 'Stop!'; feet stomp to accentuate the beat and allude to the Supremes' 1965 hit 'Stop in the Name of Love'. This was a whirlwind of sound, tailored for the group and it suited them down to the ground.

26
NOTHING RHYMED
EVERYBODY KNOWS
GILBERT O'SULLIVAN
M.A.M.
8
The sight of Gilbert O'Sullivan, dressed in schoolboy short trousers with a short back and sides haircut and a depression era flat-cap on his head, was attention grabbing in itself, but his appearance was nothing as compared to the shock when he sat at his piano and began to perform this song. Opening with his strident piano style and strings playing a winning melody, O'Sullivan takes us on a journey that is poetic but with a constant hint of pathos; totally original and quite fantastic.

25
YOU'VE GOT ME DANGLING
ON A STRING
I'LL COME CRAWLING
CHAIRMAN OF THE BOARD
INVICTUS
5
The second single by Chairman of the Board, put together by the same team who had delivered 'Give Me Just a Little More Time', but this track is a little more supercharged and insistent and General Johnson gives a less theatrical vocal on this occasion that sounds no less desperate for his restraint.

24
SIGNED SEALED DELIVERED
I'M YOURS
I'M MORE THAN HAPPY (I'M SATISFIED)
STEVIE WONDER
TAMLA MOTOWN
15
Still only 20 years old, Stevie was already a veteran with a stack of hits to his name, but he harboured ambitions to express himself more fully. This self-written track was the first he was allowed to produce. In a sign of the confidence in his own ability the utilisation of a guitar, with a sitar effect placed on it, as the main instrument in terms of carrying the melody. Stevie, who is possibly my favourite singer, of course delivers magnificently in that department, totally natural and unrestrained. If this wasn't quite a masterpiece, it was moving in the direction of future triumphs.

23
I HEAR YOU KNOCKING
BLACK BILL
DAVE EDMUNDS
M.A.M.
1
Having planned to record a version of Wilbert Harrison's 'Let's Work Together', Dave Edmunds discovered he'd been beaten to the punch by Canned Heat, whose version was ready for release. Luckily he heard Smiley Lewis's 1955 hit 'I Hear

You Knocking' on his car radio and had one of those eureka moments. Deciding to record that instead, replacing the piano-led blues shuffle of the original with a more basic guitar-led rock & roll style, Edmunds, who played all the instruments, added a slide guitar part that acted as a hook between verses and recorded his voice through a telephone line, which added to the atmosphere and helped create a timeless hit.

22

DIDN'T I BLOW YOUR MIND
THIS TIME
DOWN IS UP, UP IS DOWN
THE DELFONICS
BELL RECORDS
22

The Delfonics teamed up with writer/arranger/musician/producer Thom Bell in the mid-60s and began a run of hits, in 1968, with 'La La Means I Love You', featuring William Hart's falsetto. By the time they came to record 'Didn't I Blow Your Mind This Time', the formula had been perfected. Hart's falsetto again took the lead; layers of lush strings supported his voice; the songs were unhurried, cool and sophisticated. What became known as the Philly Sound was being created and, for a while in the 70s, became the dominant musical sound influencing the likes of David Bowie and Elton John. This was the sound of magic in the air.

21

GROOVIN' WITH MR BLOE
GET OUT OF THIS TOWN/
71-75 OXFORD STREET
MR BLOE
DJM
2

'Groovin' With Mr Bloe' was a fabulous instrumental dance track with prominent harmonica as the featured instrument. It started life as the B-side of a single by an American studio band named Bo Gentry. It was played, inadvertently, on the radio and heard by the head of DJM (or, to give the full title, Dick James Music) to whom Elton John was signed. Unable to lease the original version, a studio band was put together to record the UK release. Elton played piano on the first attempt, which wasn't deemed 'right', and an Elton-less second version was created, using the musicians who became Hookfoot (though here they were the mysterious and anonymous Mr Bloe). Elton did get to have two tracks he had written used as the B-side though, so he was quids-in when this became a monster hit.

TOP 50 - 11ᵀᴴ JULY 1970

1	1	1	IN THE SUMMERTIME Mungo Jerry, Dawn Maxi DNX 2502
2	2	3	ALL RIGHT NOW Free, Island WIP 6082
3	3	2	GROOVIN' WITH MR BLOE Mr Bloe, DJM DJS 216
4	9	18	UP AROUND THE BEND Creedence Clearwater Revival, Liberty LBF 1
5	8	13	IT'S ALL IN THE GAME Four Tops, Tamla Motown TMG 736
6	5	6	COTTONFIELDS Beach Boys, Capitol CL 15640
7	4	5	SALLY Gerry Monroe, Chapter One CH 122
8	6	7	GOODBYE SAM HELLO SAMANTHA Cliff Richard, Columbia DB 86‹
9	15	21	LOVE OF THE COMMON PEOPLE Nicky Thomas, Trojan TR 7750
10	10	10	THE GREEN MANALISHI Fleetwood Mac, Reprise RS 27007
11	13	9	ABRAHAM, MARTIN AND JOHN Marvin Gaye, Tamla Motown TMG
12	12	14	DOWN THE DUSTPIPE Status Quo, Pye 7N 17907
13	16	32	SOMETHING Shirley Bassey, United Artists UP 35126
14	11	8	HONEY COME BACK Glen Campbell, Capitol CL 15638
15	7	4	YELLOW RIVER Christie, CBS 4911
16	22	–	LOLA Kinks, Pye 7N 17961
17	17	16	I WILL SURVIVE Arrival, Decca F 13026
18	14	11	EVERYTHING IS BEAUTIFUL Ray Stevens, CBS 4953
19	28	37	LADY D'ARBANVILLE Cat Stevens, Island WIP 6086
20	–	–	THE WONDER OF YOU Elvis Presley, RCA 1974
21	18	12	UP THE LADDER TO THE ROOF Supremes, Tamla Motown TMG 73‹
22	26	23	GROUPY GIRL Tony Joe White, Monument MON 1043
23	19	26	AMERICAN WOMAN Guess Who, RCA 1943
24	29	30	LOVE LIKE A MAN Ten Years After, Deram DM 299
25	31	49	BIG YELLOW TAXI Joni Mitchell, Reprise RS 20906
26	25	22	KENTUCKY RAIN Elvis Presley, RCA 1949
27	39	–	(It's Like A) SAD OLD KINDA MOVIE Pickettywitch, Pye 7N 1795¹
28	20	17	QUESTION Moody Blues, Threshold TH 4
29	23	17	BET YER LIFE I DO Hermans Hermits, RAK 102
30	45	–	I'LL SAY FOREVER MY LOVE Jimmy Ruffin, Tamla Motown TMG ‹
31	27	19	I DON'T BELIEVE IN IF ANYMORE Roger Whittaker, Columbia DB ‹
32	48	–	NEANDERTHAL MAN Hotlegs, Fontana 6007 019
33	34	36	PSYCHEDELIC SHACK Temptations, Tamla Motown TMG 741
34	40	44	MY MARIE Engelbert Humperdinck, Decca F 13032
35	44	–	WHERE ARE YOU GOING TO MY LOVE Brotherhood of Man Deram DM 298
36	24	15	BACK HOME England World Cup Squad, Pye 7N 17920
37	35	28	DAUGHTER OF DARKNESS Tom Jones, Decca F 13013
38	33	24	DON'T YOU KNOW Butterscotch, RCA 1937
39	50	–	THE LETTER Joe Cocker, Regal Zonophone RZ 3027
40	37	29	HOUSE OF THE RISING SUN Frijid Pink, Deram DM 288
41	32	24	SPIRIT IN THE SKY Norman Greenbaum, Reprise RS 20885
42	21	34	ABC Jackson 5, Tmta Motown TMG 738
43	41	42	MY WAY Frank Sinatra, Reprise RS 20817
44	–	–	SONG OF JOY Miguel Rios, A & M AMS 790
45	49	–	HERE COMES SUMMER Dave Clark Five, Columbia DB 8689
46	30	34	WHAT IS TRUTH? Johnny Cash, CBS 4934
47	36	31	VEHICLE Ides of March, Warner Bros WB 7378
48	38	33	ALL KINDS OF EVERYTHING Dana, Rex R 11054
49	–	–	SUGAR BEE Canned Heat, Liberty LBF 18350
50	43	47	RAINDROPS KEEP FALLIN' ON MY HEAD Sacha Distel, Warner Bros WB 7345

20

ONLY LOVE CAN BREAK
YOUR HEART
BIRDS
NEIL YOUNG
REPRISE
DID NOT CHART

Neil Young has the knack of making the simple profound and the profound simple. This song, reputedly written for Graham Nash after his relationship with Joni Mitchell broke down, is a perfect example. It is a simple song, not much to it at all, and yet it is perfect. Everything that needs to be said is said, and no more. Equally, the music suits the lyric; it fits like a glove. There is no adornment because any adornment would be wholly unnecessary and superfluous. This is a brilliant, iconic song by a brilliantly iconic artist.

19

YOUNG, GIFTED AND BLACK
PEACE OF MINE
BOB AND MARCIA
TROJAN
5

Written by Nina Simone and Weldon Irvine Jr, and performed magisterially by Nina Simone, this celebration of black pride and the striving for equality was an important song. It was not though, a song likely to reach the ears of the working classes in dreary conservative Britain, where racism was rife and unchallenged. Enter Bob Andy and Marcia Griffith, who turned the track into an up-tempo Reggae piece. Trojan Records in London licensed the cream of the Jamaican releases and issued them in the UK, often adding strings to sweeten them, as was the case here. The record became a big and significant hit appealing, as it

did, to teenagers bombarded by negative images of black people. For a proportion of the white youths who danced and sang along to this, the message got through as well, and this opposing point of view to racial stereotyping began to be taken up and championed by a generation ready for change.

18

PARANOID
THE WIZARD
BLACK SABBATH
VERTIGO
4

Black Sabbath, at their brutal best, could have been the British equivalent of The Stooges. Wisely, in terms of their career, they didn't follow that path and instead became a multi-millionaire soap opera, playing overlong, tedious pieces masquerading as meaningful art. Who could blame them? This, though, is titanic. It is a monstrous juggernaut of angst, powered by a pummelling riff and sung dementedly by idiot-savant Ozzy Osborne, who apparently didn't have a clue what the song was about.

17

UP AROUND THE BEND/
RUN THROUGH THE JUNGLE
CREEDENCE CLEARWATER
REVIVAL
FANTASY
3

The high-pitched guitar figure that opens 'Up Around the Bend' acts as a clarion-call and invitation to the gathering of good people, creating an idealised alternate society, a world away from the problems we city-dwellers encounter. "Leave the sinking ship behind" sings John

Fogerty, and if the music in this idyll was all as uplifting as this, the rat race would be rejected, no doubt about that. 'Run Through the Jungle' is equally good... great even. It is an almost cinematic masterpiece, painting a frightening picture of the disturbing reality of the amount of guns in people's hands in the USA. The song moves steadily along; it is as if we are passengers cruising along in a car, looking out on the horror of the urban jungle.

16

THE GREEN MANALISHI
(WITH THE TWO-PRONG
CROWN)
WORLD IN HARMONY
FLEETWOOD MAC
REPRISE
10

Fleetwood Mac were a sensational band and their leader, Peter Green, was a man of rare talent; a superlative guitarist who conveyed great emotion in his playing, an intriguing lyricist, unafraid to address his own fears and frailties, and a fabulous natural singer to boot. Drugs though, in the form of large quantities of LSD, had undermined Green's psyche; he was a conflicted man in pain. This was the final track he recorded with the band before leaving, upset that they would not give away their earnings, which he now considered immoral. This parting shot is his masterpiece. 'The Green Manalishi' equated to money and therefore the devil. It is an anguished scream, though beautifully constructed, rumbling menacingly at one moment, before erupting violently. The drums and bass pound high in the mix, while Green and Danny Kirwan play shrieking guitars of devastating intensity. Atop all

this, Green delivers a spooked, eerie vocal performance that couldn't be faked, culminating in him howling animalistically at the demons that, for him, were very real.

15

BRONTOSAURUS
LIGHTNING NEVER STRIKES
TWICE
THE MOVE
REGAL ZONOPHONE
7

The Move were proven hit-makers, and guitarist Roy Wood a proven hit-writer, but this single was a game-changing new beginning. Singer Carl Wayne had left, at odds with the experimentalism of Roy Woods approach; in came Jeff Lynne who would, with Wood, launch the Electric Light Orchestra. This signalled a huge sonic departure. Nothing, in fact, sounded like this; a huge, supercharged, aggressive bass-riff dominates proceedings. Lynne contributed guitar and piano while Wood sang in his distinctive style. 'Brontosaurus' was the perfect title for this stomping, big-beast of a record. Another event that predicted the future was when, appearing on *Top of The Pops* for the first time as a front-man, the extremely shy Roy Wood took to hiding behind makeup, predicting his image two years later as leader of Wizzard.

14

DOWN ON THE STREET
I FEEL ALRIGHT (1970)
THE STOOGES
ELEKTRA
DID NOT CHART

The Stooges didn't deal in utopian visions and had no truck with the 'love and peace' movement. Their lives were dictated by their environment, by the urban grind in which they existed; that reality was always what powered and informed their music and attitudes. Here, the band lock into an unrelenting groove like the sound of a factory production line. Within it the singer grunts and hisses, he speaks of his lusts and passions, and stakes a claim for his individuality. The music is unrelenting, unchanging; in what passes as a chorus, the velocity is increased, the decibel level rises and releases some of the built up tension... and then, back to the groove, back to the grind, back to the world of The Stooges. By the way, the record company bigwigs thought it worth adding Doors-style electric organ to this single in an attempt to commercialise the sound of The Stooges. It was a complete failure.

13
THE WONDER OF YOU
MAMA LIKED THE ROSES
ELVIS PRESLEY
RCA
1
Recorded live in Las Vegas at the beginning, this is Elvis's at the start of a heartbreaking and inescapable run of performances, as he was sold over and over again by his despicable manager Tom Parker. Here he was still fresh, taking this often-recorded song and making it his own, imbuing it with joy and filling it with his spirit; it is stirring and celebratory. Elvis performs it magnificently but without any hokey reverence, without resorting to pomp and bombast. This was an absolute blast, this was superb.

12
YOU CAN GET IT IF YOU
REALLY WANT
PERSEVERANCE
DESMOND DEKKER
TROJAN
2
Jimmy Cliff wrote and released his own version of this song, only to find that, two weeks later, Desmond Dekker had put out a competing version. Cliff's version is wonderful and was included in the 1972 film *The Harder They Come*. Dekkers take was more pop friendly, more up-tempo, sung in a higher register, sunny and bright. He was the one who carried this anthem of positive thinking into the mainstream.

11
BAND OF GOLD
THE EASIEST WAY TO FALL
FREDA PAYNE
INVICTUS
1
Another Holland-Dozier-Holland plus Ron Dunbar, written and produced single - Freda Payne, then nearly 30-years old, initially refused to sing the song, believing it more suitable for a much younger woman. She was finally persuaded and handled it superbly. Riding on a distinctive electric sitar riff, it tells the tale of a couple of newly weds, their marriage vows unconsummated, splitting up and sleeping in separate rooms. Was he gay? Impotent? The debate rumbled for decades before Ron Dunbar revealed that lyrics had been cut from the single, which explained that the young woman simply hadn't been ready, and was left regretting her choice.

10

REFUGEES
THE BOAT OF MILLIONS OF YEARS
VAN DER GRAAF GENERATOR
CHARISMA
DID NOT CHART

Optimistic and pastoral, which is not typical of VDGG, this floats hymn-like on a gentle cello and flute arrangement, while the often strident Peter Hammill sounds almost mellow as he recounts the tale of Mike and Susie, leaving all they have known and loved behind them and heading west together as refugees, to be alone and grow old together.

9

BRIDGE OVER TROUBLED WATER
KEEP THE CUSTOMER SATISFIED
SIMON AND GARFUNKEL
COLUMBIA
1

The professional partnership between Paul Simon and Arthur Garfunkel was approaching its end but, as a final act, this single would take some topping. Hugely inspirational, this gospel-infused *meisterwerk* was sung to perfection by an initially reluctant Arthur, persuaded by Paul to sing as if he were in a church. Arthur, in turn, persuaded Paul to write the last verse and grand finale, where the two voices come together in a powerful crescendo, which the curmudgeonly Mr Simon has claimed never to like. Utilising elements of the famous wall of sound, found on Phil Spector's greatest creations, and the 'Wrecking Crew' as musicians (who played on not just Spector's hits, but those of the Beach Boys too) this record was enormous and epic on the outside, and deeply moving at its core.

8

LET IT BE
YOU KNOW MY NAME
THE BEATLES
APPLE
2

The last UK Beatles single was this church-like hymn, evoking the spirit of his mother to guide him through darkness, delivered from the gilded pen of Paul McCartney. Beatle John once apparently accused Beatle Paul of being "all pizza and fairy stories" – and thumbs aloft, smiling Paul could indeed be a little cheesy. But here, and elsewhere, when sentimentality was kept in check, his genius shone and criticism was surely born out of spitefulness and malice rather than a fair-minded assessment of his work's true value.

7

PACHUCO CADAVER
WILD LIFE
CAPTAIN BEEFHEART
AND HIS MAGIC BAND
BIZZARE
DID NOT CHART

"A squid eating dough in a polyethylene bag is fast and bulbous. Got Me?" So speaks Beefheart before the incredibly tightly-drilled Magic Band take-off on some deliberately out-of-kilter boogie, setting the tone for the good Captain to rejoin proceedings with his patented brand of surrealistic word play, before producing his horn for some Ornette Coleman-style improvisation. Alas, all too soon, our fun-filled adventure into Magic Band Land comes to a close, but what a fabulous outing away from the conventional and mundane.

6

MILES RUNS THE VOODOO DOWN
SPANISH KEY
MILES DAVIS
CBS
DID NOT CHART

Miles Davis was revolutionising music in 1970. With the album *Bitches Brew* he ceased to be classified as simply a jazz musician and transcended the genre. He became hugely influential to acts like Sly and the Family Stone and War, but also a touchstone for bands like Can and Pink Floyd. This single was an edited cut from *Bitches Brew* and if you heard this and never heard the rest of the album, it would still enlighten, such is its utilisation of space and tone. It is music that transports you, music that evokes strong images, it is language between musicians, it is devastatingly good.

5

GET UP (I FEEL LIKE BEING A)
SEX MACHINE PART 1
GET UP (I FEEL LIKE BEING A)
SEX MACHINE PART 2
JAMES BROWN
POLYDOR
32

With his brand-new band, the JBs, horn-section having little in the way of experience, a change in style was called for in their first studio session. So, the tried and trusted formula of horns leading the song, such as in 'Papas Got a Brand New Bag' or 'I Got You (I Feel Good)', was jettisoned in favour of a persistent and insistent riff, played by the Collins brothers on guitar and bass and Jabo Starks remarkable drumming. James Brown, and long time sideman Bobby Byrd, push the musicians along with their vocal interplay, exhorting each and all to "get on up, like a sex machine", before announcing the outro of the track by singing the phrase "shake your moneymaker", borrowed from bluesman Elmore James. The spontaneity of the song, which had been conceived on the back of a bus, unrehearsed before entering the studio, gave it incredible energy and rightly placed

James Brown at the forefront of the new sound. He became the 'First Minister of the Superfunk' to add to his numerous other titles.

4

RIDE A WHITE SWAN
IS IT LOVE/SUMMERTIME BLUES
T REX
FLY
2

So, Tyrannosaurus Rex was gone, replaced by the snappier T Rex. The tentativeness of the previous single, 'By the Light of The Magical Moon', had disappeared too. This time around the sound was sharp and the song was concise. Marc Bolan claimed it was written after he had been spiked with LSD and the imagery evoked is suggestive of that. The band still consisted of just Marc and Mickey Finn, but Marc played bass as well as guitar and a synchronised tambourine and handclaps substituted for drums. Bolan had finally hit on a winning formula and indeed, it sounded like nothing else on earth. The sound slowly seduced the nation's youth as it took eleven weeks from entering the charts for it to reach its peak position. By that time, the tiny, curly-haired front-man, who pouted and lisped his way through TV performances, was a star.

3

INSTANT KARMA
WHO HAS SEEN THE WIND?
JOHN LENNON WITH THE
PLASTIC ONO BAND
APPLE
5

LENNON

INSTANT KARMA!

APPLES 1003

Written, recorded and released within ten days at the beginning of January, two months before Paul McCartney announced the Beatles split, this was a monster single with a monster sound. Alan White's drums, drenched in echo at the front of the mix, pounded pianos, a chorus of nightclub revellers, recruited into the studio and conducted by George Harrison, and a message that mankind must take responsibility for its own actions because karma (just like coffee) is now instant.

2

LOLA
BERKELEY MEWS
THE KINKS
PYE
2

This was a highly controversial release at the time and was indeed banned by, or censored by, various broadcasters around the world. Its subject matter, about a man's attraction to a transgender woman in a Soho nightspot, was indeed an eye-opener for many, but that alone is not what makes this a great record. What truly makes it great is Ray Davies's eye for detail within the lyric. He creates a picture so vivid that the listener is transported to the scene. There is also the tenderness and empathy for the characters, recognising them as people with real emotions rather than comic book caricatures. We feel genuine sadness as the story plays out with no happy ending. Atop that is the musical setting created with Ray's sibling Dave Davies' unique clanging guitar sound demanding attention, along with the structure of the song which lends weight and resonance to the story as it ebbs and flows.

1

VOODOO CHILE
HEY JOE/
ALL ALONG THE WATCHTOWER
JIMI HENDRIX
TRACK
1

Recorded and released as the last track on the *Electric Ladyland* album, this was issued in 1970 as a single, after the guitarist's death. At the heart of the song is a basic blues figure; that, though, is simply the launching pad for what is a psychedelic, sonic adventure played out over an insistent and unrelenting riff. Lyrically, the song is hugely intriguing as Hendrix adopts

the role of voodoo preacher and his otherworldly style makes pronouncements on a grand scale – "if I don't see you no more in this world, then I'll meet you in the next one and don't be late, don't be late", before announcing "I'm a voodoo chile, lord knows I'm a voodoo chile". This is delivered so matter-of-factly that we are tempted to believe him.

1970 - Here I am, a traumatised 11 year-old after my first day at secondary school. It was a bit of an eye-opener!

1971 - School Photo, Aged 12 - and possibly the last time I smiled in that place

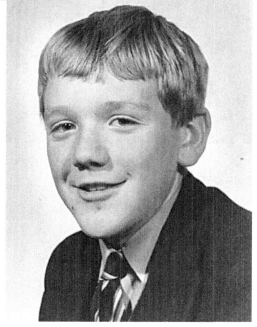

1971 - WEST END ROVERS

I made sure I was next to United European Cup winner David Sadler rather than City captain Tony Book.

1971

- 66 people die in a crush on the stairs as fans left the Rangers v Celtic football match on 2nd January in what became known as the Ibrox Disaster
- General Idi Amin deposes President Milton Obote in a military coup in Uganda
- Charles Manson and three members of 'the Family' are found guilty of the Tate-LaBianca murders
- Rolls Royce is declared bankrupt and is nationalised
- In the Vietnam War, South Vietnam, backed by the US military, invaded Laos
- The UK and Republic of Ireland introduce decimalisation
- Joe Frazier defeats Muhammad Ali in 15 rounds in the 'Fight of the Century' at Madison Square Garden to defend his World Heavyweight title.
- The first Starbucks coffee shop is opened in Seattle.
- United States President Richard Nixon declares a 'war on drugs'.
- 40,000 people attend the George Harrison organised 'Concert for Bangladesh'.
- Disneyworld opens in Florida.
- Greenpeace is founded.
- In Cambodia, Phnom Penh is attacked by Khmer Rouge forces.
- Stanley Kubrick's film *A Clockwork Orange* is released.
- The UK raises the number of troops deployed in Northern Ireland to 11,000.
- Manchester United sign Ian Storey-Moore from Nottingham Forest for a club record fee of £200,000 and appoint Frank O'Farrell as manager. Arsenal win the league and cup double.

NOTABLE BIRTHS

Pep Guardiola; Snoop Doggy Dogg; Tupac Shakur; Mariah Carey; Elon Musk; Pete Sampras; Johnny Vegas

NOTABLE DEATHS

Diane Arbus; CoCo Chanel; Gene Vincent; Igor Stravinsky; Jim Morrison; Louis Armstrong; Audie Murphy; Duane Allman

NOTABLE FILMS

A Clockwork Orange; McCabe and Mrs Miller; Dirty Harry; Death in Venice; Get Carter; Straw Dogs; Shaft; Harold and Maude; Diamonds are Forever; Walkabout

NOTABLE BOOKS

Fear and Loathing In Las Vegas – Hunter S Thompson
Post Office – Charles Bukowski
The Dice Man – Luke Rhinehart
The Room – Hubert Selby Jnr
Beneath The Underdog – Charles Mingus
Tarantula – Bob Dylan
The Anarchist Cookbook – William Powell
In a Free State – V.S. Naipaul
Adolf Hitler: My Part in his Downfall – Spike Milligan

THE MUSIC

There was a Beatles-sized hole in the music scene and it was desirable to the industry that it be filled… but where do you start looking for a new Beatles? The obvious first stop was to check on The Rolling Stones, for so long the undisputed, second-most important band around. The Stones, though, were never cut out to be leaders who could shoulder the responsibility to constantly innovate since they were, at heart, a blues and R&B combo who had somehow struck a rich seam of creative gold; in any case they seemed creatively drained as well. Spooked by the spectre of death that they had come to know first-hand, following the demise of Brian Jones and the horror of Altamont, Richards and Jagger coped in different ways: Keith sought solace in narcotics whereas Mick, with his marriage to socialite Bianca, infiltrated the social elite of aristocrats and polite society. The 'Glimmer Twins' were becoming separate entities. It was the start of the Stones turning into a commercial branding operation rather than a creative musical group.

Mega-sales figures suggested that Led Zeppelin were every

bit as big as the Beatles had been, but their sphere of influence was much narrower and they possessed none of the charisma required to reach out to the wider world. Creedence Clearwater Revival churned out hit after glorious hit, but their demeanour was dull and their game-plan did not appear to include world domination. It would be a far less likely figure who stepped into the breach, in the form of a diminutive, Tolkien quoting hippy with ambition... Marc Bolan. During this year of his ascension there was an abbreviated band name, a change from acoustic to electric guitar, a dash of satin and a glitter daubed cheekbone. This was enough to see him, and T. Rex, transformed from student union fodder to teen-sensation. T. Rextasy swept the nation and heralded the birth of the Glam Rock movement. Also, one of Bolan's old friends, David Bowie, was experimenting, out of sight, with a style that would soon spawn glam's ultimate hero, 'Ziggy Stardust', utilising the pseudonym of Arnold Corns to distance himself from failure should the plan backfire.

Out on the streets, the Skinheads hair was growing. They were on the way to becoming 'smoothies' or 'suedeheads', a more conformist and socially acceptable grown up version of their teen selves that saw smart brogues and tonic trousers replace boots, jeans and braces. These smarter 'bovver boys' dropped their fickle regard for reggae as they transformed themselves into nice types their mothers could be proud of. Reggae was too strong to fade away and die from neglect though. This was the year that the feature film *The Harder They Come* hit the silver screen, in it Jimmy Cliff played 'rude boy' Ivan, the film's anti-hero. Following his adventures through the tenement yards of Trenchtown was a brilliant soundtrack of roots music that was simply incredible. It was exciting and new and set many on their way to a voyage of discovery to hear more of what was happening in Jamaica.

In truth Soul music was this year's dominant sound. Artists were stepping away from record company straight-jacketing and seizing the right to be artistically free and true to themselves. Marvin Gaye created the uncompromising, but steadfastly beautiful *What's Goin' On?*; Isaac Hayes, the street-smart symphony that was 'Theme from Shaft'; Curtis Mayfield exhorted us to 'Move On Up' while Al Green captivated with

'Tired of Being Alone'. Genius records all but topped by Gil Scott-Heron, whose fiery erudition made him a must-hear artiste. As for those Beatles? Well, they hadn't been dubbed the 'Fab Four' without justification and each one of them treated us to superb solo singles.

MY 1971

Entering my teens, I was extremely short of confidence and suffered from low self-esteem. I did, though, harbour belief in the courage of my convictions and was true to them and true to myself. I didn't pretend to be what I wasn't and didn't pretend to like the same things as my classmates. I observed my peers effortlessly conforming as a means of fitting in, using compromise as a way to make life easier and court popularity. I stuck to my guns, which put me in a lonely place. I stood apart from the herd where only music soothed my damaged soul. I learned to accept that I was 'different'; I was a misfit. What friends I had were fellow misfits. I bought what records I could afford from my pocket money and immersed myself in them, and also, at last, I went to see a concert. Manchester's Free Trade Hall was the venue, a place I would frequent many hundreds of times in the coming years after this initiation into the world of live gigs. Slade, who were in the charts with 'Coz I Luv You', were the headline act. Supporting them were Status Quo whose 'Down the Dustpipe' and 'In my Chair' singles had made me something of a fan. It was a brilliant experience, magical and liberating. I thoroughly enjoyed both bands' performances and the thrill of the volume which I'd never imagined could be so exhilarating. But that was only a part of what excited me. Not only was this special and new to me but, crucially, it was cheap and accessible. Admission had cost 60p, which even then was not a large amount. I had simply turned up and purchased a ticket, with no need for pre-planning, and enjoyed the fact that in the barely half-full hall I could wander around to my heart's desire. During Slade's set I had been befriended by an attractive female who had snogged me lustily. I had found a place where I effortlessly fit in; where I wasn't a misfit. Music was my saviour and I discovered that fellow music enthusiasts welcomed me. Before the year was out I'd see, amongst others, The Faces, Humble Pie, The Kinks and

Donovan, whose lyric about a caterpillar shedding its skin to find the butterfly within, suited me just fine.

100
DIANA
THE LOST QUEEN'S EYE/
WINTER IS A COLOURED
BIRD
COMUS
DAWN
DID NOT CHART

Comus were what I can only describe as a psychotic folk band who seemed to revel in their songs of brutal murder, mental illness, or, as is the case here, the rape of a young, virgin girl. All these themes were played out against a backdrop of beautifully played acoustic guitar, violin, flute and delicate female vocals, along with the strange and compelling voice of Roger Wootton recounting these often repulsive tales. Diana was the band's first release, preceding the *First Utterance* album, and laid their cards on the table from the off, and powered by wild (in the extreme) percussion, this was a most remarkable single.

99
KEEP ON DANCING
ALRIGHT
BAY CITY ROLLERS
BELL
9

This U.S. 'Garage band' hit for the Gentrys, from 1965, was chosen as the debut single to launch Scottish teen-band the Bay City Rollers. Produced by Jonathan King, it was sunny and energetic high-quality pop with a great stop-start false ending. The follow-up single flopped and singer Nobby Clark was replaced with Les McKeown before the Rollers returned to the charts and the girls began screaming.

98
ME AND MY ARROW
ARE YOU SLEEPING?
NILSSON
RCA
DID NOT CHART

The Point was an album of songs accompanied by delightful animated film that sprang from the mind of Harry Nilsson during an acid trip. It was a fable concerning a character called Oblio who is the only round-headed person in his village, where everyone and everything must have a point; Oblio and his faithful canine companion Arrow are banished. 'Me and my Arrow' is their theme song. It is a lovely piece, sung simply over a tinkling piano background, about the bond between the two. It is irresistible to big softies such as myself.

97
SIMPLE GAME
YOU STOLE MY LOVE
THE FOUR TOPS
TAMLA MOTOWN
3

This song was plucked from a Moody Blues B-side and transformed into a trademark, storming Four Tops single, with its message that "we are one, we are all the same" forcefully hammered home by the winning combination of gritty lead vocals and effortlessly cool group harmonies.

96
DORA THE FEMALE
EXPLORER
EVERYMAN
STACKRIDGE
MCA
DID NOT CHART

I felt, and continue to feel, a great deal of affection for Stackridge. They were good-natured eccentrics and, in my mind, that was a laudable combination. Here, on their first single, plucked from their delicious debut album the tale of the elusive Dora is recounted over a jaunty barn dance-style backing. "Wet and windy weather rarely keep her in" they chime, for Dora is gone, pursuing her need to explore. Capturing the sound and atmospherics that ten years later would make XTC a much venerated proposition, this single is testimony to the very English loveliness of Stackridge.

95
BABY JUMP
THE MAN BEHIND
THE PIANO/LIVE FROM
HOLLYWOOD
MUNGO JERRY
DAWN
2

It's hard in these times to imagine a record so rocking, raucous and downright rude reaching the higher echelons of chart-land... but these were very different days. Mungo Jerry pulverise the piano keys, hammer along on Troggs-style guitar and bass, and simply foot-stomp out the rhythm. Singer Ray Dorset whoops, hollers, wails and screams out the lusty tale evoking da Vinci, Lady Chatterley and Lolita along the way. "Awright awright awright now!" he shouts as the music grinds to a halt, only to jerk back once again into gear; priceless.

94
BLACK-SKINNED BLUE-EYED
BOY
AIN'T GOT NOTHING TO
GIVE YOU
THE EQUALS
PRESIDENT
9

The UK's first major interracial band – very pointedly named the Equals – were the vehicle that propelled a young Eddie Grant into our consciousness. Here he writes, produces, plays guitar and sings this paean to racial diversity, linking it to the then current anti-Vietnam war sentiments being expressed globally. A nagging guitar riff, incessant congos, a spat-out vocal and an unforgettable chorus conspire to make this a fabulous single.

93
SATORI PART 1
SATORI PART 2
FLOWER TRAVELLIN' BAND
ATLANTIC
DID NOT CHART

Now a fully-formed and focused unit, Flower Travellin' Band were playing a brand of acid-drenched heavy metal that was blowing the socks off their Western contemporaries; leaner, cleaner and more experimental. King Crimson, in the moments they dropped their pastoral loveliness and bared their teeth, were the closest comparison I could make. This is a mind-trip of a record that surges with electricity from the opening scream to the power chord riffs and the almost yodelled vocal. Unmissable, this is a record that makes it feel good to be alive.

92
KEEP ON KEEPING ON
IF I COULD ONLY BE SURE
NF PORTER
LIZARD
DID NOT CHART

With a riff famously filched by Joy Division, Nolan Porter's single became a huge, enduring hit across Britain's 'Northern Soul' scene – not least for that riff, because it is absolutely magnificent; it practically issues an invitation to dance. Equally though, Mr Porter's breathy, desperate-sounding vocal is divine as he implores one and all "to keep on keeping on, no matter how hard it is". The whole thing is relatively simple and minimalistic, but is delivered with such panache and relentless insistence that it is a true classic.

91
MR BIG STUFF
WHY I KEEP LIVING THESE MEMORIES
JEAN KNIGHT
STAX
DID NOT CHART

Its offbeat bass line gives this soul/ funk strut its irresistible swagger, further accentuated by carefully placed parping horns but it is Jean Knight's delivery of this sassy put-down of unwanted male attention that is the key to this record's greatness. She sings with such a hint of glee as she rebuffs and rebukes her over-privileged admirer. This blow for female empowerment not only made its point but was a barrel-load of fun as well.

90
JIG A JIG
MARCUS JUNIOR
EAST OF EDEN
DERAM
7

Released on Decca's progressive-rock imprint Deram, not even the most optimistic company marketing man could have expected this violin-dominated sound to become a huge hit. It is in fact not a jig at all, but three traditional reels combined and then underscored by bass and drums to give it a 'rock' feel. This celebratory delight filled dance floors across the land. One listener, impressed by this single, was Pete Townshend of The Who; he invited East of Eden violinist Dave Arbus to produce something similar for a song he was recording – which is why the epic 'Baba O'Riley' concludes with a wild violin reel.

89
DRAW YOUR BRAKES
DRAW YOUR BRAKES (VERSION)
SCOTTY
CRYSTAL
DID NOT CHART

Adapted from the Keith and Tex rocksteady hit 'Stop That Train', Scotty exclaiming over 'the riddim' breathes new life into the track. It was utilised, to stunning effect, on the film soundtrack for *The Harder They Come*, introducing the 'toasting DJ' style to an incredulous wider world.

88
SULTANA
SING FOOL SING
TITANIC
CBS
5

A proto heavy-metal band from Norway, inspired by Santana, conjured up this dance-classic sound-alike that filled dancefloors from New York gay clubs to British provincial youth clubs. A near-instrumental (save for a chanted intro and outro) drums, congas and maracas push the beat, and organ is the intoxicating lead instrument. They never came close to repeating this success but continued releasing singles and albums until 1979, before splitting and reforming several times.

87
GET DOWN AND GET WITH IT
DO YOU WANT ME?/GOSPEL
ACCORDING TO RASPUTIN
SLADE
POLYDOR
16

Desperate for a first hit, Slade entered the studio intent on recreating their live energy. Duly this Bobby Marchan written number, modelled on a version by Little Richard, was completed in one take, replete with handclaps and the stomping of boots. Singer Noddy Holder exercised his razor of a larynx exhorting all and sundry to let go and let rip, stamp their feet and get down and get with it! Meanwhile, behind him, the band thundered. It wasn't subtle, nor was it meant to be, but it was totally unpretentious aural hooliganism on a grand scale; loud, proud and hugely exciting. The ball had started rolling and seventeen consecutive hits would follow.

86
BLOOD AND FIRE
MUD AND WATER
NINEY THE OBSERVER
BIG SHOT
DID NOT CHART

Winston Holness was nicknamed 'Niney' after losing a thumb in an engineering accident. He became 'the Observer' in deference to his friend and mentor Lee Perry's adoption of the title 'the Upsetter'. Like Perry, he was a performer as well as studio wizard and 'Blood and Fire' is his claim to immortality. Over the most catchy reggae beat imaginable, with a bass that slithers beneath the vocal, 'Niney' warns us "judgement has come and mercy has gone" and he pronounces that we should allow Babylon to "burn, burn, burn". Incidentally, there was a brilliant reggae reissue label named after this timeless and ageless single.

85
HIGH TIME WE WENT
BLACK EYED BLUES
JOE COCKER
CUBE
DID NOT CHART

This was a shift for Joe Cocker; much less rock and much more blues and soul – a hybrid that was unique in 1971. A crack band had been assembled and this was a confident, swaggering dance piece, sounding not dissimilar to the Happy Mondays 20-years later. Cocker counts down the hours over a churning, rolling groove. A hit in the USA, this did little business in the U.K. Cocker was in the commercial wilderness but was making some of the best music of his career.

84
I AM I SAID
DONE TOO SOON
NEIL DIAMOND
UNI
4

Painfully autobiographical, this was Neil Diamond expressing his angst in a most public way. It is a song about displacement and feelings of loneliness and emptiness. Neil Diamond was a consummate hit-writer and his tunesmith's knack had not deserted him here, making this, despite the terrible "even the chair" lyric, a compelling single that demanded attention and remains much loved.

83
YOURS IS NO DISGRACE
THE CLAP
YES
ATLANTIC
DID NOT CHART

The all-too-often insipid Yes were, on this occasion, vital and topical with this dramatic anti-war song suggesting that the soldiers sent to Vietnam should not be held responsible but had no choice other than to fight and suffer, while people more privileged condemn them as they simultaneously enjoy the high life. Instrumentally too this was a tougher piece, with Steve Howe's virtuosity as a guitarist, utilised to the benefit of the song, carrying a menacing edge.

82
YOU'VE GOT A FRIEND
YOU CAN CLOSE YOUR EYES
JAMES TAYLOR
WARNER BROTHERS
4

Written by Carole King and recorded for her own *Tapestry* album, James Taylor was simultaneously recording his own album *Mud Slide Slim and the Blue Horizon* utilising a number of the same musicians. Hearing this near-perfect gem, Taylor related strongly to it and recorded his own, very similar, version to King's – the main difference being in their voices; King's much rawer than Taylor's honeyed, warm, technically-gifted tone. The song, an expression of universal sisterly/brotherly love that is unconditional, reassured and resonated. It has deservedly come to be regarded as a standard with the power to touch souls.

81
STAY WITH ME
DEBRIS
THE FACES
WARNER BROTHERS
6

Overdue success came for The Faces on the back of singer Rod Stewart's solo breakthrough, so although it offered vindication of their shambling rock 'n' roll burlesque, the taste must have been at least slightly bittersweet. The two sides of the single show the two sides of the Faces, both equally great. The A-side is a foot-to-the-floor raver with each musician walloping their respective instrument, Ian McLagen opening proceedings with a rippling distorted Wurlitzer electric piano before Ron Wood slips and slides on guitar as Kenny Jones hammers out a beat. Over this stop – start – stop – start cacophony, the gravel-voiced Rod Stewart roars his lewd and lusty story, before a series of heart-stopping false endings precede the true finale. On the B-side is Ronnie Lane's quite wonderful and wistful 'Debris', which is full of tenderness and world-weary wonderment.

80
TAP TURNS ON THE WATER
SAVE THE WORLD
CCS
RAK
5

Although their primary source of material was covers of rock and blues hits given a big band makeover, the collective had a strong writing team in their midst in the shape of Alexis Korner and John Cameron. And so, after having hits with songs by Willie Dixon ('Whole Lotta Love') and Donovan ('Walking'), came this self-composed effort which proved to be their defining and best remembered single. Sung in highly individualistic style by the gravelly-toned Alexis Korner, although the lyric is vague and hard to read, it is full of arresting imagery. The musical arrangement matches this, with acoustic guitar interludes cutting through the horn riffs, and a minimalistic, close to tribal, drum beat being the foundation for the song.

79
SUPERSTAR
BLESS THE BEASTS AND
CHILDREN
THE CARPENTERS
A&M
18

Written by Delaney and Bonnie Bramlett, in cahoots with Leon Russell, the original version of this song nestled on the B-side of their 1969 'Coming Home' single. Richard Carpenter heard the song performed by Bette Midler on a TV broadcast and set about creating an arrangement for The Carpenters to

record. The song, about the loneliness felt by young girls who fell into the arms and beds of itinerant musicians only to be left behind the morning after, was somewhat risqué for an act with such a clean-cut image but after one minor lyrical change, it was cut utilising the famed Wrecking Crew as musicians. Karen sang the piece with such empathy during the run through that there was no need for another take and the guide vocal was used for the record.

78
HE'S GONNA STEP ON YOU
AGAIN
SOMETIMES IT'S NOT
ENOUGH
JOHN KONGOS
FLY
4

This sounded alien and exotic when it first began to be transmitted over the airwaves. Its chattering tribal drums and heavily treated guitars set it apart and the chanted chorus sounded ominous and slightly sinister while the rest of the lyric was obscure and mystifying. It certainly struck a chord with many listeners who propelled it upwards on the chart. A few months later this alien, who it transpired was from South Africa, was back with the equally arresting Tokoloshie Man before being swallowed by obscurity.

77
MY BROTHER JAKE
ONLY MY SOUL
FREE
ISLAND
4

Written by Andy Fraser and Paul Rogers; Fraser explained he had written the lyric as a pick-me-up message to his friend, reggae singer Horace Faith. Thinking that 'My Brother Horace' didn't sound great, 'Horace' was transmuted into 'Jake'. This was cut at a session just before the band split but whatever tensions existed were kept at bay on this piano-based knockabout which was one of the highlights of Free's exceptional tenure. Free were a cut-above most of their peers; they had something soulful at their core and grooved rather than rocked. Where many bands of a similar makeup were macho in the extreme, there was a tender femininity evident in the music made by this remarkable group.

76
IT DON'T COME EASY
EARLY 1970
RINGO STARR
APPLE
4

Ringo's first post-Beatles single, co-written with the uncredited George Harrison, had been attempted numerous times in 1970 before this version was selected as the 'keeper'. It was then inexplicably sat-on for 12-months before being released to out-sell concurrently released singles by his three ex-bandmates. Harrison was in the producer's chair and provides an epic sound that packs a punch. He also provides a superb cutting guitar performance and instrumental hook that helped lodge the song in the memory. The B-side too is of note, being almost an open letter to his ex-band mates, expressing the fact that he misses and needs all three; Ringo, being the ex-Beatle who took the split the worst being 'shattered' and finding himself adrift.

75
LET'S SEE ACTION
WHEN I WAS A BOY
THE WHO
TRACK
16

Pete Townshend's 'Lifeboat' project had been scuppered and the most choice material utilised for the *Who's Next* album. Three further tracks, 'Join Together', 'Relay' and this, became a run of stand-alone singles. The song reflects the influence of Townshend's guru and teacher, Meher Baba. It is a soul-searching piece and yet again a rallying cry for people not to passively accept their lot in life but strive to change it. An excellent and fascinating single, particularly for avid Who fans such as myself; but somehow, somewhere, some zip and verve was being lost; as what the songs gained in depth, they lost in equal parts vigour and youthful exuberance. The Who were on the verge of growing old.

74
FIREBALL
DEMON'S EYE
DEEP PURPLE
HARVEST
15

I loved this from the moment I heard it. The record starts with the sound of an air-conditioning unit being switched on; it sounds like a rocket leaving the launch-pad. Next, the drums kick in; they are absolutely relentless and push the souped-up combination of organ, bass and guitar headlong in a speedy rush with no time to draw breath. It is supercharged rock 'n' roll with the singer, Ian Gillan, approximating Little Richard at points. No guitar solo here, which was highly unusual for Deep Purple, a fact which no doubt had the redoubtable Ritchie Blackmore spitting plectrums. Instead there is a hammered-out bass solo followed by the organ, which has been keeping pace with the drums, mutating in a weird and wonderful echo effect.

73
AMAZING GRACE
I PITY THE POOR
IMMIGRANT
JUDY COLLINS
ELEKTRA
5

This Christian hymn had been taken up by civil rights marchers in the 1960s, protesting against the endemic racism in the US. Folk singer Judy Collins took to playing it in her set and it soon became her most requested number. She struggled with alcohol abuse and found the song strengthened and comforted her as she addressed her problems. Eventually she was persuaded to record the song and chose an *a cappella* arrangement where her crystalline voice gave absolute clarity to the words. It was a marvellous performance and the song became an unlikely worldwide hit.

72
LISTEN TO ME/HARD TIMES
BABY HUEY
CURTOM
DID NOT CHART
James Thomas Ramey had a glandular disorder which contributed to him being heavily overweight. Adopting the name Baby Huey from a giant duckling cartoon character, he and his band, the Babysitters, followed the lead of Sly and the Family Stone and adopted a psychedelic sound and

look – Huey donning African robes and spinning rhymes as part of his act. They were seen by Donny Hathaway who recommended them to Curtis Mayfield who only wanted Huey and not the band. Still, a contract was signed and a record started with Mayfield producing and the Babysitters contributing. Huey, now with a heroin habit and an alcohol problem, had swelled further in size and before the album was complete – he died of a heart attack aged 26. His album and this single were released posthumously and barely sold but, over time, the tough funk concoctions became recognised for their vitality and content; they were gritty and real. Now he is frequently sampled by rap crews and his music is seen as being hugely important in the development of hip hop .

71
HAVE YOU EVER SEEN THE RAIN/HEY TONIGHT
CREEDENCE CLEARWATER REVIVAL
FANTASY
36
The hard evidence showed that, for two years, Creedence had outsold even the Beatles and in a sales sense were now the 'biggest' band on planet Earth. And yet John Fogerty, who had written and sung all their hits (and there were plenty) felt the resentment of his band-mates whom, despite having achieved more than they could have ever have dreamed, felt unhappy and mutinous. 'Have You Ever Seen the Rain' was written in response to this situation and was a warning that the sunny days would soon be over for them. It is, as usual, absolutely top notch and is performed brilliantly; John Fogerty

in particular managing to capture his disappointment and powerlessness in the situation. Double A-side 'Hey Tonight' is a storming, glorious hoedown of a song that seemed to effortlessly roll off the production line.

70
I'M GONNA RUN AWAY FROM YOU
THE BOY NEXT DOOR
TAMI LYNN
MOJO
4

If this energetic stomper had a retro feel, it was hardly surprising, as at the instigation of Atlantic Records bigwig Jerry Wexler this track was cut in 1965 – Tami being paired with songwriter/producer Bert Berns. Inexplicably it wasn't released as a single until 1971 when it was picked up by the Northern Soul crowd before becoming a genuine hit. It proved to be a one-time solo success for Tami who had worked as an opening act for John Coltrane, Ella Fitzgerald and Miles Davis but her career never stopped and she sang on all Dr John's albums and the Rolling Stones *Exile On Mainstreet*, as well as working with Wilson Pickett, Sonny & Cher and Miles Davis.

69
LET YOUR YEAH BE YEAH
MORE LOVE
THE PIONEERS
TROJAN
5

The Pioneers were a notable and prolific Jamaican act from the mid-60s onwards. Their first international hit had been with 'Longshot Kick da Bucket', about the death of an overworked racehorse after its 203rd

race; it was beloved of the skinheads of the era and was later covered by the Specials. 'Let Your Yeah Be Yeah' became their next big hit. It was written and produced by Jimmy Cliff. It was a no-nonsense plea for straight talking – "you speak with a plastic smile, you're telling me lies" was just one lyric that told it like it was, on this top-class reggae/pop crossover hit.

68
HOCUS POCUS
JANIS
FOCUS
POLYDOR
20

'Hocus Pocus' was the opening track of the album *Moving Waves* and, in an edited form, was released as a single which sank without trace. Focus though were a band full of wit, verve and invention; too good to be ignored forever, they ploughed on. A break came when they appeared on the BBC rock show *The Old Grey Whistle Test* performing 'Hocus Pocus' where the combination of a dynamic track featuring Jan Akkerman playing exquisite guitar runs and Thijs van Leer playing organ and flute while scat singing and yodelling, all performed with manic intensity, proved irresistible. 'Hocus Pocus' was re-issued and now the time was right; and so, in early-1973 Focus had a worldwide hit.

67
TOTAL DESTRUCTION TO YOUR MIND
THE WORLD BEYOND
SWAMP DOGG
VOGUE
DID NOT CHART

Jerry Williams was a suit-and-tie

soulman. Some of his records were big on the Northern Soul scene but he was relatively obscure and more than a mite dissatisfied with, as he put it, "playing second banana". So, assisted apparently by an acid-trip and a love of Frank Zappa's use of satire, Jerry was re-invented as Swamp Dogg. Addressing any topic he cared about, Swamp Dogg took the counter-culture and immersed it in funky, southern soul and R&B. This was the title track of the Dogg's first album and its 7-inches are a brilliant introduction to the man's oeuvre. Over the bubbling funk beat, guitars scorch and horns blaze while Swamp Dogg sounds thrillingly alive and re-charged on madcap vocals.

66
HOTEL ROOM/
CALL ME A LIAR
EDGAR BROUGHTON BAND
HARVEST
DID NOT CHART
Although stating that he "despised everything they stood for" Tony Blackburn made 'Hotel Room' his 'Record of the Week'. Alas, despite this exposure, the British public ignored this fabulous double A-sided wonder in their droves. 'Hotel Room' is a dreamy, intriguing exercise in existentialism with a lead guitar playing a delicious blues-lick over a meandering, acoustic bed of loveliness. 'Call me a Liar' is the exact opposite; a stinging, hard-hitting Beefheart-like slab of proto punk.

65
WITCH QUEEN OF NEW
ORLEANS
"CHANT: 13TH HOUR"
REDBONE
EPIC
2
Written by the two native-American brothers in the band, Lolly and Pat Vegas, 'Witch Queen of New Orleans' is concerned with voodoo priestess, Marie Laveau. The sound was something I'd never heard before, drawing on influences from New Orleans Mardi Gras and the atmosphere of the bayou, combined with a hard-rock approach and native-American style chanting.

64
NATHAN JONES
HAPPY (IS A BUMPY ROAD)
THE SUPREMES
TAMLA MOTOWN
5
There was a distinct change of sound introduced on this Supremes single. It was much more rock orientated than previous releases with the 'Funk Brothers' backing track heavily phased at points. Added to that was the fact that the three Supremes, aided by Clydie King, sing in unison rather than in their more usual cross-harmony style. This gives the track an immediacy and, in view of the lyric about refusing to accept back a man who had walked out a year before, a hard-edged and emphatic strength.

63
THE KNIFE (PART 1)
THE KNIFE (PART 2)
GENESIS
CHARISMA
DID NOT CHART
This was a bolt-from-the-blue for any

Genesis fan who had become used to a gentle and pastoral sound with lyrics both poetic and obscure. Peter Gabriel claimed he wanted to write something as powerful as 'Rondo' by The Nice, and indeed 'The Knife' features a militaristic organ and drum opening as well as a challenging lyric of vicious phrases, conveying the belief that all violent revolutions lead to dictators using violence to support their position. This was the point at which Genesis finally began to fulfil their potential, stretching out, challenging themselves and their audience. Soon, with new recruits Phil Collins and Steve Hackett replacing John Mayhew and Anthony Philips, Genesis had the line-up that, before the departure of Gabriel, made them essential listening.

62
REMEMBER ME
HOW ABOUT YOU
DIANA ROSS
TAMLA MOTOWN
7

Ashford and Simpson served Diana Ross well as both producers and writers at the beginning of her solo career and this was simply stunning. The song is written from a mature point of view, after a break up, with the narrative of a woman wishing a departed lover well, and reminding him to think back on her as a good thing. It needs a nuanced and mature performance to pull off a song like this and Diana delivers with ease as she moves away from the effervescent pop soul of the Supremes towards the durability of adulthood, while retaining her appeal to her audience.

61
HOT PANTS PT. 1
HOT PANTS PT. 2
JAMES BROWN
PEOPLE
DID NOT CHART

This ode to the eye-catching clothing item, which had appeared on the market the year before, featured James and the JBs in fine, playful, almost laid-back style. Simple in concept is not necessarily simple to perform, and this is a genius groove, sampled endlessly by acts from Public Enemy to the Stone Roses – and most notably Eric B. and Rakim on their track 'Paid in Full'.

60
HAVE YOU SEEN HER
"YES I'M READY
(IF I DON'T GET TO GO)"
THE CHI-LITES
BRUNSWICK
3

This is almost doo-wop as the harmony vocalists support the half-sung, half-spoken lament to loneliness and regret, and the protagonist wanders the streets and parks to fill his time. At one point, in anguish, he cries "I'm lost, I'm lost", all the time hoping for news of the woman who has moved on and who he believes holds the key to his happiness. The Chi-Lites were a strong and versatile act from Chicago, and this sentimental single was not typical but some magic was captured in the recording studio – even my dad liked it – and he didn't like pop music at all!

59
MOONAGE DAYDREAM
HANG ON TO YOURSELF
ARNOLD CORNS
B & C
DID NOT CHART

In an attempt to try out material he wasn't at that stage convinced by David Bowie took an existing trio called Rungk and re-christened them Arnold Corns in tribute to Syd Barrett's song 'Arnold Layne', and wheeled them off to the studio where Bowie himself produced and sang. The songs were put down quickly and are, it has to be said, quite ramshackle. Bowie too delivers an extremely poor vocal performance, perhaps due to attempting to disguise his voice. The single was issued and clothes designer Freddie Burretti was credited as vocalist. The band, and single, disappeared quickly, but there had been enough strange magic in the songs that, before the end of the year, they were being recorded again, this time with Bowie's regular band. Now tighter and louder, they would be cornerstones of the ground-breaking *The Rise and Fall of Ziggy Stardust and the Spiders from Mars.*

58
INNER CITY BLUES
(MAKE ME WANNA HOLLER)
WHOLY HOLY
MARVIN GAYE
TAMLA MOTOWN
DID NOT CHART

A slow, meditative blues on the state of American inner-cities and the way the government chose to prioritise space-travel, for example, over raising living-standards for the poorest in society. Each word is enunciated clearly so the message is not lost. This was an important and majestic single.

57
GYPSIES, TRAMPS AND THIEVES
HE'LL NEVER KNOW
CHER
MCA
4

This song-story, with adult themes, gave Cher's faltering career a shot in the arm; and well it might as it was a masterful and memorable record, dealing, as it does, with racism, prostitution and teenage pregnancy. The tale is of a travelling family, despised and persecuted, but as Cher sings "every night the men would come around, and lay their money down". The song begins and ends with a verse in which the only change is that the father is now a grandfather. Apart from that, for these persecuted people, nothing has changed.

56
ONE OF THESE DAYS
FEARLESS
PINK FLOYD
HARVEST
DID NOT CHART

I must lay my cards on the table here – I don't like Pink Floyd. From the moment Syd Barrett departed I found the music of those he left behind largely dreary and miserable. When Johnny Rotten was photographed in a "I hate Pink Floyd" shirt, I smiled happily knowing that somebody else shared my feelings. Of course there are always exceptions, and I like to think myself open-minded enough to recognise these exceptions; so here are my favourite two Pink Floyd tracks, amazingly issued on one fantastic single. The largely instrumental 'One of These Days' is a vibrant slice of space-rock and 'Fearless' is a wistful, atmospheric beauty.

55
TEENAGE HEAD
EVIL HEARTED ADA
THE FLAMIN' GROOVIES
KAMA SUTRA
DID NOT CHART
The Groovies could do no wrong for me; theirs was a sound of vitality, revolution and high spirits. Here they are at their greasy best, sound-wise somewhere between the Rolling Stones and the Stooges with a bratty, lip-curling vocal by Roy Loney, spitting out lines like "I'm a child of atom bombs, and rotten air and Vietnams". This is part of the reason why the Groovies are not just another band... but an iconic band.

54
BE MY LOVER
YOU DRIVE ME NERVOUS
ALICE COOPER
WARNER BROTHERS
DID NOT CHART
This was the first Alice Cooper record I shelled out for from my meagre funds. Was it worth it? Oh yes indeed! What I got was a variation on the Velvet Underground's immortal riff from "Sweet Jane", a singer with a sneer attached to his vocal chords, self-aggrandising verses and a massive chorus. Brilliant, dumb rock & roll; I couldn't have wished for more.

53
DRAGONFLY
THE PURPLE DANCER
FLEETWOOD MAC
REPRISE
DID NOT CHART
Peter Green was gone and Jeremy Spencer was soon to follow, so this first single since the epic 'Green Manalishi' was recorded by a stripped back line-up of Danny Kirwan, Mick

Fleetwood and John McVie. Written by Danny Kirwan, with lyrics taken from a poem by W. H. Davies, it was a glistening, fabulous single. The guitar chords shimmer and the quiet vocal suggests a gentle fragility that is rarely captured. It failed to sell anywhere around the world and a dark cloud descended which seemed to be hovering over Fleetwood Mac.

52
HOT LOVE
WOODLAND ROCK/
KING OF THE MOUNTAIN COMETH
T. REX
FLY
1
With a bass player and drummer added to the band, T. Rex suddenly sounded huge. This was released in February as a stand-alone single and the changes made inside a year since the last Tyrannosaurus Rex single were myriad. The song rides in with an almost spaghetti western feel to the instrumentation, with a string arrangement by producer Tony Visconti adding to the atmospherics. Marc Bolan has adopted a leaner lyrical style; gone are the multi-syllabled mouthfuls of poetry – now the words are simple and sung in an unhurried style. Verse follows verse follows verse with no discernible chorus, but at the mid-point of the song we hit a "la la la la la la la" outro which swells, becoming enormous and seemingly endless. It is gorgeous and jubilant. Marc appeared on *Top of the Pops* to perform 'Hot Love' and revealed another change. For the first time he wore the satin suit with glittered cheekbones; he looked divine. 'Glam Rock' had begun.

51
SOLDIER BLUE
IT'S TIME FOR YOU TO GO
BUFFY SAINTE-MARIE
VANGUARD
7

This was the title-song to a film depicting the barbarous slaughter of native Americans by the US cavalry. Suppressed and pulled from cinemas within days of its release, the Nixon administration were having no truck with a re-telling of how the West was really won. As a native American woman, Buffy Sainte-Marie was a perfect choice to write and record this song. Her voice is incredible; it displays strength and pride. She sings "this is my country" and she sings of her love of it; a love not of its leaders and of the nation state, but of its lands, its rivers and trees. This is a marvellous single, one of a kind, full of emotion and full of questions that the listener cannot fail to be touched by.

50
SMILING FACES SOMETIME
THE LOVE I NEED
THE UNDISPUTED TRUTH
GORDY
DID NOT CHART

Norman Whitfield and Barrett Strong provided the Temptations with a raft of strong songs to record in the Whitfield-produced psychedelic soul idiom. 'Smiling Faces Sometime' was duly recorded as a 12-minute epic on the Temps *Sky's the Limit* album. However, plans to issue an edited version as a single were scuppered when Eddie Kendricks quit the band. Undaunted, Whitfield dropped the song into the lap of his new discoveries, the Undisputed Truth. This song, about people's deception

hidden behind smiling faces was exceptional, as was the group's performance and the track that was constructed to frame it. The similarly themed O'Jays single 'Backstabbers' acknowledged the influence in a lyric quoting this single.

49
HOLY HOLY
BLACK COUNTRY ROCK
DAVID BOWIE
MERCURY
DID NOT CHART

The recently released *Man Who Sold the World* album was deemed not to have any tracks worthy of release as a single, and so back into the studio went Bowie. He cut this with bass playing producer Herbie Flowers, credited as "Blue Mink", replacing Tony Visconti in both roles. With Marc Bolan's star in the ascendancy, Bowie adopts some of the vocal mannerisms and style of his friend/rival, making this a curious sounding item in his back catalogue. Of course it sank like a stone and was Bowie's last release on Mercury. The song stuck around and a more up-tempo version was recorded for inclusion on the *Diamond Dogs* album, before being dropped and used as a single B-side.

48
BETTER MUST COME
BETTER MUST COME
(VERSION)
DELROY WILSON
JACKPOT
DID NOT CHART

Delroy Wilson, known as the 'Cool Operator', cut this reggae classic about striving for betterment even as one suffers with producer Bunny Lee. It was chosen by Michael

Manley's People's National Party as the campaign song in the Jamaican elections of 1972. Probably best known in the U.K. for being name-checked by The Clash on their 'White Man in Hammersmith Palais' single, Wilson's early to mid-70s work was formidable and well worth checking up on.

47
JEEPSTER
LIFE'S A GAS
T. REX
FLY
2

Here Marc Bolan filches a Willie Dixon blues tune called 'You'll be Mine' that he had heard performed by Howlin' Wolf, and runs amok with it. The original lyrics are junked for sexual metaphors utilising car imagery, and the drive and attack utilised are supercharged. This rattles and shakes and kicks up a storm; it was irresistible. The flip-side too is wonderful since 'Life's a Gas' is quite simply one of Bolan's greatest ever songs. The fact that Fly released this without Bolan's permission caused some controversy at the time but, in truth, such was its explosiveness that it did absolutely demand to be a single.

46
UNDER MY WHEELS
DESPERADO
ALICE COOPER
WARNER BROTHERS
DID NOT CHART

A gleefully sick-humoured concoction from the ghoulish and fiendish Alice Cooper group, this is a quick-as-a-pistol hard rocker with horn flourishes. A hen-pecked Alice imagines taking his revenge and mowing down the object of his suffering. The song is played at breakneck speed but doesn't sacrifice melody; and it swings too. Meanwhile, Alice delivers the lyric half-way between a howl and an ironic Vegas-style croon – the cherry on the top of this delightful and tasty treat.

45
IN MY OWN TIME
SEASONS
FAMILY
REPRISE
4

Roger Chapman roars; Roger Chapman roars again, this time over drums that herald the arrival of something special. The drum-beat becomes a throb, clipped guitar chords jar the listener and Chapman begins imparting his philosophical lyrics. A piano is thrown into the mix and the intensity levels are ratcheted up. Roger Chapman roars again and the whole thing winds down to a full-stop; fabulous. There was no other band quite like Family.

44
STRANGER IN BLUE SUEDE
SHOES
STARS
KEVIN AYRES
HARVEST
DID NOT CHART

Kevin Ayres was the star determined to elude stardom and anytime it tried to creep up on him he would hotfoot away. His reputation was built on delicious records like this which became one of his best loved releases. The 'Sweet Jane' riff is recycled once more to great effect as Kevin, a creature of the counter-culture, recounts the tale of a man worn down and made rude and uncaring by his menial job. Having been won over by Kevin's kindness and hashish, the man determines to rediscover his love for life and leave behind his miserable existence − "filling the boss's bags with bread" as he puts it. The song ends with him heading out "into the sun and rain, to feel the wind on my skin again".

43
LOOK WOT YOU DUN
CANDIDATE
SLADE
POLYDOR
4

Slade had arrived with 'Get Down and Get With It' at the beginning of the year and this third hit had the confident stamp of seasoned hit-makers. Written mostly by Jim Lea and drummer Don Powell, it borrowed the percussive piano-style of John Lennon's 'Instant Karma' and included Powell's heavy-breathing during the choruses, which added to the generally unruly sound.

42
THE MAN IN BLACK
LITTLE BIT OF YESTERDAY
JOHNNY CASH
CBS
DID NOT CHART

This is not a sentimental song at all. It is, in fact, a litany of the wrongs and injustices suffered by poor people at the hands of rich unscrupulous politicians. It seems fair to say that Johnny Cash had little truck with US President Richard Nixon and the continuing war in Vietnam. No, this is not a sentimental song at all and yet, each time I hear it, my eyes fill with tears for the dignity and nobility of the man performing it and the sentiments he expresses. Aligning himself with the weak against the powerful, he ends the song with the lyric "I'll try to carry off a little darkness on my back, 'till things are brighter I'm the man in black"; and I believe he never stopped caring. He was one of a kind was Johnny Cash.

41
OPEN YOUR BOX/
POWER TO THE PEOPLE
YOKO ONO AND THE PLASTIC
ONO BAND
JOHN LENNON AND THE
PLASTIC ONO BAND
APPLE
6

Lennon's side of this double-header was the one that gained radio play and generated sales, but the truth was it was horribly glib, if well intentioned; simply rhetoric without any heart and soul or real belief in it. On the other hand, Yoko's 'Open Your Box' was sensational; a bomb! Clever, sassy, years ahead of its time and a wailing banshee of a record. Instruments rage around her, pumping out a humongous riff that never wavers and Yoko screams that we need to open up. The moral watchdogs were irate about the line "open your legs", but this was more about opening our minds to possibilities and our eyes to see what was going on, rather than a sexual tease. This was one of the great records; it was a huge shame it was hidden by Lennon's lazy sloganeering and the censors of the day.

40
SURF'S UP
DON'T GO NEAR THE WATER
BEACH BOYS
BROTHER/ REPRISE
DID NOT CHART

Composed by Brian Wilson for the ill-fated *Smile* album, which would never see the light of day, this was the crown jewel of the project. Tantalisingly played solo by Brian on piano during a TV appearance in 1967, the song became legendary. In 1971 the Beach Boys made it the title song of their latest album. It was fleshed out by the band and it was truly special; gentle, shifting as if the sea's currents determined its course. The lyric, written by Van Dyke Parks, was impressionistic, Brian's main vocal is haunting and the harmonies around it blissful. Issued as a single, with the fantastic, eco-aware 'Don't Go Near the Water' on the reverse, it is hard to fathom how it didn't chart here or in the USA.

39

YOU DON'T HAVE TO BE IN THE ARMY TO FIGHT IN THE WAR
THE SUN IS SHINING/
WE SHALL BE FREE/O'REILLY
MUNGO JERRY
DAWN
13

This was the fourth single from Mungo Jerry and the last to include founding members Colin Earl and Paul King whom, having gone to their managers demanding singer Ray Dorset be sacked, were instead handed their P45s. 'You Don't Have To Be In The Army' was a modern take on the blues, as the singer recounts his woes from spousal desertion, homelessness, joblessness and police brutality. All are delivered in a light-hearted, tongue-in-cheek fashion. Nonetheless the point, that for most of us our lives are capable of unravelling swiftly, had been made.

38
20TH-CENTURY MAN
SKIN AND BONE
THE KINKS
RCA
DID NOT CHART

From the Kinks high-watermark album *Muswell Hillbillies* came this stinging single where Ray Davies critiques the modern world, describing it as a "mechanical nightmare" and himself as "a paranoid, schizoid product of the 20th Century". It is a remarkable song, and the singing performance of Ray Davies is perfect for this tale, carrying an edge of desperation.

37
BACK SEAT OF MY CAR
HEART OF THE COUNTRY
PAUL AND LINDA
MCCARTNEY
APPLE
39

One of the absolute highlights of McCartney's career; "Back Seat of My Car" displays all his melodic gift, his genius arranging skills as the song moves between sweeping widescreen beauty to sharp rock 'n' roll and, crucially, a fine lyric, which is not always the case with McCartney. The lyric can be read in two ways: there is the face-value interpretation – the song is about a couple driving and loving, leaving the objections of overprotective parents behind them. Equally, the song can be seen as a cry for freedom from the Beatles and the court cases surrounding that divorce, with lines such as "We believe that we can't be wrong", a criticism of John and Yoko, and "Listen to daddy's song" aimed at the manager he opposed, Alan Klein. Whatever the truth of the matter, the fact remains that this is, in every sense, a truly great record.

36
BACK STREET LUV
EVERDANCE
CURVED AIR
WARNER BROTHERS
4

Curved Air were as prog as prog got, with a folk-tinged sound, a heavily prominent electric violin and an archetypal female 'hippy' singer, the strikingly attractive Sonja Kristina, dressed in chiffon and silks. Somehow they conjured up this top-5 single based on ex-convent girl Sonja telling of how she became attracted to, and seduced, a married ex-convict. Its musical backing, featuring a grinding synthesizer, was a perfect accompaniment to the sorry story of the lyric and makes this a most memorable sound from the early 70s.

35
SPLIT (Part 2)
SPLIT (Part 3)
GROUNDHOGS
UNITED ARTISTS
DID NOT CHART

There was probably not a more exciting sound in the UK than that made by The Groundhogs. Led by guitar-player Tony McPhee, they were an unapologetically loud jam band. Their music was frenetic, as drums were clattered maniacally and bass and guitar fought to keep up. The guitar, heavily distorted, provided any melody in the midst of the twisting,

screaming bombardment. Here McPhee is addressing a drug-induced mental breakdown and emptying his disturbed mind in a series of primal screams. This was music as cathartic free-expression.

34
HEART OF GOLD
SUGAR MOUNTAIN
NEIL YOUNG
REPRISE
10

Although 'Heart of Gold' is the highest-selling single of his career, and recognised as a standard, its success didn't sit comfortably with Neil. He described himself as "driving too close to the middle of the road" and instead decided to "drive into a ditch where you meet more interesting people". I'm glad Neil saw things that way and decided to explore the idiosyncratic path he chose, but it must be said that 'Heart of Gold' is a fabulous record that touches my soul to this day.

33
STRAWBERRY LETTER 23
ICE-COLD DAYDREAM
SHUGGIE OTIS
EPIC
DID NOT CHART

Pre-dating Prince by the best part of a decade, 'Strawberry Letter 23' is precisely the variety of psychedelic funk/soul that would make the man from Minneapolis a world star. Shuggie Otis didn't seem to want that kind of recognition, despite being held in such high-esteem that Billy Preston was sent along to sound him out about joining the Rolling Stones in 1974. In addition, Quincy Jones was asking to produce him. Shuggie turned them both down, preferring to play sessions on his father's (Johnny Otis) albums. This release wasn't to be the hit it deserved to be but in 1977 the Brothers Johnson recorded a near-replica version of the song and put it on the hit parade.

32
LOVE THE ONE YOU'RE WITH
TO A FLAME
STEPHEN STILLS
ATLANTIC
37

This is a fine song written by Stills who acknowledges that the phrase "if you can't be with the one you love, love the one you're with" was often employed by Billy Preston; Stills asked if he could use it and the keyboard wizard was happy to acquiesce. Stills performs the song magnificently; it is one of those that always makes my heart skip a beat on hearing it. Such is the strength of the song, it has been a hit several times over for artists such as the Isley Brothers, Luther Vandross and Bucks Fizz.

31
BURUNDI BLACK PART 1
BURUNDI BLACK PART 2
BURUNDI STEPHENSON
BLACK
BARCLAY
31

This was the creation of Michael Bernhoic, a French pianist and record producer, who heavily exploited and sampled (without acknowledgement or payment) 25 Burundi drummers from an album *Musique de Burundi* released in 1968, adding treated keyboards and guitars and releasing the track into the pop market. The result was a startled public embracing the tribal beats and guttural chanting and it became a floor-filling discotheque era classic.

30
DO IT/THE SNAKE
THE PINK FAIRIES
POLYDOR
DID NOT CHART

Two glorious sides of ramshackle brutality from The Fairies, featuring a double-drum line-up and Paul Rudolph's out-of-left-field, completely over-the-top guitar wrangling. Unrefined, unrestrained and unrepentant, this was the band's first release and, not knowing if it might also be their last, they keep nothing in reserve. These freaks simply stampede through both sides of this proto-metal, proto-punk rave-up. 'Do it' is dementedly screamed throughout by Twink until he gives up, his voice wrecked, and climbs back behind his drum kit. 'The Snake' approximates the sound of the MC5 for around half its length, and is quite tight before Rudolph, perhaps bored with the relative restraint, throws a wobbler and unleashes a death-ray guitar solo of surging power.

29
GOD'S CHILDREN
MOMENTS
THE KINKS
PYE
DID NOT CHART

From the soundtrack of the film *Percy*, about a penis transplant, 'God's Children' issues a warning concerning our reliance on technology. The song is delivered in ballad-style and is a plea for sanity and a return to simplicity; it is a touching and tender song, full of grace. Little wonder that both Ray Davies and fellow Kink John Gosling have both opined that it is amongst their personal favourites.

28
ANOTHER DAY
OH WOMAN OH WHY
PAUL MCCARTNEY
APPLE
2

Paul's first solo single was 'Another Day'. It harked back to the observational, story-telling style of 'She's Leaving Home' and 'Eleanor Rigby' from Beatles days. Here, the subject is a woman saddened by the repetitive drudgery of her personal and professional life; she is lonely and unfulfilled. Musically, McCartney's melodic bass-line is high in the mix and, along with acoustic guitar, pushes the song along briskly suggesting the relentless pace of a city at work. The B-side, 'Oh Woman Oh Why' is another piece of genius; a rocking, funky beast of a song with screamed vocals and pistol shots echoing in its thrilling coda.

27
REASON TO BELIEVE/
MAGGIE MAY
ROD STEWART
MERCURY
1

Rod Stewart went from nearly-man to superstar in a single-stroke with this record. Originally 'Reason to Believe' was the side pushed; written by Tim Hardin and relying heavily on Faces bandmate Ian McLagen's dramatic piano playing to strike a suitably gloomy feel, Rod sang it with convincing pain and pathos. However radio stations began playing Rod and Martin Quittenton's mandolin-powered 'Maggie May' instead, which charmed the birds from the trees. A *Top Of The Pops* appearance with The Faces in tow, and an embarrassed looking John

Peel 'pretending' to play mandolin, turned into an impromptu football kick-about and Rod, as 'one of the lads', became an unofficial national treasure.

26
JUST MY IMAGINATION
(RUNNING AWAY WITH ME)
YOU MAKE YOUR OWN
HEAVEN AND HELL RIGHT
HERE ON EARTH
THE TEMPTATIONS
TAMLA MOTOWN
8

Resting on 'Funk Brother' Bob Babbitt's elegant bass-line, this Norman Whitfield/Barrett Strong creation is disarmingly light and beautiful, but the lyric, delivered supremely by Eddie Kendricks on his last Temptations single, adds weight and gravity to proceedings, being sung from the perspective of a man imagining a relationship with a woman he desires. His fantasy offers him consolation from the fact she doesn't even know him; his life is dream-like as he is overwhelmed by his imagination, even while reality tortures him. This conflicted man, we realise, is doing huge emotional damage to himself. This is a song of such subtlety and depth that I could never tire of listening to it.

25
MY SWEET LORD
WHAT IS LIFE
GEORGE HARRISON
APPLE
1

George emerged from the shadow of Lennon & McCartney with 'My Sweet Lord'. It must have felt sweet, until the plagiarism law-suit from Phil Spector arrived. Delaney

Bramlett also laid claim to his part in the songwriting process. Nonetheless, 'My Sweet Lord', if one can stomach the piety, is just fine. Better though was 'What Is Life', hidden on the rear of the single. This one moves, has a brilliant, ringing guitar motif, a joyous vocal from George and winning energy and enthusiasm.

24
DEVIL'S ANSWER
THE ROCK
ATOMIC ROOSTER
B&C
4

While George Harrison was looking to the heavens for guidance, Vincent Crane and the ever-changing line up of Atomic Rooster were seeking answers in darker places. This soul-tinged prog that you could actually dance to proved to be a winning formula. Squealing guitar licks, evoking licking flames from the abyss, compete for our attention with Crane's tortured Hammond organ assault. Meanwhile, enigmatic words pour forth as if from a dark, mysterious spell being incanted. No wonder people say "the devil has all the best tunes".

23
IF YOU REALLY LOVE ME
THINK OF ME AS YOUR SOLDIER
STEVIE WONDER
TAMLA MOTOWN
60

Now 20-years old, Stevie not only wrote and produced this single and its parent album, *Where I'm Coming From*, but played most of the instruments too; Moog bass, synthesiser, drums and piano were handled by him, with the Funk Brothers contributing the rest.

This would be the last time he would use Motown's pool of musicians to record, as he subsequently moved operations to New York and made his own choices. Why this was such a lowly-selling single in the U.K. is something of a mystery. Maybe the tempo changes meant it wasn't really a number to dance to? Still, it hit big in the States and is a joyful, hand-clapping slice of exuberance, with future wife Syreeta Wright not just co-writing but heavily featured as a vocal foil.

22
MOVE ON UP
BROTHER OF MINE
CURTIS MAYFIELD
BUDDAH
12

In 1965 Curtis Mayfield had written and recorded the socially-conscious anthem 'People Get Ready' for his band, the Impressions. Curtis was an artiste of great substance; he started his solo career with the album *Curtis* from which this was extracted. Full of insight and concern about the socio-political state of America in his insightful lyrics, while never neglecting the need for it to be listened to and enjoyed, 'Move On Up' is a slice of positivity in its exhortations to live life to the full and not allow expectations to be trampled on. Utilising blazing horns, swooping strings, an instant rhythm played on conga and voiced by the magnificent, spine-tingling falsetto that was his trademark, this is Curtis Mayfield at the peak of his powers.

21
TRENCHTOWN ROCK
GROOVING KINGSTON
BOB MARLEY AND THE
WAILERS
GREEN DOOR
DID NOT CHART
Initially modelled on Curtis
Mayfield and the Impressions, by this
point Bob, Bunny and Peter, who
collectively made up the Wailers, had
developed their own voice and style.
This was the first of their records I
heard, and I recall it fascinating me.
Where is, and what is "Trenchtown",
I wondered. There was much for me
to learn. What I did know for sure
though was that I liked this music.
It was a celebration of the classless
universality of these sounds that reach
in and touch our souls. "When it hits,
you feel no pain", sang Bob Marley,
and that is a universal truth no matter
what walk of life we are from; "Be
you big fish or sprat", music lightens
our souls and eases our burdens.

20
COZ I LUV YOU
MY LIFE IS NATURAL
SLADE
POLYDOR
1
Apparently written in a half-hour
by Jim Lea and Noddy Holder, and
influenced by the style of the Django
Reinhardt/Stephane Grappelli 'Hot
Club' repertoire, it was a lighter,
more melodic piece than they were
comfortable with but with foot-
stomping and hand-clapping added
to the mesmerising sound of Jim Lea's
electric violin, it caught the attention
of a mass audience and Slade had
their first, and in my opinion best,
number one hit.

19
JOHNNY TOO BAD
TOO BAD
THE SLICKERS
PUNCH
DID NOT CHART
The salutary tale of a 'rude boy' set
to a genuinely brilliant rocksteady
rhythm, voiced with matter-of-fact
restraint by the Slickers – everything
about this record is perfect. There
is no glamorizing the lifestyle of
Johnny; he is using violence as a way
to rise in Kingston's tough streets, but
it is clear to all that he is heading for
a fall. It is the authentic voice of those
streets that we hear and this is a classic
of Jamaican music.

18
BROWN SUGAR
BITCH/LET IT ROCK
THE ROLLING STONES
ROLLING STONES RECORDS
2
Written by Mick Jagger and recorded
in Alabama in late-1969, 'Brown
Sugar' was debuted at the Altamont
Speedway show that effectively ended
the 1960s hippy dream, as 18-year-
old Meredith Hunter was murdered
in front of the stage. Released as
a single in April 1971, this had a
groove beyond compare, along with
a kaleidoscope of controversial lyrics
concerning race, rape, slavery, heroin
and sex. Perhaps understandably, the
Rolling Stones would never sound as
vital and as dangerous ever again.

17
RESPECT YOURSELF
YOUR GONNA MAKE ME CRY
THE STAPLES SINGERS
STAX
7
Stax soul-singer Luther Ingram,

frustrated by the state of the world around him, stated to songwriter Mack Rice that, "black folk need to learn to respect themselves". Impressed by the power and sentiment of the comment, Rice began constructing a song based upon it that would advocate self-empowerment through self-respect. The song was offered to the Staples Singers by producer Al Bell. They agreed to record it and were teamed with the Muscle Shoals' rhythm section and the Memphis Horns. Lead vocals were handled by the incredible Mavis Staples and her father Pops. It was a powerful statement aligned to an equally powerful slice of funk and it rightfully put the Staples Singers in the charts.

16

WON'T GET FOOLED AGAIN
I DON'T EVEN KNOW MYSELF
THE WHO
TRACK
9

The sixties counter-culture had delivered no answers; there had been glib statements of no discernible substance and Pete Townshend was thinking deeply about this. He befriended a group of anarchist squatters and questioned them on their beliefs. They disappointed him; offering no solutions, serving up nihilistic anger and no more. This seems to have fed into 'Won't Get Fooled Again', a glorious rock noise with a synthesised pulse and perhaps the greatest scream in music history, courtesy of Roger Daltrey. If lyrically it seems confusing, that may well have been Townshend expressing his own confusion, although ultimately he seems to be saying that power corrupts and merely knocking one

figurehead off his pedestal, only to be replaced by a new one, will not elicit change.

15

AIN'T NO SUNSHINE
HARLEM
BILL WITHERS
A&M
40

With a spare arrangement and backing, unobtrusive strings and nothing more, the performance of the unknown Bill Withers was a revelation. His bluesy, lived-in voice was full of tenderness and expression; his song was full of yearning and bruised beauty. The whole thing possessed a simple wisdom and compassion. We found out that Bill Withers was a 31-year old factory worker and if anyone thought 'Ain't No Sunshine' was a flash-in-the-pan, they merely had to play the B-side, 'Harlem' and they would surely be awestruck by this remarkable talent.

14

ULTIMA THULE PART 1
ULTIMA THULE PART 2
TANGERINE DREAM
OHR
DID NOT CHART

Screeching guitar, thundering bass, drum fills which never allow momentum to flag, and swelling Mellotron drone on top, this was Tangerine Dream as an unrecognisable entity from their later much more successful 'Virgin' years; here they are loud, heavy and fabulous.

13
IT'S TOO LATE/
I FEEL THE EARTH MOVE
CAROLE KING
A&M
6

'It's Too Late' is a minor-key meditation on the sadness of a romantic breakdown, with a lyric by Toni Stern, written the day after she (Stern) split from James Taylor. It is a sincere sounding confessional, handled with great sensitivity, without being maudlin. 'I Feel the Earth Move', on the other hand, is a celebratory hoot to carnal joys; Carole King's singing is warm and joyful as she feels happiness and anticipation about being close to her lover, and her piano-playing captures the feeling of excitement and arousal as it races like a beating heart.'

12
SPANISH HARLEM
LEAN ON ME
ARETHA FRANKLIN
ATLANTIC
14

They didn't nickname Aretha 'Lady Soul' without good reason. She had the knack of getting to the heart of a song and totally inhabiting it; in this case 'Spanish Harlem', written by the unlikely combination of Phil Spector and Jerry Lieber. This was first a hit for Ben E King in 1961; in his hands it was a gentle and romantic rhumba but when Aretha cut this in 1971, with a little help from Dr John on keyboards, she transformed it and made the song her own. It was delivered in a more sombre style, and now seemed to comment on the injustices and hardships commonly seen on the hot streets of Harlem.

11
FAMILY AFFAIR
LOVE 'N' HAIGHT
SLY AND THE FAMILY STONE
EPIC
15

More a Sly solo record than a band effort, only sister Rose from the Family Stone participated in the making of this record, he sings a deliberately off-key lead vocal over his programmed rhythm track, adding bass and guitar, while Billy Preston played piano. Both the attractive and the unappealing aspects of family life are trawled through in the brief but pointed lyric. It was a world away from earlier up-tempo hits such as 'Dance to the Music', but this snail-paced downbeat funk was every bit as beguiling.

TOP 30 - 8TH MAY 1971

1	1	7	DOUBLE BARREL	
			Dave and Ansell Collins	Technique TE 901
2	3	5	KNOCK THREE TIMES Dawn	Bell BLL 1146
3	4	3	BROWN SUGAR/BITCH/LET IT ROCK	
			Rolling Stones	Rolling Stones RS 19100
4	7	4	IT DON'T COME EASY Ringo Starr	Apple R 5898
5	6	5	MOZART SYMPHONY No. 40	
			Waldo de los Rios	A&M AMS 836
6	2	11	HOT LOVE T. Rex	Fly BUG 6
7	9	6	REMEMBER ME Diana Ross Tamla Motown TMG 768	
8	8	8	(Where Do I Begin) LOVE STORY	
			Andy Williams	CBS 7020
9	16	7	SOMETHING OLD SOMETHING NEW	
			Fantastics	Bell BLL 1141
10	6	9	BRIDGET THE MIDGET Ray Stevens	CBS 7070
11	15	5	ROSETTA Fame and Price Together	CBS 7108
12	20	6	INDIANA WANTS ME	
			R. Dean Taylor	Tamla Motown TMG 763
13	14	9	FUNNY FUNNY Sweet	RCA 2051
14	11	8	IF NOT FOR YOU Olivia Newton-John Pye 7N 25543	
15	22	4	JIG-A-JIG East Of Eden	Deram DM 297
16	10	11	WALKING CCS	RAK 109
17	12	12	ROSE GARDEN Lynn Anderson	CBS 5360
18	25	4	IT'S A SIN TO TELL A LIE	
			Gerry Monroe	Chapter One CH 144
19	26	6	SUGAR SUGAR Sakkarin	RCA 2064
20	18	7	MY LITTLE ONE Marmalade	Decca F 13135
21	13	8	THERE GOES MY EVERYTHING	
			Elvis Presley	RCA Victor 2060
22	27	3	DIDN'T I (Blow Your Mind This Time)	
			Delfonics	Bell BLL 1099
23	45	2	MALT AND BARLEY BLUES	
			McGuinness Flint	Capitol CL 15682
24	50	2	MY BROTHER JAKE Free	Island WIP 6100
25	48	2	HEAVEN MUST HAVE SENT YOU	
			Elgins	Tamla Motown TMG 771
26	17	8	JACK IN THE BOX	
			Clodagh Rodgers	RCA Victor RCA 2066
27	28	5	MAMA'S PEARL	
			Jackson Five	Tamla Motown TMG 769
28	32	3	UN BANC, UN ARBRE, UNE RUE	
			Severine	Philips 6009 135
29	23	22	AMAZING GRACE Judy Collins	Elektra 2101 020
30	29	5	SILVERY RAIN Cliff Richard	Columbia DB 8774

10

GET IT ON
THERE WAS A TIME/RAW RAMP
T. REX
FLY
1

This time around Marc Bolan borrowed a little Chuck Berry style riffage, acknowledged in his ad-libbed use of the phrase "and meanwhile I'm still thinking" lifted from Berry's 'Little Queenie'. Prog legends Rick Wakeman of Yes and Ian McDonald of King Crimson added piano and saxophone parts (in Wakeman's case, he desperately needed the £9 session fee to pay his rent). It is a barnstorming record, full of spirit, of which Bolan was justifiably proud. However, his once closest ally, John Peel, was not impressed by the new heavyweight T. Rex. He took unjustified offence at this single and criticised it on-air, which signalled the end of what had been a firm friendship.

9

DECLARATION OF RIGHTS
DECLARATION VERSION
THE ABYSSINIANS
COXSONE
DID NOT CHART

Following the extraordinary 'Satta Massagana', the second Abyssinians single was, at the very least, its equal. Converts to Rastafarian beliefs, at a time when this was seen as being deeply subversive, here they do not hold back in calling for justice; "Get up and stand up for your rights" is the refrain, whilst in the verses the blight of slavery is addressed and the wise advice that "fussing and fighting amongst ourselves" will achieve nothing, is offered. This is a radical 'great leap forward' for Jamaican music, and an essential listen for anyone who loves music in general.

8

WATCHING THE RIVER FLOW
SPANISH IS THE LOVING TONGUE
BOB DYLAN
CBS
24

Dylan had scuttled out of the city to his Woodstock retreat, in large part to escape the crazies who stalked him and expected him to carry the mantle of "spokesman for his generation". They pressured him and felt they needed him to protest on their behalf. It drove him crazy, but after three albums of country rock he seemed to be growing restless for a new adventure, a different sound. To that end he recruited Leon Russell to produce him and assemble a band. From the resulting sessions emerged this high-powered single, somewhere between a canter and a gallop, with thrilling guitar licks adorning Russell's rollicking piano playing. Dylan gives voice to his thoughts on his retreat; comparing himself to the rolling river, he sees his life reflected in it as it rolls on by. "If I had wings and I could fly, I know where I would go, but I just sit here on this bank of sand and watch the river flow" is a lyric that suggests he misses his old life, but realises things have changed and for now, he must bide his time and observe from the outside.

7

DOUBLE BARREL
VERSION 2
DAVE AND ANSELL COLLINS
TECHNIQUE
1

Written and produced by Winston Riley, who put Dave Barker behind the microphone, this was one of those eureka moments for me. When I first heard its incessant piano-driven groove, the hairs on the back of my neck stood up; I loved this record. The few lyrics present are nonsensical but delivered with great panache. It altered the way I walked; I was possessed by its rhythm and still feel a thrill whenever I hear that first cry of "I am the magnificent!". Incidentally an 18-year old drummer,

Sly Dunbar, later of Sly & Robbie, made his first appearance on record here.

6

THEME FROM SHAFT
CAFE REGIO'S
ISAAC HAYES
STAX
4

Isaac Hayes was persuaded to compose a film score by director Joel Freeman, with the promise of an audition for the part of the lead character in the film that would become *Shaft*. As it transpired the part was cast without Hayes getting his audition, but he completed the soundtrack anyway. The film became a runaway hit, and though no single had been scheduled for release, demand grew and an edit of the theme was released. Regarded by many as the first disco record, Hayes had put it together quickly utilising an unreleased song he had written and a drum break he'd heard on an Otis Redding session he'd played on. With prominent wah-wah guitar and a synthesised keyboard, played by Hayes, this was a unique sound; indeed it was ground-breaking. Using dialogue from several voices, rather than a sung lyric, it was impressionistic and the risqué nature of that dialogue was bold and daring. So, as much as this record was gorgeous in sound, it had street smarts and shock-value as well.

5

TIRED OF BEING ALONE
RIGHT NOW RIGHT NOW
AL GREEN
HI
4

What a talent Al Green was; he wrote his own material, and had a voice of incomparable beauty and grace which he combined with a grit that broke hearts when he sang. And in producer Willie Mitchell he had the perfect foil... so *simpatico* with Green's oeuvre that it was uncanny. Add to that the Hi Records house-band, assembled by Mitchell, who gave wonderful performances on Al Green's recordings, full of restrained power and subtle nuance. All of these elements came together on 'Tired of Being Alone' to create a complete classic.

4

RIDERS ON THE STORM
CHANGELING
THE DOORS
ELEKTRA
22

A travelogue of sorts, through the underbelly of the American dream: the road is full of danger, serial killers, psychopaths and death, and the pain of being born is pondered as the magisterial pace of the journey remains unhurried and unaltered. This was one of The Doors finest records; a real ensemble-piece where each component adds substantially to the whole. It was the last song ever recorded by the band during Jim Morrison's lifetime and they conspired to save their best for last.

3

WHAT'S GOING ON
GOD IS LOVE
MARVIN GAYE
TAMLA MOTOWN
80

"This is the worst thing I've ever heard in my life", was the alleged reaction of Motown-boss Berry Gordy to Marvin Gaye after being presented with 'What's Going On'. Gaye promptly went on strike and refused to record any material until the song was released. Anxious for product from Gaye, Motown sales Vice-President Barney Ales, without Gordy's knowledge, pressed-up the single and released it. The song was originally written by Renaldo 'Obie' Benson (of the Four Tops) and Al Cleveland, after Benson witnessed police brutality against anti-war protesters. Benson took it to his fellow Four Tops who refused to record it and Gaye was offered the song. He changed the melody and re-wrote part of the lyric, reflecting conversations he had with his brother Frankie, who was a serving soldier in Vietnam. And so, after being dissuaded from giving the song away to the Originals by Benson, Marvin recorded his masterpiece, his plea for peace, his call for love – and in doing so, made the world a better place for those who listened.

2

THE HARDER THEY COME
MANY RIVERS TO CROSS
JIMMY CLIFF
ISLAND
DID NOT CHART

From the film of the same name, Jimmy Cliff's classic, backed by another classic on the B-side, did little business in the UK. That does not reflect on the quality, or our appreciation, of the record. 'The Harder They Come' is a song about defying the odds, about determination and self-belief. It is massively inspirational and musically superbly conceived, with the instrumental hook giving pause between the verses of cascading words, articulating the singer's refusal to quit in his quest. "I'd rather be a free man in my grave, than living as a puppet or a slave" sings Jimmy, giving voice to Ivan, the film's lead character; and we can feel nothing but admiration for his spirit as he fights against the forces who try to kill his hopes and dreams.

1

THE REVOLUTION WILL NOT
BE TELEVISED
HOME IS WHERE THE HATRED IS
GIL SCOTT HERON
FLYING DUTCHMAN
DID NOT CHART

The phrase "The Revolution Will Not Be Televised" is firmly in the lexicon these days; it has been neutralised, becoming nothing more than a snappy slogan but in 1971 those words carried an implicit threat, or warning, depending on your viewpoint. This proto-rap was highly articulate as it attacked the totems of middle-class America, making point after point after point. It marked Gil Scott-Heron as a remarkable talent, possessed of

great dignity and of huge significance; a man who would not be moulded into becoming a family entertainer. Here was an artist who made it his mission to speak the truth. This was aural electricity that hit with a mighty charge, and the final statement "there will be no re-runs, the revolution will be live", was both thrilling and shocking at the same time.

1972

EVENTS

- The United Nations appoints ex-Nazi Kurt Waldheim as Secretary-General
- Japanese Soldier Shoichi Yokoi is discovered in Guam, where he has spent 28 years in the jungle unaware that the Second World War has ended
- Bloody Sunday: 14 unarmed nationalist civil rights marchers are massacred by the British Army in Derry
- Miners Strike: British Government declare a State of Emergency
- U.S. President Richard Nixon visits China and meets Chairman Mao Zedong
- 7 people murdered by I.R.A. bomb in Aldershot
- *The Godfather* film starring Marlon Brando is released
- The Burundian Genocide begins: more than half-a-million Hutu people will be murdered
- Ulrike Meinhof and Gerhard Muller of the Red Army Faction are arrested in West Germany
- In June five White House operatives are arrested for a burglary at the Democratic National Committee Headquarters in the Watergate Hotel. Having successfully covered up his involvement, Richard Nixon is re-elected as President of the United States, defeating George McGovern in a landslide.
- American Bobby Fischer and Russian Boris Spassky compete for the title of World Chess Champion in Reykjavik. Fischer wins to become the first US champion
- Bloody Friday: 22 I.R.A. bombs explode in Belfast; 9 people are murdered and 130 are injured
- Idi Amin expels 50,000 Asians from Uganda
- At the Olympic Games in Munich 11 Israeli athletes are murdered by the Black September terrorist group; 5 terrorists and a policeman also die.
- Atari launches the first generation of video games releasing an arcade version of 'Pong'

- A tea-house named 'Mellow Yellow' opens in Amsterdam as the first legal outlet for the sale of cannabis in the Netherlands
- Apollo 17 is launched: it is the last manned flight to the moon to date
- Swedish Prime Minister Olaf Palme compares the American bombing of North Vietnam to Nazi atrocities; the US breaks diplomatic relations with Sweden. Two days later on December 25, the Christmas Day bombing of North Vietnam causes widespread criticism of the United States and President Richard Nixon
- Manchester United sack Frank O'Farrell as manager following a 5-0 defeat to Crystal Palace. Derby County win the First Division title, Leeds the FA Cup.

NOTABLE BIRTHS

Eminem; Zinedine Zidane; DJ Shadow; Cameron Diaz ;Vanessa Paradis; Luis Figo

NOTABLE DEATHS

Charles Atlas; M.C. Escher; J Edgar Hoover; Rory Storm; Ezra Pound; Billy Murcia; Danny Whitten; Havergal Brian; Harry Truman

NOTABLE FILMS

Cabaret; Aguirre, Wrath of God; Fat City; The Godfather; Pink Flamingos; Superfly; Last Tango in Paris; Deliverance; Fists of Fury The Harder They Come

NOTABLE BOOKS

Watership Down – Richard Adams
The Stepford Wives – Ira Levin
Surfacing – Margaret Atwood
The Joy of Sex – Alex Comfort
We Can Build You – Philip K Dick
Banco – Henri Charriere
Erections, Ejaculations, Exhibitions and Takes of Ordinary Madness – Charles Bukowski
Profession of Violence – John George Pearson
Dissemination – Jacques Derrida

THE MUSIC

It hadn't taken long for the optimism of the sixties to give way to a creeping air of despondency and despair. The news worldwide and domestically was all bad, from the escalation of 'The Troubles' in Ireland, to the war being waged between trade-unions and the Tory government. The U.K. was a tired and grim place; clothes, furniture and cars were coloured predominantly beige and brown. Class divisions were deeply entrenched and racism was a pernicious evil embedded in the national psyche, to the point that expressing anti-discriminatory views was seen as being subversive and unpatriotic. America was, if anything, even more divided than the U.K. It was a country tearing itself apart on pro- or anti-Vietnam war arguments. Its racism was even more blatant than the British variety, and to top it all they had a narcissistic President who was secretly engaged in criminal activity.

A new generation of Germans were opposing their rulers, many of whom were ex-Nazis. Most militant were the Baader Meinhof/Red Army Faction, who waged a campaign of terror and violence against the establishment. Asia, Africa, South America and the Middle East were all highly turbulent and human life seemed to be a cheap commodity with casual mass slaughter seemingly on the news every day. Perhaps because of this state of affairs a lot of the music we heard strove to give voice to the concerns of the people. Perhaps the vibrancy that was undeniable in music was a backlash to the dull, oppressive wider world. Certainly throughout many completely different genres, this year was one of great quality and undoubted substance. Artists were connecting with listeners on an emotional, intellectual and political level; the world itself was a dark place, but the world of music was full of colour.

Into this musical world 'Glam' erupted; David Bowie emerged into the mainstream as a fully-fledged genius impossible to ignore or dismiss. His talent was only matched by his sartorial influence which saw Elton John, Slade and the Rolling Stones all applying a touch of make-up to enhance upbeat, uplifting singles. Bowie's lead also paved the way for the undoubtedly talented Roxy Music, Alice Cooper and Lou Reed to infiltrate the mainstream; and of course at this stage Marc Bolan, who might have been wise to look over his shoulder, felt absolutely unassailable atop his perch. From Germany we received music that stunned us from a new breed of artists, including Can, Neu and Faust, who were all intent on creating a sound that owed nothing to the British or American influence. From America came The Carpenters with an easy-listening sound that captivated not only traditionalists but also, because of its undeniable quality, anyone with an open mind. There emerged too the subtle and subversively sly pop of Steely Dan, whilst soul acts such as Bobby Womack, Billy Preston, Harold Melvin & the Bluenotes and James Brown, released absolute classic singles. Established acts too contributed singles that reminded us of their enduring quality; The Kinks, The Move, The Who, Van Morrison and Derek & the Dominoes were all at this point alive and still kicking, while the less established likes of Thin Lizzy, Hawkwind, Genesis and 10cc were emerging and making their mark.

MY 1972

I was, in many ways, coming into my own and my character was developing, due in part to my ability with a football being recognised. I had lacked the confidence to go and join teams but my reputation as a player meant that now I was approached and asked to play. I was never out of my depth and teams flourished and won trophies with my inclusion. I was appreciated and respected in this sphere. I was also going to lots of gigs – both good and bad. I saw terrible performances from Procol Harum and ELP for instance, but equally there were life-affirming gigs that were instrumental in shaping my outlook on life by, amongst others, David Bowie, Kevin Ayres and Lou Reed.

My school work, meanwhile, went rapidly downhill. I was in open conflict with one teacher in particular, a bully who was attempting to crush my spirit. I arrived one day with my hair pushed up into spikes and dyed a bright orange colour. It scandalised the whole establishment; never had a pupil turned up looking like this before. It was 1972 in the industrial North West! It just wasn't done… I was tall and assured enough to pass for 18 and therefore I could be served alcohol in pubs, and

I started finding myself in dangerous situations. In a club, in Manchester's gay sector, I was sexually abused by a group of men. This event scarred me, diminished me and caused considerable emotional damage but, as always, music in the form of records was the balm to my soul and I also acquired an ally. My younger brother now shared my passion, and between us we built a collection of fantastic records by the likes of Spirit, Love, Robert Johnson, Pearls Before Swine, King Crimson, MC5 and the Velvet Underground. These were my spirit guides; they opened up doors of enlightenment to me; they were my true teachers. I learned more about life listening to the first Velvet Underground LP than I did in five years of schooling. Music was shaping me; it was my oxygen and I was gulping it down hungrily.

100
GARDEN PARTY
SO LONG MAMA
RICK NELSON
MCA
41

Rick (or Ricky as he had been) Nelson was an early-60s, clean-cut pop star who had several hits including 'Hello Mary Lou' however by this point he was making his mark playing a hybrid of country and rock with his well-respected Stone Canyon Band. 'Garden Party' is a recollection of going to play an "oldies show". Unrecognised, he felt like a human jukebox and when he tried to play his contemporary music he received catcalls and jeers. The sour-taste in his mouth moved him to write this put-down of those "oldies" events. The concluding line summed up his feelings succinctly... "If memories were all I sang, I'd rather drive a truck". Well said that man!

99
DOCTOR MY EYES
LOOKING INTO YOU
JACKSON BROWNE
ASYLUM
DID NOT CHART

A teenage Jackson Browne had accompanied Velvet Underground chanteuse Nico upon her departure from that band and contributed to her solo debut 'Chelsea Girl'. Now, in his early twenties, his own debut album was released with this as the obvious single. A striking up-tempo piano piece, with backing vocals from David Crosby and Graham Nash, the song was about experiencing misery and coming out the other end numb and concerned that now there is no feeling left at all. A year later the

Jackson 5 recorded a version that was a big UK hit.

98
ROCKET MAN
HOLIDAY INN/
LADY SAMANTHA
ELTON JOHN
DJM
2

Well established by this point, but with only one previous hit-single to his name – 'Your Song' (1970) – Elton John must have known this would be a sensation. It shares similar inspiration to David Bowie's 'Space Oddity' in its tale of an astronaut lost and lonely out in space. It even shared, in Gus Dudgeon, the same producer. It is handled in ballad-style with some electronic effects but what makes it special, and separated it from Elton John's earlier work, was the use of the other musicians to harmonise with, which they do to stunning effect, lifting the song considerably. Lessons were clearly learned, and scoring hits became much less of a problem from this point onward.

97
WALKING IN THE RAIN WITH THE ONE I LOVE
I SHOULD HAVE KNOWN
LOVE UNLIMITED
UNI
14

Love Unlimited were a female R&B trio put together by writer/producer Barry White, and this was their first single. It was lush and lavish and, of course, deeply romantic. Notable too for Barry White's first public vocal performance, as his soon-to-be unmistakable voice is used as the lover who is heard during a telephone conversation. This was a multi-million selling single worldwide and would give Barry White the confidence to build-on this sound and become one of the most enduring artists of the era.

96
ROCK AND ROLL
BOX OF OLD ROSES
DETROIT
PARAMOUNT
DID NOT CHART

The Mitch Ryder-fronted 'Detroit' were formed when Ryder disbanded his legendary high-powered soul outfit The Detroit Wheels. In came demon guitarist Steve Hunter, and this glorious song (about the redemptive power of rock 'n' roll) from the pen of Lou Reed, via the swansong Velvet Underground album *Loaded*, was given a high-octane arrangement by Hunter, under the auspices of producer Bob Ezrin. It gained some attention in the USA, but nothing here in dear old Blighty. However, in the strange way that wheels work within wheels, both Bob Ezrin and Steve Hunter would go on to work with Lou Reed (and Alice Cooper) and, incidentally, on the sole Detroit album there appeared a version of "It Ain't Easy", a Ron Davis song covered by David Bowie on his 'Ziggy Stardust' album. Was, I wonder, noted Reed/Velvets fan Bowie checking these guys out too? One can only wonder...

95
YOU WEAR IT WELL
LOST PARAGUAYOS
ROD STEWART
MERCURY
1

"If it ain't bust, don't fix it" seems to have been the motto when it came to this release. Rod followed up the success of 'Maggie May' with similar arrangement co-authored by the mandolin-wielding Martin Quittenton. This time around the song has a fiddle-break and is more reliant on Ron Wood's individualistic guitar sound. The main change, however, was in the lyric; 'You Wear it Well' is written in the form of a letter sent to a lost love, reminding her of the good times and expressing his regret for causing their break up. It is tender and wistful and contains some fabulous lyrical couplets; "Do you remember that birthday gown that I bought in town, when you sat down and cried on the stairs, you knew it didn't cost the Earth but for what it's worth, you made me feel a millionaire". Appearing on *Top of The Pops* with the Faces once again in tow, an unrehearsed Rod sang the lyrics from a sheet of paper. Unprofessional to many, but we loved him for it. He seemed 'real', with feet still firmly on the ground.

94
BREAK
BABYLON
APHRODITE'S CHILD
VERTIGO
DID NOT CHART

Boasting future international superstars Demis Roussos and Vangelis in their ranks, Aphrodite's Child had achieved a good deal of European success with a prog/pop sound similar to that of the Moody Blues. By this point though, relations within the band were deteriorating. Roussos was beginning a solo-career and so Vangelis took the tiller and steered the reluctant band into stranger, more psychedelic territory. Taken from the resulting double album *666*, 'Break' is a wonderful, cosmic ballad. A muted, percussively played piano supplies the rhythm; a world-weary and enigmatic vocal delivery sits atop that, before a flourish of guitar decorates the mid-section and allows the build of a sound-swell that takes the song to its conclusion. By this point the band had split, but what a fabulous finale this was.

93

WHISKEY IN THE JAR
BLACK BOYS ON THE CORNER
THIN LIZZY
DECCA
6

The original three-piece Thin Lizzy were, in my opinion, far and away the best incarnation of that band; but… they were going nowhere. Despite their talent as players, performers and writers, and even with the charismatic and eye-catching Phillip Lynott as front-man, prospects were grim. In rehearsals, for fun, they had played around with the old Irish folk song 'Whiskey in the Jar', concerned with highway robbery, betrayed love and treachery that results in jail. Someone suggested it was "pretty good" and should be recorded. Issued as a single, with the fabulous rocker 'Black Boys on the Corner' as the flip side, the record struck a chord and was swept into the charts, having the unfortunate effect of embarrassing and "freaking out" the purist in guitar player Eric Bell, who hated miming on silly TV shows. So, at the moment of their first triumph, Thin Lizzy lost the first of a long list of guitar-slinging rockers as Bell quit the band.

92

SYLVIA'S MOTHER
MAKIN' IT NATURAL
DR HOOK AND THE MEDICINE SHOW
CBS
2

Dr Hook and the Medicine Show were a band from New Jersey who, in their early incarnation, played a lot of humorous songs often written by poet Shel Silverstein. This, though, is not a fun song, but a sad autobiographical account of a failed relationship that Silverstein went through. It is however performed as a loving parody of late-50s, early-60s teen-romance songs, with the spurned lover hearing his ex is to leave town and be married. In desperation for one last chance he calls her mother who is matter-of-fact in informing him "thank you for calling but please don't you call back again" – the pathos lies in the fact that he knows the daughter is in the room with her mother but doesn't know who it is she is speaking to.

91

JUST A CONVERSATION
JUMPING JONAH
SLAPP HAPPY
POLYDOR
DID NOT CHART

An Englishman (Anthony Moore), an American (Peter Blegvad) and a German woman (Dagmar Krause) walked into a recording studio, accompanied by the rhythm section from the band Faust. Ostensibly they were there to cynically take the piss out of manufactured pop music, which they thought stupid and beneath them. The song was written by Moore and Blegvad in twenty minutes flat… but something very strange happened when Dagmar Krause added her voice; the song was transformed, gaining levity through the inherent sadness of her singing. It was fabulous; they had accidentally stumbled across a magical formula to create 'naive pop'.

90
TAKE ME BAK 'OME
WONDERIN'Y
SLADE
POLYDOR
1

I am well aware that it may seem churlish, but on hearing this as the 'brand new' Slade single, I was less impressed than I would have liked to have been. It was still good; it was absolute smash-your-head-against-a-wall powerful… but it seemed a bit regressive to me, a little bit obvious. Plus, I was already irritated by the misspelled titles; were they subliminally suggesting their own audience were thick? There we are – I was growing tired of Slade, but I had to admit I still liked this more than most other things… and it did still kick like a mule.

89
JOIN TOGETHER
BABY DON'T YOU DO IT
THE WHO
TRACK
9

Like Slade, The Who were a band I had adored and felt an affinity with. They had seemingly articulated so many personal feelings I was unable to articulate myself. I trotted off to the record store (Headstoned in Haughton Green) and purchased this, and I liked it. I played it to death, and sang and clapped along, though in my heart-of-hearts I knew The Who

were not simply running on the spot but sliding backwards in terminal decline; a superfluous synthesiser part, as a nod at modernity, couldn't disguise that sad fact. Still great, just about, but not as great as they had previously been.

88
POPCORN
AT THE MOVIES
HOT BUTTER
INTERFUSION
5

If you were going to use a synthesiser, this was the way to do it. 'Popcorn' had been written and recorded by Gershon Kingsley as early as 1969. He released the single twice; once as the 'Popcorn Makers', and again with his band the 'First Moog Quartet', without achieving the success he had hoped for. However, 'First Moog Quartet' member Stan Free had much better luck when he released the track under the name 'Hot Butter'; at last the songs irresistible charms found the audience they deserved. Insanely catchy, the song is basically the melding of two parts; the rapid-fire popping effect, which is cut by a quite grandiose sweeping section. It is, as is often the case, very simple… but in this simplicity and economy lay genius.

87
MY FRIEND THE SUN
GLOVE
FAMILY
REPRISE
DID NOT CHART

I visited the Buxton Festival – think bleak moorland, high winds and incessant rain – where Roger Chapman and Charlie Whitney of Family played 'My Friend The Sun' to us poor, soaked, shivering, foolhardy wretches dotted around the landscape. Mid-song Chapman stretches for a high note as he sings "it's there in the distance, if you care to see" with his finger pointed at the sky and at that instant the clouds part and the sun breaks through, illuminating and warming performers and audience alike for the remainder of the song. That was a mind-blowing thing to witness. How could I then not fail to love this uplifting song with its promise of better times ahead?

86

TALKIN' LOUD AND SAYIN' NOTHING (part 1)
TALKIN' LOUD AND SAYIN' NOTHING (part 2)
JAMES BROWN
POLYDOR
DID NOT CHART

Just one of JB's superlative early-70s singles, as he seemed to have gained a considerable second-wind and was setting the musical agenda in terms of funk and proto rap. This loose-limbed groove puts us on the good foot, whilst James and co-vocalist Bobby Byrd trade-off lines condemning the exploitation of people by loud-mouths on soapboxes; politicians and jive-artists alike. Mid-song James commands the band to stop while he and Bobby Byrd vocalise the rhythm, treating us to an early example of a dance track "breakdown".

85

CROCODILE ROCK
ELDERBERRY WINE
ELTON JOHN
DJM
5

Between the release of 'Rocket Man' and this, the most excellent

'Honky Cat' had been released as a single. It wasn't the most commercial choice being a loose, funky piece with no chorus. Still, it had charted, albeit modestly. Elton had certainly arrived as a pop star and 'Crocodile Rock' would put the top-hat on that status. It is a loud, proudly silly piece that is infectious fun, harking back to a golden era of rock 'n' roll, and throwing in a "Speedy Gonzales" pastiche as the chorus hook. This was bright and gaudy music for fun-fairs and it cheered even the most curmudgeonly among us.

84

SLARK
PURPLE SPACESHIPS OVER YATTON
STACKRIDGE
MCA
DID NOT CHART

Opening with a mid-paced 'olde-English' style riff, we are led into the morbid deliciousness of the tale of "Slark", a monster who plucks the narrator from his car and carries him aloft to an ancient Queen, who takes him by the hand to drown at the bottom of an enchanted lake. This is eccentric whimsy, wearing a cloak of darkness and it enchanted me.

83

GOODBYE TO LOVE
CRYSTAL LULLABY
THE CARPENTERS
A&M
9

If you had put a utility bill into the hands of Karen Carpenter and asked her to sing it, she may well have reduced you to tears such was her ability to express emotion. Give her a song as good as this, which is what composers John Bettis and her brother Richard did, and you get something extraordinary. Add to that a stunning fuzz-guitar solo courtesy of Tony Peluso (much encouraged by Richard Carpenter himself) and what results is a single that is astonishing and very moving. You have also created the musical concept of the power ballad.

82
SUPER
NEUSCHNEE
NEU
BRAIN
DID NOT CHART

Ex-Kraftwerk members, drummer Klaus Dinger and guitar player Michael Rother, re-emerged as Neu, a wilder but equally inventive and adventurous outfit, pioneering the "motorik", a rigid 4/4 drum-beat that drove their sound and grew to be hugely influential. This single preceded their second album *Neu 2* and is a precursor of the 'punk' sound of later in the decade. The drums are relentlessly battered, the guitar buzzes like a power-tool and the occasional vocals are hoarsely shouted to create a droning, hypnotic and extremely exciting single.

81
WISHING WELL
LET ME SHOW YOU
FREE
ISLAND
7

Free, who had been an exceptional band, were falling apart. Andy Fraser had quit and Paul Kossoff, as soulful a guitar-player as can be imagined, was disintegrating as a person, dependent on hard drugs and increasingly erratic and unreliable. That still left powerhouse drummer Simon Kirke

and vocalist/writer Paul Rogers. They pulled together to make a good farewell album, *Heartbreaker* and this final wonderful single 'Wishing Well' which, although generously credited to the full band, was penned by Rogers about a friend with a drug problem, possibly Kossoff, possibly not. It is angry and yet loving; it is about accepting there is nothing that can be done to help and the consequent feeling of sadness and frustration. It is raw, it is passionate, it is heartbreaking and somehow, quite magically, Paul Kossoff delivers a performance that no-one could have expected, as the guitar practically cries with the emotion captured in his playing.

80
WATCHER OF THE SKIES
WILLOW FARM
GENESIS
CHARISMA
DID NOT CHART

Inspired by Arthur C Clark's *Childhood's End* science-fiction novel, and named by taking a line from John Keats's poem *On First Looking Into Chapman's Homer*, this was mostly written by Tony Banks and Mike Rutherford. It is an apocalyptic tale of aliens observing an Earth destroyed by mankind. It zips along in an awkward staccato carried by Phil Collins' nimble but powerful drumming over which Tony Banks utilises Moog and organ, and Peter Gabriel throws himself into the role of watcher with a strident vocal.

79
REGGAE ON BROADWAY
GONNA GET YOU
BOB MARLEY
CBS
DID NOT CHART

Before Island Records came calling Bob Marley was, for this one single only, on the CBS roster as they aimed to see if Marley could make in-roads into the UK market. Cut in America when Marley, on sabbatical from the Wailers, was working with Johnny Nash (who would take Marley's 'Stir It Up' into the charts). This uses Nash's band as musicians and so it sounds like no Bob Marley record before or since; it has a brash rock sound and big production. Underneath the noise is a fine song, with Marley singing as well as ever. This was a mis-step, but a fascinating part of the journey from ghetto to global icon.

78
LADY ELEANOR
NOTHING BUT THE
MARVELLOUS IS BEAUTIFUL
LINDISFARNE
CHARISMA
3

This gem was first released in 1970 as part of the first Lindisfarne album *Nicely Out Of Tune*, and then in 1971 as a single. That flopped but on the back of interest created when the band had a hit with 'Meet Me On The Corner' it was issued again, and this time made it into the top-three. Alan Hull wrote the song based on Edgar Allan Poe's short story, *The Fall of The House of Usher,* and captures the atmosphere of gothic horror quite masterfully. Ray Jackson's mandolin playing is at the fore of the songs arrangement and the ensemble singing is sublime.

77
DO IT AGAIN
FIRE IN THE HOLE
STEELY DAN
ABC
39

Walter Becker and Donald Fagen were the antithesis of the hippy sixties vibe that people were still trying to cling to. There was no lazy, glib sermonising from these two; they were collectively as sharp as a tack and determined to do things their own way. This was a nasty song dealing with obsessive behaviour and its consequences. It slides along with Fagen's whining, acid-laced vocal perfectly suiting the quick-witted lyric. An electric sitar solo is featured, but here there is no hint of gimmickry. This grabbed my attention and made me want to hear more.

76
HI HI HI/
C MOON
WINGS
APPLE
5

Beatle Paul had put the final nail in the coffin of his sixties band and formed a new outfit. The first two releases had failed to excite; there had been the patronising and trite 'Give Ireland Back to the Irish', followed by the saccharine 'Mary Had a Little Lamb'. This third single was more like it; 'Hi Hi Hi' was a 'Helter Skelter' style raving rocker with risqué lyrics. The BBC dutifully banned it. 'C Moon' then picked up the airplay; it was a playful and tuneful reggae piece – a form Paul had experimented with before, and one he seemed to comprehend to a much greater degree than other white rock musicians, who dabbled with it without ever getting to grips with the rhythmical complexities of playing on the off-beat.

75
DONNA
HOT SUN ROCK
10CC
UK
2

Hotlegs had morphed into 10cc and strange happenings were afoot in Stockport. This was their first single, cooked-up in their sound laboratory Strawberry Studios. It is a very subtle parody of doo-wop but, having a degree of genuine affection, it never strays into novelty territory nor, heaven forbid, grovelling tribute. It features Lol Creme's falsetto vocal contrasting with Kevin Godley's ultra-deep baritone, and the way they handle the knowingly inane and nonsensical lyrics without flinching makes this a thing of beauty.

74
I'VE BEEN LONELY FOR SO LONG
LEAN ON ME
FREDERICK KNIGHT
STAX
23

Sweet the sound may be; a beautiful guitar-motif shapes the body of this slice of southern country soul, but Frederick Knight's voice is seemingly wracked in pain as he pours out his tale of woe. No chorus, just a deep-voiced interjection of "won't somebody help me please?" punctuates the verses. This is absolutely sublime and incredibly moving.

73
ELECTED
LUNEY TUNE
ALICE COOPER
WARNER BROTHERS
4

Alice Cooper went from being outcast freaks to fêted pop sensations seemingly overnight. Once they had refined their craft they were unstoppable. A consummate singles band they packed rebellious and satirical bombs full of hooks and killer choruses that were absolutely in tune with the misfit army of teens who adored them. This followed their anthem 'School's Out' and was, in fact, an updated version of their debut single from 1969, 'Reflected'. Then it sold in hundreds; now in its souped-up form, mocking and parodying the promises and lies of politicians seeking election, it sold in the hundreds of thousands. It was brash, it was loud, it offended the pompous; it was brilliant!

72
PONCHO AND LEFTY
HEAVENLY HOUSEBOAT DUES
TOWNES VAN ZANDT
POPPY
DID NOT CHART

Townes Van Zandt was a guitar-picking singer-songwriter who utilised a country style. 'Poncho and Lefty' is his most famous, and some consider his finest, song. Whether that is true or not is a debate for another time but what is self-evident is that 'Poncho and Lefty' is without doubt a song of perceptive genius. There are layers of emotion and intrigue within its words; it speaks in the opening verses of Poncho, a young idealist leaving home, and how his heart hardens. He becomes a bandit and is shot down. Lefty is then introduced; Poncho's brother or perhaps a friend? Whatever he had been, he now becomes the betrayer, and on the day Poncho is killed he heads for anonymity with the reward money, but without happiness or honour. It is all delivered with some panache in Van Zandt's world-weary style. It is not a song, once heard, you are likely to forget; it is immortal.

71
THE MESSAGE
ZION
CYMANDE
JANUS
DID NOT CHART

Cymande were a British band who utilised a funk-style as the basis for their music, though it also contained strong elements of African, Caribbean and reggae as well. They went unnoticed in the U.K. but this single put them into the American charts. They became the first British act to headline at the Harlem Apollo, and appeared on the influential *Soultrain* TV show. 'The Message' was their debut release and it is a slice of rhythmic, percussive funk with a chanted chorus. Their music, for a long while, became a footnote and nothing more; but their obscurity ended in the 1980s as hip-hop acts such as Grandmaster Flash and De La Soul began using their records to sample. Director Spike Lee placed 'The Message' in his 2002 film *25th Hour* and Cymande, finally receiving deserved credit, got themselves back together too.

70
JACKIE WILSON SAID
YOU'VE GOT THE POWER
VAN MORRISON
WARNER BROTHERS
DID NOT CHART

Dexy's Midnight Runners would have huge success with this song in the 1980s and while their version is excellent, this version by the song's composer is definitive. Name-checking soul legend Jackie Wilson, and quoting from his hit 'Reet Petite', Van Morrison was acknowledging the influence on his own singing style and the pleasure he got from listening to the soul legend. Beyond that the song is an attempt to capture, in music, the euphoric state of unalloyed elation. Recorded in a single take, it achieves everything that it set out to.

69
MONEY IN MY POCKET
MONEY LOVE (By Joe Gibbs and the Professionals)
DENNIS BROWN
PRESSURE BEAT
DID NOT CHART

Described by Bob Marley as "my favourite singer", Dennis cut this classic aged 15, by which time he was already a veteran having cut numerous sides since his debut aged 11. Who wrote the song is difficult to ascertain, but it was originally recorded by Niney Holness for Joe Gibbs. Those two oversaw this recording too. Dennis would re-record the song in 1978 and have a huge international hit, but this lighter, airier original is far superior.

68
O CAROLINE
SIGNED CURTAIN
MATCHING MOLE
CBS
DID NOT CHART

Robert Wyatt's most gorgeous song; this tender display of vulnerability was written as an open letter to Caroline Coon, with whom he had recently broken-up. Matching Mole were the band Robert had formed after leaving Soft Machine featuring contemporaries who had played in bands such as Quiet Sun and Caravan. They were a treat to listen to; excellent musicians who replaced the ego-driven showing-off prevalent of the era, with superb ensemble playing.

67
HOLD YOUR HEAD UP
CLOSER TO HEAVEN
ARGENT
EPIC
5

After the demise of the Zombies, bass guitarist Chris White continued to assist singer Colin Blunstone in his solo endeavours, and also aided keyboard player Rod Argent with his immodestly titled band - Argent, and so it came to pass that Chris White gifted the song 'Hold Your Head Up' to Argent. Opening with a marching bass line supported by a gritty-sounding guitar, Russ Ballard then begins to sing verses of encouragement, not to ever quit when facing negativity; these are followed by the gospel-like chorus and then an organ break by Rod Argent which was praised by no less than Rick Wakeman as "the greatest organ solo ever!". This all conspired to give Argent their signature-song,

and an iconic and enduring hit.

66
BETCHA BY GOLLY WOW
EBONY EYES
THE STYLISTICS
ATCO
13

This "Philly soul" hit broke the Stylistics in the UK and started a love affair with their silky, sophisticated music. With voices to die for, and featuring the glorious falsetto of Russell Thompkins Jnr, the Stylistics were recipients of the songcraft of Linda Creed and Thom Bell, plus Bell's mastery in the art of production. Their sound was almost liquid, intoxicating. The hits went on well into the decade, but this was the best and was covered fantastically by Prince in 1995.

65
CALIFORNIA MAN
DO YA/ELLA JAMES
THE MOVE
HARVEST
7

This is rock 'n' roll gloriously resurrected and souped-up, wearing a wide smile. This crackled with all the energy of Little Richard at his wildest as Roy Wood and Jeff Lynne trade-off vocals in a moment of short-lived harmony. On the flip were 'Ella James', which had been a withdrawn single, and Lynne's 'Do Ya', which was made the A-side in the USA where it was a hit in its own right.

64

HARRY HIPPIE/
I CAN UNDERSTAND IT
BOBBY WOMACK
UA
DID NOT CHART

This was originally, although a tremendous record, regarded as a musical 'joke' about Bobby Womack's laid-back, anti-materialistic brother Harry, who had no great ambition or drive and was simply content to roll through life, playing some music and having a good time. The emphasis of the song changed dramatically when Harry was brutally murdered by a jealous girlfriend. 'I Can Understand It', the double A's other side, picked up the radio play - a delicious, funky, chugging piano groove with Bobby's famous gravelly voice sweetened by the presence of female backing. A fiery guitar part adds further delight to what became one of this great soul man's signature songs.

63

BACK OFF BOOGALOO
BLINDMAN
RINGO STARR
APPLE
2

Ringo wrote much of it, but George Harrison finished it off and then produced and played guitar on it. Ringo offered the song to Cilla Black, who said thank you very much… but no! So it was released as a single by Ringo himself. It was certainly inspired by Marc Bolan, and has a glam-rock meets wall-of-sound vibe. Football commentator Jimmy Hill, with his descriptive use of the word "tasty", inadvertently provided some inspiration too. Some of the lyrics are thinly-veiled attacks on Paul McCartney, although Ringo

denies that interpretation (but in the immortal words of Mandy Rice Davies at the Old Bailey, "he would say that, wouldn't he"), it's a cracking record in any case.

62

I'M STILL IN LOVE WITH YOU
OLD TIME LOVIN'
AL GREEN
HI
35

As John Peel famously said of the Fall, "always different, always the same"; and so it was with Al Green in his 70s prime. Whenever I went out to buy an Al Green single I knew what I was getting, but there were always delightful surprises each time. This, though superficially close to 'Let's Stay Together', is more romantic still, and has an instrumental lift that makes my head spin with sheer ecstasy. Al Green was operating on a higher level, it seemed, than any other soul singer; two albums per year and no filler, as well as a clutch of high-class singles. He was leading the pack.

61

BURLESQUE
THE ROCKIN R's
FAMILY
REPRISE
13

Swaggering almost out of control, this was Family at their unhinged best. A riff of titanic proportions lurches like a drunken man on a wrecking spree and sounds like the best fun in town as Roger Chapman wails out the lyrics about a night of "rolling and tumbling". They were streets ahead of their peers – one only has to open one's ears to be convinced of that statement. Family were capable of being fierce but subtle, hard and gentle, intelligent and primal; what they couldn't be was easily categorized. This contributed to their relative lack of success which, by this point, was making them consider the wisdom of continuing.

60
EVERYTHING I OWN
I DON'T LOVE YOU
BREAD
ELEKTRA
32

One of the songs of the year, and indeed of any year, was 'Everything I Own' written by David Gates whose band, Bread, with their soft-rock approach, were doing big-business. While many would sneer at their "middle-of-the-road" stylings, and the blandness of much of their material, Gates was, when he put the effort in, a brilliant songwriter. This was written in the manner of a love song, but on closer inspection it has an unusually profound depth of emotion. It is, in fact, a song written after his father's funeral and is a cry of loss. A year later Ken Boothe recorded a brilliant reggae version and had a number one single with it then in 1987 Boy George too would hit number one with this masterful song, in a style very much copied from Ken Boothe.

59
CONQUERING LION
CONQUERING LION
VERSION
VIVIAN JACKSON AND THE
RALPH BROTHERS
VIVIAN JACKSON (YABBY
YOU)
DID NOT CHART

Instantly recognisable from the first note, 'Conquering Lion' is one of the great leaps forward in the reggae genre. Vivian Jackson had a hard early life; malnutrition left him with partially crippled legs and money was a struggle. He lived and hustled on the streets. Nicknamed "Jesus Dread" for his Christian beliefs, he claimed to have found music during a period of hospitalisation. It was King Tubby who made this single a reality, and with its chanted intro of "be you, yabby yabby you", it earned Vivian Jackson the name of "Yabby You" for the rest of his musical career.

58
I DON'T BELIEVE IN
MIRACLES
I'VE ALWAYS HAD YOU
COLIN BLUNSTONE
EPIC
31

Ex-Zombies vocalist Colin Blunstone was blessed with a breathy, high-octave vocal range such that, when the material was suitable – as was the case here – he could transport we mere mortals to celestial heights. It is pure pleasure to hear the genuine quality in his singing. This piano and string arrangement of a song gifted by Argent front man, Russ Ballard, is almost minimal in truth, but Blunstone renders every word of the song with such gravitas that the effect is emotionally shattering.

57
SUGARMAN
INNER CITY BLUES
RODRIGUEZ
A&M
DID NOT CHART

From Rodriguez's 1970 album, this song has had multiple releases as a single, but the European major-label release seems to be from 1972. It is a chugging folk-blues with some added hints of psychedelia and a ragged, pained vocal from Rodriguez as he sings of waiting for his dealer to bring the "jumpers, coke, sweet Mary Jane" so that the tired and weary user can partake and "make questions disappear".

56
IF YOU DON'T KNOW ME BY NOW
LET ME INTO YOUR WORLD
HAROLD MELVIN AND THE BLUE NOTES
PHILADELPHIA INTERNATIONAL
9
'If You Don't Know Me By Now' was one of the first hits for the Philadelphia International label launched by Kenny Gamble and Leon Huff. These writer/producers, with considerable assistance from long-time collaborator Thom Bell, redefined soul music, bridging the relatively simple late-60s sounds and those of the disco era, with their sophisticated string-laden productions. They offered this song to female trio Labelle, who declined the opportunity; Harold Melvin and the Blue Notes however, did not. Recorded at Sigma Sound Studios (where a few years later David Bowie would cut his "Philly Soul" *Young Americans* album) the Blue Notes, with Teddy Pendergrass on lead vocals supported by a sumptuous three-part harmony, had their first iconic hit record under their belt. In 1989 English band Simply Red had a number 1 with their interpretation of the song.

55
SANTA DOG (2 x 7-inch singles)
FIRE/AIRCRAFT DAMAGE/ EXPLOSION/LIGHTNING
THE RESIDENTS
RALPH
DID NOT CHART
1972 saw this debut release crawl out from San Francisco by a group called The Residents; an intriguing double-single in Christmas wrapping. 'Santa Dog', it was noted, was a not-too-difficult to decipher anagram of 'Satan God'. It was our first taste of the mangled, mutated, mutant rock & roll from these avant-garde pranksters, whose identities were, then as now, unrevealed. They sounded like nothing else on Earth; intriguing and highly entertaining in equal measure.

54
THE NIGHT
WHEN THE MORNING COMES
FRANKIE VALLI AND THE FOUR SEASONS
MOWEST
DID NOT CHART
(number 7 when reissued 1975)
A spooked-voiced Frankie Valli begins the song backed by an eerie organ track as he pleads with the girl he has lost to look properly at the man she has replaced him with because he isn't good for her. It has an air of suffocating darkness and even though the song kicks, and bass, brass and drums propel it along, the feeling it conveys is of dizziness and confusion. Totally ignored by the mainstream, 'The Night' found favour on the Northern Soul scene where it was a dancer's dream. The interest, in the end, saw it re-released in 1975 when it became the hit it deserved to be first time around.

53
PAPA WAS A ROLLIN' STONE
PAPA WAS A ROLLIN' STONE
THE TEMPTATIONS
TAMLA MOTOWN
14

'Papa Was a Rollin' Stone' was released as a single by The Undisputed Truth at the beginning of the year however that version only proved to be a dry-run for this much superior take on the song by The Temptations. Written by Norman Whitfield and Barrett Strong and produced in Whitfield's psychedelic-soul style it quickly led to a stand-off between producer and band who wanted to return to their 1960s work practice with more emphasis on voices and less on production techniques and resulted in a parting of the ways. The sad fact remains that as a result of this parting of the ways this was the last truly great record ever made by The Temptations.

52
TOO MUCH TIME
LO YO-YO STUFF
CAPTAIN BEEFHEART
REPRISE
DID NOT CHART

Beefheart's pursuit of some commercial success brought around this soulful groover, with added harmony vocals from the Blackberries, sweetening the Captain's crooned choruses. It was delicious but lines about "heating up old stale beans and opening cans of sardines" probably alienated the public at large, more used to sugar-coated romantic imagery than anything Beefheart was inclined to offer up.

51
SKYLARKING
SKYLARKING VERSION
HORACE ANDY
BONGO MAN
DID NOT CHART

Laid down at the legendary Studio 1 right at the beginning of Horace Andy's half-century long musical career, his heart-stopping falsetto bemoans the lack of opportunity available to the youth of the tenement yards of Kingston. Despite the years of acclaim, and success as a featured vocalist for Massive Attack, it is testament to the quality of this single that it remains the signature-song of this golden-voiced musical icon.

50
JOURNEY
IN A MIST
DUNCAN BROWNE
RAK
23

Opening with picked flamenco-style guitar before mutating into an updated traditional 'square dance' underpinned by a rock-bass and drum section courtesy of Jim Rodford and Rob Henrit of Argent, is added Duncan Browne's beautiful and posh (and very English) vocal and an intriguing lyric, then there's a synthesiser solo from go-to guy of the early-70s, John 'Rabbit' Bundrick (who worked with Johnny Nash, the Wailers, Free and many more) which is garnished with wailed backing vocals (courtesy of Suzi Quattro) and what you have is a very tasty and eccentric pop gem.

49
OUTA SPACE
I WROTE A SIMPLE SONG
BILLY PRESTON
A&M
44

As a youngster Billy had been named the "wildest organ in town". He had played on Beatles sessions – indeed was credited as a performer on 'Get Back' – he had played on Sly and the Family Stone's seminal *There's a Riot Goin' On* and on George Harrison's *All Things Must Pass*. Through all of this he had maintained a solo career; now, from his sixth album came this. My ears had never encountered anything like it… it was sensational. Born out of studio experimentation, he had put a clavinet through a wah-wah pedal, located a groove and let rip, shouting out chord changes to the band so they could follow. That spontaneity infuses the piece with energy and lifts my spirits each time I hear this record. A year later Billy toured as a musician with the Rolling Stones, and played a support set including 'Outa Space'; I was overjoyed to be there, just to hear this monster groove loud and live.

48
OH WOT A DREAM
CONNIE ON A RUBBER BAND
KEVIN AYRES
HARVEST
DID NOT CHART

This is Kevin's ode to his friend Syd Barrett. The pair shared a delightful, eccentric musicality which is clearly on display here. Syd was yesterday's man and all but forgotten by 1972, and so Kevin shining a spotlight on the reclusive genius was a nice gesture, and this warm tribute was lovely, sunny and possessed of the playful spirit of its inspirational figure. However the B-side is where the real magic lies; it is a version of 'Clarence in Wonderland', a track from Ayres' *Shooting at the Moon* album. Here Kevin is backed by Trojan Records hit-makers Greyhound in a reggae style that fits like a glove; marvellous stuff indeed.

47
ROCK AND ROLL PART 1
ROCK AND ROLL PART 2
GARY GLITTER
BELL
2

It is tempting to omit Gary Glitter from this book due to his heinous crimes against vulnerable children; but that would be a Stalinesque rewrite of history. So here is the first Gary Glitter single, moulded by producer/writer Mike Leander – it is where the Glitterbeat originates. That rhythmic device was the basis of every record made by Gary Glitter and its influence is immeasurable.

46
MOTHER AND CHILD
REUNION
PARANOIA BLUES
PAUL SIMON
CBS
5

The Simon & Garfunkel partnership having ended, this was the first solo single that followed. While hugely commercial and joyful sounding, it was a born of abstract thought. Simon was a huge reggae fan in the days when reggae was perceived in the 'white' media as being inferior to even the worst efforts of the blues-rock plank spankers. Thus he went to Kingston, Jamaica to record the track using Jimmy Cliff's band. He drew inspiration for the lyrics from the death of his dog, and also a menu in a Chinese restaurant. Putting these elements together, he created an outstanding and uplifting single of great potency.

45
ORDINARY JOE
GOLDEN CIRCLE OF YOUR LOVE
TERRY CALLIER
CADET
DID NOT CHART

Terry Callier was a Chicago native and childhood friend of Curtis Mayfield, Jerry Butler and Major Lance. His music contained elements of folk, jazz and soul. His songs were striking and intelligent, but he was difficult to classify and was allowed to slip into obscurity. This single, which displayed all of his strengths, kept his name alive. Picked up, in the first instance, by DJs on the British Northern Soul scene due to its danceability, in the late-1980s a new breed of British DJs, of the "rare groove" variety, re-discovered this superb record, and the mounting interest lured Terry Callier out of retirement to enjoy some well deserved time in the spotlight.

44
ALL FALL DOWN
WE CAN SWING TOGETHER
LINDISFARNE
CHARISMA
34

The third album in two years saw a clearly jaded Lindisfarne going through the motions. It was a disappointing record where the songwriting, in particular, was not of the quality previously shown. The one exception was "All Fall Down", possibly the band's finest moment, which came from the pen of Alan Hull and was released as a single. It is a battle cry against the "Councillors, magistrates and men of renown" – it is a warning to the "Politicians and planners to look what they've done" – it is an angry broadside aimed at those with no regard for the ecological and social impact that their money-making schemes ignore. "One day the machine might turn on" suggests Hull, "and we'll dance on their graves until the flowers return". A voice of sanity, passionate and humane; a great song, a great single!

43
10538 OVERTURE
FIRST MOVEMENT
(JUMPING BIZ)
ELECTRIC LIGHT ORCHESTRA
HARVEST
9

Opening with an awe-inspiring guitar-riff, followed by a bombardment of cello sawing, '10538 Overture' had a sound previously unheard in the pop music firmament. When they had begun work on the song it had been intended as a track for The Move; by the time they had finished Roy Wood and Jeff Lynne knew that they had the debut single for the band they had previously discussed forming... the Electric Light Orchestra. It had been birthed in a spirit of unity, with both singing on the track, but by the time the single was climbing the chart Wood distanced himself from Lynne's ideas and soon quit to form Wizzard.

42
SLIPPIN' INTO DARKNESS
NAPPY HEAD
WAR
UNITED ARTISTS
DID NOT CHART

War, with their melding of Latin and African rhythms into the exotic funkiness that was their stock-in-trade, didn't mean much in the UK. They were, though, a superb band. Cut down to almost half its playing time in morphing from album track to single, this lost little or nothing in the process. The lyric concerns itself with the consequences of behaviour that can only be negative; in this instance a friend who has lost his life in a fog of alcoholism. His plight is hammered home in the hypnotic refrain "slippin' into darkness, slippin' into darkness". This is high-calibre funk of a very heavy variety.

41
ALONE AGAIN NATURALLY
SAVE IT
GILBERT O SULLIVAN
MAM
3

Thank goodness this wasn't written autobiographically! Starting with the narrator contemplating suicide after being "stood up at the altar" on his wedding day, and finishing with the death of his grieving, broken-hearted mother, this is a song about loneliness and the unnoticed despair that people suffer. Performed with wonderful empathy by the 21-year old O'Sullivan, I struggle to remain dry-eyed even thinking about it. This was a gem from a precocious talent that shone brightly, before being squandered in the pursuit of mass appeal.

40
WHY CAN'T WE LIVE
TOGETHER
FUNKY ME
TIMMY THOMAS
MOJO
12

Sparse and stripped to the bare bones, this was recorded in mono, which emphasises the minimalism of the recording that features pulsing organ and an early example of what a rhythm-box could provide. The backing feels space-age and antiseptically clean but the vocal is full of human emotion and soul. The lyric is minimal, just a few repeated phrases, rendering the whole track wide open, uncluttered by anything superfluous. A brilliant conceptual piece that still sounds contemporary today, back then it felt like listening to the future.

39
URBAN GUERRILLA
BRAINBOX POLLUTION
HAWKWIND
UNITED ARTISTS
39

The single opens with the lyric "I'm an Urban Guerilla, I make bombs in my cellar" – it proved to be an ill-timed provocation; just as the record was released the IRA launched a bombing campaign on mainland Britain. Written and sung by Robert Calvert as a satirical piece, in truth the production and mix left something to be desired in terms of sonic attack; it sounded thin and brittle, but it was a good song with a pre-punk feel. It was, of course, doomed by events, and almost inevitably and without protest, after just three weeks availability, the record was withdrawn from sale.

38
STICK BY ME
IT'S A PLEASURE
JOHN HOLT
JACKPOT
DID NOT CHART

John Holt was a Jamaican child-star, entering and winning radio broadcast talent-shows as a 12-year old (a route employed by several reggae singers). He recorded and released dozens of singles throughout the 1960s and spent time as a member of The Paragons, for whom he wrote the classic "The Tide is High". However his biggest Jamaican hit was this cover of a song from 1962 by Shep and the Limelights which stayed on the chart for an incredible 33 weeks. 'Stick By Me' is one of those sublime moments where a singer finds a song that suits so well, that it seems effortless and natural; they simply belong together. John Holt was, by this stage, a Jamaican national-treasure and would go on to great success with his album *1000 Volts of Holt* and scoring a UK top-5 hit covering 'Help Me Make it Through the Night'.

37

AN AMERICAN TRILOGY
SAN FRANCISCO MABEL JOY
MICKEY NEWBURY
ELEKTRA
42

'An American Trilogy' was recorded by Mickey Newbury as part of his *Frisco Mabel Joy* album. It was his arrangement of three 19th-century songs pertaining to the American Civil War; 'Dixie' represented the South, 'The Battle Hymn of the Republic' the North and 'All My Trials' the slaves. It was a startling and moving piece, and was issued as a single. Banned by some radio stations as unpatriotic, Newbury was steadfast in opposing censorship. But just as the song was gaining positive attention, a cover version was released by none other than Elvis Presley. The emphasis of quiet introspection was drastically changed; Presley's version was louder, brasher, bigger and a bombastic flag-waver. It did, of course, claim the larger share of chart action.

36
SUPERFLY
GIVE ME YOUR LOVE (LOVE SONG)
CURTIS MAYFIELD
BUDDAH
52

This was the tale of "Youngblood Priest", the cocaine-dealing pimp and central character of the film *Superfly*, played over the end credits and telling of Priest's ruthless ambition to succeed, but also of the damage to his soul caused by the lifestyle of do or die. "Time is running out and there's no happiness" sings Curtis, towards the end of the song, as congas rumble beneath strings and wah-wah guitar.

35
LAYLA
BELL BOTTOM BLUES
DEREK AND THE DOMINOS
POLYDOR
7

Feelings of a powerful, unrequited love and the gift of a seventh century Arabian Book — *The Story of Layla and Majnun* — gave Eric Clapton the inspiration for this song. It has a marvellous descending riff that sets pulses racing but in truth, beyond that 'Layla' isn't much of a song; the lyrics are no more than perfunctory, and a little clichéd. What Layla is though is a great record; and that is down to the power and passion of the performance. Clapton sings as though his life depends upon delivering his message; he is raw and on edge. The rhythm section are perfectly in-sync and groove, while Clapton and Duane Allman, on twin lead guitars, play as though their fingers are being guided and they create a sound full of fire. The genie was caught in the bottle, and indeed the feat was replicated on B-side 'Bell Bottom Blues' which is equally outstanding.

34
I SAW THE LIGHT
BLACK MARIA
TODD RUNDGREN
BEARSVILLE
36

This, the opening track on the first album to be released bearing his name, shows Todd Rundgren announcing his arrival in grand fashion. He stated in the sleeve notes that he was putting "the hit" at the front of the album in the same way Motown kicked off their albums. It was a deserved hit, of course, when the single was inevitably issued, but 'I Saw the Light' was even more than that. It was a sublime pop song that endures; a mini-epic, crafted with the kind of care Brian Wilson once applied to the Beach Boys greatest recordings.

33
BACKSTABBERS
SUNSHINE
THE O'JAYS
PHILADELPHIA
INTERNATIONAL
14

The O'Jays were one of the jewels in the crown of Philadelphia International Records, as they set about supplanting Motown as the pre-eminent soul label of the day. They had a solid history of releases going back to the mid 1960s and were a formidable act. Furnish them with songs as good as 'Backstabbers' and they were dynamite! A rolling piano phrase acts as the intro and over a steady rhythmic bed the O'Jays warn men that they "better beware" of those friends who aim to deceive, with the intention of stealing away their wives and girlfriends. Written by Leon Huff with recording and writing team McFadden and Whitehead, the imagery of the lyric is startling; "The blades are long, clenched tight in their fists, aiming straight at your back, and I don't think they'll miss". There is a nod to the inspiration of The Undisputed Truth as the band sing "smilin' faces sometimes tell lies", so remember what they do… "They smile in your face, all the time they want to take your place, the Backstabbers".

32
RUN RUN RUN
TAKE IT EASY
JO JO GUNNE
ASYLUM
6

After playing in the often exotic-sounding and experimental Spirit, this represented a back-to-basics approach when Mark Andes and Jay Ferguson formed Jo Jo Gunne, named after a 1958 Chuck Berry single. This debut single was incredible, full of vitality and joy. 'Run Run Run' is the aural equivalent of racing a bobsleigh on a downhill slalom whilst slugging on a bottle of bourbon; it is fast, reckless and on the verge of being out-of-control as it seemingly goes faster and faster and faster. The vocals are gleefully shouted and two guitar solos are thrown in before the whole thing careers to a screeching halt.

31
KING HEROIN
THEME FROM KING HEROIN
JAMES BROWN
POLYDOR
DID NOT CHART

'King Heroin' was a poem by Manny Rosen, an anti-drug piece written from the point-of-view of the drug itself. James Brown set it to music and set about narrating its graphic horrors, detailing how it destroys looks, renders virile men impotent and, ultimately, brings death. "This is a revolution of the mind", exclaims James – "Get your mind together and get away from drugs" he continues. This was JB at his socially-conscious best.

30
CELLULOID HEROES
HOT POTATOES
THE KINKS
RCA
DID NOT CHART

Lesser-known than the big 1960s hits but far superior to most of them, here The Kinks muse over the notion of stardom and its effects on people caught in the spotlight's harsh glare. "Don't step on dearest Marilyn, she's not very tough, she should have been made of iron or steel but she was only made of flesh and blood" we are cautioned, while making the point that fame is no protection against insecurity. The song sprawls over its elegant piano backdrop and reaches several crescendos as we wind our way down Hollywood Boulevard, led by Raymond Douglas Davies. We meet not just Ms Monroe, but

Bette Davies, Mickey Rooney, Greta Garbo and Rudolph Valentino amongst others, the latter who "looks up ladies dresses as they sadly pass him by". Finally Davies concludes that he wishes his life could be "a non-stop Hollywood movie show", because "celluloid heroes never feel any pain, and celluloid heroes never really die". This is a tour-de-force of quite exquisite musicality and lyrical insight.

29
A THING CALLED LOVE
DADDY
JOHNNY CASH
CBS
4

Johnny Cash enjoyed his greatest European success with 'A Thing Called Love', a song originally recorded by Jerry Reed in 1968, and in the interim covered by a multitude, including Cash's old Sun Records alumnus, Elvis Presley. Handled in a simple country-style, with his famous deep, rich and warm baritone perfect for the good-natured, matter-of-fact tone of the song, this was a delight.

28
WHEN MY BABY'S BESIDE ME
IN THE STREET
BIG STAR
ARDENT
DID NOT CHART

Like its parent album, Big Star's debut single sank without trace when first released before critical re-assessment saw the band, and their sadly slim body of work, rightly heralded. The principal creative spark came from Beatle-influenced pair Alex Chilton (who as an ex-Box Top had been a teen-star) and Chris Bell, each contributing to the other's songs.

'When My Baby's Beside Me' is a good example; it's a tough rocker from Chilton with a sweet-coating added by Bell. A ringing guitar opens proceedings before a riff to-die-for intrudes. Chilton then adds his remarkably soulful voice and we are transported into the realm of guitar-pop heaven, that very few are capable of emulating.

27
I'LL TAKE YOU THERE
I'M JUST ANOTHER SOLDIER
THE STAPLES SINGERS
STAX
20

With a supple bass-line, shared with Harry J and the Allstars reggae hit 'Liquidator', Al Bell's 'I'll Take You There' conjures imagery of a hard-won ideal of equality and justice. It is, as such, a perfect piece for civil rights commentators The Staples Singers. Dignity is ever present in their performance of the song; they are quite clearly serious and sincere. This adds considerable weight to lines such as "Ain't no smiling faces, lying to the races, I'll take you there". But this is not simply polemic; it is music to put a smile on our faces and put a spring in our step. This is music that manages, in a small way, to make the world seem a better place to live in.

26
COULDN'T I JUST TELL YOU
WOLFMAN JACK
TODD RUNDGREN
BEARSVILLE
DID NOT CHART

Todd had rather immodestly named his new album *A Wizard A True Star*, and nobody challenged the veracity of the claim. The boy-genius was at the top of his game; a veritable one-man band, effortlessly knocking out shining pop jewels from the rich and fertile seam of his creative mind. Here he sets the template for every "power pop" record that follows in its wake. This is the level of quality to aim for; it is the holy grail; many have tried but none have come close to matching this mix of twelve-string guitar, pumping bass, lead guitar line, effects-laden breakdown and impassioned vocal that combine in a heady, adrenaline-pumping rush of pure pleasure and thrills.

25
I CAN SEE CLEARLY NOW
HOW GOOD IT IS
JOHNNY NASH
CBS
5

Credit Johnny Nash with seeing the enormous talent and potential possessed by Bob Marley. The two had worked closely together and Nash had taken Marley's 'Stir It Up' into the charts earlier in the year. 'I Can See Clearly Now' was recorded without the Jamaican's assistance, but his influence is all over the mellow reggae groove that Johnny Nash incorporates into this incredibly positive and spiritual song. Blessed with a soulful, crooning-style of vocalising that carries the uplifting message of the song in an easy, unhurried style, this is a truly great and beautiful single. As a personal postscript to that statement, 'I Can See Clearly Now' was the soundtrack to one of the most unpleasant and harrowing episodes I have experienced in my life; yet still its glory transcends the negative memories I associate with it.

24
SO FAR
IT'S A BIT OF A PAIN
FAUST
POLYDOR
DID NOT CHART

I was smitten by Faust at first hearing – and first hearing for me was this single. The A-side was a fabulous instrumental piece, approached differently to any music I'd ever heard before; rhythmic, subtle and modern, with a horn playing a simple and naive two-note hook whilst strange noises bubbled beneath the surface. It was thrilling and fed my imagination – which I'm was the intention. The other side of the single, 'It's A Bit of a Pain', was a more conventional type of song but "noise" was used as a counterpoint to the delicately played melody. This was revolutionary stuff to me and very exciting.

23
TUMBLING DICE
SWEET BLACK ANGEL
ROLLING STONES
ROLLING STONES RECORDS
5

'Tumbling Dice' is based around a killer-riff that refuses to be hurried; it creates a strange and sensual groove that innocent bystanders are in danger of being sucked into if they fail to keep up their guard. Keith Richards, Charlie Watts and Mick Taylor (playing bass on this one) keep this churning thing in motion, with Mick Jagger adding his underrated guitar skills as well as a tongue-twisting vocal, as he somehow makes a seemingly unsingable lyric fit with consummate ease.

22
SLOW DEATH
TALLAHASSEE LASSIE
THE FLAMIN' GROOVIES
UNITED ARTISTS
DID NOT CHART

The Flamin' Groovies might just have 'outstoned' the Stones with this masterpiece of a record. Cyril Jordan plays a slide-guitar figure that sounds dangerously malevolent while Roy Loney, on what was his last recording with the band, alternates between an anguished yowl and a snarled yelp of a vocal as he recounts this low-life account of narcotic abuse gone much too far. Cut by these San Franciscan refugees in Monmouthshire with studio wizard Dave Edmonds at the controls, this was, and remains, a towering testament to the greatness of the Groovies, as well as being one of the best guitar records ever released.

21
RUNNIN' AWAY
BRAVE AND STRONG
SLY AND THE FAMILY STONE
EPIC
17

On the one hand this is sweet, summery pop with an almost Bossa nova rhythm, and a horn section that Herb Alpert might well have approved of; but there is a darkness here too. The thin, brittle sound is an indication that not all is as it seems. This is a bold, conceptual device for a song seemingly about paranoia. As Orson Welles had done with cinema, Sly Stone was doing with music; he was audacious and pushing at barriers ever harder, operating way beyond orthodoxy; but at what personal cost?

20
CHILDREN OF THE
REVOLUTION
JITTERBUG LOVE/SUNKEN
RAGS
T. REX
T. REX WAX CO
2

By the time 'Children of the Revolution' was released, T. Rex had enjoyed four consecutive number 1s in the UK; they were the nation's favourite. This was a barnstorming single too. By this stage T. Rex singles sounded enormous, the meticulous production a work of art and Marc's rhyming couplets memorable as well as being terrific fun. That 'Children of the Revolution' only reached number 2 should have sounded alarm bells that the formula was wearing thin, and a 'Starman' who would "let the children boogie" was waiting in the sky ready to pick up the plaudits – and the audience – slipping from Marc Bolan's loosening grip.

19
METAL GURU
THUNDERWING/LADY
T. REX
T REX WAX CO
1

Marc Bolan himself stated that this song was about a 'God figure', "all alone without a telephone" – and in the next sentence, conceitedly and dangerously began comparing himself to this God. It was a fabulous single though; superbly tuneful guitar-pop that was certainly noticed by the young Johnny Marr, who would pillage it in the 1980s for The Smiths hit 'Panic'.

18
PAPER PLANE
SOFTER RIDE
STATUS QUO
VERTIGO
8

Glitter characterises much of the early 1970s British music scene. Glam was accessorising all sorts of unlikely and shameless acts; but rising at the same time were re-born boogie machine Status Quo. Bedecked in double-denim, without even a hint of blusher, they were in many ways truly representative of the working class hordes who came to worship them. Unrelenting, unyielding, unsubtle… but powerful and unpretentious too, Quo were The Ramones before The Ramones. Derided as dumb and repetitive, they had stripped-away the artifice that surrounded so much music, reduced it to its core components and made it sound exciting and fresh. 'Paper Plane' is the genius moment when what they had been working towards all came together. It is a record comprising a killer riff and (dare one say this when talking about Quo?) a smart, perceptive lyric about self-delusion.

17
WITHOUT YOU
GOTTA GET UP
NILSSON
RCA
1

Written by Pete Ham and Tom Evans of Badfinger, 'Without You' was recorded and released on their 1970 album *No Dice* not yet fully-realised and largely unnoticed. That was until Harry Nilsson heard it at a party and decided to record the song utilising every tool at his disposal. He created a huge-sounding, ultra-dramatic thing of awe-inspiring beauty that revealed all of the song's hitherto hidden depths. The brilliant melody and superb lyric were brought to the fore by the widened, soaring production and the magnificent singing voice of Nilsson. Ham and Evans, on hearing a playback of their humble song re-cast as magisterial power ballad, were reputed to have wept with joy and overwhelming emotion. Hundreds of artists have recorded this song in the intervening years, but none have matched the heights reached by Harry Nilsson.

16
LOVE TRAIN
WHO AM I?
O'JAYS
PHILADELPHIA INTERNATIONAL
9
The magic from writer/producer duo Gamble and Huff, the expertise of "MFSB" (the house band for Philadelphia International records) and the trio who comprised the O'Jays were all present and correct when this pre-disco dance sensation was recorded. It is a wildly infectious call for unity between nations, set to an irresistible track constructed to simulate forward motion, this was positivity made euphoric.

15
GIRL FROM GERMANY
BEAVER O'LINDY
SPARKS
BEARSVILLE
DID NOT CHART
Confirmed anglophiles Sparks toured the UK on the back of their album *A Woofer in Tweeter's Clothing*, which attracted cult attention. Whilst here they appeared on the BBCs deadly-

dull rock program *The Old Grey Whistle Test* where they glistened like diamonds in a dark and desultory mine. Keyboard playing brother Ron Mael, wearing a Chaplin/Hitler-style moustache, jerked and twitched when he deigned to move at all, but beyond that simply glowered rigidly while teen heart-throb styled singing brother Russell cavorted and hammed-up the songs while singing in an operatic falsetto. They performed 'Girl from Germany' and I loved it. It is one of the most audacious, slyly funny, superbly observed songs I've ever heard. The next day I bought the single – I treasure it still.

14
LOUIE LOUIE
PRESSURE DROP 72
TOOTS AND THE MAYTALS
TROJAN
DID NOT CHART
I was drawn to Toots and the Maytals almost as soon as I began listening to music with any discernment, probably as a 10 or 11-year old; their tunes thrilled me and reggae captivated me from the off but what made them stand out was the voice! Toots Hibbert, like Otis Redding and Levi Stubbs, has that something special in his vocal inflection that pulls at the heart strings; he seems to invest whatever he sings with significance and emotion. For this single, garage-rock staple 'Louie Louie' is mashed up into a joyous reggae concoction that wears a very wide smile. Flip the record over and we get a bigger, badder, louder 'Pressure Drop', a remake of their own 1968 classic.

13
VITAMIN C
I'M SO GREEN
CAN
UNITED ARTISTS
DID NOT CHART

Germany was throwing up very intriguing sounds from bands whom it was difficult to get much information about. One such band were Can – now regarded as seminal, but back in 1972 they confused the hell out of the rock crowd their music was aimed at. This single is a perfect example; it is about as orthodox as Can could be – under 4 minutes in length with a recognisable song structure. They were playing funk but this was unlike anything funky that had ever emerged from America. Can were playing funk as if the form had originated back in Cologne. The drum-pattern is incredible and mesmerising; indeed, each component part of the song adds some unique flavour. Japanese vocalist Damo Suzuki seemingly plucks phrases out of thin air that deliciously add to the already rich texture, it's a wonderful listen and wonderful to dance your ass off to as well.

12
TELEGRAM SAM
CADILLAC/BABY STRANGE
T. REX
T. REX WAX CO
1

The apex of T. Rextasy on 7-inch single is undoubtedly 'Telegram Sam', the first single on Marc Bolan's own record label. This also provided the hat-trick of number one chart hits that Marc had strived and hustled so long and so hard for. A genius single full of instantly memorable hooks, and the James Brown style self-aggrandising lyric of "Me I funk, but I don't care, I ain't no square with my corkscrew hair" which so delighted the legion of fans. Elsewhere, the lyrics deal with a litany of characters such as "Bobby" (Dylan?) who is "a natural born poet" and, of course, "outta sight". None of these though measure up to the "main man", the titular 'Telegram Sam', who is believed to be Marc's manager – and cocaine supplier – Tony Secunda.

11
SCHOOL'S OUT
GUTTER CAT
ALICE COOPER
WARNER BROTHERS
1

'Alice', the horrible and evil-looking rag-doll of a singer, and Alice Cooper, the long-haired, malevolent droog-like band, exploded out of the underground into the national consciousness with this perfect teenage anti-authoritarian rampage of a single. Gleefully they attack the totem of repression – the school – "we can't even think of a word that rhymes" they jeer, whilst mocking the failure of the system. They were too knowing and arch to be truly threatening, but their quick-witted and gentle subversions were very welcome anyway. Alice Cooper created scores of superb tracks, but this would forever be their signature.

10

FEEL THE NEED IN ME
THERE IS A LOVE
FOR ME SOMEWHERE
THE DETROIT EMERALDS
WESTBOUND
4

The fact this was a UK chart hit for no fewer than six different acts speaks volumes for the calibre and enduring durability of this song. Written by Abrim Tilmon, one of four brothers in the original line-up, the band were not actually from Detroit, as their name suggests, but from Little Rock, Arkansas, and only became the Detroit Emeralds when they signed for the Ric-Tic label to release their 'Show Time' single (which gained some traction with the UKs Northern Soul fraternity) before moving to Westbound Records for whom the grooving 'Feel The Need In Me' was recorded. The song is an aching soul showcase of vocal prowess and harmony, containing a horn part that lifts into the chorus, and a riffing string section. It is an unforgettable performance of an unforgettable song. A few years later the Detroit Emeralds returned to the song once again and recorded an extended disco version, which gave them a second top-ten hit in 1977.

9

SILVER MACHINE
SEVEN BY SEVEN
HAWKWIND
UNITED ARTISTS
3

It was almost unthinkable that ultimate festival favourites and freak band Hawkwind, could reach the higher echelons of the chart, but they crashed the party spectacularly with 'Silver Machine', which is perhaps best described as "cosmic space boogie mixed with punk rock". Several group members had been tried on lead vocals, before it was decreed that Lemmy Kilmister's unlovely rasp best suited the song. They were beamed into our homes on television by the BBC, and they looked incredible simply by being themselves; this was an iconic TV moment and 'Silver Machine' was an iconic record. Speaking of which, icons of all things punk, The Sex Pistols, would later doff their proverbial caps and perform the song during one of their lucrative reunion jaunts.

8

VICIOUS/
SATELLITE OF LOVE
LOU REED
RCA
DID NOT CHART

The incredible 'Walk on the Wild Side' had been issued as a single from ex-Velvet Underground legend Lou Reed's *Transformer* album, produced and glammed to the gills by David Bowie and Mick Ronson. How could it fail? Nobody knew, but fail it did, picking up no airplay and very few sales. Plan B was to issue this 'camp as Christmas' sub-Velvets rocker, featuring brilliant, violent guitar from Ronson, while Lou cooed "You hit me with a flower". This was backed by the fabulous 'Satellite of Love', where the boys sang "Bom, Bom, Bom" as if auditioning for the Shangri Las. This single bombed too… what to do next?

7

WALK ON THE WILD SIDE
PERFECT DAY
LOU REED
RCA
10

"If at first you don't succeed, try, try and try again" goes the old adage and so, though it had already flopped once, 'Walk On The Wild Side' was re-promoted as a new single… and this time Lou's guided-tour around the dive bars of New York and his introductions to a whole raft of Warhol "Superstars" began to sell. In doing so Lou was belatedly established as a major artist. Spare a thought for Herbie Flowers the next time you hear this record, for it was he who invented the intricate and hypnotic bass-line that underpins the record, for which he received no writer's credit – just his £17 session-players daily fee. The B-side is worthy of mention too; 'Perfect Day' was Lou's delicious and very suave love song, in honour of his drug of choice, heroin. "You're gonna reap just what you sow" he drawled through the outro. Amazingly, in a re-recorded form, featuring a cast of singing stars and major celebrities (including Lou himself and David Bowie) the song was issued as a charity record that celebrated the BBC and became a 1997 number 1 hit – its original meaning buried and forgotten.

6

SUPERSTITION
YOU'VE GOT IT BAD GIRL
STEVIE WONDER
TAMLA MOTOWN
11

The lead single taken from Stevie's album *Talking Book*; this signalled to anyone with ears that the Motown child genius, 'Little' Stevie Wonder, was a big boy now. The song was very nearly gifted to Jeff Beck in return for his participation on the album until corporation bigwigs cautioned Stevie about giving away this particular gem. 'Superstition' is built on a squelching riff played by Stevie on Moog bass and clavinet, and anchored by a solid drum pattern (again played by Stevie) along with added tenor sax and trumpet. The track was complete save for Stevie's wild and exuberant vocal. The sounds created for 'Superstition' were a world away from the accepted norms of soul and funk but for Stevie rules were there to be broken; he was creating a brand-new musical language.

5

LEAN ON ME
BETTER OFF DEAD
BILL WITHERS
A&M
18

One might imagine that 'Lean on Me', one of the most brilliant songs of the latter part of the 20th-Century, would have been an enormous hit but oh no – it charted modestly, but no more than that. It was written by Bill Withers whilst living in Los Angeles as he found himself reminiscing over the sense of community which, though absent in LA, had been what he was used to as he was raised in the poor part of Slab Fork, a mining town in West Virginia. Using several members of the Watts 103rd St Rhythm Band as studio musicians, as well as an elegant string arrangement, the song is musically rather unobtrusive; it is tender and reflective. 'Lean on Me' was also lyrically quite sparse and kept deliberately simple; each sentence is unambiguous and straight to the point – looking after each other when times are tough. It has a hymn-like quality and Withers's steadfast vocal is full of dignity and the goodness that resides in the human spirit.

4

VIRGINIA PLAIN
THE NUMBERER
ROXY MUSIC
ISLAND
4

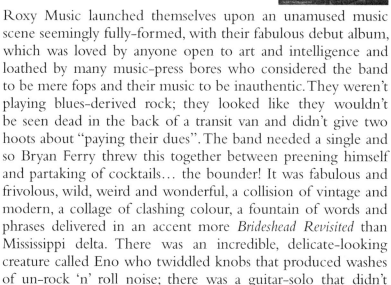

Roxy Music launched themselves upon an unamused music scene seemingly fully-formed, with their fabulous debut album, which was loved by anyone open to art and intelligence and loathed by many music-press bores who considered the band to be mere fops and their music to be inauthentic. They weren't playing blues-derived rock; they looked like they wouldn't be seen dead in the back of a transit van and didn't give two hoots about "paying their dues". The band needed a single and so Bryan Ferry threw this together between preening himself and partaking of cocktails... the bounder! It was fabulous and frivolous, wild, weird and wonderful, a collision of vintage and modern, a collage of clashing colour, a fountain of words and phrases delivered in an accent more *Brideshead Revisited* than Mississippi delta. There was an incredible, delicate-looking creature called Eno who twiddled knobs that produced washes of un-rock 'n' roll noise; there was a guitar-solo that didn't sound like a guitar solo and a caveman beating up on a drum kit. Pure, unadulterated genius – it was a 'My Generation' for my generation!

1 (Jointly)

CHANGES
ANDY WARHOL
DAVID BOWIE
RCA RECORDS
DID NOT CHART

STARMAN
SUFFRAGETTE CITY
DAVID BOWIE
RCA RECORDS
10

JOHN I'M ONLY DANCING
HANG ONTO YOURSELF
DAVID BOWIE
RCA RECORDS
12

THE JEAN GENIE
ZIGGY STARDUST
DAVID BOWIE
RCA RECORDS
2

ALL THE YOUNG DUDES
ONE OF THE BOYS
MOTT THE HOOPLE
CBS
3

David Bowie started 1972 as a nobody in terms of public recognition, and ended the year as perhaps the most recognisable figure in the country. More importantly, within 12-months he had proved himself to be, and was widely accepted as, the most important musical figure in the country. The chart placings for his singles hardly support that statement, but because his records were somewhat ahead of their time, a gestation period was needed so that people could assimilate the content and come to eventually value their worth.

'Changes' was released in the first week of the year and signified a new beginning. This was Bowie's first single for RCA and was a great leap forward from 1971's Bolan-imitating 'Holy Holy'. For the first time on record Bowie seemed confident in his own voice and comfortable in his own skin; so comfortable in fact that he is able to manipulate his persona to his own artistic ends, making "ch ch ch changes" as and when he feels appropriate. "Look out you rock 'n' rollers" he exclaims, and with that single phrase distances himself from the prevailing orthodoxy. 'Changes' is, of course, an amazing song, but beyond that it is an amazing record; incredibly sure-footed and brilliantly produced by Ken Scott, it is built upon the pounding, dancing piano-part performed heroically by Rick Wakeman. The band; consisting of drummer Woody Woodmansey, bass guitarist Trevor Bolder and Mick Ronson who was simultaneously an extraordinary guitarist, a genius arranger and all-round musical foil - all perform superbly. Bowie's own saxophone parts are crucial too. Tony Blackburn, the arch-conservative BBC Radio 1 DJ, chose 'Changes' as his Record of the Week on his flagship Breakfast Show, giving it huge exposure; and yet, the record-buying public were resistant to its charms… for now.

'Starman' followed in April and if 'Changes' acted as the foreshadowing of what was to come, this made the breakthrough. A new look had been adopted by Bowie and the band, now known as The Spiders from Mars and heavily influenced by Stanley Kubrick's cinematic version of *A Clockwork Orange* (given an androgynous and futuristic makeover) they looked, as was intended, like nothing on earth. This visual representation of the new music was not only striking and eye-catching, but it strengthened the concept, making it whole. For many of us, the unveiling of this startling image took place via an appearance on *The Old Grey Whistle Test* in February, just as the Ziggy tour began. We were excited and our attention had been seized. 'Starman' was written to be released as a single at the behest of RCA and replaced a version of 'Around and Around', a Chuck Berry number, on the *Ziggy Stardust* album. Sales were, once again, initially disappointing; nevertheless, the single sold consistently over a long period to keep it hovering around the chart. The tour was helping, an appearance on Granada TV's *Lift Off With Ayesha* assisted further and then, two months after the single's release, on 6th July 1972, Bowie and the Spiders appeared on *Top of the Pops* and the world changed; it was impossible not to have an opinion, and 'Starman' sped up the charts. Its strummed acoustic guitar, its "Judy Garland meets the Supremes" chorus and the promise of an extraterrestrial being who would like to "blow our minds" was irresistible. Our mundane, suburban lives were transformed for ever.

'John I'm Only Dancing' was the stand-alone single chosen to follow 'Starman', and hopefully consolidate Bowie's hard-won position as a chart act. It was a strategy not without a degree of risk; the single was not released in America, considered far too risqué for that uptight market, and even in the UK a video filmed to promote the release featuring Lindsey Kemp's mime troupe was banned as obscene by the BBC. The song itself was a kind of up-tempo R&B shuffle, with Ronson adding searing lead guitar fills. Lyrically the song was quite ambiguous, but many people believed it was sung from the perspective of a gay man reassuring his male partner that he is "only" dancing with a girl and has no sexual interest in her. It may not have won many new converts, but for those of us already fascinated by Bowie, it was glorious reaffirmation of our faith.

High-quality songs were pouring out of Bowie's fertile mind, and with great generosity of spirit he wrote and donated the outstanding 'All The Young Dudes' specifically for floundering rockers Mott the Hoople, as a last-ditch effort to boost their prospects and prevent their dissolution. Not only that, but along with the song came Mick Ronson and Bowie himself as producers. As a musical piece 'Dudes' was magnificent while as a performance, in particular that of vocalist Ian Hunter, it went even beyond that magnificence into the rare musical territory of great significance and importance – Mott had seized the opportunity that Bowie had given them. The song itself is played dirge-like and name checks the old-guard whom, though not so old in reality, are already, in Bowie's mind, "yesterday's

men": T. Rex, The Beatles and The Rolling Stones are all viewed negatively, all as failures, false prophets and discredited soothsayers. This is because they do not grasp the truth as the youth now know it; "All the young dudes, carry the news" is the anthemic chorus... and the news they carry is that we are on the brink of apocalypse.

'Jean Genie' was released at the end of November and was confirmation to anyone who had doubted that David Bowie was now the pre-eminent musical artist of the age. He had conquered old sparring-partner Marc Bolan and knocked him off his perch. He had hammered nails into the coffin of the 1960s and made the totems of that decade seem redundant. Big selling acts, such as Elton John and Rod Stewart, intuitively knew their place was beneath Bowie in the grand-scheme of things and even hard-rockin' blues-thieving pirates such as Led Zeppelin were now culturally unimportant; they were stuck in a past that Bowie had left behind, a past that was dull and imprisoning. 'Jean Genie' was big and bold – a year of touring had added muscular bulk to the Spider's playing, and Bowie drove this juggernaut of high-powered repetition playing wailing harmonica and celebrating the explosive, uninhibited talents of Iggy Pop and Jean Genet. "Let yourself go!" he exclaimed... and 'Jean Genie' was a wild bacchanal in salute of a triumphant year.

1973

EVENTS

EVENTS

- The U.K. enters the EEC (European Economic Community)
- George Foreman defeats Joe Frazier to become World Heavyweight Boxing Champion
- USA ends its involvement in the Vietnam War by signing the Paris Peace Accords
- Israeli fighter planes shoot down a Libyan Arab Airlines flight killing 108 passengers and crew
- Value Added Tax introduced in U.K.
- U.S. Vice-President Spiro Agnew resigns after being found guilty of Income Tax evasion
- The American Psychiatric Association removes homosexuality from its list of mental illnesses
- The 'Three Day Week' is introduced in the U.K. to reduce electricity consumption during the Miner's Strike
- Tommy Docherty's Manchester United shed George Best, Bobby Charlton and Denis Law and replace them with Tony Young, George Graham and Trevor Anderson; they play the most defensive, dour and negative style of football in the club's entire history! Liverpool win the league while Second Division Sunderland pull off one of the biggest shocks in football history beating Leeds to win the FA Cup

NOTABLE BIRTHS

Ole Gunnar Solskjaer; Larry Page; Pharrell Williams; Sachin Tendulkar; Peter Kay; Rufus Wainwright; Nas; Paula Radcliffe

NOTABLE DEATHS

Lyndon Johnson; Noel Coward; Pablo Picasso; Betty Grable; Veronica Lake; Lon Chaney Jnr; Bruce Lee; J.R.R. Tolkien; Victor Jara; Gram Parsons; Sister Rosetta Tharpe; Gene Krupa; Bobby Darin

NOTABLE FILMS

Badlands; The Exorcist; Don't Look Now; Mean Streets; The Wicker Man; Enter The Dragon; The Last Detail; Pat Garrett and Billy The Kid; The Sting

NOTABLE BOOKS

Breakfast of Champions – Kurt Vonnegut Jnr
Gravity's Rainbow – Thomas Pynchon
Fear of Flying – Erica Jong
The Honorary Consul – Graham Greene
The Rachel Papers – Martin Amis
Crash – JG Ballard
Child of God – Cormac McCarthy
The Princess Bride – William Goldman

THE MUSIC

By 1973 the music scene was totally fractured. Record companies were clueless as to which way things were moving and therefore began a process of musical regurgitation; re-issues of 60s hits, re-packaged and re-marketed, were swamping the racks as executives saw safety and security in looking backwards. There arose a trend of bands, made up of what seemed to be unemployed holiday-camp entertainers, issuing toothless, neutered rock 'n' roll facsimiles, based on the success at the cinema of *American Graffiti* and *That'll Be The Day*. Shabby also-rans such as Gary Glitter and Mud, who cared not one jot about dignity, were churning out hit after hit and being dressed up like turkeys at Christmas whilst being marketed as wholesome and safe pop stars for young teens. From across the Atlantic a tidal wave of bland dross began washing up on our shores.

The singer-songwriter scene had been sanded down and smoothed over until its sound was little more than aural mush. Into our homes, oozing from transistor radios, came John Denver, Linda Ronstadt, Bread and The Eagles – all-American and saccharine sweet. Rock music was big business too and talentless dorks chugged and noodled to stupid and stoned pretend hippies in stinking Afghan coats, as a lucrative career choice. Meanwhile. on the streets of the UK, young, middle-aged and elderly men alike grew collar-length hair and wore flared trousers, while a double brushed denim trouser and shirt combination was considered high style and favoured casual wear. Females adopted a look of shapeless smocks, often in brown, or else Crimplene trouser-suits in pastel shades. The mainstream was largely fucked.

Thank goodness then for the bravado and derring-do of David Bowie, Roxy Music and Alice Cooper; thank the Lord in Heaven for Al Green, George Clinton and Bootsy Collins; praise Jah for The Wailers and Big Youth, because beyond the crass commerciality of marketing departments, dreadfully mimed performances on children's TV shows and the mountains of tinsel and tat it came wrapped in, there remained, thankfully, enough substance, attitude and excitement to nurse a horrified young teen through the nightmare landscape of Britain in 1973.

MY 1973

I was part of the last group of school pupils who had the choice of leaving after four years or staying for a fifth and sitting exams. I chose the latter, more because I wasn't yet ready to make a career choice than because I believed a few CSE certificates would pave my way towards a brighter future. Most of my peers chose to leave, and those who stayed on were uniformly made prefects – except for one individual... me. I was by now regarded as a pernicious and seditious presence. I had turned-up at a school function as drunk as could be, I had edited the school magazine and included unflattering cartoon drawings of some teachers I disliked, one of whom had reacted by grabbing me by my jacket lapels, pinning me against the wall and threatening to "do me". Actions, of course, speak louder than words, and another teacher took his revenge in a staff versus pupils rugby match by inflicting a severe groin injury upon me that went untreated, and caused me pain and illness for several years afterwards. My football career too had hit the buffers - I had been attached to a professional club and had become seriously disenchanted by a lot of what went on... e.g. being told to remove my shorts to have an ankle injury attended to rang serious alarm bells in my head. My behaviour became rebellious and my on-field performances bad tempered; I was released and felt very disillusioned.

Predictably, my exam results were poor – I received good

grades only in Art, English Literature and History. I then attended a few interviews for jobs that I didn't really want to be offered and wound-up starting work on my 16th birthday as a trainee handbag designer. I didn't much like my work, though in hindsight I realise it was actually pretty free and easy. Being at heart quite shy I found it difficult, initially, to develop friendships with my colleagues, although they were kind and courteous towards me. There was one exception; a lad of my age was a fellow music-buff and we were soon lending each other records. He provided me with a schooling in up-to-date American soul, whereas I led him towards an appreciation of Roxy Music and David Bowie. I queued all-night, in the rain, to purchase front-row tickets to see the Rolling Stones. I was impressed by them as I watched, but what I liked best was that they were far from perfect – they made mistakes and it humanised them in my eyes.

Despite seeing these living-legends, my undoubted musical highlight of the year happened a couple of weeks into my working-life when, one lunchtime, rifling through the record racks of a shop in Ashton-under-Lyne, I came across a copy of *Fun House*, an album by The Stooges. It was a record I had searched for and desired beyond all others. It cost me 50p and it changed my life; I was totally inspired. I didn't know a single other person who had heard of The Stooges, let alone owned a record by them. Henceforth I often smiled inwardly knowing I had this fantastic and secret music inside my head that contained a transformative power that made me feel truly alive. I formed a band with a pair of friends; I sang. We played songs by The Kinks, The Who, The Beatles and Eddie Cochran. It only lasted a couple of months but I was again nourished by music. I met Ray Davies of the Kinks who was kind and patient with me, and we conversed for 20 minutes or more. He showed me the human face of a serious musician who I could see was vulnerable and insecure too. This was a world away from the untouchable rock star image that I already distrusted and loathed. Records were bought on every single pay day; more and more gigs were attended. I had become a popular boy, who on the surface was fine, but beneath the façade I was fractured and frightened. Without music I was nothing... thankfully I had music.

100
DAMNED FLAME
HOPE
BLAST
MAJESTIC RECORDS
DID NOT CHART

There is little known about this band, beyond the fact that they were from Belgium, recorded and mixed this single in two hours (which sold between 300 and 500 copies) and recorded nothing else ever again. So why is this record on my list, you may well ask… ? The answer is that it is absolutely fabulous. 1973 was three or four years before punk and a decade before speed metal, and yet both forms are contained within this record. Essentially they were playing in styles that hadn't yet been invented. They sound crude but committed, as though they're experiencing the best adrenaline rush of all time. Their enthusiasm makes them play faster and faster; the drummer just keeps speeding things up and his energy is contagious. Listening to them even now, I just can't sit still.

99
ALSO SPRACH
ZARATHUSTRA
SPIRIT OF SUMMER
DEODATO
CTI
7

'Also Sprach Zarathustra' was a tone-poem composed by Richard Strauss in the last decade of the nineteenth-century. It was memorably used by Stanley Kubrick as part of the soundtrack for his film *2001: A Space Odyssey* and from that point onward entered popular culture, no longer the sole property of orchestral concert halls and so in 1973 Brazilian jazz pianist Eumir Deodato recorded a heavily 'funked up' jazz version of the piece, along with notables such as bassists Ron Carter and Stanley Clarke, along with Billy Cobham on drums. It was a brilliantly conceptual piece, magnificently realised, that delightfully brought the music of Strauss into the mirror-balled discotheques and dancehalls of the great proletariat masses…

98
CALIFORNIA SAGA (ON MY
WAY TO SUNNY CALIFORNIA)
FUNKY PRETTY
THE BEACH BOYS
BROTHER
37

'California Saga' was a ten-minute plus opus, written by Al Jardine, contained on the Beach Boys album *Holland*. For this single version, the latter section of the song was re-mixed and it featured vocals by Brian Wilson which were unheard on the album. It is a sunny, countrified shuffle celebrating the great outdoors. The record heralded the Beach Boys acceptance by a younger, less preppy, audience than they had previously appealed to, as they sing about playing the 'Big Sur' folk-festival, along with Country Joe McDonald, who sang of liberty "and the people there, in the open air, (who) were one big family".

97
MARLENE
EVERYBODY SAYS
KEVIN COYNE
VIRGIN
DID NOT CHART

'Marlene' was the first single issued by Virgin Records and featured the distinctively-voiced Kevin Coyne, author and performer of several genuinely frightening, insightful songs about mental health institutions and other subjects generally considered to be taboo at the time. "Marlene" is not one of those; it is a wonderful jaunty piece, highlighted by organ and guitar, which concerns the singer's longing for the aforementioned lady. "Everybody Says", on the reverse side of the single, is the complete opposite. Simply backed by acoustic guitar, Coyne laments life's disappointments and injustices, and his continual suffering as people encourage him with false hope – "Everybody says I'll be flying high someday" he sadly observes. The lament concludes with these very same encouraging people weeping by his graveside as he is laid to rest in "the sodden barren ground".

96
GIMME THREE STEPS
MR BANKER
LYNYRD SKYNYRD
MCA
DID NOT CHART

Playing good-time rock 'n' roll licks and singing about a misunderstanding over a woman's favours in a hostile bar, this sounded like The Faces transported from the West End of London to the American Deep South. However, there was a crucial difference; whereas The Faces tales of bad behaviour, ending with ejection from the premises, employed much artistic licence, Lynyrd Skynyrd were playing a song written by Ronnie Van Zant about a real-life incident in a biker-bar in Jacksonville, when an irate Hells Angel threatened him with a loaded pistol.

95
WILD IN THE STREETS
LON CHANEY
GARLAND JEFFRIES
ATLANTIC
DID NOT CHART

Garland Jeffries was a pre-Velvet Underground acquaintance of Lou Reed and later he would work with John Cale on his *Vintage Violence* album. He was certainly keeping good company, and on the evidence of this debut single, was no slouch himself. Written about a pre-teen rape and murder that had taken place in the Bronx, the single featured Dr John on clavinette, as well as some of New York's finest and most in-demand session players - it had a swagger and an edge that was highly impressive.

94
MY COO CA CHOO
PULL TOGETHER
ALVIN STARDUST
MAGNET
2

Chunky-jumpered, bespectacled, nice-guy songwriter Peter Shelley had co-founded Magnet Records. In the studio he cooked up a catchy glam-influenced single and issued it under the Bowie-esque pseudonym Alvin Stardust. It began rising up the charts, but having no interest in performing he began seeking somebody to adopt the role of 'Alvin' and take on the requisite promotional duties. Enter Bernard Jewry, who in pre-Beatles days had scored a few minor hits as Shane Fenton. Dressed up in black leather, with hair slicked back in imitation of Vince Taylor, 'Alvin' had arrived just in time to glower, waggle his finger and lip sync to 'My Coo Ca Choo' on *Top of the*

Pops and a star was born!

93
5-15
WATER
THE WHO
TRACK
20

Quadrophenia, the album from which this single was lifted, marked the start of The Who's slow death. It was uneven, overblown and too verbose for its own good. No matter that it spawned a film which in turn spawned a Mod revival (a misnomer if ever there was one) and no matter that it eventually earned Pete Townshend a shed-load of cash, it would have made a better short-story than a 2-disc concept album. Despite this '5-15' was, thankfully, a rollicking good single, noisy but tuneful. Although Roger Daltrey still roars out the lyric as though it is of vital importance, when isolated from the rest of the narrative the words are rendered rather meaningless. The Who were still an incredible live act; their history together had created a musical chemistry that was just thrilling but sadly as good as it was, '5-15' didn't come close to matching 'I Can See For Miles', 'Substitute' or 'My Generation'. The Who had entered their terminal, but seemingly never ending, decline.

92
ANGIE
SILVER TRAIN
ROLLING STONES
ROLLING STONES RECORDS
5

Largely written by Keith Richards, this gentle, lovelorn ballad was widely speculated to be about David Bowie's wife Angela, who was rumoured to have had a fling with Mick Jagger. In truth, it was more probably a name chosen randomly that simply scanned well. It was a softer and blander Rolling Stones single than we had heard before; was the rot beginning to set in here as well?

91
DEAR ELAINE
SONGS OF PRAISE
ROY WOOD
HARVEST
18

'Dear Elaine' is a gentle, slightly eccentric nugget with a baroque feel. It was written and produced by Roy Wood, who also played every instrument on the record, including several from the classical domain. Here he created a lovely, offbeat single that lightens my soul whenever I hear it.

90
SATURDAY NIGHT'S ALRIGHT FOR FIGHTING
JACK RABBIT/WHENEVER YOU'RE READY (WE'LL GO STEADY AGAIN)
ELTON JOHN
DJM
7

Elton was at the artistic pinnacle of his career, full of ideas and enthusiasm and enjoying being a pop star. However, soon enough a combination of cocaine and it's inevitable symptom, an inflated ego, would turn him into a dull, bloated, irrelevant bore. On 'Saturday Night's Alright for Fighting' he successfully evokes the nasty flash of small-town Britain in the early 1960s; the motorbike boys, greasy hair, warm beer, loud music and gratuitous violence to end the night's revelry. Musically this is as aggressive as Elton ever got. The band take a highly prominent role in proceedings, with the piano battling valiantly for pre-eminence amongst them. Vocally, Elton is as strong as ever, and although the singer's tongue was surely firmly in his cheek, the delivery never crosses the line into comedy territory.

89
MR SKIN
NATURE'S WAY
SPIRIT
EPIC
DID NOT CHART

Spirit released their fourth LP, from which these two tracks derive, in 1970. The album *Twelve Dreams of Dr Sardonicus* didn't sell well initially but proved to be an enduring piece of work that sold steadily over several years which is why, 3 years after the album release, this single appeared. 'Mr Skin' is a fabulous record featuring blaring horns, a slightly jazz feel, captivating lyrics and a "Na Na Na Na" chorus that adds buoyancy. The B-side, 'Nature's Way', is perhaps Spirit's best known song and is a work of startling genius.

88
STONED OUTTA MY MIND
SOMEONE ELSE'S ARMS
CHI–LITES
BRUNSWICK
DID NOT CHART

With its floating groove, punchy horns and falsetto-voiced lead vocalist, this could easily be mistaken for the work of Curtis Mayfield; in fact it was performed by fellow Chicago soulsters the Chi–Lites. Although its title may indicate that 'Stoned Outta My Mind' has a drug theme, it is actually a song of lost

love and heartache written by lead singer Eugene Record and label mate Barbara Acklin. The quality of the song is clearly indicated by the heavyweight cover versions it has attracted, from the likes of John Holt, the Mighty Diamonds and besuited punkers, the Jam.

87
FRANKENSTEIN
UNDERCOVER MAN
EDGAR WINTER
EPIC
18

No vocals, an ominous, lumbering riff, synthesiser manipulations, funky bass (courtesy of future disco star Dan Hartman) a double drum solo, featuring Chuck Ruff, all supported with admirable restraint by guitar hero Ronnie Montrose and Edgar Winter himself on percussion, what else could this mutant-hybrid of art, rock and dance be titled but... Frankenstein!

86
RUBBER BULLETS
WATERFALL
10CC
UK
1

Toying with sounds and styles in their self-contained bubble, 10cc came up with this playful, slightly subversive take on cheerful jailhouse numbers such as 'Jailhouse Rock'. In this instance, the prisoners are not rocking but rioting, hence the call to "load up with rubber bullets", perceived by some as a comment on British Army tactics in Northern Ireland, even though the song is chock-full of Americanisms. As inventive as ever, a double-speed guitar solo is thrown like a Molotov Cocktail into the mix, and when the dust had settled we were left with a pop single of quite startling quality and distinction.

85
BROTHER LOUIE
I WANT TO BE FREE
HOT CHOCOLATE
RAK
7

A brave attempt to address an issue that was barely whispered about in polite society, namely fraternisation between men and woman of different colours and the nightmare world of interracial couples facing persecution from both sides of the racial divide. Hot Chocolate tackle the issue with sensitivity and, crucially, without losing their pop smarts. This meant that their message was transmitted over the radio into households all around the country. A great cameo vocal from Alexis Korner is thrown in for good measure too.

84
RELAY
WASPMAN
THE WHO
TRACK
21

The third stand-alone pre-Quadrophenia single in a row from The Who, all salvaged from the aborted *Lifehouse* project, 'Relay' speaks about the electronic transference of information, and the impact upon our lives of what seemed a far-fetched prospect in pre-internet 1973. On this track the guitar was fed through a synthesiser to give the piece a modern sheen and, admittedly, it moved along quite nicely; but even composer Pete Townshend noted that the once vital Who were beginning to sound a little

bit jaded. Better, much better in fact, was the B-side 'Waspman', which consists of a simple, repetitive guitar riff, pounding drums and songwriter Keith Moon shouting "waspman sting" in an almost Captain Beefheart-esque slice of conceptual strangeness.

83
PILLOW TALK
MY THING
SYLVIA
VIBRATION
14

Sultry and sensual, there was no doubt that 'Pillow Talk' was about sex. Sylvia Robinson wrote the song and offered it to Al Green, but it was too near the knuckle for him and somewhat offended his religious sensibilities. Unperturbed, Sylvia resurrected her dormant performing career and recorded it herself. Lush sounding with a disco feel, and replete with orgasmic moaning, 'Pillow Talk' was a forerunner of a new genre of music. Robinson was also a businesswoman who ploughed her money into her own record label, and as disco dawned All Platinum Records released hit after hit. Later, of course, Sylvia who was always willing to give a chance to what she believed in, went on to form Sugarhill Records and was a major part of bringing hip-hop into the public eye via acts such as the Sugarhill Gang and Grandmaster Flash and the Furious Five.

82
THE BALLROOM BLITZ
ROCK AND ROLL DISGRACE
THE SWEET
RCA
2

The Sweet were a bunch of macho-rockers squeezed into ludicrous satin-and-tat outfits and plastered in makeup. They aspired to be taken seriously, like Uriah Heep or Budgie, but had sacrificed their dreams and dignity for the wealth and fame that came from being a blank canvas for songwriting bubblegum record producers Nicky Chinn and Mike Chapman. Remarkably, after a run of some of the silliest, most lightweight and childish singles ever made ('Wig Wam Bam', 'Co–Co', 'Little Willy' and numerous other atrocities) Chinn and Chapman decided to crank the power and volume up and compete with the likes of Slade and Gary Glitter. Remarkably, it worked; the new sound, with drums to the fore and anthemic, though empty slogans as choruses, made for glorious fun pop. 'The Ballroom Blitz' was about an incident that occurred when the band were performing in Kilmarnock; the show was halted by a barrage of bottles aimed at the group. In a flash of lateral thinking that has to be admired, Chinn and Chapman turned the debacle into a triumph, a crowd-driven wild with excitement, and so 'The Ballroom Blitz' was created. It offered no insight and had no depth… but it was big, brash, loud and genuinely exciting.

81
SYLVIA
LOVE REMEMBERED
FOCUS
POLYDOR
4
Oh what joy! The audible exuberance and gusto in the playing, combined with a supremely uplifting melody, go a long way to making this such a pleasurable listen. The rhythm section interlocks perfectly and Thijs van Leer's organ is propulsive.

He also provides a brief yodelling section, but the cherry on the cake is the incredible guitar playing of Jan Akkerman which is a marvel of harmonic expression, combined with admirable restraint and wonderful technique.

80
SHE
THAT'S ALL IT TOOK
GRAM PARSONS
REPRISE
DID NOT CHART
After creating what he described as American cosmic music (though others simply called it country rock) and spending a dissolute time as part of the Rolling Stones entourage – until they grew tired of his excesses and sent him packing – Gram Parsons set about recording some pure country music. Failing to recruit Merle Haggard as producer, but hiring Elvis Presley's TCB band – led by Glen D Hardin – and the then unknown Emmylou Harris as a backing vocalist, he cut the album *G.P.*, which featured this gorgeous single. 'She' tells a tale of the Deep South where Parsons was raised. The "she" in question is a plain, lonely woman, doing back-breaking work in the cornfields beneath the Delta sun. Her release, and her standing in the community comes from her singing voice: "Oh she sure could sing" is the refrain at the end of each verse. The piece is full of melancholy, and ghosts seem to inhabit the darkest corners of this beautiful song, yet it is played with an elegant half-swing, full of grace, and sung with tenderness and empathy by the doomed soul that was Gram Parsons.

79
LAMPLIGHT
WE ALL INSANE
DAVID ESSEX
CBS
7

'Rock On' catapulted David Essex to major-league stardom, after close-on a decade's worth of flops. 'Lamplight' was a sure-footed follow-up of dub-like echo, "dragnet" horns and a suggestive lyric delivered in heavily-soaked reverb vocal. His looks ensured that he was a teeny-bopper idol, but his music owed more to the sonic experiments taking place in Jamaica and Germany than the production line pop of David Cassidy or Donny Osmond.

78
MIND GAMES
MEAT CITY
JOHN LENNON
APPLE
26

John's album *Mind Games* was mostly appalling; a morose trudge through banal preaching. Two songs were good, 'Bring On the Lucie' and 'Meat City' – they had both energy and enthusiasm. Only one song was great... the title track and unsurprisingly it was chosen to be released as a single. 'Mind Games' is a song of positivity, calling for unity and peace. It originated as a Beatles-era song called 'Make Love Not War', with the melody coming from another aborted song called 'I Promise'. John comes alive on this more than any other recording of the era; we sense that he is truly comfortable with the song and its content. "Yes is the answer" is the opening line of the chorus, and is a tacit acknowledgement of Yoko's influence in his thinking, this key word being the title of her ceiling-art exhibit where they first met. Love is a huge part of the message and is intrinsic to the song; it is in the lyric and in its gentle, blissful tune. It didn't sell well, but this was a single John could be proud of.

77
RIGHT TIME WRONG PLACE
I BEEN HOODOOD
DR JOHN
ATLANTIC
DID NOT CHART

New Orleans resident Mac Rebennack, known to the outside world by his stage persona of Dr John, was already a legendary figure when he recorded 'Right Time Wrong Place'. He was highly regarded, with a rich catalogue of wonderful music that warranted respect but this tongue-twister of a song became one of his key, and best known, works. Deliciously funky and good-natured, it is brimful of goodness, including a needle-point guitar section and the esteemed Dr John's chuckling vocal. The inclusion of the equally legendary band The Meters is another key to the record's success, as the alchemy produced by singer and players is, quite simply, aural gold.

76
BALLAD OF EL GOODO
BALLAD OF EL GOODO
BIG STAR
ARDENT
DID NOT CHART

From opening note to final flourish this is a totally captivating single. The song flows easily and naturally; all of its changes belong, nothing is superfluous. This is close to perfection and a thing of shimmering beauty. Alex Chilton, with his bruised but still golden voice, sings words of defiant self-resolution; "Ain't no-one gonna turn me round" – he repeats to emphasise his reliance on his own decisions. The band harmonise like fallen angels and the production serves the song, displaying all the nuance with crystal clarity.

75
CAN THE CAN
AIN'T YA SOMETHING HONEY
SUZI QUATRO
RAK
1

Bass-playing singer Suzi was spotted by Mickie Most, with her band the Pleasure Seekers, during a visit to the USA . He signed her on a solo-artist deal and she relocated to the UK to join the Mickie Most roster of artists on his RAK record label. Her first single flopped, and so, for the second, Most brought in hit-makers Chinn and Chapman to write and produce, his protégé. They gave Suzi the up-tempo, aggressive sounding 'Can the Can', and allowed her to use the band put together for live shows she had played with the likes of Slade and Thin Lizzy. Her bass rumbles like thunder, the band kick-up a bit of a storm, and then Suzi opens her mouth and emits a mighty roar; this is followed by all manner of yelps and squeals as she attacks the lyric like a banshee. As a piece of production-line pop, it was pretty thrilling and primal.

74
SATURDAY NIGHT
MARLENA
BAY CITY ROLLERS
BELL
DID NOT CHART

The third consecutive flop since 'Keep on Dancing' had charted in 1971, 'Saturday Night' opens with the word 'Saturday' chanted phonetically over a hammered-out drum part, before a buzz-saw guitar riff leads into the song and the sweet chorus. It's a cheap-sounding and brash record, which is exactly what gives it a degree of endearing charm; it sounds like it's made by kids who you might find hanging around the local parks or shops, passing a fag around and looking for something to do. It is full of innocent enthusiasm and has an unpolished energy – in that sense, though not in terms of the song's soppy sentiments, 'Saturday Night' is a true precursor of punk. Little wonder then that The Ramones gleefully ripped it off for their own 'Blitzkrieg Bop'.

73
CALL ME
WHAT A WONDERFUL THING
LOVE IS
AL GREEN
HI
DID NOT CHART

Al Green was, by now, untouchable and unchallenged as the pre-eminent soul star. 'Call Me' is magnificent in every sense; an intelligent song about unhurried seduction and the promise of more. The sound is delivered by the team of producer Willie Mitchell, the trusted Hi Records rhythm section and, of course, Al Green's voice, which mostly simmers, but when emphasis is needed, shifts to a devastating falsetto. With country and gospel elements in the make-up of the song, and in its production, we are gifted something beautiful and substantial, containing real deep-rooted grit and passion.

72
PHOTOGRAPH
DOWN AND OUT
RINGO STARR
APPLE
8

'Photograph' was the third single in a row written by Ringo and George Harrison, although it was the first to formally credit Harrison. It was a song that had been around for a couple of years, and when the time finally came for recording it was overseen in America by producer Richard Perry who did a great job utilising a stellar cast including Starr and Harrison themselves, Nicky Hopkins, Klaus Voorman and arranger Jack Nitzsche. It is a soaring song with a contagious, sing-a-long chorus which disguises the sadness of the lyric about accepting permanent loss, with only a photograph remaining which causes as much pain as it gives consolation. Ringo's best ever song without a doubt, but also one of the best songs by any ex-Beatle in this or any other year, since the mothership had crashed.

71
S-90 SKANK
TRUE TRUE TO MY HEART
BIG YOUTH
MAFIA
DID NOT CHART

Teenage producer Gussie Clarke brought out the best in Big Youth. He understood the importance of giving the exuberant toaster room to express himself, and they duly hit with 'The Killer', using Horace Andy's 'Skylarking' rhythm. Keith Hudson had been trying out various toasters for his rhythms and Big Youth was the man of the moment. So, offering the rhythm from Hudson's own 'True True To My Heart', Big Youth was set loose on the subject of the S-90 Honda motorcycle. These were highly popular with the youth of Trenchtown and one of the prized machines was even brought into the studio to be revved-up, thus creating an authentic sound effect for the track. It was a stunt, but it made for an electrifying opening to the record.

70
TOP OF THE WORLD
HEATHER
THE CARPENTERS
A&M
5

From their 1972 album *A Song For You*, this was never earmarked as a single. That changed when Lynn Anderson had a big country music hit with her version of the song and so the Carpenter's original 'Top of the World' was belatedly issued. Opening with a steel guitar figure, the song moves unhurriedly, and in an uncluttered fashion, with unobtrusive strings the only adornment; Karen Carpenter's crystal-clear voice does the rest. We are led into a beautiful chorus of such deep joy and open-hearted wonder that it actually feels cleansing to hear it.

69
COME ON FEEL THE NOIZE
I'M MEE, I'M NOW AN' THAT'S ORL
SLADE
POLYDOR
1

"BABY–BABY–BABY", roars Noddy Holder as an introduction and then a wall of deafening noise hurtles out of the speakers. It was calculated, it pandered to audience expectation, it was far from subtle –

but it came with a memorable tune and was undeniably exciting, there is a hint of an insurrectional message in the huge chorus; "We go wild, wild, wild" they cried… and the band's loyal audience of working-class kids screeched along.

68
THE ROCKER
HERE I GO AGAIN
THIN LIZZY
DECCA
DID NOT CHART
Tongue-in-cheek cartoon violence in the lyric, a razor-edged guitar attack, drums that thunder and a swaggering vocal from Philip Lynott, expounding on his credentials as rocker extraordinaire; this single also includes a nice name check for Ted Carroll's "Rock On Records" emporium in Camden Town. Sadly, after this high-watermark moment, the original and best Lizzy line-up would fragment.

67
JET BOY
VIETNAMESE BABY
NEW YORK DOLLS
MERCURY
DID NOT CHART
The Dolls were the real deal; they lived rock 'n' roll lives amid the squalor of the streets, strutting their exotic stuff. Meanwhile, the fêted rock rebels of yore hid away in gated mansions in total detachment. The Dolls sashayed out on a limb to display their rejection of the orthodoxy of the music scene – "mock rock" sneered the ludicrous *Old Grey Whistle Test* presenter Bob Harris, proving that he was hopelessly out of touch. The Dolls jumbled up their Bo Diddley, Rolling Stones and Shangri-Las influences to create a big,

loud, glorious sound, accompanied by melody and flash. 'Jet Boy' is one of their classics; written by the erudite David Johansen and bad-boy guitar slinger Johnny Thunders, it doesn't aim to say anything apart from "Jet boy flies around New York City all night"… but it says it with extreme style and attitude. The 'Blank Generation' was almost upon us.

66
CONCRETE JUNGLE
REINCARNATED SOUL
THE WAILERS
ISLAND RECORDS
DID NOT CHART
Stuck in a British winter whilst decamped in grey London, physically and emotionally a world away from the sunshine, blue skies and green fields of Jamaica, Bob Marley wrote 'Concrete Jungle' about the alien environment in which he found himself. "Darkness has covered my light" he comments on the gloom of urban city living. Recorded for the *Catch a Fire* album on Island Records, the track featured a guitar solo by American Wayne Perkins, brought onboard to sweeten the Wailers' sound for Western ears, since international approval was sought for the band's music. This single wouldn't provide that breakthrough, but it was quite wonderful to hear Marley's soulful lead vocal, supported by the uniquely inventive Peter and Bunny as they harmonised over the delicious groove laid down by the Barrett brothers.

65
GHETTO CHILD
WE BELONG TOGETHER
THE SPINNERS
ATLANTIC
7

The Spinners had relocated from their native Detroit to Philadelphia's Sigma Sound Studio to work with masterful producer Thom Bell and there they recorded this excellent single, full of aching melancholy. Featuring lead vocals from each of the Spinners in turn, the lyric, concerning a young boy's escape from a town "filled with narrow minds and hate", tugs at the heartstrings. His tale of moving from place to place, without ever finding anywhere he can call home, is handled exquisitely and without overt sentimentality.

64
NUMBERS (TRAVELLING BAND)
DRINKING SONG/
ONE OFF PAT
ALAN HULL
CHARISMA
DID NOT CHART

Lindisfarne didn't have the resilience to withstand setbacks; they had come together in a marriage of convenience and the chemistry that binds old friends together simply didn't exist. And so, after the relative failure of 1972 album *Dingly Dell* cracks appeared that couldn't be repaired and the group splintered into factions, allowing principal songwriter Alan Hull to go off and record *Pipedream*, a splendid solo album. From the album came the single 'Numbers', a life-on-the-road song, written from the point of view of a weary, jaundiced, travelling musician who finds himself on a treadmill of hangovers, greasy-spoon cafés, boring journeys from town to town and guest houses. He doesn't know how to get off and lives for the hour on stage when he can play "music from a dream". The whole piece is performed in an almost surreal fashion, with various pieces of musical exotica utilised to create the sad, washed-out feel of the song and the emptiness felt by the narrator.

63
SMALL TOWN TALK
GROW TOO OLD
BOBBY CHARLES
BEARSVILLE
DID NOT CHART

Bobby Charles arrived in upstate New York, from Louisiana, to record an album utilising the talents of various members of The Band and their producer John Simon. Charles and Rick Danko wrote 'Small Town Talk', an unassuming, though finely-crafted marvel. It is a wonderful, observational song, taking in the "tittle tattle" of gossiping for gossiping's sake, and the hurt it can cause – all delivered without histrionics and conveying a wry understanding of the situation. Bobby Charles sings it perfectly, and the lurching, organ-dominated groove is used as a springboard from phrase to phrase.

62
ALL THE WAY FROM MEMPHIS
BALLAD OF MOTT
MOTT THE HOOPLE
CBS
10

Totally rejuvenated by their hit with David Bowie's gift of 'All The Young Dudes', they were now confident enough to decline further assistance and plot their own course. 'Honaloochie Boogie' had been a success, but 'All The Way From Memphis', its follow-up, was so seriously excellent that no-one would ever doubt them again. The band may have been uncomfortable in their new glittery outfits, but the glam sparkle added to their already potent music and set it alight. 'All The Way From Memphis' had so much going on; Ian Hunter's travelogue lyric of mishaps, a potent piano–guitar led track that surged with unleashed energy and, on loan from Roxy Music, Andy Mackay coaxed an extraordinary saxophone solo from the ether, all combining to make this a dizzying, roller coaster ride of a record.

61
I LIKE YOU
EARTH SIGN MAN
DONOVAN
EPIC
DID NOT CHART
Donovan had a knack of making records that sounded profound and full of deep significance, but on closer inspection said very little. He put together words beautifully but they were habitually added to gentle, often portentous sounding melodies; the songs were therefore saccharine sweet but empty of meaning. That is very much the case with 'I Like You'. Its huge, overpowering sweep seems full of emotion and it has a sense of heartfelt sadness in the swells of sound; and yet it is not the soul-baring exercise initially imagined, but simply a delicious, ornate abstraction that nonetheless is hugely pleasurable and enchanting.

60
LOOSE BOOTY
A JOYFUL PROCESS
FUNKADELIC
WESTBOUND
DID NOT CHART
Hip-shakingly propulsive, this was a satirical put-down of hard drug use and its disastrous consequences, told in nursery-rhyme style. Only Frank Zappa came close in terms of dealing with serious subjects whilst using humour to make his point. Frank though wasn't nearly as concise, or a fraction as funky, as George Clinton and his extraordinary crew.

59
CARIBBEAN MOON
TAKE ME TO TAHITI
KEVIN AYERS
HARVEST
DID NOT CHART
Flutes and piccolo flutter over the sound of waves lapping on a golden beach; a very inauthentic sounding calypso begins, and Kevin sings of "The wind blowing in the coconut tree" and the "Rum-lime honey" he has found underneath the Caribbean moon. It's all very silly, delightfully so in fact, and the ludicrous backing vocals during the song's sing-a-long outro are genuinely funny. There we have it, the thinking man's credible take on 'Viva España'.

58
THE SHOW MUST GO ON
TOMORROW
LEO SAYER
CHARISMA
2
Dressed as a Pierrot clown and borrowing from "Entrance of the Gladiators", Leo Sayer launched into his song detailing life's

disappointments, utilising the guise of circus performer as metaphor. It was audacious but it was judged perfectly; the pain and anguish of the song meant that no-one was laughing at this sad clown. On and on he details the injustices and betrayals heaped upon him – "I've been so blind, I've wasted all my time" he realises – but now he will make a stand, now he will control his own destiny... and now, in a subversive inversion of the song's title, he "won't let the show go on".

57
RUMOURS
MAN LOVES A WOMAN
HOT CHOCOLATE
RAK
44

Hot Chocolate were, at this point, releasing some very questioning singles, touching on themes not often found in mainstream pop. Here, with a string arrangement influenced by 'Superfly' and 'Shaft', a tale of paranoia concerning the Watergate scandal unfolds in restrained, half-whispered lyrics, as a chant of "Rumours, rumours, rumours" echoes over a primitive conga beat; it is as if the narrator has these conflicting voices battling within his head. A string flourish heralds the arrival of a positively nasty sounding wah-wah guitar, and the malevolence of poisonous tongues dispatching misinformation to fuel the rumours that refuse to abate.

56
BLOCKBUSTER
NEED A LOT OF LOVIN'
THE SWEET
RCA
1

It was a little confusing that the numbers one and two on the pop chart shared almost identical riffs, but 'Blockbuster' and David Bowie's 'Jean Genie' were practically conjoined twins in that respect. If Bowie aimed at a higher artistic sensibility, it has to be said that The Sweet's record was much more fun. The lyric was gibberish but delivered with earnest seriousness by Brian Connolly; sirens wail and periodically Steve Priest is heard chirping "We haven't got a clue, what to do". Neither had we, the listeners, it was fair to say, but we did know that we should beware of a man if we have "long black hair" – and we were told with urgent emphasis that "We must find a way to block-buster"...

55
DON'T YOU WORRY
'BOUT A THING
BLAME IT ON THE SUN
STEVIE WONDER
TAMLA MOTOWN
DID NOT CHART

From the period of Stevie's artistic searching and experimentation, 'Don't You Worry 'Bout A Thing', with its feel of spontaneity and unbridled joy, was an unqualified success in everything except sales. It is all about the power of positive thinking and Stevie is at his exuberant and playful best. He jives through an opening dialogue over a Latin-flavoured piano piece, throws out the phrase "Todo está bien chévere" and away we go into the song proper, almost skeletal in its construction, relying as it does on the interplay between percussion and piano. In summary, the piece conveys a fresh and cheerful feeling which is further enhanced by Stevie's easy-on-the-ear vocal.

54
SHOWBIZ KIDS
RAZOR BOY
STEELY DAN
MCA
DID NOT CHART

Known generally for their subtlety, 'Showbiz Kids' is not subtle at all. It is a powerful indictment of the gap between the 'haves' and the 'have-nots', delivered over an unchanging riff which is given added potency with the addition of Rick Derringer on slide guitar; this complements the almost percussive piano played by Donald Fagen whose vocal carries the hint of a sneer as he details the lives of the privileged rich... "The showbiz kids making movies of themselves, you know they don't give a fuck about anybody else".

53
SEE MY BABY JIVE
BEND OVER BEETHOVEN
WIZZARD
HARVEST
1

There was magic in the air when Roy Wood cooked up 'See My Baby Jive' in his wizard's cauldron. This is a record that, whilst paying glorious homage to the past, seems so fantastical that it is surely sent from the stars; every aspect is gleefully exaggerated, suggesting a total lack of restraint, a wild and free celebration. Of course, it's nothing of the sort; Wood, being a master pop craftsman,

conducts from the centre of the maelstrom, ensuring that he is in complete control of the shifting gears of the song, its ebbs and flows and twinkling chorus. In Stockholm, the fledgling Abba were busy taking note and designing their breakout hit, 'Waterloo', based upon this wonder from Wizzard.

52
RADAR LOVE
JUST LIKE VINCE TAYLOR
GOLDEN EARRING
TRACK
7

The 4/4 snare drum beat, the riveting bass line adding propulsion and the choppy power-chords of the guitar combine to create a rhythmic, forward moving whole. Snaking and accelerating with the drum beat doubled, this is taut and we feel the tension mounting as the narrator, who drives through the night, picks up telepathic signals from his girlfriend who is distressed; "It's my baby calling saying I need you here" is the message he receives, and his desperation to be with her pushes him through the exhaustion with his eyes on the road and his hands wet on the wheel, as he journeys onward, pushing himself and his machine to the limit. A song of conceptual genius – in fact the ultimate driving song – this single is iconic and instantly recognisable; it has not withered or aged at all.

51
LOVES ME LIKE A ROCK
LEARN HOW TO FALL
PAUL SIMON
CBS
39

Although it is a very slender song,

lyrically 'Loves Me Like A Rock' manages to speak volumes about a mother's unequivocal love for her son, and how important that steadfast support is to him. Whether it be a little boy facing temptation, or the American President dealing with Congress, the certainty of a mother's love gives him strength. Featuring vocals from a black Baptist gospel group – the Dixie Hummingbirds – which give flavour to the song, 'Loves Me Like A Rock' is a resounding, uplifting success.

50
BAD MOTOR SCOOTER
ONE THING ON MY MIND
MONTROSE
WARNER BROTHERS
DID NOT CHART
Hard rock of the highest order here from the band put together by guitarist Ronnie Montrose after he left Edgar Winter's White Trash. Written by teenage vocalist Sammy Hagar, 'Bad Motor Scooter' has none of the braggadocio of much of this genre, as Hagar encourages the object of his desire to "Get on your bad motor scooter and ride" from her home to his house – as he confesses, "I'd come to your place but I'm afraid of your dad". It is all attacked with a good deal of gusto, and the noise that comes out of the guitar-amp is thrilling in its filthy nastiness.

49
SAIL ON SAILOR
ONLY WITH YOU
THE BEACH BOYS
BROTHER/ REPRISE
DID NOT CHART
In the view of the suits at Reprise the Beach Boys hadn't got a track worthy of being a single on *Holland*, the

album they had recently submitted; it was decreed that the album wouldn't be released until a suitable single was forthcoming. Happily, at this point, the band remembered 'Sail On Sailor', a song that Van Dyke Parks and Brian Wilson had written in 1971. Following some lyrical additions from Brian's friends, the song was recorded by the Beach Boys. Brian began to tinker, searching for perfection as he had done with *Smile*. On this occasion however, he was told that he would not be allowed to follow his muse. The next task was to decide who would sing the song. Dennis Wilson half-heartedly tried a lead vocal before going surfing; brother Carl had a go and concluded that his voice was unsuitable. Eventually the band's guitar player, Blondie Chaplin, was given the task; his soulful voice was a perfect fit. Brian, now completely divorced from the process, failed to turn up at the studio to record backing vocals but instead phoned in instructions. Under these circumstances this could easily have been a disastrous record; instead it stands as the Beach Boys last true classic. Its rolling melody perfectly conjures a journey across an ocean, and that is the lyrical metaphor used to describe the struggle through life's travails without becoming discouraged and capsizing in a sea of woe.

48
I'M DOIN' FINE NOW
AIN'T IT SO
NEW YORK CITY
CHELSEA
20
Under the tutelage of Philly soul producer Thom Bell, New York City recorded two albums and hit big with

this single. 'I'm Doin' Fine Now' was one of those seemingly effortless, pre-disco dance-floor fillers that Thom Bell was issuing almost weekly. This one is sturdily anchored by drums and a superb horn figure punctuates the honey sweet vocals; there is, however, much more going on than is revealed via a superficial listen. New York City's touring musicians, the 'Big Apple Band' found themselves seeking a new path when, in 1975, New York City split. Two of them, Bernard Edwards and Nile Rogers, formed a new group; called Chic.

47
HELLO HOORAY
GENERATION LANDSLIDE
ALICE COOPER
WARNER BROTHERS
6

'Hello Hooray' was written by Rolf Kempf and recorded by Judy Collins as part of her 1968 *Who Knows Where The Time Goes* album. Resurrected by Alice Cooper as a grand, glam showstopper in the manner of 'Cabaret', producer Bob Ezrin had recent form in capturing that kind of vibe, having worked with Lou Reed on his *Berlin* album; it served him well. 'Hello Hooray' is striking from its elegant guitar intro and stately-paced grace; there are grand piano flourishes adorning the track and Alice reveals a fabulous singing voice displaying hitherto unheard subtlety and restraint, before unleashing all of his power in the bombastic, soaring finale to this untypical, but glorious, record.

46
THE DEAN AND I
BEE IN MY BONNET
10 CC
UK
10

John Milton's *Paradise Lost* is name-checked; the Beach Boys are referenced; Kevin Godley (who I would often see out-and-about during this period) repeatedly sings "Humdrum days and humdrum ways" and Lol Creme sweetly croons about a world of ups and downs, and finally more ups – "It's a wonderful world, when you're rolling in dollars, now!". The song finishes; we can only hazard a guess as to its meaning… if indeed it has one. But, after catching our breath, let us be thankful that 10cc weren't following anybody's rules but their own as they served-up the kookiest and most eccentric of pop delights.

45
THE JOKER
SOMETHING TO BELIEVE IN
STEVE MILLER BAND
CAPITAL
DID NOT CHART 1973
(Number 1 Reissue 1990)

'The Joker' is an amalgam of a song; Steve Miller is magpie-like in his plundering. The tune is lifted from 'Soul Sister' by Allen Toussaint, and lyrically Miller dips into his own back catalogue and references 'Space Cowboy', 'The Gangster of Love' and 'Enter Maurice', as well as utilising lines from The Clovers 1954 hit 'Lovey Dovey'. All of this fits together perfectly to create something striking. Throw in the wolf-whistle slide guitar part and the inventive use of the prominently placed made up word "pompatus" and 'The

Joker' becomes a once heard, never forgotten song, that grew, grew and grew again in popularity.

44
CINDY INCIDENTALLY
SKEWIFF (MEND THE FUSE)
THE FACES
WARNER BROTHERS
2

With its lolloping rhythm and rolling piano this is unmistakably Faces fare. From the opening bars it's a lovely vignette of a man feeling the need to move on, to leave the safety of the suburbs and get to where the action is. He is engaged in trying to persuade 'Cindy' to join him; he points out that "The street outside is just a little too quiet and the local paper has run out of news". Finally he encourages her with the lines "Cindy get your coat on, leave the rent with the gent up in the penthouse" before proposing that they "drink a round to this town and bid goodbye". Their all-action style perhaps obscured the fact that Faces songs were often excellently written and insightful; 'Cindy Incidentally' was a fine example of this, though sadly it was also Ronnie Lane's last record with the group.

43
DON'T LIE TO ME
WATCH THE SUNRISE
BIG STAR
ARDENT
DID NOT CHART

Penned by Chris Bell and packing a punch, 'Don't Lie To Me' is basically a couple of churning riffs, minimalist verses and big choruses; some songs just don't need any more. Near perfection was achieved here, though not many folk were listening.

42
PERSONALITY CRISIS/
TRASH
NEW YORK DOLLS
MERCURY
DID NOT CHART

Take your pick – whichever side of the record the needle drops onto, you're on a winner. 'Trash' and 'Personality Crisis' are two enormous slabs of big-hearted but sleazy rock 'n' roll. 'Trash' leaps out of the speakers and straight into a shouted chorus; it is deeply ambiguous but at the centre of things are a low-life couple getting on with the business of surviving and retaining their humanity. 'Personality Crisis' just might have been the finest song and performance of the Dolls' truncated career. David Johansen is the star of the show with a vocal of passion and humour that spits in the face of the concept of restraint. Equally unrestrained drummer Jerry Nolan manages to hold the beat together so the song doesn't go crashing off the rails as Johnny Thunders and Syl Sylvain trade-off dangerous sounding guitar licks, and the icing on the cake is the demented, Jerry Lee Lewis style piano-part played by producer Todd Rundgren.

41
YOU'RE SO VAIN
HIS FRIENDS ARE MORE
THAN FOND OF ROBIN
CARLY SIMON
ELEKTRA
3

This is a needle-point, forensic attack on an ex-lover and a brilliant song that, in some ways, has become overshadowed by the subject of her accusations. It is a fun game to speculate I suppose, but it doesn't really matter since this record will endure longer than the singer or the subject. A superb, bubbling bass line from Klaus Voorman leads into the song, and from there the string arrangement delights as she observes and condemns. Each verse builds toward a soaring chorus, where Mick Jagger provides some edge as he lends his unmistakable voice to the proceedings.

40
SEBASTIAN
ROCK AND ROLL PARADE
COCKNEY REBEL
EMI
DID NOT CHART

As a first-ever release for Cockney Rebel, they aimed high – very high indeed – with the epic 'Sebastian'. This is seven minutes of moody and magnificent gothic splendour, poetic word play, a huge orchestral arrangement and choir. Steve Harley, the songwriter and singer, wrings every scrap of drama from the song, seemingly spiralling towards madness from the opening piano trills to the closing crescendo. Harley was not modest, and 'Sebastian' was massively ambitious and arrogant but his audacity brought out the bitchy worst in the music press who relished the record's failure to chart. However Cockney Rebel had laid down a marker, a signifier of what was to come, and they had created quite an impression on those seeking dark, twisted and esoteric thrills.

39
SORROW
AMSTERDAM
DAVID BOWIE
RCA
3

After his famous "retirement" speech,

prior to the final song of the *Ziggy* tour at Hammersmith Odeon, Bowie headed to France to record *Pin Ups*, an album of cover versions. This was only a partial success since the majority of songs did not match up to the originals; the one obvious exception was 'Sorrow'. It had been a US hit for The McCoys and a UK hit for The Merseys, whose version was the blueprint for Bowie's interpretation. It's a laid-back and languid song which suited Bowie's voice. The treatment is respectful and subtle, with Mike Garson typically excellent on piano, and a string arrangement (by the ever versatile and impressive Mick Ronson) adding texture. The B-side too was a real treat for fans; a recording of 'Amsterdam' made in 1971 during the *Ziggy Stardust* sessions. This is one of two brilliant Jaques Brel songs – the other being 'My Death' – that regularly featured in live performances by Bowie around this time.

38
FUNKY WORM
PAINT ME
OHIO PLAYERS
WESTBOUND
DID NOT CHART

These funksters, who had been playing together since the early 1960s, were getting seriously abstract about this time, rivalling Funkadelic as the most groovesome Dadaists on the planet. 'Funky Worm' is a highly entertaining and individualistic single, with its cartoon vocalised story of a worm playing guitar with no hands, it also includes synthesiser solos that have been sampled to death by the hip-hop community.

37
CELEBRATION
OLD RAIN
PFM
MANTICORE
DID NOT CHART

Premiata Forneria Marconi were an Italian progressive-rock band that formed at the beginning of the 1970s and had a big continental hit with a record called 'È-Festa'. They came to the attention of Emerson, Lake and Palmer who signed them to their own Manticore label and put them in the hands of Pete Sinfield (lyricist for King Crimson/ELP and Roxy Music producer). He decided to shorten their name to PFM and re-wrote the lyrics to their past material which were then re-recorded utilising bigger, better studios. 'È-Festa' was duly re-worked and became 'Celebration'; synthesiser-led, it was a glorious, up-tempo piece containing elements of symphonic sound and European folk. It shifted through distinctly different passages, never losing its relentless pace, before slowing down to permit a short vocal interlude. The pace is then picked up again before a sudden and unexpected full-stop. The overall effect was as if one had been spun around on a very pretty, ornate fairground ride… great fun.

36
BOOK OF RULES
VERSION
THE HEPTONES
ISLAND
DID NOT CHART

Contemporaries of The Wailers and The Maytals, vocal harmony trio The Heptones transitioned through ska and rocksteady into the reggae era with ease, and bass player/singer Leroy Sibbles was one of the major talents shaping Jamaican music. 'Book of Rules' was largely the work of Barry Llewellyn, who sang the lead part and developed the song from an American poem called 'A Bag of Tools' by R.L. Sharpe. The song is possessed with steadfastness and innate nobility, dealing as it does with the unfair apportioning of menial and manual work upon the poorer classes.

35
WIRED UP
AIN'T GOT TIME
HECTOR
DJM
DID NOT CHART

This is an unpretentious, thumping glam racket. With their energised sound and subject matter, Hector were closer to punk than they were to Bowie or Roxy Music. 'Wired up' is all blazing guitars, crunching drums and a wildly over-the-top synthesiser solo. The production, in truth, is appalling – particularly in regard to the vocals which are softened, presumably so as not to cause offence, whereas they should, of course, have been aiming to offend. The band were also hindered by the ludicrous outfits they were dressed in which made them look like a half-witted, country bumpkin version of the Bay City Rollers.

34
ACROSS 110th STREET
HANG ON IN THERE
BOBBY WOMACK AND PEACE
UNITED ARTISTS
DID NOT CHART

The title-song of a film, 'Across 110th Street' is one of Bobby Womack's finest songs and performances. Over a lean groove of wah-wah guitar with horns used to emphasise changes, Womack paints an unflinching portrait of ghetto-life and points out how widespread the problem of urban deprivation along the racial divide was… and remains. In every city you find the same thing going down, and Harlem is the capital of every ghetto town. He offers no solutions and doesn't pretend to have any; solutions need to come from politicians and he is just a guy on the street trying to break free of the cycle of poverty and degradation. This was music based on reality; an articulation of a subject that needed addressing. A truly great single.

33
MOONSHAKE
FUTURE DAYS
CAN
UNITED ARTISTS
DID NOT CHART
The music of Can existed in a sphere of its own and 'Moonshake' is unmistakably their work; the sound was resolutely un-American. Can helped me, as a young, untravelled schoolboy, to feel European. They helped me feel a kinship with people on a landmass I'd never set foot on. As usual, drummer Jaki Liebezeit is to the fore, his style totally unmistakable – a brilliant creator of the groove. Each of the other players add to the piece and Damo Suzuki sings beautifully. On this occasion Can are light and breezy; there is a distinctly pop flavour to be found in 'Moonshake', albeit a pop that is slightly esoteric and otherworldly but also refreshing and highly stimulating.

32
LA GRANGE
JUST GOT PAID
ZZ TOP
WARNER BROTHERS
DID NOT CHART
An electrified blues boogie rhythm, handled in ZZ Top's own inimitable style, replete with growled vocal and a stunning guitar solo from Billy Gibbons. The subject matter of the song is the La Grange brothel in Texas, and it lends a loose, sleazy vibe to this exemplary guitar music. Place this on a loop and play it repeatedly; it is so good that no sane person would ever tire of it.

31
SCREAMING TARGET
CONCRETE JUNGLE
BIG YOUTH
GRAPE
DID NOT CHART
The sound of Big Youth is one of positive energy; there is vitality aplenty in his work. 'Screaming Target' is the record that established his name outside Jamaica and brought the whole DJ phenomenon to the wider World's attention. This particular track is full of the ingredients that make Big Youth so irresistible. Recorded with long-time friend Gussie Clarke and using K.C White's rhythm from 'No, No, No', Big Youth chants and screams his way through the piece, offering pearls of wisdom such as advocating schooling and literacy as a way out of a life of crime, and of self-improvement.

30
NO MORE MR NICE GUY
RAPED AND FREEZIN'
ALICE COOPER
WARNER BROTHERS
10

Billion Dollar Babies, the album from which this single was plucked, was almost a greatest hits collection, full of memorable songs with hooks aplenty. 'No More Mr Nice Guy', over a great, taut rock riff, tells the story of a man shunned, and often persecuted, by all and sundry – including the family dog. With even the local preacher joining in and punching him on the nose, he comes to the conclusion that his only option is to fight back; hence 'No More Mr Nice Guy'. My mother, who was fast approaching the age of 50 when this was released, would cackle in glee when this record was played, and sing along as happy as a lark. Forty years later, as she lay unconscious in the hours before her death, I held her hand and sang this song, hoping that somehow she could hear or sense it...

29
REELIN' IN THE YEARS
ONLY A FOOL WOULD SAY THAT
STEELY DAN
ABC
DID NOT CHART

For a cynic, Steely Dan were huge fun; they gleefully displayed their disdain for human failing – and such failings were lampooned with a sarcasm that could draw blood. Their attitude was an antidote to the bland, inoffensive pap being peddled by manipulators who selected the radio playlists. 'Reelin' in the Years' was a brutal put-down of an ex-partner who was found wanting. It had a musical buoyancy at odds with the nature of the song, and an absolute killer guitar solo from session player Elliott Randall. Walter Becker and Donald Fagen were curmudgeons for sure, but in infiltrating the pop mainstream with their seditious and sardonic wit, they were providing a very essential and enjoyable alternative to the bland mediocrity we were encouraged to swallow.

28
TSOP
SOMETHING FOR NOTHING
MFSB (featuring the Three Degrees)
PHILADELPHIA INTERNATIONAL
22

MFSB stood for Mothers, Fathers, Sisters, Brothers; they were a pool of around thirty studio-musicians who worked at Sigma Sound with producers Gamble & Huff and Thom Bell. They provided backing for acts such as The O'Jays, The Stylistics and Harold Melvin & The Bluenotes. MFSB recorded TSOP (an abbreviation of "The Sound Of Philadelphia") as a largely instrumental piece, comprising a combination of horns and very lush strings. Written by Gamble & Huff and featuring The Three Degrees purring the lines "Let's get it on, it's time to get down", this became the theme-tune to American TV show *Soul Train*, and it captures the spirit of the age to perfection.

27
STREET LIFE
HULA KULA
ROXY MUSIC
ISLAND
9

For the first time in the UK, Roxy Music used an album track as a single; it was also the first release since Brian Eno had been replaced by Eddie Jobson. The strangeness of earlier releases makes way for a more orthodox loud guitar led sound and a generally more solid song structure. However, 'Street Life' was still top drawer material and a perfect choice for a single, with Bryan Ferry's vocal performance every bit as refreshingly anti-rock as on previous outings.

26
I SHOT THE SHERIFF
PUT IT ON
THE WAILERS
ISLAND
DID NOT CHART

Bob Marley's outlaw song, 'I Shot the Sheriff', tells the simple story of a man planting seeds that the authorities kill before they grow. The perceived injustice leads to him taking the law into his own hands and gunning down the Sheriff – a crime to which he readily admits; though he will not take the blame for the death of the Deputy Sheriff. This was a tale Marley had told in an earlier single, 'Keep On Movin', but this insanely catchy tune gathered more attention. Still it wasn't a hit, although a dull and watered down version by Eric Clapton would score heavily just a year later.

25
HELEN WHEELS
COUNTRY DREAMER
WINGS
APPLE
12

One of the most thrilling sounds in popular music is that of Paul McCartney letting rip in his Little Richard style voice over a hard-driving rock 'n' roll beat; 'Helen Wheels' is one of the occasions when he did just that. 'Helen Wheels' is a play on the nickname that he and Linda McCartney had given to their Land Rover (Hell on Wheels) and it is a driving song in the style of 'Route 66', transported across the Atlantic. The song describes a road trip from Scotland to London; perhaps name-checking Carlisle (describing it as pretty was stretching artistic license to the limit) but all was forgiven on this occasion because the record was oh, so very good.

24
FAITH HEALER
ST ANTHONY
THE SENSATIONAL ALEX HARVEY BAND
MOUNTAIN
DID NOT CHART

The Sensational Alex Harvey Band were one of the great "live" acts – and anybody who saw them would agree – but in making that statement the thing that is often overlooked is that it is impossible to be a great "live" act unless one actually has great songs. The Sensational Alex Harvey Band did have great songs… and 'Faith Healer' was the greatest of them all. It builds slowly with brooding keyboards before Zal Cleminson provides a coiling guitar line and Alex enters with "If your body's feeling bad". Harvey acts out the role of shamanistic healer – "Can I put my hands on you?" – and in concert he would stretch out his arms towards his audience as if he truly believed he could take our pain away. All too soon this unforgettable song reaches its dramatic climax and the only remedy is to put the needle back in the groove and listen to it all over again.

23
SUCH A NIGHT
LIFE
DR JOHN
ATLANTIC
DID NOT CHART
Dr John's gloriously charming piano blues is sung with the matter of fact resignation of a lothario who simply cannot help himself. The piano keys practically twinkle, like the stars beneath which the seduction takes place – never hurried and moving no faster than a romantic stroll through the moonlight. This was an utterly beguiling single.

22
A HARD RAIN'S A-GONNA
FALL
2HB
BRYAN FERRY
ISLAND
10
Bob Dylan wrote 'A Hard Rain's A-Gonna Fall' as a poem in the style of Arthur Rimbaud, supposedly in response to the Cuban Missile Crisis when the world teetered on the brink of nuclear destruction. Ferry took this sacred tract and afforded it zero respect and turned it into a vamped-up pop masterclass. Utilizing a heavily mannered vocal, Ferry delightfully played with the song's

symbolist imagery; it became frothy, bubbly and uncontainable. All-in-all a brilliant subversion of what was regarded as a deadly serious piece, turned into a joyous romp and, in truth, an improvement on the original.

21
STUCK IN THE
MIDDLE WITH YOU
JOSE
STEALERS WHEEL
A&M
8
Gerry Rafferty and Joe Egan, who essentially were Stealers Wheel, generally had a Beatles-y, *Rubber Soul* era style. Here, though, they lovingly lampoon Bob Dylan, placing him at a music business dinner where he grows uncomfortable with the unctuous company in which he finds himself. Rafferty sings, using borrowed Dylan-style phrasing, while Egan harmonises. What takes 'Stuck in the Middle' out of the realms of parody is the strength of the song in its own right; both musically and lyrically it is top-notch, and producers Leiber and Stoller create a warm, intimate feeling of closeness between performers and listener.

20
IF YOU WANT ME TO STAY
THANKFUL AND
THOUGHTFUL
SLY AND THE FAMILY STONE
EPIC
DID NOT CHART
Sinuous, loose-limbed and funky; this is from the album *Fresh*, which contained more flesh-on-the-bone than most recent releases from Sly and Co. The superb rumbling bass and horns have such clarity that they

feel raw and spontaneous while Sly, singing in a low moan, is clearly energised and manages to convey a sense of playfulness as he explains, in the form of a letter to a girlfriend, that for their relationship to survive, he must be able to feel free and be true to himself.

19
HALLOGALLO part 1
HALLOGALLO part 2
NEU
BRAIN
DID NOT CHART
Without sharing a friendship, because they were such opposites as people, Michael Rother and Klaus Dinger had a telepathic musical rapport and in producer Conrad Plank, who, crucially, they respected as both a conductor and mediator. 'Hallogallo' is the band's crowning glory; its influence was soaked up by Hawkwind and Joy Division to name but two. It suggests perpetual motion; it is at once austere and expressive, stark but dreamy, as the layers of guitar paint pictures in the mind over the hypnotic pulse.

18
HIGHER GROUND
TOO HIGH
STEVIE WONDER
TAMLA MOTOWN
29
Stevie sings from the viewpoint of a man who has been re-incarnated and learned from his past experiences. He looks at the people around him living their lives "believin', warrin', dyin'" while he seeks (spiritual) higher ground. Again, he plays all the instruments, cooking up some brand-new and exciting sounds as he experiments and the vocal is simply

incomparable. Overall, an immaculate and absolutely unrestrained delight.

17
CAROLINE SAYS 2
CAROLINE SAYS 1
LOU REED
RCA
DID NOT CHART
'Caroline Says 1' is an up-tempo song that describes (from Jim's perspective) the wreckage of a relationship between "Jim" and "Caroline". He describes how she constantly belittles him, but to him she is still "a German Queen". 'Caroline Says 2' is her account of the relationship – this time the song crawls out of the speakers. She speaks of the beatings she endures at Jim's hands, and her escape from this pained life into a fog of drugs, before cutting herself badly by putting her fist through a window pane. This was Lou at his finest, trawling the underbelly of society and holding up a mirror to a hidden world of shameful denial.

16
LIVE AND LET DIE
I LIE AROUND
WINGS
APPLE
9
Reunited with Beatle producer George Martin – who produced, arranged and orchestrated – this was the theme-song to the Bond movie of the same name. McCartney clearly understood the need for something that shifts dramatically through the gears, and so he delivers orchestral bombast, a hint of reggae, a winning melody and some vocal interplay between McCartney and his wife Linda. The movie moguls wanted to hand the song to Shirley Bassey

or Thelma Houston to perform, but McCartney insisted that if they wanted the song, it would have to be Wings' version playing over the opening credits. He won the day and they should have thanked him; the song was a lot better than the film.

15
LET'S GET IT ON
I WISH IT WOULD RAIN
MARVIN GAYE
TAMLA MOTOWN
31

Marvin Gaye became a huge sex-symbol with the release of this single; it is the ultimate seduction record. In truth, this is a somewhat slight piece, resting on a magnificent drum pattern and Eastern-flavoured guitar; strings and horns then enter the mix contributing to a heightening sense of sexual release. The dominant instrument however is the voice of Marvin Gaye, which purrs over the quite delicious background vocals, also provided by Marvin himself.

14
ROCK ON
ON AND ON
DAVID ESSEX
CBS
3

Appearing in the musical *Godspell* had made David Essex a teen heart-throb and pin up; the release of a single was inevitable, and it was thought equally inevitable that it would be a hit. Therefore, any production-line, pap knock-off would have sufficed... but Essex had higher artistic ambitions than that. Having teamed-up with unknown American producer called Jeff Wayne they sculpted 'Rock On', with a sound having echoes of both Ennio Morricone and Joe Meek. It was impressionistic, innovative rock 'n' roll that, while having roots in the past, was looking toward the future. Simultaneously Essex was launching a film career starring opposite Ringo Starr in *That'll Be The Day*, which was something of a gritty, British classic. 'Rock On' played over the end-credits, and for a while David Essex had the world at his feet.

13
THAT LADY PART 1
THAT LADY PART 2
ISLEY BROTHERS
EPIC
14

Times had changed; the Isley Brothers had not had a substantial hit in four years when, bolstered by the fresh blood of family members Ernie and Marvin Isley, along with Chris Jasper, they entered the studio to re-cut their own 1964 hit 'Who's That Lady?'. Incorporating the style of Santana and other contemporary acts, they opted for Latin percussion, a heavy organ sound and more prominent guitar; the older Isleys even revamped their harmonies and the sound was thrilling. A truly wonderful change had been made with no loss of dignity; everything slotted into place and then the whole thing was taken up yet another gear as Ernie Isley went into his guitar solo – it scorched as if the spirit of former Isley stage guitarist Jimi Hendrix had possessed him. This was one of those occasions when the hairs on the back of your neck stand on end after hearing this superb record for the first time; repeated plays have not dulled its magic.

12

DRIVE IN SATURDAY
ROUND AND ROUND
DAVID BOWIE
RCA

3

'Drive in Saturday' is a perplexing single; it has a duality between a retro-leaning doo-wop style, and the futuristic feel of a man looking backwards at our present time from a post-apocalyptic landscape where people watch ancient pornographic films to teach them how to make love. Mick Jagger, Twiggy (who would feature on the cover of *Pin Ups*) and psychologist Carl Jung are all name-checked along the way as jazz player David Sanborn plays fluid tenor saxophone on a song that remains absolutely fascinating and which, oddly, Bowie tried to give away to Mott The Hoople; odder still they turned it down! The B-Side, 'Round and Round', is a Chuck Berry rocker that was a Ziggy Stardust leftover – it is scorching!

11

NUTBUSH CITY LIMITS
HELP HIM
IKE AND TINA TURNER
UNITED ARTISTS

4

Written by Tina Turner as an ode to the town she was raised in (although, as a town, it didn't actually have any city limits), it is a hard-driving, funky monster with inventive guitar playing – rumoured to have been the work of Marc Bolan – and a throat-grabbing Moog synthesiser break from Ike Turner that made this single absolutely impossible to ignore.

TOP 50 - 1ST SEPT 1973

#	LW	Wks	Title / Artist / Label
1	16	2	YOUNG LOVE Donny Osmond MGM 2006 3
2	2	8	YESTERDAY ONCE MORE Carpenters A&M AMS 7(
3	1	6	I'M THE LEADER OF THE GANG (I AM) Gary Glitter BELL 13
4	8	5	DANCING ON A SATURDAY NIGHT Barry Blue BELL 12
5	7	6	YOU CAN DO MAGIC Limmie & The Family Cookin' Avco 6105 (
6	5	7	SPANISH EYES Al Martino Capitol CL 154
7	3	5	48 CRASH Suzi Quatro RAK 1
8	4	14	WELCOME HOME Peters & Lee Philips 6006 3
9	14	4	SMARTY PANTS First Choice BELL 13
10	6	8	ALRIGHT ALRIGHT ALRIGHT Mungo Jerry Dawn DNS 1(
11	18	4	RISING SUN Medicine Head Polydor 2058 :
12	17	4	SUMMER (THE FIRST TIME) Bobby Goldsboro United Artists UP 35!
13	19	4	LIKE SISTER AND BROTHER Drifters BELL 1:
14	11	7	TOUCH ME IN THE MORNING Diana Ross Tamla Motown TMG I
15	9	6	YING TONG SONG Goons Decca F 13(
16	24	4	I'M FREE Roger Daltrey/ LSO & Chamber Choir ODE ODS 66:
17	12	6	BAD BAD BOY Nazareth Mooncrest Moo
18	15	6	ALL RIGHT NOW Free Island WIP 6(
19	13	9	LIFE ON MARS David Bowie RCA 2:
20	23	6	I'M DOIN' FINE NOW New York City RCA 2:
21	10	7	GOING HOME Osmonds MGM 2006
22	28	3	FOOL Elvis Presley RCA 2
23	25	4	SAY, HAS ANYBODY SEEN MY SWEET GYPSY ROSE Dawn BELL 1
24	21	10	HYPNOSIS Mud RAK
25	38	3	DEAR ELAINE Roy Wood Harvest HAR 5
26	27	9	FREE ELECTRIC BAND Albert Hammond MUMS 1
27	20	9	GAYE Clifford T. Ward Charisma CB
28	29	25	TIE A YELLOW RIBBON Dawn BELL 1
29	22	10	RANDY Blue Mink EMI 2
30	49	2	PICK UP THE PIECES Hudson Ford A&M AMS 7
31	46	2	ROCK ON David Essex CBS 1
32	–	–	THE DEAN AND I 10 CC (UK
33	35	3	I THINK OF YOU Detroit Emeralds Westbound 6146
34	31	19	AND I LOVE YOU SO Perry Como RCA 2
35	–	–	ELECTRIC LADY Geordie EMI 2
36	36	4	BAND PLAYED THE BOOGIE CCS RAK
37	30	8	SATURDAY NIGHTS ALRIGHT FOR FIGHTING Elton John DJM DJX
38	41	2	I'VE BEEN HURT Guy Darrell Santa Po PN
39	43	3	URBAN GUERILLA Hawkwind United Artists UP 35
40	32	9	SKWEEZE ME PLEEZE ME Slade Polydor 2058
41	26	10	PILLOW TALK Sylvia London AL 1(
42	44	15	RUBBER BULLETS 10 CC U!
43	34	13	SNOOPY VERSUS THE RED BARON Hot Shots Mooncrest Moo
44	45	2	RUMOURS Hot Chocolate RAK
45	33	12	BORN TO BE WITH YOU Dave Edmunds Rockfield RC
46	–	–	FOR THE GOOD TIMES Perry Como RCA 2
47	47	2	NATURAL HIGH Bloodstone Decca F 13
48	40	12	LIVE AND LET DIE Wings Apple R E
49	37	11	TAKE ME TO THE MARDI GRAS Paul Simon CBS 1
50	–	–	OUR LAST SONG TOGETHER Neil Sedaka MGM 2006

10

CAROLINE
JOANNE
STATUS QUO
VERTIGO
5

The claim that Francis Rossi and Bob Young wrote this in five minutes on a table-napkin over breakfast in a Cornish hotel is easy to believe – there is nothing fancy happening in this song, there is no message, it is as basic as it gets… and yet it is brilliant! This is more mid-tempo than out-and-out rocker, but the simple, yet tuneful, guitar riff is touched with genius. The verses sound like choruses and the choruses are a supercharged sing-a-long, perfect for an audience to roar right back at the band during their gigs, which very often felt like a tribal gathering.

9

20TH CENTURY BOY
FREE ANGEL
T. REX
T. REX WAX CO
3

Everything that was good and great about T. Rex was contained within this stand-alone single. It has a magical riff, the kind that Marc Bolan seemed able to conjure-up effortlessly, and a lyric that quotes Muhammad Ali – "I sting like a Bee" lisps Marc deliciously. Finally it contains a chorus that, once listened to, is remembered for all eternity; '20th Century Boy' is quite simply great.

8

GET UP STAND UP
SLAVE DRIVER
THE WAILERS
ISLAND
DID NOT CHART

Peter Tosh and Bob Marley co-wrote this statement song that

was a stand-out, defining moment in both their careers and a song that, for me, was a shot in the arm when I first heard it. The articulation and clarity of its message gave me plenty of food for thought; do I accept what I believe to be false for the sake of an easy life or do I oppose it and seek to tread the more problematic path of righteousness? That was the dilemma; as the Wailers put it – "You can fool some people sometimes, but you can't fool all the people all the time, so now we see the light, we gonna stand-up for our rights". This record drew a line-in-the-sand with the power to change: 'Get Up Stand Up'… wow!

7

KNOCKIN' ON HEAVEN'S DOOR
TURKEY CHASE
BOB DYLAN
COLUMBIA
14

'Knockin' on Heaven's Door' was written for Sam Peckinpah's smouldering and violent Western in which Bob Dylan acted. It contains just two stanzas – one gives voice to the titular outlaw *Billy the Kid*, the other to Pat Garrett, his friend, who is employed to kill him. The acclaimed wordsmith here condenses into two simple verses, and a six-word chorus, a whole dissertation upon the nature of life and death, guilt, betrayal and remorse. The simplicity and conciseness speak volumes, and convey real depths of emotion and sad resignation.

6

SEARCH AND DESTROY
PENETRATION
IGGY AND THE STOOGES
COLUMBIA
DID NOT CHART

A song that opens with the savage proclamation "I'm a street walking cheetah with a heart full of napalm" is laying its cards on the table from the off. This is not for the peace and love crowd; as it plainly states, this is for "the world's forgotten boys" – all the misfits, the non-conformists and the geeks shunned by the homogeneous masses. It is a howl of pain mixed with determined defiance from arch-Stooge Iggy, along with "dum dum boys" Ron and Scott and living "skull" James Williamson. It is a ticking time bomb that will eventually detonate beneath the smug and complacent industry types, and though not quite powerful enough to blow them all away, will certainly leave them feeling bruised and highly uncomfortable!

5

LIVING FOR THE CITY
VISIONS
STEVIE WONDER
TAMLA MOTOWN
15

One of Stevie's greatest records, 'Living For The City' tells the sorry story of a family in Mississippi who experience discrimination at every turn and an uphill fight to survive. The son uproots and moves to New York City seeking a better life, only to find more poverty as he trudges the streets choking on not just pollution but the injustice of life for black people. The world is cruel to him, but he hasn't abandoned hope that a change will come, that lessons will be learned to create a better tomorrow for the generations that follow him. The record incorporates street sound, which was revolutionary at the time, amid the symphonic funk of the stunning musical backing. Stevie turns in a vocal that is a mix of grief and anger; it jolts the listener and absolutely demands more understanding and compassion.

4

I CAN'T STAND THE RAIN
BEEN THERE BEFORE
ANN PEEBLES
HI
41

Sat in a restaurant with future husband Don Bryant and DJ Bernie Miller, the heavens opened and Ann Peebles exclaimed "I can't stand the rain!". Bryant, a staff songwriter at Hi Records, found inspiration in the phrase and began picking out a melody on the restaurant piano. Peebles and Miller threw in suggestions for lyrics, and the song was presented to Willie Mitchell the next morning. He assembled Hi's crack team of musicians and added the distinctive electric timbale, which mimicked the sound of a raindrop. Ann Peebles sang her part incredibly well, riding the emotional tide of the song; it was sweet, soul perfection.

3

LIFE ON MARS
THE MAN WHO SOLD THE WORLD
DAVID BOWIE
RCA
3

Mysterious and lyrically cryptic, beautiful and musically stirring, Bowie cooked this gem up between listening to Frank Sinatra performing 'My Way' (parodying its grandiosity) and having his heart broken by Hermione Farthingale (trying to understand how the break-up occurred). He then applied William Burroughs's cut-up technique to find himself with a series of abstract and surreal images that, when put together, created something thought-provoking and quite magical. Rick Wakeman contributed a magnificent piano part, and modest genius Mick Ronson created a superb string arrangement. Bowie brings to the song an absolutely magisterial vocal performance; it is sheer brilliance. It took the marketing department at RCA two years to realise the song's obvious potential to become an iconic hit... better late than never I suppose.

2

HERCULES
GOING HOME
AARON NEVILLE
MERCURY
DID NOT CHART

Aaron Neville would go on to finally achieve overdue success in the 1980s and 1990s; his golden voice came, at last, to be appreciated for the thing of wonder it truly is. Back in 1966 he'd had a huge hit with 'Tell It Like It Is', which had been adopted as an anthem by the Black Panthers – but in 1973 he was practically invisible when this, his absolute masterpiece, was released. It was produced by New Orleans legend Allen Toussaint and it is reasonable, I think, to presume that the musicians who play on the record are The Meters. What we are served up is a slow, almost ominous, Bayou funk that is totally arresting, and then Neville opens his mouth to sing... and oh, what words he sings. The song is about surviving; surviving temptation to do yourself, and others, wrong; surviving the pressure from every side and trying to keep hold of compassion... "I beg, steal or borrow, somehow I've got to make it to tomorrow". He knows exactly what a hole he is in and he knows he needs the strength of 'Hercules' to keep from going under.

1

PYJAMARAMA
THE PRIDE AND THE PAIN
ROXY MUSIC
ISLAND
10

In 1973 Roxy Music were out on their own; they were simultaneously the act who had their finger on the pulse of the present, and they were futuristic too – indeed, their music from this period has never seemed to age. In 1973 Roxy Music would record and release two ground-breaking albums, *For Your Pleasure* and *Stranded*. Between those twin peaks, Bryan Ferry would also issue his stunning solo album *These Foolish Things* – but the first Roxy release of the year was the stand-alone 'Pyjamarama' single, which gave some indication of the changes taking place. Firstly, John Porter replaced Graham Simpson on bass and brought into the band a quasi-funk groove; secondly, the band began to record with producer Chris Thomas, who introduced a whole new layer of sonic splendour to proceedings after the fragility and brittleness of Pete Sinfield's art-rock leaning sound. 'Pyjamarama' was a brave single in that it had none of the showiness or exuberance of 'Virginia Plain'; whereas that single had screamed out "Look at me!", 'Pyjamarama', by contrast, was positively demure... it seemed to come with an attitude of take it or leave it. Although the track opens with

a startling guitar chime, the song soon moves into a swaying groove. Ferry, sounding thicker-voiced and yet even more suave and elegant than previously, begins to sing in eloquent and colourful couplets about devotion to a romantic ideal, rather than mere flesh and blood. Paul Thompson, the rock of the band, propels the song along from his drum kit, while the contributions from saxophonist Andy Mackay, who serves up an audaciously madcap solo, and Phil Manzanera on spine-tingling guitar, are immense and showcase the strength of the whole. Eno is somewhat peripheral on this occasion, but nonetheless the bleeps and drones from his arsenal of electronic devices add to the atmosphere. This was Roxy Music at their most adventurous, and at that time they were, without doubt, the most intriguing group of musicians in the entire Western World.

1973 - MUFC FAN CLUB CHRISTMAS BASH

L to R Sam, Derek, Paddy Crerand, me (in glittering Mary Quant bowtie), unknown and manager Tommy Docherty in the background.

1973 - myself and little brother get borderline Glam!

*1974 - Blackpool Tower ballroom following
my first singing performance.*

1974

NOTABLE EVENTS

- American heiress Patty Hearst is kidnapped by the Symbionese Liberation Army in Berkeley, California
- With the country in the midst of an economic crisis Britain holds two General Elections - the first in February sees a hung parliament after which Prime Minister Edward Heath resigns while the second in October sees a small majority for Harold Wilson's Labour of just 14 seats
- The Ulster Volunteer Force murder 33 people and wound 300 more in car-bomb attacks in Dublin and Monaghan in the Republic of Ireland
- The Turkish military invade Cyprus
- Tapes reveal a conversation between President Richard Nixon and Chief of Staff H. R. Haldeman plotting to use the C.I.A. to obstruct the F.B.I. investigation into Watergate just days after the initial break-in. The president resigns in August and Gerald Ford replaces him. Ford quickly issues a pardon to his predecessor
- In a Heavyweight contest dubbed the 'Rumble in the Jungle', Muhammad Ali knocks out champion George Foreman in Zaire to regain his title seven years after it was stripped from him for his refusal to join the US military and be shipped to Vietnam
- McDonald's opens its first UK outlet in Woolwich, London
- In Birmingham two pubs are bombed by the IRA and 21 people are murdered. Six innocent Irishmen are convicted and given life-sentences that are quashed many years later
- John Lennon makes his last-ever concert appearance at New York's Madison Square Gardens Arena as a guest during a show by Elton John
- Manchester United are relegated into the Second Division of the Football League for the first time since the war. Leeds win the league, Liverpool defeat Newcastle 3-0 to win the FA Cup. West Germany win the World Cup beating Johan

Cruyff's Netherlands 2-1 in Munich

NOTABLE BIRTHS

Kate Moss; J Dilla; Alanis Morissette; Tim Henman; Leonardo DiCaprio; Meg White; Allesandro Del Piero; Ryan Adams

NOTABLE DEATHS

H.E. Bates; Samuel Goldwyn; Candy Darling; Georges Pompidou; Duke Ellington; Mama Cass Elliot; Lightnin' Slim; Charles Lindbergh; Harry Partch; Nick Drake; Jack Bennyl; Tex Ritter

NOTABLE FILMS

The Night Porter; Stardust; The Parallax View; The Conversation ; Chinatown; Blazing Saddles; Texas Chainsaw Massacre; The Towering Inferno; Foxy Brown; A Woman Under The Influence

NOTABLE BOOKS

Tinker Tailor Soldier Spy – John Le Carre
The Bottle Factory Outing – Beryl Bainbridge
A Pagan Place – Edna O Brien
The Honorary Consul – Graham Green
Gravity's Rainbow – Thomas Pynchon
Zen and the Art of Motorcycle Maintenance – Robert M Pirsig
Helter Skelter: The True Story of the Manson Murders – Vincent Bugliosi
The Lost Honour Of Katharina Blum – Heinrich Boll

THE MUSIC

These were grim times; conflicts all around the globe were reported on a daily basis. Here, in the UK, the atmosphere was poisonous and depressing; power cuts and the three-day week were unpleasant indicators of where we were as a nation - unenlightened, the British were scrambling around in the dark as if we were cave dwellers. We struggled to comprehend the battleground that Northern Ireland had become. Indeed, that war was now also being conducted on mainland Britain as the Provisionals began a campaign of indiscriminately bombing civilian targets.

We weren't alone in feeling total confusion, the US was shaken to the core in the aftermath of the Vietnam War; deep divisions remained between the pro- and anti-war factions. For the pro-war lobby, the fact that their country (which they had perceived to be invincible) had been defeated was a bitter pill to swallow; there was a deep sense of shame and returning service personnel were shunned as embarrassing failures. To add to the trauma there was the Watergate scandal where President Richard Nixon was proven to have abused and dishonoured his office and the American people.

This provoked a musical yearning for escapism which brought about the release of inane, manufactured pop dross and a wave of pretty-boy teen-idols whose musical styles were safe, conservative and extremely dull; step forward David Soul, Donny Osmond and David Cassidy. As mainstream pop-radio stations transmitted this bland, socially-controlling dross, we looked elsewhere for inspiration to find that lots of the so-called progressive bands were churning out grandiose, bloated, conceited magnum opuses that bore no relevance to the lives of ordinary people. Hard-rock too was done for; it had become a predictable, cliché-driven embarrassment of monumental bad taste. Yet beneath this toxic mix something was stirring – a rearguard action of higher aesthetic leanings was countering the unenlightened with political and revolutionary thought. In America acts as diverse as Neil Young, Smokey Robinson, The O'Jays, Patti Smith and The New York Dolls pushed the envelope in terms of content and concept. The UK saw the birth of a grass-roots 'back to basics' scene, featuring the likes of Dr Feelgood and Kilburn and the Highroads, along with emerging vibrant acts such as The Sensational Alex Harvey Band and Queen; these were harbingers for a sweeping away of much that was tired and redundant. Reggae and funk continued to flourish and make sonic advances, and perhaps most significantly, Kraftwerk put away all traditional instruments and hit-upon their singular approach to music-making that would arguably prove to be the most significant and influential act of musical inventiveness in the entire decade.

MY 1974

Between my 16th and 17th birthday, in June 1974, I gained 3-stone in weight. This was, in some part, due to the injury I'd suffered at the hands of a schoolteacher; my body was struggling with the trauma. It was also – in a larger part – down to my drinking which, as soon as I started receiving a wage, had become very regular and heavy. I was sad; I suffered hugely with lack of self-esteem and I required medical treatment for depression. This cycle of negative thought and behaviour spiraled into bouts of self-loathing. I would sit in a dark unheated room, in a fog of whisky and barbiturates, listening to Fripp and Eno's *No Pussyfooting* album or Nick Drake's *Pink Moon*, and then I would cut my arms with a razor blade so that, as the blood ran across my skin, the pain was taken out of my head and externalised. Like most depressives, I was good at compartmentalising and hiding my true-self. At weekends, I would go to clubs and seem perfectly happy, dancing to The O'Jays or Barry White. I went to lots of gigs too, and these could sometimes make me genuinely happy. I saw The Who, Alice Cooper, Wings, 10cc and, memorably, Kevin Ayres, John Cale, Nico and Eno all performing together. All these occasions were memorable in a good way. I was interviewed on Red Rose Radio about an award I'd won, connected to my job, and whilst there I met Ian Dury and the rest of his band, Kilburn and the Highroads. Less fun was a beating I received from bouncers at a Wizzard gig on the Isle Of Man. Thankfully, my inebriated state meant I felt little of the assault. I was assaulted too at the Buxton Pop Festival for no apparent reason where, very disappointingly, The New York Dolls scheduled appearance was cancelled. Still, there was The Faces, Mott the Hoople, Lindisfarne, Humble Pie and Charlie Whitney and Roger Chapman, formerly of Family. I made a stage debut at Blackpool's Tower Ballroom in a talent competition and sang songs written by Chuck Berry and Eddie Cochran. I polarised the audience; the majority hated my venomous performance, but one gnarled 'Teddy Boy', with tears in his eyes, showered me with praise, compared me to Gene Vincent and bought me several pints of Tartan bitter. I loved being on the stage; I experienced a feeling approaching euphoria as I snarled out the songs… I'd do it again one day.

100
ONLY YOU
OUT OF MY BODY
FOX
GTO
DID NOT CHART
(reissue 1975, number 3)
With a reggae-ish lilt, and a tropical feel to the instrumentation, 'Only You' was an arresting proposition from the opening bars; but what made a truly indelible mark was the voice of the singer, Noosha, who delivered her lines in a kooky, sensuous purr, with a gurgling effect that pre-dates other female stylists such as Kate Bush and Bjork. The combination of music and voice worked a treat – the song was not unpleasant either, which made this a winner.

99
EMMA
MAKIN' MUSIC
HOT CHOCOLATE
RAK
3
Having addressed the issue of mixed-race relationships and the Watergate affair that toppled President "Tricky Dicky" Nixon, Hot Chocolate now incorporated the theme of suicide into a pop single. Singer and lyricist Errol Brown, drawing upon his painful experience in relation to his mother's death, tells the tale of a young girl, Emma, who dreams of being a star. She is married to her first love who tries to support her emotionally as she is constantly rejected when she auditions for roles in plays. Eventually, all hope extinguished, she takes her own life. He reads her suicide note in anguish and literally howls in his suffering and grief.

98
ROUGH KIDS
BILLY BENTLEY
(Promenades Himself in London)
KILBURN AND THE
HIGHROADS
DAWN
DID NOT CHART
This Ian Dury-led combo were an odd-looking ensemble who were nobody's idea of a commercial proposition in 1974 and their sound was distinctive and raw in the extreme. Dury had a carnival character style of delivery, Davey Payne blew avant-jazz sax, future 999 man Keith Lucas delivered speedy, aggressive guitar solos and fine artist Humphrey Ocean was a better painter than bass player. Still, the songs were good and earthy, based on real people and real lives. 'Rough Kids' ticked lots of boxes; it was unique and untidy – who cared about perfection? The Kilburn's opened for The Who, and the next day I met them at Blackburn's Red Rose Radio Station where they and I were separate guests on the same programme. I liked them; they impressed me with their unpretentious good humour.

97
SHOO-RAH SHOO-RAH
TONIGHT IS THE NIGHT
BETTY WRIGHT
RCA
27
Betty Wright was one of that breed of American soul singers who emerged from the gospel tradition before transitioning to R&B. As a young teen she took on backing vocal duties for several major acts, as well as beginning a solo career. She charted with 'Clean Up Woman' in 1971, but then waited three years for this

next success. 'Shoo-Rah Shoo-Rah' is a sassy piece of strutting, southern funk from the inexhaustible supply of songs written by Allen Toussaint; its rhythm is punched out by horns and there is a smiling, playful vocal from Betty Wright. This record provided much in the way of dancefloor temptation and it was a great listen as well.

96
VA VA VOOM
SPACE ACE
ANCHOR
BRETT SMILEY
DID NOT CHART

Glam rock brought out the peacock in lots of pretty boys (and not-so-pretty men who should have known better). Androgyny was de-rigueur, and by far the prettiest and most androgynous glam-rocker on the face of the earth was delectable American Brett Smiley, managed by former Rolling Stones Svengali Andrew Loog Oldham. Smiley's career didn't amount to much beyond a one-off TV appearance on *The Russell Harty Show* and this solitary single; a rather splendid, frothy romp of piano, saxophone and guitars, which appropriated the sound of The New York Dolls and over which breathless Brett emoted in mock-serious style. It was over the top, camp as Christmas… but wonderful fun nonetheless.

95
FIRE
TOGETHER
OHIO PLAYERS
MERCURY
DID NOT CHART

Unrestrained joy is on offer here: blaring fire sirens, choppy guitar riffs, blazing horns and a smoking rhythm section with call and response vocals. The Ohio Players were so incredibly tight and so supremely talented – and to top it all, they were obviously having a great time. Their records sounded like the best party ever; the vibe was contagious and unbelievably funky.

94
DECK OF CARDS
DECK OF CARDS
PRINCE FAR I
JOE GIBBS
DID NOT CHART.

"The Voice of Thunder" was an appropriate nickname for the mighty Jamaican 'chanter' Prince Far I. Having recorded as Prince Cry Cry with no success, Michael James Williams took time-out working as a security guard and bouncer before returning to music in 1974. His deep baritone sounded earth-shaking and he dealt with important subjects – criticising the government and quoting from scripture, as he does on this single, which was later included on his classic *Under Heavy Manners* album.

93
SEVEN SEAS OF RHYE
SEE WHAT A FOOL I'VE BEEN
QUEEN
EMI
10

Announcing itself with a distinctive, arpeggiated piano intro, 'Seven Seas of Rhye' erupts into a series of guitar power-chords while drums crash and the singer begins to recount, in a strong, refined voice, some kind of mythical story using portentous imagery. Has Led Zeppelin gone glam I wondered ? I was suspicious of the bombast. Of course it wasn't them and on closer inspection the more subtle moments of the song hinted at what would lie ahead. A closing sing-a-long of "Oh I do like to be beside the seaside" showed a dash of style and bravado as well. I decided I liked it and so went out and bought it. Up the charts it went and Freddie Mercury, the song-writing singer, felt enough confidence to quit his day job on Camden Market and fully concentrate on Queen.

92
LET'S EAT (REAL SOON)
FITTER STOKE HAS A BATH
HATFIELD AND THE NORTH
VIRGIN
DID NOT CHART
Hatfield and the North were part of what was known as the Canterbury scene. Indeed, they were something of a supergroup, with members having played in the likes of Gong, Egg, Matching Mole and Caravan. They created cheerful, idiosyncratic and unmistakable English music. 'Let's Eat' bore all of those trademarks – there's the slippery organ of Dave Stewart, the anti-rock guitar from Phil Miller and a vocal as light as a summer breeze from Richard Sinclair, where he seems, in a romantic sales pitch, to compare himself to a wholesome meal.

91
YOU TORE ME DOWN
HIM OR ME
FLAMIN' GROOVIES
BOMP
DID NOT CHART
The legendary San Franciscan band's first release since Roy Loney was replaced by Chris Wilson saw a marked change in direction. Previously they had a hard, savage edge, but 'You Tore Me Down' showed the more tuneful Byrds-like and Beatlesque side of the band. In came chiming 12-string guitars and harmony vocals. It was a new-era for the Flamin' Groovies – different yes, but still highly potent.

90
THEME FROM THE GUN COURT
NO PAROLE
MBV AND MUDIES ALL STARS
MOODISC
DID NOT CHART
I remember buying this single on spec, simply because the title fascinated me; my instincts did not fail me that day. Opening with a wicked cackle and a proclamation that "This is the team from the gun courts", the rest of the track is instrumental. Moving through a section of 'dragnet-style' horns over a wicked, rocksteady rhythm, sax and trombone are then given solos before a final announcement that the verdict of the court is "indefinite detention".

89
FOXY FOXY
TRUDI'S SONG
MOTT THE HOOPLE
CBS
33
They worked so hard to gain success, and when it was achieved realised it wasn't all it was cracked up to be. In short order organist Verden Allen and guitarist Mick Ralphs quit the band. Replacements were drafted in and success continued, but the soul of the band was irreparably damaged. This was a stand-alone single, and a fine one too, albeit in a rather eccentric fashion. It came with a curious, washed-out Phil Spector-

ish production style, exaggerated showbizzy female backing vocals, sleigh bells and horns playing the riff and a never-ending chorus. 'Foxy Foxy' was very good, very quirky; it could have passed as a single by Roy Wood's Wizzard – the trouble was that Mott had lost something of themselves in making it.

88
WALK ON
FOR THE TURNSTILES
NEIL YOUNG
REPRISE
DID NOT CHART

The album *Harvest* and the single 'Heart of Gold' had turned Neil Young into a big-selling star. If he wanted more success, more money, more back slapping and praise, all he had to do was release something similar, something comfortable and comforting for his legion of new-found fans. What he did release, as a form of insightful self-sabotage to ensure his continued artistic freedom and integrity, was the album *On The Beach* and the single 'Walk On'. It worked; the press and public alike gave it the thumbs down and ignored it in droves. 'Walk On' is a fabulous song – it's a stripped-back, chugging piece, adorned with angular guitar figures as Neil dismisses criticism of himself as inconsequential and just not worth getting bogged down in. He had drawn ire from south of the Mason–Dixon Line by pointing out in the song 'Southern Man' that slavery had been abolished long-ago and it was high-time the fact was recognised. There was disapproval too from his record company over the album *Tonight's the Night*, which at this point was recorded but unreleased. 'Walk On' was stating that

he had no time for raking over the coals of an already extinguished fire – he expressed himself thus: "Some get stoned, some get strange, sooner or later it all gets real… Walk on".

87
IRE FEELINGS (SKANGA)
FEELING HIGH
RUPIE EDWARDS
CACTUS
9

The first dub track to reach the charts, 'Ire Feelings' was by veteran Rupie Edwards, who had been releasing records since 1962. This was recorded with Errol Thompson – the renowned mixer from Studio 1 – over the rhythm from Johnny Clarke's 'Everyday Wondering'. It seemed incredible that this utilisation of space and echo, with Rupie dementedly shouting "Skanga", could possibly breach the citadel of the top 10. I remember laughing about it and feeling a little" smug. Of course it had sold as a mere novelty, so King Tubby and Augustus Pablo were hardly likely to suddenly become household names. Still, it was a start, and all revolutions have to start somewhere.

86
NO OTHER
THE TRUE ONE
GENE CLARK
ASYLUM
DID NOT CHART

From the album of the same name – which was lambasted and under-promoted before being deleted in 1976 – this was one of a pair of singles; it is a superlative record. Gospel tinged and very funky – supposedly Sly Stone was present at the session and, if so, his influence was certainly felt – there is not a hint of the country-tinged folk at which Clark was so adept. In an interview given at the time his album was released, Clark stated that he was obsessed with Stevie Wonder's *Innervisions* and the Rolling Stones' *Goats Head Soup* albums and was guided and influenced by them. This single, more than anything else on the album, tallies with that ambition, as over the groove Clark sings as if entranced. His haunted voice brings to mind Robert Johnson; Clark seems to be searching for meaning and spirituality, meanwhile more earthy and sensual female voices seem intent on steering him into the dark and murky places where temptation lies.

85
LITTLE DARLIN'
BUFFALO GAL
THIN LIZZY
DECCA
DID NOT CHART
With Eric Bell departed, Gary Moore, who had been playing incredible guitar in the band Colosseum, briefly joined and positively lit-up this barnstorming single. 'Little Darlin' is quick out of the traps, as a horn section augments the core trio; the previous incarnation of the band had never sounded so hard and heavy. Thankfully, Philip Lynott had lost none of his melodic sensibility, nor the swagger in his vocal delivery. Moore went as quickly as he had arrived, but left this fine single as a permanent legacy.

84
THE MAN WHO SOLD THE WORLD
WATCH THAT MAN
LULU
POLYDOR
3
David Bowie believed that Lulu had a great voice suitable for more challenging songs than she was routinely given to perform. He invited her to France during the sessions for his *Pin Ups* album where they cut the tracks on this record using Bowie's band. Bowie and Mick Ronson produced and Bowie also acted as backing vocalist and saxophonist. Lulu was encouraged to smoke cigarettes during breaks to add further rasp and thickness to her voice. What they cooked-up was a slick, disco-sound with a decadent, distinctly European sensibility. It was a shame that the pairing of Bowie and Lulu was a one-off; there was, on the evidence of this artistic and commercial success, plenty of potential that could have been explored.

83
RED SHIFT PART 1
RED SHIFT PART 2
PETER HAMMILL
CHARISMA
DID NOT CHART
Taken from *The Silent Corner and the Empty Page*, one of the finest albums of Hammill's long and productive career, this single features the galactic guitar of Randy California, along with Hammill's colleagues from Van der Graaf Generator. The song appears to be about impending and inevitable death; it is described in Hammill's fascinating, oblique word play and delivered in that crystal,

operatic voice that was, and remains, quite unique. There are shades of what people may presume to be 'the David Bowie sound' here – in fact the opposite is true; the magpie star only borrowed from the best and he was certainly influenced by Peter Hammill.

82
#9 DREAM
WHAT YOU GOT
JOHN LENNON
(with the Plastic Ono Nuclear Band)
APPLE
23

Lennon claimed that this song was about nothing in particular and that it came to him in a dream; he simply scribbled it down on awakening. His obsession with the number 9 – which he felt had recurred throughout his life – gave him a title and the chorus consisted of made-up words… "Bowakawa poussé, poussé". The dream theory seems highly plausible when listening to the song; it floats and shimmers and boasts a beautiful, almost psychedelic production, redolent of 'Strawberry Fields Forever'.

81
OOH LA LA
GONE TOMORROW
JOBRIATH
ELEKTRA
DID NOT CHART

Declaring himself "Rock's truest fairy", Jobriath undoubtedly had talent to burn and a quite incredible back story which included being called-up into the army and deserting, being sacked from a Los Angeles production of *Hair* for the crime of upstaging the other performers, and fronting a folk-band named Pidgeon

before being arrested and jailed for his army desertion. Later he suffered a breakdown and ended up working as a prostitute before signing a music contract – thus making himself the first openly gay man to ink a major solo record deal. Masses of money was spent on recording and promotion; it smacked of hype to many and pretty soon Jobriath was being dismissed as exactly that. The shame is that he was truly talented and this single reveals that fact. It is a brash, manic, rip-snorting and theatrical rocker. The piano is attacked venomously while Jobriath out-drawls Mick Jagger with an off-the-top-board and into the deep-end vocal. He was clearly the real thing; I remember pirouetting around my parent's parlour in gay abandon as I span this on the Dansette.

80
THE IN CROWD
CHANCE MEETING
BRYAN FERRY
ISLAND
13

Fanning the flames of the critics' prejudicial thinking, Bryan Ferry must surely have allowed himself a chuckle when he decided to record this anthem to style and exclusivity for his *Another Time Another Place* album of cover versions. Originally a hit in 1964 for Dobie Gray, every aspect of the song was stretched and exaggerated; the inherent snobbery is made explicit, the riff played by original Roxy Music guitarist Davy O'List is enormous and powerful, the finger-clicked intro is way up high in the mix, and last but not least, Ferry's vocal is a masterclass in snooty disdain for anyone who doesn't measure up to the exacting standards of the 'in crowd'. However you look at this record – as a conceptual joke or a straight, glammed-up version of a classic – it worked.

79
UPON THE MY-OH-MY
MAGIC BE
CAPTAIN BEEFHEART
VIRGIN
DID NOT CHART
In this period, the promise of easy-pickings made by his new management saw Captain Beefheart forgo much of his integrity, both personal and artistic, and – with the most unmagical of all Magic Bands to back him – make the dullest, most uninspiring and formulaic music of his career. Fortunately, the one track that sparkled from two albums of dross was released as a single; 'Upon The My-Oh-My' is the sound of a sea-shanty set to a voodoo incantation. It is playfully delivered and grooves sweetly and sensually as it rhythmically sways in a manner not too dissimilar to Dr John's 'I Walk on Gilded Splinters'.

78
GET DANCIN'
GET DANCIN' (Part 2)
DISCO-TEX
AND THE SEX-O-LETTES
CHELSEA
8
Disco-Tex and the Sex-O-Lettes comprised of famed hit songwriters Bob Crewe and Kenny Young (The Four Seasons, Mitch Ryder, Labelle etc) plus Cindy Bullens (who had just featured on Gene Clark's *No Other* album) and extravagant front man Monti Rock III (a former celebrity hairdresser turned ordained minister). They served-up this early disco

classic which was effervescent and fun. It set a template for other acts to follow with its willingness to embrace excess and dispense with traditional song structure. My clubbing days had just begun and this was the mightiest of floor-fillers.

77
THE MAN WHO COULDN'T
AFFORD TO ORGY
SYLVIA SAID
JOHN CALE
ISLAND
DID NOT CHART
John Cale makes brilliant pop records that are unpopular: 'The Man Who Couldn't Afford To Orgy' is quintessential in that regard. It has a pleasant, undemanding lilt and mid-tempo pace; Cale is on his best behaviour, singing in that lovely Welsh baritone, rather than (as was often the case) maniacally screaming; Judy Nylon purrs each chorus in full-on temptress mode; Phil Manzanera throws in a wonderfully restrained guitar solo and the lyric seems to be about desire, disappointment and the arbitrary nature of choice. So, nothing controversial there… except for that single word – orgy. If anyone, be it Cale himself or the Head of Marketing at Island Records, thought that in the prudish Britain of 1974 – where only sexual *innuendo* was permitted – the uptight and repressive BBC would allow this word to be carried over the nation's airwaves, they were living in a fool's paradise.

76

SALLY CAN'T DANCE
ENNUI
LOU REED
RCA
DID NOT CHART

They loved him as an appendage of the Bowie phenomenon, but when he presented them with the pure Lou of *Berlin* they hated him. Of course, there was zero chance that he would yield and give them more 'glam Lou'. Now here he was with a funky soul concoction – a lyric of little substance, but a cool nagging hook. It was, in that respect, like the pre-Velvet Underground single 'The Ostrich'. Pretty much ignored in the UK, 'Sally Can't Dance' was one of those singles that inexplicably failed to garner radio play or sales. One man who was listening intently however was David Bowie, who would soon use similar soulful stylings to extricate himself from the glam cage he was starting to feel imprisoned in…

75

I'M A BELIEVER
MEMORIES
ROBERT WYATT
VIRGIN
29

Robert Wyatt is a man who clearly enjoys the incongruous and absurd, which is the reason the wheelchair-bound, ex-Soft Machine man came to record a cover version of 'I'm a Believer'–the Neil Diamond-written Monkees hit – utilising, amongst others, musicians Nick Mason, Fred Frith and Richard Sinclair (of Pink Floyd, Henry Cow and Caravan respectively). A fabulous version it is too, with frenetic drumming from Mason and intriguing violin patterns from Frith that superbly accompany

Wyatt's wonderfully touching vocal, conjuring up a feeling of lost innocence. Incidentally, 'I'm a Believer' was recorded by mistake; Wyatt had intended to record 'Last Train to Clarksville' instead, but somehow that intention was hijacked by confusion and the mistake was serendipitously embraced.

74

AIN'T NO LOVE IN THE
HEART OF THE CITY
TWENTY-FOUR HOUR BLUES
BOBBY BLAND
ABC
DID NOT CHART

The great soul-bluesman had become a marginal figure when he released his album *Dreamer* in 1974. The opening and stand-out track was 'Ain't No Love In The Heart Of The City' which was chosen to be the single. It is, of course, a complete and utter classic that one supposes would have been a huge hit but the sad truth is that it bombed and cover versions mopped-up whatever success there was to be had. This is, ostensibly, a slow, bluesy love song, but the lyrics are ambiguous enough to suggest social comment about injustice and exploitation – and of course, sung by a vocalist of the calibre of Bobby Bland, who unfailingly locates the emotional heart of a song, it is a delight to listen to.

73

ROCK THE BOAT
ALL GOIN' DOWN TOGETHER
HUES CORPORATION
RCA
6

Energetic and punchy, 'Rock the Boat' initially floundered when first released as a single, before becoming popular in New York's discos from whence it then spread contagiously across the Atlantic. Although inconsequential, the lyric is lean and memorable and the lightness in the voice of lead vocalist Fleming Williams is ideal for the song's verses, leading into the big chorus where H. Ann Kelley's more powerful voice dominates. Musically, the song's supple strength comes as no surprise when one learns that the celebrated 'Jazz Crusaders' (Wilton Felder, Joe Sample and Larry Carlton on bass, piano and guitar respectively) provided the backing while Jim Gordon, famed for his work with Derek and the Dominoes, Traffic and Frank Zappa, provided the back beat.

72
ALL I WANT IS YOU
YOUR APPLICATION'S FAILED
ROXY MUSIC
ISLAND
12
Although not as revolutionary sounding, nor perhaps as audacious as previous singles, 'All I Want Is You' is still a marvellous record. Phil Manzanera's stylish way with a guitar dominates the sound as Paul Thompson propels the song forward on the drum kit. Bryan Ferry, his rhyming couplets as witty and concise as ever, delivers with considerable aplomb and the mid-song instrumental breakdown is magnificent – pure Roxy Music magic.

71
SO JAH SEH
NATTY DREAD
BOB MARLEY AND THE
WAILERS
ISLAND
DID NOT CHART
This was an extraordinarily left-field choice of single to launch the 'solo' Bob Marley, after the departure of Peter Tosh and Bunny Livingstone from The Wailers. It reflects the singer's burgeoning embrace of Rastafarian thought and belief. Bob Marley, the great humanist, is growing more militant and urgent in his message; "Not one of my seed shall sit on the sidewalk and beg your bread" is the opening line of the song, which pretty much lays down a marker as to his conviction that the injustices he encounters must be challenged. He then asks, "Cause puss and dog get together, what's wrong with loving one another?" The folk-wisdom he imparts is delivered over a jazz-tinged arrangement, heavy on horns with free-form guitar and synthesiser aiding the message as it is carried along to the wider world.

70
MIDNIGHT AT THE OASIS
ANY OLD TIME
MARIA MULDAUR
REPRISE
21
Smooth and extremely sensuous, 'Midnight at the Oasis' is a very suggestive song, full of playful innuendo and sexual metaphor utilising imagery of sand and camels to hint at carnality… and somehow it manages to not sound ridiculous! Sung in a languid, almost liquid flow by Maria Muldaur, she teases as she plays the temptress. The remarkable

guitar solo, used as a bridge, succeeds in not altering the mood or flow of this impossible not-to-love gem.

69
(WHAT'S SO FUNNY
ABOUT) PEACE, LOVE AND
UNDERSTANDING
EVER SINCE YOU'RE GONE
BRINSLEY SCHWARZ
UNITED ARTISTS
DID NOT CHART
Written and sung by Nick Lowe, this song is full of fine sentiments about opposing the prevailing cynicism in favour of embracing "peace, love and understanding". Not only is it a splendid and stirring lyric (that often brings an emotional tear to my eye) but it rattles along with no studio adornment in fine toe-tapping style; it is transformative rock 'n' roll of the finest kind. Little wonder then that this song has become so popular in the decades since this brilliant single was such a resounding flop.

68
GONNA MAKE YOU A STAR
WINDOW
DAVID ESSEX
CBS
1
Less sonically adventurous than previous singles, this was still superbly produced by Jeff Wayne in a pleasingly uncluttered style. The song rests simply on a warm, strummed acoustic guitar, drums and synthesised horns. Essex, in the uncomfortable position of being treated as teen fodder, was simultaneously amused and dismayed by this state of affairs. Here, he couldn't resist inserting some cynicism into his lyrics, along with a very tongue-in-cheek approach to delivering them − "Oh is he more,

too much more than a pretty face?" he enquires, before answering himself in theatrical cockney, "I don't fink so". Ultimately he didn't rebel; he merely nibbled at the hands that fed him as all the while he smiled and twinkled his eyes for the camera. In that sense he was a true professional and a great pop star, and 'Gonna Make You A Star' was his first number 1 and a great pop record.

67
ANTHEM PART 1
ANTHEM PART 2
THE SENSATIONAL ALEX
HARVEY BAND
VERTIGO
DID NOT CHART
Dramatising all of his Scottish pride, Alex Harvey plays the part of a poor man unjustly arrested and incarcerated, without trial, by the occupying English Army. He pleads his case to be set free in order to "Chase the wild goose", promising to be of no more trouble... "I would not do you wrong" he states. However, we are left in no doubt at all that given half-a-chance, 'wrong' would be precisely what he would do. The story is acted out over a martial drum beat, a stirring female choir and, finally, a troupe of pipers, as the pressure gradually rises throughout the appropriately titled 'Anthem'.

66
RIKKI DON'T LOSE THAT
NUMBER
ANY MAJOR DUDE WILL TELL
YOU
STEELY DAN
ABC
58
No disguised subtext here, no hint of subversion, just a song of lost love told

by Donald Fagen in a straightforward and accessible manner. 'Rikki Don't Lose That Number' is, nonetheless, one of Steely Dan's greatest songs; sung by Fagen with a real sense of regret in his voice, the song moves along elegantly, incorporating marimba and a guitar solo of great lyricism from Jeff 'Skunk' Baxter.

65
LOVER LOVER LOVER
WHO BY FIRE
LEONARD COHEN
COLUMBIA
DID NOT CHART
This period saw Leonard Cohen move away from the folk sound that had made his name but was, frustratingly, not allowing him to fully express himself. So, with a new set of musicians and a new producer, he moved towards a more supple and sophisticated sound that, though still sparse, utilised a wider range of instruments; this better supported his voice and allowed for a more nuanced performance. Here the singer is asking for a new beginning and an escape from the shame he feels due to his emotional cowardice, but he is told that, in order to find enlightenment, it is he himself who must pull down the barriers that he has erected. All this is vividly recounted in verses which are separated by a simple, repetitive chorus to create a gloriously hypnotic effect suggestive of prayer and the age-old conflict between faith and flesh.

64
SILLY LOVE
THE SACRO-ILIAC
10 CC
UK
29
Avant-pop masters 10cc did 'wry' wonderfully well; they were an aural version of the Marx Brothers – clever in a funny way, quick witted and a little bit zany. 'Silly Love' combines heroic rock guitar with an excursion into pianoforte and a touch of jungle-drumming… all this while surgically lampooning and dissecting the ludicrous clichés surrounding the art of love.

63
THE SIX TEENS
BURN ON THE FLAME
THE SWEET
RCA
9
By this stage The Sweet were desperate to be taken seriously and their albums and single B-sides, which were self-written, gave them some degree of credibility. The job of providing hits however still fell to the writing and production team of Chinn and Chapman, who had grown adept at tailoring material specifically for the band. 'The Six Teens' was a perfect song for the Sweet; a Bowie-like acoustic verse structure, followed by what can only be described as a gigantic and anthemic chorus. This wasn't as big a hit as previous singles and as a result is something of a neglected classic.

62
BOOGIE ON REGGAE WOMAN
SEEMS SO LONG
STEVIE WONDER
TAMLA MOTOWN
12

Despite the title, 'Boogie On Reggae Woman' neither "boogies" or "reggaes"; it does, however, move along in a sprightly fashion propelled by a pulsing, squelching Moog Bass. This was perfect for the dance floor with its rhythmic groove and, despite its risqué content, a radio favourite too. It is a sexually suggestive and flirty number, balanced by a light-hearted, good-time feel and Stevie's harmonica accompaniment which is, as ever, unmistakable.

61
AFTER THE SHOW
THANK YOU VERY MUCH
KEVIN AYRES
ISLAND
DID NOT CHART

Another slightly ragged and wine-drenched tale of late-night longing, this one doesn't veer toward the melancholic but retains a cheerful optimism as the narrator winds his way homeward; it is charming and quite lovely, but better is to be found on the B-side. 'Thank You Very Much' is a sparse piece, just voice and acoustic guitar, about wistful loneliness, delivered in Kevin's most devilish, deepest drawl. I picture him in an armchair, savouring a fine cognac, and between each line taking a long, satisfying pull on a herbal cigarette!

60
FREEBIRD
DOWN SOUTH JUKIN
LYNYRD SKYNYRD
MCA
43 (Charted in 1979)

Lynyrd Skynyrd's most iconic song – and one of the absolute classics of 1970s rock – appeared on the band's first album in 1973. Edited down, it was an obvious single and is truly great; but if somehow the whole nine minutes could have been pressed onto a single, rather than just half the song, then it would have been even greater. Essentially a power ballad and guitar symphony about our inherent desire for freedom; this is an awe-inspiring piece of music where every single word and note counts.

59
WESTBOUND TRAIN
SCAVENGER
DENNIS BROWN
OBSERVER
DID NOT CHART

We hear a distinctive guitar figure and then 'chugga, chugga' goes the lurching rhythm. The soulful voice of Dennis Brown reveals the contents of a letter from his "Cherry baby", who is leaving him on the 'Westbound Train'; he can't face life without her and off he goes in pursuit. It is hardly original in composition, but that doesn't matter when a song is executed as well as this. It has a freshness and sprightliness that sets it apart, and a universality which makes it special.

58
A DREAM GOES ON
FOREVER
HEAVY METAL KIDS
TODD RUNDGREN
BEARSVILLE
DID NOT CHART

Sounding as if it was recorded in some kind of enchanted toy shop – indeed, each instrument is played *with* as well as being actually *played* – 'A Dream Goes On Forever' is touched by magic, as Todd, influenced by a bout of psychedelic drug taking, explores the importance to our well-being of unrelinquished dreams. Sung sweetly and openly, there is a wide-eyed, childlike charm to this that feels, in the parlance of the day, cosmic and mind-blowing… but also absolutely sincere.

57
KNOCK ON WOOD
PANIC IN DETROIT
DAVID BOWIE
RCA
10

Bowie was engaged on his mammoth *Diamond Dogs* tour; he rearranged his songs seeking different ways to perform them as he looked for a way to move on from glam. Midway through the tour this Eddie Floyd/Stax Records' classic was introduced into the set. Recorded in Philadelphia and taken from the *David Live* album, 'Knock On Wood' was released as a single. It is fairly faithful to the original as far as the rhythm section is concerned, and Bowie, his voice hardened by the touring schedule, sounds gritty and at ease with the song. By contrast, Earl Slick (having replaced Mick Ronson on guitar) substitutes the original's horn-riffs with shards of noise from the fretboard. For Bowie, this was a symbolic burial of Ziggy and a glimpse into the future by visiting the past.

56
I WANT TO SEE THE BRIGHT
LIGHTS TONIGHT
WHEN I GET TO THE BORDER
RICHARD AND LINDA
THOMPSON
ISLAND
DID NOT CHART

Ex-Fairport Convention guitarist Richard Thompson and his wife Linda combine to excellent effect on this song about the desperate need of the female narrator to dance and drink and escape the drudgery and grimness of the working week. Taken at a stately pace, with the sound of a brass band cut into the track, we find her seeking not restrictive, lady-like sophistication, but the rawness and release of the taverns and dance halls. As she yearns for a sense of freedom in these low places, she notes that "There are crazy people running all over town" and "The big boys are all spoiling for a fight". The picture is vividly painted and Linda's perfectly clear voice has great strength. Coming from the female perspective, we are reminded that the back-breaking work in the mills was undertaken by not just the men, but women and children too; the whole town coming alive only at the weekend and seizing the opportunity with lusty relish.

55
ROCK YOUR BABY
ROCK YOUR BABY PART 2
GEORGE MCCREA
TK
1

George McCrea found himself in

the right place at the right time; just about to abandon his singing career and return to college, he stepped into the breach to record 'Rock Your Baby' when his wife, Gwen, missed a studio session. The song, written by Richard Finch and Howie Casey of KC and the Sunshine Band, was committed to tape in 45 minutes. Utilising an early drum machine, the participants realised the combination of the irresistible rhythm and falsetto voice was dynamite. Songwriters of the calibre of John Lennon, and Abba's Benny and Bjorn, acknowledged that they had borrowed the 'Rock Your Baby' chord progression for their own hits, 'Whatever Gets You through the Night' and 'Dancing Queen' respectively.

54
HOW COME
TELL EVERYONE/
DONE THIS ONE BEFORE
RONNIE LANE
GM
11

Ronnie Lane had quit The Faces as a result of them being increasingly treated as Rod Stewart's backing group and put together his own band, Slim Chance, that had a revolving door membership, but here featured the soon-to-be-famous in their own right Gallagher and Lyle. 'How Come', the first single, has an East End pub sing-a-long vibe, as well as a folk feel – mandolin and accordion feature prominently. Ronnie himself is in sparkling form as he sings about a list of mishaps that have aroused in him strongly superstitious feelings, even as he sings "I ain't a superstitious fella, but it worries me".

53
DIZZY DIZZY
SPLASH
CAN
UNITED ARTISTS
DID NOT CHART

Damo Suzuki having departed, the vocals here come from Michael Karoli (as well as the prominent violin part that runs throughout the track). 'Dizzy Dizzy' is another of those strange dance tracks that nobody danced to – a genre at which Can were consummate masters. Here, they sound like avant-garde cousins of Parliament/Funkadelic, with the chanted "Got to get it up, got to get it over" worming its way into the psyche just as infectiously as any P-Funk mantra.

52
YEAR OF DECISION
A WOMAN NEEDS A GOOD MAN
THE THREE DEGREES
PHILADELPHIA INTERNATIONAL
13

If one can blank the mental image of Prince Charles 'frugging' to this single across the opulent shag-pile carpeting of Buckingham Palace, and simply listen, we are rewarded by an absolutely superlative example of the greatness of the Philly Sound as created by Kenny Gamble and Leon Huff, who wrote and produced this smooth but highly soulful three minutes of encouragement to greater self-determination. It is delivered with panache and great aplomb by the Three Degrees, who would be forever damned by their Royal patronage.

51
BILLY PORTER
SEVEN DAYS
MICK RONSON
RCA
DID NOT CHART
He had the ability, he had the looks, he had the management backing... but despite all of this, Mick Ronson lacked the will or the ego to be a solo star; he never seemed comfortable taking centre stage. This third solo single might well have thrust him into the limelight, but inexplicably, even though it was excellent and had great commercial potential, the song never received much radio play and therefore flopped. It was written by Ronson after a conversation with Lou Reed, in which Reed described being mugged in New York. We, the listeners, walk hand-in-hand with Ronson as he walks the mean, urban terrain, becoming increasingly threatened and frightened, before the titular 'Billy Porter' takes him under his wing and teaches him that street survival depends on him becoming a "roughneck". Played at heart beating pace by his comrades from Bowie's old band, and with female backing vocals, saxophone and police sirens all used to add colour and drama, this is a great demonstration of the huge talent possessed by the spider with platinum hair.

50
QUEEN OF CLUBS
DO IT GOOD
KC AND THE SUNSHINE BAND
TK
7
It makes perfect sense that KC and the Sunshine Band came out of Florida; they had a warm, breezy sound and a lightness of touch that one might associate with that state. On 'Queen of Clubs', which has an up-tempo Latin feel, they replicate the formula that had worked so well on 'Rock Your Baby' by having the uncredited George McCrea hitting those glorious high notes in the chorus. Lyrically, it is a mindless, hedonistic and celebratory record – not a song to analyse but simply to enjoy. Musically though, it was a steaming, funky, horn-blazing call to the dance-floor; close to disco perfection.

49
DOLPHINS
HONEY MAN
TIM BUCKLEY
DISCREET
DID NOT CHART
'Dolphins' was written by Fred Neil, the uber-talented doyen of the Greenwich Village folk scene who quit music in 1970 to move to Florida and work as a dolphin conservationist. His songs lived on in the hands of other performers and 'Dolphins' was one that attracted plenty of cover versions. Tim Buckley had shared management with Fred Neil and had been performing 'Dolphins' while still in his teens. Buckley's magnificent, rich and soaring voice was perfect for a song as subtle and dream-like as 'Dolphins'; there is a shimmering and incandescent beauty to this performance.

48
DIAMOND DOGS
HOLY HOLY
DAVID BOWIE
RCA
21
Six minutes of post-apocalyptic imagery over a relentless Stooges-type

riff was pushing it a bit for a single, but nonetheless the title track of the George Orwell influenced album was issued and became a hit. The song is stuffed full of memorable lines and also introduces the "Halloween Jack" character, showing that Bowie had definitively moved away from "Ziggy" who had almost consumed him; my favourite moment here is when Bowie delightfully barks "Bow wow, woof woof". The B-side, 'Holy Holy', was a heavily glammed and rocking take on the 1970 single which had been cut twelve months later with the Spiders From Mars in their glorious pomp.

47
TEENAGE DREAM
SATISFACTION PONY
MARC BOLAN AND T. REX
T. REX WAX COMPANY
13
In a blizzard of cocaine Marc Bolan's megalomania became gigantic, and as he grew to be increasingly detached from reality, his music suffered terribly. His last two albums, *Tanx* and *Zinc Alloy and the Hidden Riders of Tomorrow* had sounded dull and lacking in inspiration; the one exception was this melodramatic epic released as a single. Containing a whirlwind of strings, distant wailing guitars and a gospel-infused chorus, 'Teenage Dream' flaunted its grandeur and pomposity. It waddled where the music had once skipped... and yet one could still admire the breadth of ambition it took to construct this grimly fascinating, titanic thing. Bolan's lyrics were more obscure and difficult to comprehend than ever, but they were entertaining and full of arresting imagery. 'Teenage Dream' was the sound of a man trapped in a gilded cage and slowly going insane – it was Marc Bolan's *Citizen Kane*.

46
WALL STREET SHUFFLE
GISMO MY WAY
10CC
UK
10
An acerbic attack on the "greed is good" culture – "Oh, Howard Hughes, did your money make you better?" they ask; the answer, of course, was no it didn't. Rothschild and Getty are name-checked too while Eric Stewart power chords away, symbolising the might felt by the super-rich. The B-side is the first public unveiling of 'the Gismo', which was a choral device attached to a guitar invented by Lol Creme and Kevin Godley, and ultimately it would split the band into two factions.

45
PICK UP THE PIECES
WORK TO DO
AVERAGE WHITE BAND
ATLANTIC
6
Although released in July 1974, it was March 1975 before 'Pick Up The Pieces' charted. It wasn't easy to gain credibility as a Scottish funk band but the Average White Band managed to do just that with this single; it has scorching horns and a genuinely smouldering groove. The little vocal the song contains amounts simply to shouted exhortations of "Pick up the Pieces", encouraging the philosophy of not giving in when the chips are down.

44
YOU'RE THE FIRST, THE LAST,
MY EVERYTHING
MORE THAN ANYTHING
YOU'RE MY EVERYTHING
BARRY WHITE
20TH CENTURY
1
By this point Barry White was a chart regular and a by-word for seductive, sophisticated, string-laden soul with a disco beat. He had become pre-eminent due to an unbelievable amount of talent and, of course, that voice that sounded like a combination of rich cream and dark chocolate. 'You're The First, The Last, My Everything' was originally written in the early 1950s by Peter Radcliffe who intended it as a country & western tune. Barry White re-wrote the lyric and sprinkled around his fairy dust to create one of the early disco scene's seminal records.

43
WHATEVER GETS YOU THRU
THE NIGHT
BEEF JERKY
JOHN LENNON
APPLE
36
John Lennon had finally arrested his artistic decline; his most recent albums *Sometime In New York City* and *Mind Games* had been, in large parts, diabolically bad. His latest, *Walls and Bridges*, though not the equal of earlier triumphs, was a considerable improvement. Of the tracks on the new album, 'Whatever Gets You Thru The Night' was the obvious choice to be released as a single, with Elton John playing keyboards and providing backing vocals. Lennon himself seemed rejuvenated and sounded like he was, at last, having

fun again; he sounded in fact like the John Lennon we loved. The single was a number one on the American Billboard Chart, and although something of a commercial flop in the UK it was, without doubt, Lennon's best single since 'Instant Karma'. Lyrically, 'Whatever Gets You Thru The Night', was inspired by an evangelical TV preacher, and musically by George McCrea's recent 'Rock Your Baby'.

42
JUDY TEEN
SPACED OUT
COCKNEY REBEL
EMI
5
'Judy Teen' gave Cockney Rebel their first hit, but it was far from a conventional single. It displays its "art" credentials from the off with what sounds like a hoover being switched on before the tinkling, waltz-like rhythm kicks in, supported by a complicated but effective drum pattern. The playful lyrics are delivered – after being chewed into different shapes – in a stylised, foppish manner by Steve Harley; there are hooks aplenty and the chorus helium filled… the whole marvellous effect is of a record slightly unhinged and amphetamine charged.

41
YOU CAN MAKE ME DANCE,
SING OR ANYTHING
AS LONG AS YOU TELL HIM
THE FACES/ROD STEWART
WARNER BROTHERS
12
The Faces had been practically semi-retired from the moment Ronnie Lane quit. He was replaced by Tetsu Yamauchi (who had played bass with

Free after the departure of that band's songwriting bass player Andy Fraser). Unfortunately Tetsu was rather too fond of a drink and therefore not very productive. To make matters worse Ron Wood was having a dalliance with the Rolling Stones and singer Rod Stewart had become a far bigger solo proposition than the band could ever hope to be; hence, for the first time, his name was placed prominently on the sleeve. Thankfully, despite the bad omens, this "goodbye" single was excellent. It was unlike any other song they'd released in that it featured prominent strings; it was also a more pop-fan friendly single than its raucous predecessors – but it still had spirit, it still had charm and it was still so cheerful and chirpy that it practically shook your hand. And so, The Faces left us in the same way they'd introduced themselves five years earlier… with a big collective smile on our faces.

40
CAN'T GET IT OUT OF MY HEAD
ILLUSIONS IN G MAJOR
ELECTRIC LIGHT ORCHESTRA
WARNER BROTHERS
DID NOT CHART

It is odd that the run of hits ELO were enjoying was interrupted when this single flopped; especially odd because this one was of a quality that they'd previously not achieved. 'Can't Get It Out Of My Head' is an enchanting fairy tale set to music – there is a sense of wonderment created as beneath the mournful string backdrop, the delicate rhythm moves us through a beautiful landscape of the imagination, as the poetic lyric is sung with great tenderness by Jeff Lynne.

39
JET
LET ME ROLL IT
WINGS
APPLE
7

Letting his imagination run wild, McCartney took the name of his Labrador puppy and his feelings of trepidation when first meeting his wife Linda's father, and moulded this into the fizzing, power-pop gem that is 'Jet'. Brilliantly executed and produced, this was McCartney right at the top of his game. There is such confidence in his voice and a real zip about the song; it is rich and full of warmth, and even as it rocks it never strays from its melodic heart.

38
KILLER QUEEN/
FLICK OF THE WRIST
QUEEN
EMI
2

Two Freddie Mercury songs as a double A-sided single that took Queen away from the hard rock style with which they'd made their name and introduced a subtlety that was hugely impressive. Suddenly Queen were superbly melodic with breathtaking harmonies and imaginative arrangements; the change allowed Freddie Mercury the space to croon and enunciate like some Noel Coward type figure, re-born as an extravagant rock star. Also, we could now discern the wit and bite of the lyrical content too, and there was still room left for Brian May to embellish the songs with tasteful guitar parts that gave the songs a strong sense of grandeur.

37
COUNTING OUT TIME
RIDING THE SCREE
GENESIS
CHARISMA
DID NOT CHART

Jaunty in the extreme, giving the sense of overcompensation for a distinct lack of confidence, 'Counting Out Time' is an amusing, step-by-step account of what is, literally, a text-book seduction. Peter Gabriel, adopting the role of narrator, describes following the directives in a guide-book he has purchased, which usher him through the right of passage towards the acquisition of carnal knowledge. He attempts to reassure his partner that he knows what he's doing – don't worry he says, "I'll get you turned on just fine", and with the mechanics of foreplay concluded, "It's time to unzip". The musical message tells us that he experiences a humiliating failure before he promises to return the guide-book to the bookstore straight away. It is a tragi-comic song and a quite supreme single.

36
IT'S BETTER TO HAVE (AND DON'T NEED)
LEAVE HIM (PART 2)
DON COVAY
MERCURY
29

A play on the hi-hat starts proceedings before a stinging guitar and piano propel us into this slice of fabulous, southern-fried soul. Brilliantly sung in call-and-response style (with the chorus serving up some homespun philosophy) this was Don Covay's only charting single in the UK, despite him being a legendary figure whose songs were covered by the

likes of Aretha Franklin and The Rolling Stones.

35
OVERNIGHT SENSATION
HANDS ON YOU
THE RASPBERRIES
CAPITAL
DID NOT CHART

From the opening bars on the piano to Eric Carmen's plaintive vocals, there is a sense of sad yearning that permeates this record, as the singer desperately desires that he will achieve his dream of having a "hit record". The music soars and the drums kick hard as if to signify optimism… only for that to be swept away as the sound subsides before the dreaming recommences; the band harmonise their voices – almost touched with religious fervour – and at the turn of a radio dial they find they have a hit. They rhapsodise in blissful happiness as the song fades, and then the drums kick in again and the sound swells gloriously one final time. 'Overnight Sensation' was an operetta played out on 7 inches of vinyl; too grandiose in its ambition for the masses but personally I adored it.

34
THE POACHER
BYE AND BYE (Gonna See The King)
RONNIE LANE
GM
36

With 'The Poacher' Ronnie Lane wore his heart very much on his sleeve. It speaks of a simple way of life that he was coming to embrace; it is a rejection of the satin and tat of the rock star lifestyle he had walked away from and an escape from an urban environment that no longer thrilled, but now seemed to choke him. 'The Poacher' is a rather slight piece of work and yet it is hugely evocative – we can picture the sun breaking through the canopy of trees and dappling the ground, we can hear the ripple of the river and smell the grass, we can picture the "old timer" who narrates and imparts to us his simple truth, "I've no use for riches and I've no use for power and I've no use for a broken heart; I'll let this world go by". Gently strummed and sensitively sung, with oboe and violin creating a vision of bucolic splendour, this beautifully idealised vision of a semi-mythical England joyously warms the heart.

33
SHA LA LA (MAKE ME HAPPY)
SCHOOL DAYS
AL GREEN
HI
20
This was written by Al Green about girlfriend Mary Woodson, and released the week after she had poured a pan of red-hot grits over his back, whilst he was in the bath, before shooting herself dead. This grim backdrop adds a good deal of poignancy to what is essentially a bright and sunny declaration of love and thankfulness for knowing somebody who can understand you. It is a gorgeous record where every component part adds to the greater whole. Green and his band, as always, locate the groove with ease. This sound might easily have been considered old-fashioned and passé compared to the symphonic soul coming out of Philadelphia, or the increasingly inventive disco sounds that were also coming to the fore; but with the talent and voice that Al

Green possessed, replacing the small ensemble with whom he worked so well would have been an act of sacrilege and cultural vandalism.

32
PINBALL
MONEY LOVE
BRIAN PROTHEROE
CHARISMA
22
Primarily an actor, Brian Protheroe found himself 'resting', in severely reduced circumstances, in a tatty, run-down flat. Picking up a guitar, looking around and musing despondently, he produced this observational rambling song with no chorus. Sung almost lethargically, Protheroe captured a feeling that had taken hold in the UK of the early 1970s – one of paralysis as we watched everything that was good sliding away, while a grim, puritanical orthodoxy increasingly held sway.

31
THE PAYBACK
THE PAYBACK PART 2
JAMES BROWN
POLYDOR
'The Payback' is a song about extracting revenge; composed for the film *Hell Up In Harlem*, it was rejected by the producers as "the same old James Brown stuff". In actual fact the track deviates from the sound that Brown was utilising during this period, relying less on the bass and horns and instead having wah-wah guitar as the dominant instrument. Infuriated by the rejection, James released this single – and an album of the same name – and let them speak for themselves… and to this very day, they stand tall as testimony to the rare talent of their creator.

30

STRANDED IN THE JUNGLE
WHO ARE THE MYSTERY
GIRLS?
THE NEW YORK DOLLS
MERCURY
DID NOT CHART

The Jayhawks and the Cadets had simultaneous 60s US hits with this song in a doo-wop style that the Dolls now incorporated into their version. Of course, this being The New York Dolls they throw into the mix a whole lot more as they playfully romp through the song, utilising a kaleidoscope of styles from Chuck Berry style guitar breaks to Cab Calloway influenced vocals. If this had been released by practically any other act it would have been a sure fire hit, but the Dolls were considered seditious by the people who controlled the media and it marked another nail in the coffin of this fabulous band.

29

DOWN DOWN
NIGHT RIDE
STATUS QUO
VERTIGO
1

This song plagiarizes their own hit 'Pictures of Matchstick Men' and it has a subtly aimed dig at Francis Rossi's ex-wife as well as the Quo-hating, snobby music press but, leaving all that aside, 'Down Down' is a stop-start sequence of choruses played relentlessly hard and fast, combined with guitar hooks in which players and listeners can actually draw a breath. This is as lean as a whippet, stripped of anything superfluous, totally unpretentious and absolutely smashing fun.

28

ME AND BABY BROTHER
IN YOUR EYES
WAR
UNITED ARTISTS
21 when re released in 1976

Like a Latin-flavoured, funk version of Status Quo, this is a piece of minimalistic genius. The riff powers the song while the chanted vocals, implying estrangement between siblings, leave much to the imagination of the listener. The organ stabs on the off-beat create a lurching momentum, and harmonica and horns add colour to create a hard, funky classic.

27

AMERICA
DANCE LITTLE GIRL
DAVID ESSEX
CBS
32

America is a big country, but in 1974 it seemed much bigger; in fact it seemed like another world. Everything about the place seemed louder, brighter, brasher and better than what we had in the dreary UK. Whereas they had *Starsky and Hutch*, we had *Z Cars*; they had shiny sky-scrapers and apartments, we had horrible tower blocks of flats; they were healthily tanned and paraded like peacocks whilst we were grey-skinned and dressed in brown... all-in-all we felt very much second-best and intimidated by our transatlantic cousins yet somehow, inside the echoing chasms of space on this record and by utilising a musical shorthand that acted as a roadmap as well as the palpable wonderment in his voice, David Essex conjured up an authentic feeling of the USA on this remarkable single. We are transported and given a taste and flavour of this amazing place where it all seems fantastic, wonderful and yet we can't shake off a nagging worry that we are a little bit out of our depth.

26

IT'S ONLY ROCK N ROLL
THROUGH THE LONELY
NIGHTS
ROLLING STONES
ROLLING STONES RECORDS
10

Credited to Jagger and Richards, the song was actually written by Mick Jagger and Faces guitarist Ronnie Wood, and was originally recorded at Wood's house with David Bowie on backing vocals, Willie Weeks on bass and Kenney Jones of The Faces on drums. When the Rolling Stones recorded the song (which incidentally was their last single with Mick Taylor in the band) they retained the rhythm track played by Weeks and Jones while future Stone Ronnie Wood played acoustic guitar. Lyrically it is Jagger having a dig at journalists for over-analyzing the band's music and taking it far too seriously – hence the genius title and chorus "I know, it's only rock 'n' roll but I like it, like it, yes I do". Good singles – and some very good – by the band have followed in the intervening decades, but this may well have been the last truly great one.

25

SLAVERY DAYS
SLAVERY DAYS (VERSION)
BURNING SPEAR
FOX
DID NOT CHART

Winston Rodney was set upon the path of a recording career when Bob Marley advised him to audition for Coxone Dodd at Studio 1. Putting together a band he named Burning Spear, Rodney's belief in the Rastafarian religion, alongside his alignment with the political views of Marcus Garvey, led to the sound and lyrical content of the music created being described as "Roots Reggae", since the themes of pan-Africanism were explored in song. This mighty track harks back to the barbaric slave trade that brought Rodney's ancestors to Jamaica from their African homeland; their suffering and plight is powerfully evoked as he wails "Do you remember the days of slavery?"

24

SWEET HOME ALABAMA
TAKE YOUR TIME
LYNYRD SKYNYRD
MCA
DID NOT CHART

'Sweet Home Alabama' is a great song with some controversial lyrical content, depending on how it is construed. The stuttering riff is the key to the song; it is unbelievably catchy without being at all obvious, and as always with the best of Skynyrd's songs, the piano part adds a melodic subtlety. Initially written as a riposte to Neil Young's album track 'Alabama' (which even Young himself declared that he didn't like when he listened back to it, calling it "accusatory and condescending" although lyricist Ronnie Van Zant certainly bore no grudges and was pictured several times clad in a Neil Young t-shirt) the more contentious lines in 'Sweet Home Alabama' concerned segregationist Governor George Wallace that were ambiguous and open to interpretation. Van Zant later commented that "Wallace and I have very little in common; I don't like what he says about coloured people" which *is* completely unambiguous and suggest that he was using heavy irony in the song lyric. It is also worthy of note that Wallace, who was confined to a wheelchair following an assassination attempt in 1972, later fore-swore his previous racist segregationist policies saying, in 1979, "I was wrong. Those days are over, and they ought to be over."

23
MACHINE GUN
THERE'S A SONG IN MY HEART
THE COMMODORES
TAMLA MOTOWN
20

Ooooh, I remember the feeling I got when I first heard 'Machine Gun'; it grabbed hold of me and shook me until my head spun; it moved me and I needed to hear it again… and fast! It was written under the title of "The Ram" and initially it was intended that a lyric would be attached, but synthesiser lines that positively burned were used instead. It was modern funk *par excellence*, and when Motown head-honcho Berry Gordy first heard it – with the prominent use of clavinet that reminded him of the sound of gunfire – he re-christened the track 'Machine Gun'.

22
NEVER CAN SAY GOODBYE
WE JUST CAN'T MAKE IT
GLORIA GAYNOR
MGM
2

Previously a hit for The Jackson 5 – and later for The Communards – it is Gloria Gaynor's disco-era take on the song that is the definitive version. It announces itself with a crescendo of strings, and from there the high-tempo, drum-led pulse is unfaltering, while Gaynor gives a soulful, vocal masterclass – always in control, her voice never hurried, it is a marvellous performance.

21
JUST MY SOUL RESPONDING
SWEET HARMONY
SMOKEY ROBINSON
TAMLA MOTOWN
35

It's never easy for a mass audience to accept change, and with 'Just My Soul Responding', Smokey Robinson was revealing a side of himself previously unseen. He had been dubbed "America's greatest poet" by Bob Dylan, Robinson had soundtracked the romances and the good times of a generation, but never before had they heard "political" Smokey. 'Just My Soul Responding' speaks of black soldiers returning from Vietnam and realising that back in the country they have been fighting for they are still regarded as second-class citizens. It speaks also of the plight of Native Americans; Tom Bee of the band XIT joins Smokey in singing a Sioux medicine-man chant during the track, which is beautifully produced by Willie Hutch; the smoothness and calm of the music giving added emphasis to the message of injustice in the lyric… "Too many roaches and not enough heat to keep my babies warm, in this land I helped to form", Smokey sings, and he was pulling no punches, speaking the same truths and expressing them as eloquently as Stevie Wonder and Marvin Gaye. But this great record was met only by critical scorn, and Smokey didn't return to social comment ever again.

20
WORST BAND IN THE WORLD
18 CARAT MAN OF MEANS
10CC
UK
DID NOT CHART

10cc straddled the fine line between humour and comedy with consummate ease, and there is perhaps no better example than 'Worst Band In The World', which in lesser hands could have seen a great idea reduced to slapstick silliness but 10cc were undoubtedly very smart and the humour they employ is often used to disguise the acidic nature of their lyricism. 'Worst Band In The World' is a subversive attack on the star-making stratagems of the music industry… and its willing puppets. Full of brilliant lines and with a structure that makes the record read like a book, this was pop music as art and vice-versa; a classic.

19
NEVER TURN YOUR BACK
ON MOTHER EARTH
ALABAMY RIGHT
SPARKS
ISLAND
13

Sparks had switched operations from the USA to the UK and had begun to have hits, but 'Never Turn Your Back On Mother Earth' was a change of gear from what had gone before. Previously they had been frenetic and hyperactive but with this song they displayed a slower, calmer and more melodic sensibility. Ron Mael dominates the sound of the track, playing an almost baroque arrangement but without it sounding at all retro. Russell sings beautifully, although quite what he is singing about is not clear, beyond a general sense of betrayal and regret.

18
I KNOW WHAT I LIKE (IN
YOUR WARDROBE)
TWILIGHT ALEHOUSE
GENESIS
CHARISMA
21

Like 1960s classics 'Hole In My Shoe' and 'Itchycoo Park', Genesis present us with some psychedelic sounding, shimmering pop, containing a fabulously entertaining and erudite lyric, a flute solo and the sound of a lawnmower being reproduced inexactly, but interestingly, by a Mellotron. The lyric tells of Jacob, a groundsman and gardener who rejects ambition and a future in the "fire escape trade" because he is content to mow the lawns and lie on the bench – "I know what I like and I like what I know" he sings, in this prog/slacker anthem.

17
BE THANKFUL FOR WHAT
YOU'VE GOT
BE THANKFUL FOR WHAT
YOU'VE GOT PART 2
WILLIAM DeVAUGHN
CHELSEA
31

William DeVaughn was in full-time employment and singing only part-time when he wrote 'Be Thankful For What You've Got'. He spent $900 dollars to get it recorded with John Davis (a member of MFSB) and the song was then taken to Sigma Sound in Philadelphia to be completed. 'Be Thankful For What You've Got' is an excellent and wise song, encouraging people to look beyond material wealth and possessiveness. It has a lightness of touch not usually associated with the Philly Sound being much more in the vein of Curtis Mayfield's brand of spare sophistication. Covered by acts of the calibre of Arthur Lee and Love, Lee Perry and Massive Attack, this record has grown to be recognised as a true classic.

16
SATURDAY GIGS
MEDLEY – JERKIN CROCUS/
SUCKER/ VIOLENCE
MOTT THE HOOPLE
CBS
41
Guitar player Ariel Bender departed, and in his place came Mick Ronson, a move that should have re-ignited the spirit of Mott the Hoople; instead, jealousies and resentment surfaced and 'Saturday Gigs' became the band's swansong. This one of Ian Hunter's long list of self-aggrandising anthems, telling the tale of early optimism turning to despair, redemption and finally break-up; a Shakespearean tragedy set to funeral-paced piano backing that leads into a trademark chorus of titanic proportions. Add in Ronson's magisterial guitar playing, along with a horn fanfare, and it all adds up to something of an emotional epic – pass the handkerchiefs.

15
ROXETTE
ROUTE 66
DR FEELGOOD
UNITED ARTISTS
DID NOT CHART
Something was happening to British music… something not seen on television, not heard on the radio and not appearing on stage in concert halls or at the university; this something was happening in pubs. It was a back-to-basics movement, and at its vanguard were Dr Feelgood who were thrillingly raw, maniacally intense, fast and loud. They dressed in suits and looked intimidating, and yet they were a much needed antidote to the blandness and mind-numbing mediocrity of many top-line acts. 'Roxette' was their first single. It was recognisable as an R&B song but it was bug-eyed and reckless; it growled aggressively, it was short, sharp and shocking in a good way. It was, in fact, just what was needed… I loved it.

14
THE BOTTLE
BACK HOME
GIL SCOTT-HERON
AND BRIAN JACKSON
STRATA-EAST
DID NOT CHART
The sheer groove and infectious beat made this an irresistible dance-floor favourite to both funk and Northern Soul aficionados, while Gil Scott-Heron's keyboard part, along with Brian Jackson's contributions on flute, add wonderful flavour too. It is, however, the lyricism of Scott-Heron that makes 'The Bottle' such a compelling record, as he surveys the people on the street and the damage that has been done to them by alcohol abuse. People from all strands of society are represented, from doctors to drug addicts. The lyric offers no easy solutions because there aren't any… all Gil Scott-Heron can do is point out the problem, give voice to his concern and hope that understanding and help will one day arrive.

13
STARDUST
MISS SWEETNESS
DAVID ESSEX
CBS
7

The theme song to the feature film of the same name, 'Stardust' opens and closes to the sound of a heartbeat that acts as a metronome. There are dramatic strings, Chris Spedding plays ice-pick guitar, and in the cavernous spaces left by producer Jeff Wayne, the voice of David Essex echoes. This is a spooky, desolate track – Essex sings of a life disintegrating and in freefall, bitterly anticipating the inevitable final crash.

12
CURLY LOCKS
GOLDEN LOCKS
(BY UPSETTERS)
JUNIOR BYLES
MAGNET
DID NOT CHART

With the departure of Bob Marley from his creative sphere, Lee Perry looked for a new singer/songwriter to work with on a regular basis. The chosen man was Junior Byles and together they created a significant body of work which often expressed Byles's Rasta faith. 'Curly Locks' though, is a gorgeous love song… of sorts. It is very melodic with a lyric in which the narrator has taken to sporting dreadlocks – a symbol of Rastafarianism which was perceived to be dangerous and anti-establishment by mainstream society. The singer's girlfriend has been forbidden by her father from seeing a dreadlock, so he, the narrator, asks her which path she will take. Will she submit to her father's will or choose a life as an outsider in the Rastafarian

way? Recorded in a light, sunny and minimalistic manner by Perry, with a correspondingly floating vocal by Byles, this is a crucial cut in the reggae genre.

11
SEPTEMBER GURLS
MOD LANG
BIG STAR
ARDENT
DID NOT CHART

For anybody who has ever loved the sound of a guitar, 'September Gurls' was manna from heaven. In fact the song, and its execution, is superlative in every way; it is slightly ragged around the edges, which only makes it sound even more exhilarating while Alex Chilton's lead vocal is breathlessly wonderful and the harmonies are warm and rich. 'September Gurls' is part of the pantheon of what came to be known as "power pop", and for a boy who had been thrilled by The Kinks, The Beatles and The Small Faces, finding this record was like discovering a seam of gold running all the way through the back garden.

10

SEVEN DEADLY FINNS
LATER ON
ENO
ISLAND
DID NOT CHART

Eno, with his post-Roxy band The Winkies, debuted on vinyl with this rampaging single which spurts from the speakers in a torrent of words, relentlessly rhythmic guitar and electronic manipulation. Throw in a doo-wop section, and then the highly camp yodelled finale, and one might be forgiven for thinking that this was quite enough. But, there is even more… as the lyric unfolds one is treated to the tale of seven Finnish gentlemen encountering a household of French ladies, and their perverse and lustful couplings in a frenzy of orgiastic excess.

9

BAND ON THE RUN
ZOO GANG
WINGS
APPLE
3

At this time Paul McCartney's relations with his fellow ex-Beatles had become much more cordial as they severed their ties with the contentious figure of manager Allen Klein. During a business meeting George Harrison alluded to the ex-band mates as "all being prisoners". The remark struck a chord with McCartney and the seed of 'Band On The Run' was sewn. The song is concerned with notions of escape and freedom and, though not explicit, was very much informed by McCartney and his generation of musicians being criminalised for their marijuana use. The song is in three sections: the opening part is contemplative before we go up a gear into a hand-clapping, funky section of yearning for release. There is then an orchestrated part (provided by Bowie/T. Rex producer Tony Visconti) that adds drama and provides the pivot of the song, before the finale of a successful escape which is played in a bright, country-rock style. McCartney was undoubtedly benefiting from the cessation of acrimony; he seemed happy and confident and was at the peak of his artistic second coming. I was fortunate to see Wings play live in this period… it was superb and memorable

8

THIS TOWN AIN'T BIG ENOUGH
FOR THE BOTH OF US
BARBECUTIE
SPARKS
ISLAND
2

Sparks stampeded their way into the hearts and minds of the British public with this jolting riot of a single. It is absolutely crammed with words: descriptive words, funny words, all kinds of words which Russell Mael manages to deliver in rapid-fire style with great panache. Meanwhile, a veritable maelstrom of piano, guitar and drum hammers away as a Wild West gunfight ensues; simply and quite literally this was breathtaking.

7

HEY JOE/
PISS FACTORY
PATTI SMITH
MER
DID NOT CHART

Inspired by the likes of Allen Ginsberg and the beat writers, along with rock 'n' rollers such as Bob Dylan and The Rolling Stones, Patti Smith was a poet who had begun presenting her material with the assistance of music critic Lenny Kaye who accompanied her on electric guitar. They were given the chance to record this single cheaply and quickly. 'Hey Joe' has its context altered, and rather than "Joe" being the one with his finger on the trigger, we are presented with fugitive heiress Patty Hearst participating in an armed robbery with the Symbionese Liberation Army, the stuff of American nightmares. 'Piss Factory' is a breathlessly delivered description of Patti Smith's time spent working in a "baby-buggy factory" and how she was singled out and bullied in an attempt to make her conform even as she steadfastly refused to buckle under and have her hopes and ambitions squashed. There were more great records to come, but never again would Patti Smith sound so incredibly, vividly raw and live.

6

MR SOFT
SPACED OUT
COCKNEY REBEL
EMI
8

'Mr Soft' is a mad vamp – the arrangement is reminiscent of what was being performed in the Weimar Republic cabarets. The Mike Sammes Singers, mainstays of light entertainment programming, are drafted in on highly prominent and eccentric backing vocals, whilst the violins saw and Steve Harley enunciates his enigmatic lyrics in a mannered English style, also utilised by Bryan Ferry and David Bowie. Critics sneered but, as usual, they were wrong and Harley's refusal to incorporate the expected Americanisms into his music was absolutely the right thing for him to do, his aesthetic was not one of tired blues rock retreads but one of experimentation and unblinkered thought .

5

HE'S MISSTRA KNOW IT ALL
YOU CAN'T JUDGE A BOOK
BY ITS COVER
STEVIE WONDER
TAMLA MOTOWN
10

Often the best way of dealing with somebody who is powerful, pompous and full of self-importance is to subject them to ridicule, and mockery, and simply laugh at them. He's Misstra Know It All' adopts this tactic with regard to US President Richard Milhous Nixon, a lying, deceitful criminal who believed he was protected by his high office. The song proceeds at an unhurried, mid-tempo pace, but never once lets up the fierce, relentless attack on Nixon; line after line details his numerous faults. Congas and handclaps provide the rhythm, along with supple bass playing by Willie Weeks, while Stevie, without ever losing his grip on the melody, has fun with the vocal phrasing – a playfulness that seems to emphasise even more the subtle dissection of the soon to be disgraced "Tricky Dicky".

4

FOR THE LOVE OF MONEY
PEOPLE KEEP TELLIN' ME
THE O'JAYS
PHILADELPHIA INTERNATIONAL
DID NOT CHART

Pushing Anthony Jackson's bass guitar through phasers and a wah-wah pedal, and then adding a touch of echo was a masterstroke of inspiration. That sonic inventiveness, aligned to the awe-inspiring bass line itself, sets the tone for this single. Written by Anthony Jackson, with crucial input from Kenny Gamble and Leon Huff, the song takes inspiration from the Bible verse which begins "For the love of money is the root of all evil". This timeless theme is then expanded upon and speaks a universal truth. The three O'Jays also have their vocals fed through an echo chamber as they combine voices to tremendous effect in order to deliver an always welcome and relevant message on the horror and iniquity of greed. The horns are punchy and the music is light-footed, which all works together to make this one of the greatest, and most essential, funk singles of all time.

3

REBEL REBEL
QUEEN BITCH
DAVID BOWIE
RCA
2

It's the unforgettable guitar riff which hits first – perhaps the greatest Rolling Stones riff they never wrote – it has a filthy, ragged sound that pre-dates punk and was played by Bowie himself. The song, with its "not sure if you're a boy or a girl" refrain, plays with gender roles and the reference to "a handful of ludes" is suggestive of destructive, drug-fuelled debauchery.; if this was "glam", it was glam dragged into the gutter. In reality, this was indeed the death of "glam" and 'Rebel Rebel' was one of Bowie's finest singles… which means it was one of *the* finest singles of the decade and beyond.

2

HURT SO GOOD
LOVING IS GOOD
SUSAN CADOGAN
MAGNET
4

Catching the ear of Lee 'Scratch' Perry, librarian Alison Cadogan was invited to the Black Ark Recording Studio where Perry renamed her Susan and cut an album's worth of material with her, including 'Hurt So Good' which had been a soul hit for Millie Jackson. The up-tempo track was laid down utilising Boris Gardiner on bass, the Zap Pow Horns and the studio magician himself on impish backing vocals. Meanwhile, Susan Cadogan sings with convincing longing for yet more pleasure mixed with pain. That the nature of the pain is sado-masochistic and the fact she is deriving sexual satisfaction from it is made quite explicit, making this a very adult-themed single that somehow eluded the censors and allowed a UK audience to enthusiastically embrace it.

1

AUTOBAHN
KOMETENMELODIE 1
KRAFTWERK
VERTIGO
11

Beyond any shadow of a doubt, the success of 'Autobahn' has to be attributed to "novelty value"; few had heard music of its like before… It was the shock of the new that persuaded many to purchase this record. However some had suspected that the moment would come when guitar's pre-eminent position in modern music would be overthrown while others simply felt

it… they sensed that what we were hearing was the sound of the future yet the majority would have scoffed if asked to believe that this record, and the band who created it, would soon be acknowledged as being of equal importance, musically, culturally and artistically as The Beatles, James Brown and David Bowie.

Written by Florian Schneider, Ralf Hütter and lyricist Emil Schult, 'Autobahn' owed a huge debt to nurturing producer Conny Plank, this was the band's first ever sung lyric. Musically it is an evocation of driving; the sounds of other vehicles, the wind and rain, brakes and gear changes, all transformed to synthesised sound with a rhythm that suggests the sensation of forward motion. It is, in concept, a form of folk music played on modern instruments, a reflection of our environment and rather than looking backwards it looked resolutely into the increasingly mechanised future. The release and success of 'Autobahn' was fundamental to the advancements made in music; it re-shaped the landscape and changed the vocabulary; it was a revolution in sound, just as 'Strawberry Fields Forever' was a giant leap forward in the 1960s , 'Autobahn' served the same function in the 1970s, it changed perceptions of what was allowed and opened up fresh possibilities inspiring and informing so much music that followed.

1975

NOTABLE EVENTS

- Margaret Thatcher defeats Edward Heath to become leader of the Conservative Party
- Teenager Lesley Whittle is kidnapped and murdered by Donald 'Black Panther' Neilson
- The Kataeb militia murders 27 Palestinian people on a bus, an incident that triggers the Lebanese Civil War
- The Khmer Rouge take power in Cambodia and begin a programme of genocide
- Communist North Vietnamese forces take Saigon and South Vietnam surrenders ending the Vietnam War
- Lord Lucan disappears and is found guilty *in absentia* of murdering his child's nanny Sandra Rivett
- *Fawlty Towers*, the John Cleese/Connie Booth written sitcom, is broadcast on BBC 2
- Two thwarted assassination attempts are made on the life of US President Gerald Ford in September
- Muhammad Ali defeats Joe Frazier in a savage re-match dubbed 'The Thrilla in Manila' – neither boxer ever fully recovers
- NBC in the US screens the first episode of *Saturday Night Live*
- The Yorkshire Ripper murders begin - Wilma McCann is the first victim
- New York City is bailed-out and receives $6.9 billion over a 3-year period to avert bankruptcy
- Newly-promoted Manchester United return to the First Division playing attacking and entertaining football. Derby County win the league and West Ham beat Fulham to win the FA Cup

NOTABLE BIRTHS

Big Boi; David Beckham; Lauryn Hill; Andre 3000; Angelina Jolie; Sufjan Stevens; 50 Cent; Jack White; M.I.A.; Tiger Woods

NOTABLE DEATHS

Dave Alexander; P.G. Wodehouse; Elijah Muhammad; Mikhail Bakhtin; Aristotle Onassis; Josephine Baker; Tim Buckley; Dmitri Shostokovich; Haile Selassie; Éamon de Valera; Pier Paolo Pasolini; General Franco

NOTABLE FILMS

Barry Lyndon; The Day of the Locust; Dog Day Afternoon; Jaws; Dersu Uzala; Monty Python and the Holy Grail; One Flew Over The Cuckoo's Nest; Salò; The Passenger

NOTABLE BOOKS

High Rise – J.G. Ballard
First Love Last Rites – Ian McEwan
The Periodic Table – Primo Levi
Dead Babies – Martin Amis
Grimus – Salman Rushdie
Something Happened – Joseph Heller
A Dance To The Music Of Time – Anthony Powell

THE MUSIC

Half-way through the decade and as a nation we trod water; we were directionless and content to wallow in our mediocrity, whilst simultaneously singing 'Rule Britannia'. Scapegoats had to be found be they Irish, black, Pakistani or gay; they all came under concerted attack and were persecuted at every turn – in the job market, in the housing market, by right-wing thugs as the National Front attracted mass support, aided and abetted by the Police, who were institutionally racist and homophobic from top to bottom, also by politicians widely perceived to be useless and out of touch. The UK was a nasty little island full of hate and violence; it was squalid, coarse and corrupt and this was all reflected in the UK music scene. Radio 1, the national flagship pop station, held sway; the DJs were sold to the public as wacky, with-it, youthful celebrities. They were, in fact, exclusively male, ultra conservative middle-aged bores who, in most cases, didn't even care about music. The thought of 'Diddy' David Hamilton or 'DLT' – the 'hairy cornflake' – attempting to inflict their singular lack of taste across the airwaves still offends, whilst the Corporation's biggest star, Jimmy Savile, was indulged and protected despite most of his employers being aware that he was a serious serial sex offender who abused his position within the institution as a weapon. Wonderful Radio 1 gave heavy rotational play to the cheesiest, blandest, lowest quality mass-produced musical garbage imaginable. Its conformist safety-first play-list policy aimed to strangle the life out of any music that could be perceived to be rocking the boat.

On TV things were equally bad; every Thursday *Top Of The Pops* was sneered at by anyone who actually liked music, and leered at by middle-aged men who liked scantily-clad young women. Meanwhile the station's serious music show was presided over by a supercilious 1960s relic who adored soft-rock and hated The New York Dolls. Thankfully though the barricades were being manned, and in clubs across the land there was a resistance movement. In the cellars we did not listen to The Rubettes and Showaddywaddy; we did not countenance Telly Savalas or Guys 'n' Dolls, and we did not groove to Smokie or Kenny. The Northern Soul scene was an enormous uncontrollable underground movement; pub rock was providing unpretentious live music in small venues, and the musical diet of even the most mainstream of nightspots was contemporary, high-quality soul and funk, mixed with the beginnings of disco. In record shops it was wise to check-out releases on the Harvest, Island and Virgin labels, as they offered a treasure trove of alternative sounds. Another tip was to buy as much reggae music as possible, because at that time the tiny island of Jamaica was arguably the musical epicentre of the planet, and a large proportion of the records emanating from the Black Ark, Studio 1 and dozens of other studios, was touched to some degree by genius. Meanwhile, whispers were reaching our ears that in America there were musicians doing some fascinating things; operating far away from the public eye were bands called Pere Ubu, Television, Devo and The Modern Lovers, whose aesthetic was closer to that of The Velvet Underground or The Stooges than to The Grateful Dead or The Doobie Brothers. This sounded promising…

MY 1975

In this year my stylistic adventures and departures mirrored my musical tastes. It appeared to me that every single male in the country aged between 6 and 60 had grown their hair to at least medium-length; every single male in the same demographic also wore flared trousers or jeans, huge collared shirts and jackets, and stacked heel shoes - so I rebelled.

I hated the Californian dross that my friends chose to listen to and instead journeyed backwards in time to get myself attuned to the 1960s sounds of The Yardbirds, The Troggs, The Pretty Things and The Small Faces, the latter of which I became obsessed with to the point that I launched a one-man Mod revival, incorporating a wardrobe of suede desert boots, sharply-pressed narrow trousers, Fred Perry polo shirts and a Steve Marriott style 'bouncy onion' haircut. I found myself – smartly attired, short-haired, clean-shaven and fresh – being called 'weird' by hairy, denim-bedecked moustachioed men tottering about on high heels. I soon grew bored and my hair was cut and shaved in the style sported by Lou Reed on his *Rock 'n' Roll Animal* album cover. I wore black, listened to The Walker Brothers and read Albert Camus before drifting towards a more recognisable normality and adopting a look copied from Kevin Ayres. I bought hundreds of records this year, from all over the musical spectrum – Dr Feelgood, Dr John, Joni Mitchell, Faust, Stevie Wonder and Toots and the Maytals – I stood outside all tribes and so musical genres didn't concern me. I saw all kinds of gigs too – John Martyn, Fairport Convention, Graham Parker and 10cc. I probably most enjoyed seeing Kevin Ayres but undoubtedly the *least* enjoyable gig I attended was a performance by Led Zeppelin at Earl's Court. I'd been to the England v Scotland football match in the afternoon, where England had won by 5 goals to 1. I had been drinking a lot of whisky (offered to me by unbowed Scots) but by the evening I was clear-headed and settled down to watch the world's most popular band. The good bits (surely there were at least some) were hard to discern since Led Zeppelin seemed intent on pummelling the audience with a barrage of tasteless bombast. The bad bits were really, truly, undeniably bad and almost coma inducing. For anybody who never saw Led Zeppelin I would say, truthfully, have no regrets; you dodged a bullet… they were an appalling spectacle.

100
DON'T CRY NO TEARS
STUPID GIRL
NEIL YOUNG AND CRAZY
HORSE
REPRISE
DID NOT CHART
Neil Young had been sailing in emotionally dangerous waters for a few years, seemingly surrounded by death and drugs. He had recorded his so-called "doom trilogy" of albums and now, on the other side, seemingly wanted to crank up his guitar and have fun alongside a band he felt comfortable playing with. To that end, 'Don't Cry No Tears' was resurrected from Young's high-school days when it had been titled 'I Wonder'. It is a slender song of lost love with just a few simple lyrics but it was rendered with passion and gusto. Young sings up a storm and plays guitar in that neo-primitive style that is completely unique while Crazy Horse provide ragged and idiosyncratic support.

99
NEW YORK GROOVE
LITTLE MISS MYSTERY
HELLO
BELL
9
On leaving Argent Russ Ballard worked on Roger Daltrey's *Ride a Rock Horse* album; he flew to New York to master the tapes and during the flight played with the phrase "I'm back in the New York groove". Upon arrival Ballard wrote out the complete song. At this point fate stepped in when Ballard's brother told Russ that he had watched a young denim bedecked band play a high-energy show and go down an absolute storm. They were called Hello and it was suggested that they be given the

chance to record the new song. In the studio with producer Mike Leander – originator of the Glitterbeat – they incorporated a hand-clapping and foot-stamping approach. The verses are half-spoken and half-sung over a Bo Diddley-style shuffle-beat which then neatly slips into a chorus that is such an eruption of joy it seems as if it could almost raise the dead.

98
GAMMA RAY Part 1
GAMMA RAY Part 2
BIRTH CONTROL
CBS
DID NOT CHART
Birth Control were formed in 1968 in Germany and named as a provocative spit-in-the-eye gesture against Pope Paul's anti-birth control stance. 'Gamma Ray' was a stand-out track on their 1972 album *Hoodoo Man* but it was only given a single release three years later. Highly percussive, with skin-scratching guitars and wild, untethered sounds being coaxed out of the organ, the band positively smokes. The lyrics describe the lack of ethics associated with the arms trade in particular, and society in general. Our narrator informs us that he wishes to be a gamma-ray flying around the world, destroying weapons and fighting against misery.

97
SILVER AND GOLD
SILVER AND GOLD VERSION
PRINCE FAR I
MICRON MUSIC
DID NOT CHART
Hearing the cavernous dub echo in combination with Prince Far I's deep, rich voice, this record sounds as if it has been excavated from the very depths of the earth itself. Here the

'chanter' is in no hurry whatsoever; it is easy to imagine him reciting his message of fire and brimstone from a tablet of stone, although such was the imposing power he possessed that it could have been a shopping list being recited and it would have sounded equally 'dread'. No hurry either from the players; they are formidable, solid and graceful. This was seriously unsettling music that was awe-inspiring in its utilisation of controlled power.

96
GET DOWN TONIGHT
YOU DON'T KNOW
KC AND THE SUNSHINE BAND
TK
21
A double-speed guitar intro gives 'Get Down Tonight' a distinctive flavour from the off, and it is employed as a hook throughout the track. The song itself is quick-stepping and the horns jab accordingly like a fast-on-his-feet middleweight boxer. With a highly repetitive vocal and insistent rhythm, this was designed for the dance floor, and it was a perfect fit for hedonistic nights of celebratory pleasure-seeking.

95
DELUXE (IMMER WIEDER)
MONZA (RAUF UND RUNTER)
HARMONIUM
BRAIN
DID NOT CHART
Harmonia was a group featuring Neu guitarist Michael Rother along with Cluster pair Dieter Moebius and Hans-Joachim Roedelius. Here they are joined by Guru Guru drummer Mani Neumeier and producer Conny Plank. Together they created

a distinctly European music and tread new ground, combining stunning and elegant synth lines of an almost classical type with the insistent motorik beat and Rother's fluid guitar playing, to create a beautiful sound that invigorates the soul as it washes over the listener.

94
SLOW DOWN
DAY TRIPPER
THE KNEES
UNITED ARTISTS
DID NOT CHART
Brinsley Schwarz couldn't buy a hit; maybe it's the name they thought... and so they began to release singles under a variety of different aliases – all of which flopped as well. Obviously the problem wasn't the name after all; nor was it the music since the records were excellent... maybe it was the haircuts? Anyway, whatever the answer to the enigma was, this is one of those secret Brinsley singles; a cover of the Larry Williams classic handled impeccably, lean and tight with no padding or studio trickery, and a fabulous vocal from (I'm guessing) Nick Lowe.

93
MAID IN HEAVEN
LIGHTS
BE-BOP DELUXE
HARVEST
DID NOT CHART
('Maid In Heaven' was the lead track on the *Hot Valves* EP which reached number 36 in 1976)
Be-Bop Deluxe played a glam/prog hybrid with flashes of muscular hard-rock guitar. They seemed to be constantly on the verge of a huge commercial breakthrough that somehow never quite arrived.

This was recorded with Queen producer Roy Thomas Baker, and so it is perhaps no coincidence that 'Maid In Heaven' shared that band's arty cleverness and displayed leader Bill Nelson's melodic gifts, along with his prowess on guitar and not unpleasant voice. Unfortunately, cramming several tempo changes into a 2 minute 27 second single was far too much for the radio station tastemakers to cope with, and thus the record failed to sell... but I for one loved its speedy madness.

92
EXPENSIVE SHIT
WATER NO GET ENEMY
FELA KUTI AND AFRICA 70
MAKOSSA
DID NOT CHART
Fela Kuti essentially took the funk of James Brown back home to Nigeria and crossbred it with traditional music and a dash of jazz. What he created was Afrobeat and on top of that he added funny and sarcastic lyrics which attacked the authorities for their brutality and corruption. They, in turn, identified him as a trouble-maker and as a public enemy. They began a drawn-out series of raids on the compound he had set-up, dealing out beatings and using false evidence to make arrests. All of this was detailed in Fela Kuti's songs and 'Expensive Shit' is a fine example. So here, in this 4-minute long edited version of a 13-minute track, we are given a taste of the fire and fury of Fela Kuti, as well as his indestructible rhythm.

91
FEEL LIKE MAKIN' LOVE
WILD FIRE WOMAN
BAD COMPANY
ISLAND
20
Anybody expecting great things from Bad Company was bound to be disappointed. Paul Rogers and Simon Kirke brought along nothing of the soulfulness that Free had in abundance to their new outfit, and ex-Mott The Hoople guitarist Mick Ralphs showed none of the flair he had previously exhibited but, and there is always an exception to the rule, with this track Bad Company, for once, scored a bullseye. 'Feel Like Makin' Love' was a song half-written by Rogers that was a leftover from Free; it had that nonchalant swagger they so often adroitly captured. He played it to Ralphs who inserted a stuttered guitar figure after the verse, and then added some wailing guitar to the walloping big chorus... bingo! A hard-rock classic that Bad Company hadn't produced before and never came close to emulating afterwards.

90
PROFONDO ROSSO
DEATH DIES
GOBLIN
CINEVOX
DID NOT CHART
Deep Red was a horror film directed by Dario Argento. After failing to persuade Pink Floyd to provide the soundtrack, he turned to Italian progressive rock band Goblin to do the honours... it was an inspired choice. Their brand of jazz-infused, gothic rock fitted the bill perfectly and it was good enough to stand alone, as this single attests. Totally

instrumental, and clearly influenced by the likes of King Crimson, Mike Oldfield and ELP, their sense of doom and drama set them apart - they are purposeful and decisive in the execution of their music – not for them the meandering passages favoured by their more famous peers. 'Profondo Rosso' opens with an ornate harpsichord figure that recurs throughout the piece, between passages of darkly-infused, keyboard-led rock that tended to disturb the casual listener.

89
SUMMERTIME
JENNY COME DOWN
THE TROGGS
PENNY FARTHING
DID NOT CHART

After seemingly falling off the edge of the world, at least as far as the media were concerned, The Troggs were reintroduced into the mainstream when appearing as guests of David Bowie on his televised *1980 Floor Show*. From there they reunited with Larry Page (the producer of their 1960s hits) and released cover versions of 'Good Vibrations' and 'Satisfaction', which, though good, sold poorly. 'Summertime', a self-written song was chosen for the third attempt to reclaim their position as hit makers… it failed, of course, but it was nonetheless a slice of prime Troggs magic. Beautifully melodic and played on acoustic guitar, Reg Presley's leering vocal dispels any notion that The Troggs had gone soft, as he suggestively recounts the various lustful reasons that he likes the summertime.

88
BYE BYE BABY
IT'S FOR YOU
THE BAY CITY ROLLERS
BELL
1

In many ways the Rollers were a younger generations Troggs, as they dumbly attacked the material they were presented with, showing great enthusiasm, but very little finesse, on their weirdly thin-sounding records. At this point that all changed, as soundscaping duties fell into the hands of The Sweet's producer Phil Wainman; he gave the band a big, full sound with more polish than they'd ever previously attained. He had them record this cover version of a Four Seasons track and it proved to be perfect for them. Showing scant respect for the original, it was sped up, played an octave lower and a guitar solo was thrown in for good measure before the whole thing turned into a giant sing-a-long; it was brash and brilliant pop music.

87
BAD BOYS
FIGHTING IN THE STREET
SPEEDY KEEN
ISLAND
DID NOT CHART

'Something In The Air' writer and singer Speedy Keen had his finger on the pulse of the simmering discontent that was being felt on the city streets when he issued this prescient single – it is full of police sirens and screeching car tyres. There is a loping reggae rhythm and a low-frequency, sinister sounding synthesiser line supporting a lyric which tells the tale of a boy gone wrong being chased through the alleyways on the run from the law.

86
DRANO IN YOUR VEINS
CIRCUS HIGHLIGHTS
POLI STYRENE JASS BAND
MUSTARD
DID NOT CHART

I know little of Poli Styrene Jass Band beyond that they came from Cleveland, Ohio and members included Anton Fier – later of the Golden Palominos – and Jim Jones, who played a long stint with Pere Ubu. 'Drano In Your Veins' reminds me in tone of The Pretty Things during their "SF Sorrow" period, but with a more experimental bent and darker subject matter (presumably the song references the "hi-fi murders" of 1974 where, amongst other horrors inflicted upon them, hostages were forced to drink highly corrosive drain cleaning fluid). In its own way this was music ahead of its time, and equally as important as the music being made simultaneously by fellow Ohio bands Pere Ubu and Devo.

85
ROCKIN' ALL OVER THE
WORLD
THE WALL
JOHN FOGERTY
ASYLUM
DID NOT CHART

John Fogerty took the patented sound he had created for Creedence Clearwater Revival and applied it to his solo recordings. Here, he came up with a simple repetitive phrase, "Rockin' all over the world", and added hillbilly rock 'n' roll guitars and a flurry of piano notes over an insistent beat – and then he sang like his life depended on it. Although this was a hit in the USA, 'Rockin' All Over The World' was practically unheard in the UK until Status Quo

recorded a version of it in 1977.

84
SOUL CITY WALK
LET'S GROOVE PT 1
ARCHIE BELL AND THE
DRELLS
PHILADELPHIA
INTERNATIONAL
13

Outside of a re-issue of 'Here I Go Again', Archie Bell and the Drells hadn't had a sniff of success since the 1960s but a move to Philadelphia International remedied that immediately. Working with songwriting/production team McFadden and Whitehead, 'Soul City Walk' was sprinkled with the fairy dust that seemed to emanate from the very walls of Sigma Sound Studios. In this case, the combination of disco beat, serene strings, horns and fabulous voices full of character made this a strutting dance-floor filler.

83
MOTORBIKING
WORKING FOR THE UNION
CHRIS SPEDDING
RAK
14

Ex-Womble and future Sex Pistols producer Chris Spedding, dressed in full leathers and with hair greased into an impressive quiff, served up 'Motorbiking' in a punk meets Eddie Cochran style. The chunky guitar, with heavy use of tremolo arm, and the spiky lyrics delivered in a couldn't care less manner, both failed to disguise what fabulous fun 'Motorbiking' was, as we were transported along the A-roads of the unglamorous UK. "Listen to me, I tell you no lie, I'm too fast to live and too young to die" he sang... and without this sounding even remotely sincere, it was still quite delicious and stood apart in its mock embrace of a nihilistic outlook.

82
ROLLING STONE
COCONUT ICE
DAVID ESSEX
CBS
5

More slow-burning studio excellence from Essex and Jeff Wayne, but this time around we are not treated to space age rock 'n' roll, but a kind of weird, ambient soul music featuring Liverpool band, The Real Thing, on backing vocals. There are hints of 'Shaft' style orchestration, which act as a bridge between the verses of the song's first half and the extended chorus of the second half.

81
IN DULCI JUBILO/
ON HORSEBACK
MIKE OLDFIELD
VIRGIN
4

'In Dulci Jubilo' is a traditional German Christmas carol dating back to the Middle Ages. Mike Oldfield recorded it as a jolly, good-natured instrumental played with snare drum, recorder, synthesiser and guitar – and with the latter, he throws in a gleeful solo. It was a lovely, bright note in a Britain that at the time was a dreary and strife-riven place. On the other side of this double-A release is 'On Horseback', which had already appeared as an unlisted final track on Oldfield's masterpiece album *Ommadawn*. This is a delightful, eccentric and whimsical song about riding in the countryside, and it features a children's choir adding

their voices to the song's climax.

80
TALKIN' TRASH
YOU AND I
BETTY DAVIS
ISLAND
DID NOT CHART

Having hipped her ex-husband, Miles Davis, to the music of her friends, Jimi Hendrix and Sly Stone (which, at a stroke, moved his and many followers' conception of what music could be, with thrilling, genre-changing results) Betty Davis then got on with her own career. She created a high-intensity, hard-funk sound, with often highly-sexualised lyrics... and she dressed like a space-aged Amazonian goddess. Without her – and this is no exaggeration – there would have been no Rick James, no Chaka Khan and no Prince (who described Betty Davis as "what we aim to be"). 'Talkin' Trash' was taken from her album *Nasty Girl* which features on the cover a symbol not unlike the one Prince would adopt for himself in the 1990s. The track was recorded with her road-band Funk House, who serve-up a stupendous, guitar-driven groove, over which Betty duets with one of the musicians in a liberated and risqué manner. Denigrated by the gentlemen of the music-press in the 1970s, time has proven that the music of Betty Davis was very much top-notch.

79
LOVE MACHINE PART 1
LOVE MACHINE PART 2
THE MIRACLES
TAMLA MOTOWN
3

This was the biggest hit of The

Miracles long career, eclipsing all the great records made with Smokey Robinson. 'Love Machine' was written by lead vocalist Billy Griffin and original Miracle Pete Moore, and the record was produced by Freddie Perren, who had been part of "the Corporation", overseers of early Jackson 5 hits, which share a similarly flirtatious and effervescent vibe as 'Love Machine'. Griffin sings a lyric that compares himself to an electronic device, to be turned on or off by his lover. Meanwhile, eccentric backing vocals are provided by Bobby Rogers who growls his part, alongside a repeated baritone "yeah, baby" from Ronnie White, and the whole piece is splendidly underpinned by a quick-fire disco beat that made the track totally irrepressible.

78
SHE DOES IT RIGHT
I DON'T MIND
DR FEELGOOD
UNITED ARTISTS
DID NOT CHART
There had been a few bands around with a street sensibility and some edge for several years, The Sensational Alex Harvey Band spring to mind; but there was a theatricality about their approach that diluted any real sense of threat – everything seemed to have a cartoon Punch and Judy feel about it. However Dr Feelgood, without even trying, were like a broken bottle or a jagged blade… they conveyed a genuine feeling of danger. Their songs, written by 'speed-freak' guitarist Wilko Johnson, contained no cartoon violence because they were essentially love songs, and 'She Does it Right' is a perfect example. Lyrically it is simply a list of compliments being paid

to a woman… but it is played at breakneck speed. The guitar stutters, drums and bass pound in lockstep and singer Lee Brilleaux spits out the words in a rapid-fire delivery; it is a whirlwind, a force of nature. The Feelgood's really were a breath of fresh air and were undoubtedly the most exciting British band around. They were making the established groups sound not merely tame, but old! The winds of change were beginning to blow stronger…

77
BOTH ENDS BURNING
FOR YOUR PLEASURE
ROXY MUSIC
ISLAND
Roxy Music no longer seemed other worldly; the most angular of their edges had been carefully smoothed away, but they nevertheless remained a highly-potent act and 'Both Ends Burning' was an intoxicating gem. Andy Mackay on saxophone, along with drummer Paul Thompson and keyboardist Eddie Jobson are well to the fore musically, though the more restrained Phil Manzanera unleashes a trademark guitar solo of astonishing intensity towards the song's conclusion. Bryan Ferry, meanwhile, sings almost in the manner of the soul men he grew up listening to as he professes his ardour in a much more passionate performance than we listeners had been used to. His ever entertaining lyrics, this time less playful but more direct, do not disappoint either.

76
YOU SEXY THING
AMAZING SKIN SONG
HOT CHOCOLATE
RAK
2

Originally the B-side of flop single 'Blue Night' but re-mixed and released as an A-side, 'You Sexy Thing' has a fairly basic construction, following a rigid verse–chorus formula, but the attention to detail in the recording make it extraordinarily potent. The first thing that grabs you is the six-note riff; trebly, overdriven and highly distinctive, then come the violin flourishes that accentuate the rhythm, further embellished by high-in-the-mix hand-drumming, as Errol Brown sings in an almost frenzied, soulful-style, adding yelps and ecstatic screams to emphasise his devotion to the titular 'sexy thing' who has saved him from his fate as "one of the lonely people". The fact that this was a hit again in the following two decades underlines just how durable and evocative a single this was.

75
HIT THE ROAD JACK
HIT THE ROAD JACK VERSION
BIG YOUTH
TROJAN
DID NOT CHART

Big Youth's version of 'Hit The Road Jack' sparkles; it is eccentric and a little surreal, almost 'alternative karaoke' as he merges the Ray Charles hit with the rhythm of 'Love Me Forever', the Studio 1 classic by Carlton and the Shoes. Then, in mid-song, seemingly for no reason other than he feels like it, Big Youth veers off to deliver a verse of Burt Bacharach's 'What The World Needs Now'. Slick this was not and all the better for retaining the

human touch. Big Youth's records, and this one in particular, had the gift of making the listener feel intimately connected, in that they somehow captured the very essence and spirit of the performer.

74
GET IN THE SWING
PROFILE
SPARKS
ISLAND
27

With its marching band beat and carnival instrumentation, 'Get In The Swing' was unconventional to say the least. It is highly repetitive too, with the titular phrase repeated and repeated to the point of being a desperate sounding mantra. Quite madcap then, even before one examines the lyric which seems to be using the spawning of salmon as a metaphor for the uphill battle that life can often be. Then, bizarrely, a divine figure appears to announce "Hello down there, this is your creator with a questionnaire"; he is answered by a worn-out and breathless Russell Mael who informs him that he just doesn't have the time…

73
LIFE IS A MINESTRONE
CHANNEL SWIMMER
10CC
PHONOGRAM
7

Any examination of the human condition by 10cc was inevitably going to be absurdist in nature, and so it proved when Lol Creme and Eric Stewart cooked up 'Life Is A Minestrone' after being handed the title via a misheard remark. Pondering on the possible meanings of this phrase they concluded that life consists of all the random experiences that we, as individuals, fill it up with. Hence we are guided around a travel brochure of the world's must-see destinations – the Leaning Tower of Pisa, the Hanging Gardens of Babylon – all of which become ingredients in the minestrone of life, "served-up with parmesan cheese". The clever lyric was set to a dizzying musical soundtrack that feels very much like a ride on a carousel. This was a brilliant single that contained an almost as brilliant flip-side in Channel Swimmer.

72
ISI
AFTER EIGHT
NEU
UNITED ARTISTS
DID NOT CHART
The musical chemistry between Klaus Dinger and Michael Rother was, by this stage, honed to perfection; they were sublime creators of a sound that is, here at least, relatively simple but which practically rolls in waves of wondrous harmonics from Rother's guitar and keyboards, alongside the disciplined but supple and propulsive beat of Dinger. Hearing music as warm as this is a rewarding and life-enhancing joy, and if the radio programmers of the day had shown even a scintilla of imagination, this might well have been a surprise hit.

71
MR RAFFLES
(MAN IT WAS MEAN)
SEBASTIAN
STEVE HARLEY AND
COCKNEY REBEL
EMI
13
The old Cockney Rebel had crashed

and burned on a tide of acrimony; in their place came a more robust, but traditional leaning outfit. Initially though their records remained fascinatingly original. 'Mr Raffles' rides along over a grand piano bed, played in a decorative, supper-club style, as synths wash over giving an impression of menace, before the jolting introduction of a deliberately exaggerated cod-reggae section. Lyrically it is as strong as anything to come from Harley's pen; his debt to Bob Dylan is obvious, as is his attraction to the post-modernist poets as he utilises the fictional master thief "Raffles" as a symbol of non-conformist sedition, whose story he sings with an air of creepy decadence.

70
WHY DID YOU DO IT
WRITE ME A NOTE
STRETCH
ANCHOR
16
Ex-Curved Air member Kirby and Elmer Gantry of Velvet Opera were approached by the management of a floundering Fleetwood Mac to act as doppelgangers to fulfil contractual obligations and tour the USA as "Fleetwood Mac", with original member Mick Fleetwood joining them to give the enterprise a degree of authenticity. They learnt the songs they were required to play and flew out to do the tour. However Mick Fleetwood did not show up and audiences soon realised that they were being cheated; after just a few dates the tour was scrapped. Out of the ashes of this debacle Kirby and Gantry formed Stretch and wrote the song 'Why Did You Do It', a scabrous, if justified, attack on Mick Fleetwood. It has a slow, grinding,

funk flavour with guitar, bass and drums locked into a tight groove, while horns are cleverly employed to gently raise the musical temperature. The lyrics, laced with contempt, are venomously growled by Gantry. Stretch came close to repeating the magic of 'Why Did You Do It' again or even settling on a defined musical style, but for the duration of this song they were spookily touched by genius.

69
50 WAYS TO LEAVE YOUR LOVER
SOME FOLKS LIVES ROLL EASY
PAUL SIMON
COLUMBIA
23

Built around a repeated drum riff, '50 Ways to Leave Your Lover' is an uncluttered masterclass in economy, as just a lone acoustic guitar supports the vocal melody in which the recently divorced Paul Simon addresses the split in a humorous manner. Lyrically the song is extremely clever and assured; it is also sung beautifully and has an upbeat chorus that is catchy and unforgettable. This was a single of the highest quality.

68
TUSH
BLUE JEAN BLUES
ZZ TOP
LONDON
DID NOT CHART

There is something about ZZ Top's best music that sounds effortless and carefree, as if the riffs upon which they build their songs just drip from their fingers; they then go on to play them in such a loose-limbed and joyful manner, without skipping a beat, that it becomes quite hypnotic and you are drawn inexorably into their groove, their pace, their world. That's exactly what 'Tush' succeeds in doing – I close my eyes as it plays and I'm inside some Texas roadhouse; there's the smell of chilli and refried beans, the taste of chilled beer and the sound of the greatest bar-band in the USA ringing in my ears.

67
CHOCOLATE CITY
CHOCOLATE CITY
(Long version)
PARLIAMENT
CASABLANCA
DID NOT CHART

Funky satire from George Clinton, Bootsy Collins and the P-Funk crew; over a drumless, rumbling groove, George Clinton delivers his spoken word vocal in the form of a presidential election report. They're sniggering behind their hands for sure, but there is a deadly serious subtext to this as they identify "chocolate cities" on their population breakdown, and draw attention to their lack of representation in high office. "Don't be surprised if Muhammad Ali is in the White House" declares George, before adding "and the name of that building is just a temporary condition". Political agitation with humour… Parliament/Funkadelic were essential listening.

66
BAADER MEINHOF BLUES
ODB
HELDON
DISJUNCTA
DID NOT CHART

Heldon were a band who played the work of French guitarist Richard Pinhas, assisted by various collaborators, some associated with the more famous Magma. 'Baader Meinhof Blues' is a stunning piece of music – absolutely ground-breaking in the way guitar and programmed synthesiser meld together to create sheets of savage noise, while the rhythm beneath them is pummelling and utterly relentless. Self-confessedly influenced by King Crimson's Robert Fripp, Pinhas incorporates Fripp's style of playing fluid, sustained notes, while the use of synth and drum pre-dates acts like Ministry and Nine Inch Nails by nearly two decades.

65

LOVE ROLLERCOASTER
IT'S ALL OVER
OHIO PLAYERS
MERCURY
DID NOT CHART

Up and down and round and round slides the slippery riff played by guitarist Leroy "Sugarfoot" Bonner, echoing the lyric concerned with problematic personal relationships. This is a fun-filled ride on the funky side, with horns parping joyously and the female backing vocalists adding honey-coated sweetness to complement the rawness of the band's gravelly tones.

64

18 WITH A BULLET
SHADOW OF A DOUBT
PETE WINGFIELD
ISLAND
7

Session man for the likes of Van Morrison and Paul McCartney, producer of Dexy's Midnight Runners, and here songwriter and performer of a lovingly constructed doo-wop parody with a very clever lyric about having a "hit first time" or, in record business jargon, entering the chart "with a bullet". It was a great summer record - very fresh and catchy with a luscious saxophone break and exaggerated vocals that stay just on the right side of comedic; one of the great one-hit wonders.

63

TRAMPLED UNDERFOOT
BLACK COUNTRY WOMAN
LED ZEPPELIN
SWANSONG
DID NOT CHART

Led Zeppelin had a policy of not releasing singles in the UK, but to tie-in with a series of concerts at Earl's Court 'Trampled Underfoot' was issued... only to be quickly withdrawn. Very strongly influenced by Stevie Wonder's 'Superstition', John Paul Jones plays the banging, relentless riff on clavinet, while guitarist Jimmy Page utilises the wah-wah pedal to fine effect. Brutalist drummer John Bonham does indeed absolutely brutalise the drum kit in caveman style, and Minnie Mouse-voiced Robert Plant squeals the lyrics, using car parts as sexual metaphors, a rip-off from Robert Johnson's 'Terraplane Blues'. Led Zeppelin were undoubtedly a powerful proposition, and when they allowed the funk to seep into their style, as they do here, they were capable of being really very good indeed.

62

I NEED A MAN
AGAIN AND AGAIN
GRACE JONES
ORFEUS
DID NOT CHART

It turned out that the distinctive

figure of fashion model Grace Jones also had a distinctive voice. Her first single was 'I Need a Man', recorded and released in France. It passed by relatively unnoticed but it is apparent how similar in style and execution the track is to the hits that elevated her to superstar status in the 1980s. Her powerful, strident vocals, matched to a flowing disco rhythm and, of course, the chorus delivered by this striking and strange looking androgyne, meant that she was soon picking up an audience from the gay club scene... and when 'I Need a Man' was re-issued in 1977, interest was growing and her time was drawing closer.

61
LETTING GO
YOU GAVE ME THE ANSWER
WINGS
CAPITOL
41
The *Venus and Mars* album that 'Letting Go' is taken from is an abomination; it is vapid and largely inconsequential, so it is something of a surprise that 'Letting Go' is the exact opposite... soulful and insightful. Paul McCartney writes about his wife Linda; still very much in love and ever more appreciative, he has had the time to realise the sacrifices she has made to assist his career by giving up her own independent work as a photographer. He understands that he has been possessive and he must now give her the space for her own creativity. The track is played in a rhythm & blues style, and new guitarist Jimmy McCulloch is given plenty of room to play some stinging licks. There is a powerful horn part used as a break, and McCartney, with material that is so personal, sings with

a passion and sense of abandon that is completely riveting.

60
KING TUBBY MEETS THE ROCKERS UPTOWN
BABY I LOVE YOU SO
AUGUSTUS PABLO
ISLAND
DID NOT CHART
Two sides of sheer brilliance that, if not quite the pinnacle of the studio art of dub, are certainly not far below the summit. Merging the talents of Tubby, the great originator, and Pablo, the man who made the melodica cool, was a master stroke. It is not easy to describe a dub instrumental without resorting to tired old cliché, so I will simply state that this is completely brilliant; if you are not familiar with this record, do yourself a favour... listen and feel uplifted.

59
NO REGRETS
REMEMBER ME
THE WALKER BROTHERS
GTO
7
'No Regrets', a lovely though simple and unadorned track in the hands of composer Tom Rush, was given the full Wagnerian effect on this first Walker Brothers single since 1967. Over country-flavoured guitar, a lush orchestral arrangement and the sound of the exquisitely-voiced Scott Walker locating, and then exposing, the very heart and soul of the lovelorn lyric is heard with an epic guitar solo as the cherry on top, and it was hard not to fall for this beautifully maudlin concoction.

58
SHACK UP
SHACK UP PART 2
BANBARRA
UNITED ARTISTS
DID NOT CHART
'Shack Up' is an absolute funk classic and so it is difficult to believe that it was both Banbarra's first and last record. The track was initially written by Moe Daniels as an instrumental piece called 'Boogie On The Other Side Of Town', but his friend, Joe "Bunny" Carter, added some words and 'Shack Up' was born. The lyric dealt with unmarried couples cohabiting, something which was considered socially unacceptable at this time. The message was delivered with great élan by Wesley Aydlett, as the phase "Shack up" was chanted in response to every line. With a simple but highly effective horn riff, combined with a massive kick on the drum, this was a loud and dramatic sounding record that should have been the start of something long-lasting for Banbarra but, like musicians before and after them, they were cheated out of their money and simply left unable to carry on.

57
YOU GO TO MY HEAD
RE-MAKE\RE-MODEL
BRYAN FERRY
ISLAND
33
'You Go To My Head' was a 1938 song that quickly became a jazz standard and was covered numerous times by the likes of Duke Ellington, Louis Armstrong and Billie Holliday. It suited Bryan Ferry perfectly, just as if it had been written especially for him: it was smokey, sophisticated, languorous and the epitome of good taste. On the flip-side, Ferry re-interprets his own composition 'Re-make/Re-model' which had been one of the stand-out cuts on the first Roxy Music album. Slowed down, it is treated like a classic soul track recorded in the near-future, as synthesisers gurgle and a full brass-section wails away while Ferry delivers his cool-as-a-cucumber vocal

56
THE LION SLEEPS TONIGHT (WIMOWEH)
I'LL COME RUNNING TO TIE YOUR SHOES
ENO
ISLAND
DID NOT CHART
Originating in South Africa as 'Mbube' (the Zulu word for Lion) the tune was given English language lyrics in the 1930s and became a popular song, particularly amongst the folk-music fraternity. Eno approaches the song from a child-like perspective, with a wide-eyed wonder that is totally disarming. What he produces is charming and very lovely; relying on Eno's un-rock 'n' roll voice to supply beautiful simplicity amidst the fabulously lush backing vocals that make this such a well-loved and iconic song.

55
WALK THIS WAY
ROUND AND ROUND
AEROSMITH
COLUMBIA
DID NOT CHART
Having been turned onto New Orleans funk maestros The Meters by fellow guitarist Jeff Beck, Aerosmith's Joe Perry found himself imitating their style as he noodled on his guitar

during a pre-gig sound check. He hit on something that sounded good, and so, with the drummer playing along to the groove, the idea began to take shape as singer Steven Tyler scribbled down some nonsense lyric to help the process along, before writing something more definitive at a later time. When that lyric eventually arrived, it further emphasised the rhythm since Tyler wrote words that fitted in almost percussively; they concerned losing his virginity to a cheerleader and there was a kind of Chuck Berry quality to them. The highly repetitive funk riff was a hook in itself, before the chorus was even added, and Tyler's lovably cheeky vocal is just one of the ingredients that go into making this single a very tasty dish indeed.

54
LEGALISE IT
LEGALISE IT VERSION
PETER TOSH
INTEL DIPLO
DID NOT CHART
The brooding, militant ex-Wailer was feeling the heat of police persecution as they reacted with raids because of his taste for herb, to which he ascribed medicinal qualities and spiritual enlightenment. Rather than maintain a diplomatic silence, Peter was, as ever, recklessly true to his nature. He chose to taunt and challenge the authorities by releasing his pro-herb anthem 'Legalise It', a portrayal in song of the benefits of marijuana use, with a chorus in which Peter sings "legalise it and I will advertise it". Recruiting 'brother' Bob Marley's band to play on the record, it had a fabulous mid-tempo feel to complement the convictions of the song's writer and singer. Tosh's

troubles and confrontations with the police would never cease, and in 1987 he was assassinated in his own home, with the finger of suspicion pointing to the authorities being his murderers.

53
THAT'S THE WAY I LIKE IT
WHAT MAKES YOU HAPPY
KC AND THE SUNSHINE BAND
TK
4
The epitome of a 'summer hit', this was disco perfection during the long, hot and sultry days that we were experiencing. As the shackles of convention seemed to be easing, dress codes relaxed and people forgot about power-cuts and three-day-weeks, there was finally the chance to have some fun, and 'That's The Way I Like It' was the sound of freedom. It was brash and brazen, it was fresh and it was funky; we danced, we smiled and we sang along… aha aha.

52
REGGAE GOT SOUL
INSTRUMENTAL VERSION
CREDITED TO THE
DYNAMITES
TOOTS AND THE MAYTALS
JAGUAR
DID NOT CHART
Opening with a horn riff that could have graced an Otis Redding or Sam & Dave record in the heyday of Stax records, before switching and hitting its stride with a biting rocksteady rhythm, 'Reggae Got Soul' was a successful hybrid of the two musical genres in which the gravel-voiced Toots excitedly lets rip as he expresses his joy in creating such an irresistible musical force.

51

BLACK FRIDAY

THROW BACK THE LITTLE ONES

STEELY DAN

ABC

DID NOT CHART

Deliciously and darkly cynical, 'Black Friday' sees Steely Dan sharply dissecting the "greed is good" culture. It tells the tale of a plot to defraud investors on the stock exchange – "I'll stand by the door and catch the grey men when they dive from the fourteenth floor" sings Donald Fagan, before he escapes any repercussions by fleeing to Muswellbrook in Australia "with nothing to do but feed all the Kangaroos". There's also a little dig at the Church and it's easily bought forgiveness, available to the wealthiest but most dubious characters. The tale is played out to a swinging, up-tempo backing, notably featuring a fiery guitar break by Walter Becker on his trusty Telecaster.

50

A FOOL IN LOVE

I KNOW WHY THE SUN DON'T SHINE

FRANKIE MILLER

CHARISMA

DID NOT CHART

Big-hatted Scotsman Frankie Miller and Andy Fraser, formerly of Free, had, at one point, attempted to put a band together. It didn't work out but a friendship was made, and on the evidence of 'A Fool In Love', a fine songwriting combination was formed as well. Recorded in America with Miller's band (which included ex-Wings guitarist Henry McCullough) and augmented by The Memphis Horns and The Edwin Hawkins Singers, 'A Fool In Love' is, from start to finish, a hard-hitting soul classic. Its staccato riff jolts and jerks like a kicking mule, but Miller rides the rhythm with ease and sings up a storm. Nigh on the perfect single, the song was covered by Etta James… but even a legendary figure such as her couldn't get close to the genius of this original version.

49

KINGS OF SPEED

MOTÖRHEAD

HAWKWIND

UNITED ARTISTS

DID NOT CHART

Hawkwind were, at this point, deep into their 'space-rock' phase, and fittingly 'Kings Of Speed' featured a lyric written by sci-fi author Michael Moorcock; it plays like a psychotic barn-dance, and "speed" (in the sense of velocity) is the subject matter of the song. B-side 'Motörhead' is written by singing, bass playing, leather-jacketed eccentric Lemmy, and it is also about "speed" – though this time it is the chemically produced amphetamine variety that is being referred to. Great stuff…

48

WHAT AM I GONNA DO WITH YOU?

WHAT AM I GONNA DO WITH YOU BABY?

BARRY WHITE

20th CENTURY

5

A more R&B flavoured single from Barry White than we had grown used to, with rock-solid drumming high in the mix alongside pounding, rhythmic piano and the ever-present string arrangement – which although highly prominent, was nothing like as ornate and expansive as was usually the case. Barry's vocal too is unadorned, and he rasps, yelps and groans quite nakedly. One could never in a million years make the mistake of thinking that a Barry White record was by anybody else; however, on 'What Am I Gonna Do With You' there was no playing safe whatsoever, as the formula was cooked-up and served in a dramatically different way.

47
WHAT A DIFFERENCE A DAY MAKES
TURN AROUND LOOK AT ME
ESTHER PHILLIPS
KUDU
20

It was widely accepted that Dinah Washington had cut the definitive version of 'What A Difference A Day Makes', hers being a stately, sophisticated and smokey jazz rendition. As far as the general record-buying public were concerned, Esther Phillips was in heroin-addicted exile… yet here she was, back to have her first hit since 1962 with this irreverent trampling of the original. Cut at a much faster tempo, with the focus shared between Phillips's astoundingly feline-sounding vocal and unashamed disco stylings, it was a huge club hit and introduced both song and performer to a brand new audience.

46
EVIL WOMAN
10538 OVERTURE
ELECTRIC LIGHT ORCHESTRA
JET
10

Jeff Lynne had gained a good deal of confidence from 1974s *Eldorado* album, where he had consciously worked on making his material more melodic. In the UK sales had been disappointing, but artistically Lynne sensed that he was progressing; suddenly ideas were coming more easily and 'Evil Woman' was reputedly composed inside 30 minutes – whether this is true or not, the song became ELO's first global hit. Full of orchestral flourishes and a wicked synthesiser line, hook followed hook to make this a truly memorable and genuinely likeable pop nugget.

45
NEW YORK CITY
CHROME SITAR
T REX
T REX WAX CO
15

Pretty much a one line lyric – "Have you ever seen a woman coming out of New York City with a frog in her hand?" – this just had to have a fantastic groove to amount to anything at all… fortunately it did. Played with panache by Gloria Jones (Marc Bolan's muse) on keyboards, she also adds soulful backing vocals to the most overtly funky of all the T. Rex singles. Bolan, drowning in cognac, cocaine and self-pity was floundering around for inspiration and decent songs; chart placings were getting lower and lower, but this was, without doubt, a high-spot in what was his lowest period. Bolan attempted to mythologise the song by suggesting that he happened to be hob-nobbing with Rod Stewart or David Bowie when he saw a lady walking along with a live frog; but Gloria Jones version of the story – that the idea came about when they saw a woman with a "Kermit the Frog" toy – which seems a lot more plausible.

44
HOW LONG
SNIFFIN' ABOUT
ACE
ANCHOR
20

I have seen thousands of bands performing during my lifetime, and perhaps the most painfully dull I ever had the misfortune to witness were Ace. I cannot abide acts who adopt a phoney transatlantic sheen for their music, and Ace were guilty of that; 'How Long' bears the same relationship to Steely Dan as America's 'Horse With No Name' had to Neil Young – it is a facsimile… no more and no less. The track is so silky; it rolls along on its keyboard groove while Paul Carrack, the vocalist, sings with smooth restraint. There is also a guitar solo that Skunk Baxter probably couldn't believe he hadn't already played; and yet… my head nods, my foot moves and I find myself mouthing along to the chorus. Yes, I know it's a total stylistic rip-off, but I'm not yet sufficiently curmudgeonly or cynical enough to deny that it is all carried-off extremely well – and at the heart of this record is really a quite wonderful song.

43
WELDING
WELDING VERSION
I ROY
WELL CHARGE
DID NOT CHART

In the 1970s when "toasters" were pre-eminent in the reggae sphere, U Roy, Dennis Alcapone, Big Youth and I Roy were the cream of the crop… and I Roy was the most eloquent and poetic of them all. Often laced with sexual innuendo, his good-natured style and fluid delivery made him very popular in both Jamaica and the UK. 'Welding' is a risqué and racy tale that I Roy, in typically expressive fashion, cut at Channel One where, at this time, he acted in a (usually) uncredited capacity as recording engineer and producer.

42
BIRTHDAY SPECIAL
SHINGLE SONG
PETER HAMMILL
CHARISMA
DID NOT CHART

The LP *Nadir's Big Chance* saw Peter Hammill put on the mask of the album's central character, Rikki Nadir, a proto-punk black-clad rocker. This single taken from the album has a ferocious attack; Hammill hurls the words like poison darts and also contributes razor-sharp guitar which slashes away wildly amidst the maelstrom produced by his Van Der Graaf colleagues as they are let loose on unhinged saxophone, blitzkrieg drums and earth-trembling bass. The party to which the title and song allude was quite clearly far from genteel and innocent… but it was, most certainly, very special.

41
LOW RIDER
SO
WAR
UNITED ARTISTS
12

A "low-rider" is a car but also a culture that was a big-deal in the Latin American community. It entailed the modification of a car with hydraulic lifts so that it could be bounced, and these cars (which often had outlandish paint jobs and swivel seats) were a source of huge pride.

War saxophonist Charles Miller just happened to be a low-rider and one day, as the band jammed in rehearsals, they hit upon such a sweet and cool groove that Miller began to ad-lib the lyric "Low rider, drives a little slower" and then develop it further; by the time the jam was over they knew they had a monster song within their grasp. With its insistent rhythm, carefully tracked by the vocal, and the saxophone riff to provide colour, this was an essential sound of the summer.

40

LONG DISTANCE LOVE
ROMANCE DANCE
LITTLE FEAT
WARNER BROTHERS
DID NOT CHART

Little Feat were a great band, though perhaps their music was better suited to the album format because singles by them were relatively scarce – and when one was released, they seemed to be very poorly chosen from what was a highly eclectic repertoire of outstanding songs. The exception to the rule is 'Long Distance Love', which is tender and achingly beautiful. Written and sung by the band's leader of sorts (as well as being the resident songwriting genius) ex-Mother of Invention, Lowell George. 'Long Distance Love' was plucked from the band's fifth LP, *The Last Record Album*, which generally betrayed a distinct lack of inspiration and sign-posted a rapid and marked decline for Little Feat, since George contributed less and less of himself as time went on. So, here was a single that was sweetly and soulfully magical played exquisitely and sung with great charm, this was Little Feat's one unarguably brilliant single… and sadly their last ever brilliant record.

39

COME ON TRAIN
COME ON TRAIN INSTRUMENTAL
DON THOMAS
VJ
DID NOT CHART

On joining the Drifters in 1969 Charles Thomas changed his name to Don in order to avoid confusion with long-standing member Charlie Thomas. Don then left the band in 1971 before eventually re-surfacing with this single which, although having zero impact in the wider world, became a record with absolutely classic status on the UK's 'Northern Soul' scene. It is a tale of lost-love, and the train represents a symbol of hope and the possibility of reconciliation. Mid-tempo, funky and imaginatively arranged, it palpably bleeds with the pain of the narrator, and as Don Thomas explores every emotional nook and cranny of the song, his hiccupping voice betrays his desperation to find the one he needs.

38

BEST DRESSED CHICKEN IN TOWN
SHE WRENG EP
DR ALIMANTADO
CAPO
DID NOT CHART

The old adage that "less is more" is certainly true in the case of 'Best Dressed Chicken in Town', which plays out over a simple, unchanging organ vamp, while the doctor's voice is echo-laden by producer Lee Perry in his Black Ark Studio heyday. Highly idiosyncratic and hugely entertaining, but also with plenty to say hidden beneath the eccentric exterior.

37
ONCE BITTEN TWICE SHY
3000 MILES FROM HERE
IAN HUNTER
CBS
14

Having split from Mott the Hoople Ian Hunter and Mick Ronson attempted to put a band together but were thwarted by the fact that they were each contracted to separate record labels and management. To solve the problem Ian Hunter became a solo act and Mick Ronson played guitar and handled production duties. 'Once Bitten Twice Shy' was their first release; from the opening "Allo" from Hunter, to the spiralling guitar-solo conclusion from Ronson, it was an impeccable pop gem with its saucy, suggestive lyric and epic chorus that pleased both old and new fans alike.

36
ROLL OVER LAY DOWN
WHERE I AM
STATUS QUO
VERTIGO
9

Two-years old by the time it was belatedly released as a gap-filling single, 'Roll Over Lay Down' was Quo at their very best. Part-written by bassist Alan Lancaster, whose songs tended to be (as this one is) of the more muscular variety, it has all the ingredients of classic Quo – the churning riff, the instrumental breakdown to almost nothing before the music peaks and surges once again and, of course, a chorus so simple and obvious that it borders either on the edge of genius or total inanity, depending very much on the listeners' perspective. 'Roll Over Lay Down' was not clever nor flashy...

but like all the best Quo records, it was fabulous fun.

35
WHEN AN OLD CRICKETER
LEAVES THE CREASE
HALLUCINATING LIGHT
ROY HARPER
HARVEST
DID NOT CHART

A eulogy for times past, a recollection of childhood memories and a metaphor for death, 'When an Old Cricketer Leaves the Crease' is a wistful and wonderful song; calm and with an almost dreamlike flow, mid-way through the Grimethorpe Colliery Band join proceedings and add further poignancy to the piece, along with an authentic sense of place – we are in the industrial North of England, the area that shaped Roy Harper and continued to resonate throughout his entire body of work.

34
BROTHER CAN YOU
SPARE A DIME
AIN'T NO LADY
RONNIE LANE
ISLAND
DID NOT CHART

'Brother Can You Spare a Dime' was a depression-era song first popularised by Bing Crosby. This version was the title song for a documentary film which examined the disparity between rich and poor during those sad and desperate times. Ronnie totally nails the song as he movingly conveys the despair and disappointment of a broken man brought to his knees, and the band capture a genuine flavour of the time with scratched banjo backing before a nervy guitar solo intrudes, followed by a saxophone part that is rich in melancholia.

33
L-O-V-E (LOVE)
I WISH YOU WERE HERE
AL GREEN
HI
24

Al Green had previously sung songs of seduction, loneliness and heartache, but with this single he sings of the concept of love as a spiritual necessity, a salvation that will set him free; he places the ideal of love upon an altar and praises it as a sacred state. Of course, with a sumptuous backing track that grooves along effortlessly, because this is Al Green, his message is delivered in that honeyed voice that could charm the birds from the trees even if he happened to be giving voice to his weekly shopping list.

32
LADY MARMALADE
SPACE CHILDREN
LABELLE
EPIC
17

The French Quarter in New Orleans is a notoriously raunchy place and 'Lady Marmalade' convincingly captures that flavour in the raw funk of the music and the sassy vocals of Sarah Dash, Nona Hendryx and Patti Labelle as they strut through a lyric about a prostitute whose explicit catch-phrase "Voulez-vous coucher avec moi, ce soir?" (Would you like to sleep with me tonight?) is used as a chorus. Written by Bob Crewe and Kenny Nolan and produced by Allen Toussaint (as were so many great southern soul records) and with The Meters serving as backing-band, this was a record impossible not to be seduced by.

31
BACK IN THE NIGHT
I'M A MAN
DR FEELGOOD
UNITED ARTISTS
DID NOT CHART

Displaying enough naked electricity to light-up the entire seafront at Southend, 'Back In the Night' was a colossal single in the classic style of early Who or Kinks. It has an insanely catchy riff that is pummelled almost to the point of extinction; meanwhile Wilko Johnson provides a funny, street-smart lyric that was straight-to-the-point and front-man Lee Brilleaux sang it like he lived it whilst throwing-in some very tasty slide-guitar. This was lean, mean and absolutely top of the class.

30
TEAR THE ROOF OFF THE
SUCKER (GIVE UP THE FUNK)
P-FUNK
(WANTS TO GET FUNKED UP)
PARLIAMENT
CASABLANCA
DID NOT CHART

From their album *The Mothership Connection*, the P-Funk crew were now inhabiting a completely different universe to the rest of us... and they operated using their own musical rules with their own musical language too. 'Tear the Roof Off the Sucker' plays as a simple, anthemic sing-a-long, but also as intuitive jazz, as the players bounce riffs around each other while the bass and drums ensure that they never once lose sight of the underlying funkiness.

29
CB200
CB200 VERSION
DILLINGER
WELL CHARGE
DID NOT CHART

Lester Bullock initially made his name working with Lee Perry, who had also been the one to suggest a name change to Dillinger, referencing the American gangster. By this point though Dillinger was recording at Channel One utilising the talents of the superb house band, The Revolutionaries, and displaying his dread vocal talents toasting over the rhythms of The Mighty Diamonds, Delroy Wilson and others. Here, on CB200, he once again displays the Jamaican own love-affair with motorbikes while Gregory Isaacs provides the launch pad for Dillinger to extemporise in a thick patois-laden style that is impenetrable to my ears, but sounds fabulous anyway, no matter what it is that I'm missing in translation.

28
HOW DOES IT FEEL
SO FAR SO GOOD
SLADE
POLYDOR
15

Writing music for the feature film *In Flame* allowed Slade to abandon the tried and tested formula that had made them much-loved stars, but which was now just crushing their creativity. With 'How Does It Feel', the film's pivotal song, they allowed themselves to write in adult style about an adult theme and express adult emotions, rather than just go on pretending to be retarded boot-boy adolescents. It must have felt hugely liberating because the change of approach yielded a strong body of work with 'How Does It Feel' standing head-and-shoulders above anything they had previously produced. Built on a simple piano-part, played by Jim Lea, the guitars take very much a secondary role to the brass section, brought in to add dynamic thrust to the song courtesy of the band Gonzales. Noddy Holder writes a downbeat, serious and poignant lyric and sings with restraint and subtlety. It was a masterful release, but the lowest charting since their hit-run had first begun. Soon they were back on the treadmill knocking out bangers… it must have been very dispiriting. By that point Slade were lacking any sort of magic, and although they were still racking-up the hits they were, in truth, languishing somewhere between very poor and absolutely atrocious.

27
LOVIN YOU
THE EDGE OF A DREAM
MINNIE RIPPERTON
EPIC
2

Once heard, never forgotten… 'Lovin' You' is an ultra-simple song; it is a declaration of love made heart-rendingly effective by Minnie Ripperton's use of her remarkable five-and-a-half octave vocal range – she hits impossible high notes that seem to be quite other-worldly. Produced by Stevie Wonder (under the pseudonym El Toro Negro) who also plays the sparkling piano-part, there are some cute bird noises and acoustic guitar played by Richard Rudolph, the song's co-writer and Ripperton's partner; these small touches are all that is required to add the finishing veneer to this spectacular track.

26
ONLY WOMEN
DEVIL'S FOOD
ALICE COOPER
ANCHOR
DID NOT CHART

It was rather startling when Alice Cooper released a ballad as a single, and even more startling when one digested the content of the song. Alice was insightfully directing a spotlight onto the subject of spousal abuse and displaying a maturity in his song-writing that had hitherto not been heard. The music came from an old song which guitar player Dick Wagner had written for his late 1960s Detroit area band, The Frost. Wagner had never been happy with the words and was delighted that Alice wished to write a new lyric. However radio stations ignored the record like the plague because of its "Only women bleed" chorus, misconstruing it to be a reference to menstruation that they felt would grievously offend the public – if only they had realised that the song was really about violence against women, that might well have been okay! And so the track sank without trace, only to be resurrected by Julie Covington a year later, who managed to achieve a number 12 hit with the song - presumably because it was being sung by a female, the BBC found it to be more palatable…

25
LOVE TO LOVE YOU BABY
NEED A MAN BLUES
DONNA SUMMER
CASABLANCA
4

Building upon her own idea, and assisted by the Munich-based production team of Georgio Moroder and Pete Bellotte, Donna Summer produced a demo and sent it along to Casablanca label boss Neil Bogart who requested an extended version up to 20 minutes long. Summer, who was not particularly keen to be the performer on the track, nevertheless went back to the studio; the lights were dimmed and she lay down and thought about her handsome boyfriend Pete… The result was 16 minutes of indubitable musical history that the BBC refused to play (even in its edited 7-inch single form) claiming that it contained the sound of no less than 23 orgasms. Musically, the track imitated Blaxploitation movie soundtrack styles, with wah-wah guitar, washes of synthesiser and a drum track heavy on the cymbals, over which Donna feigned ecstatic love-play. Boundaries had been violated and disco music was about to get very interesting indeed.

24
I DON'T KNOW WHY
TRY A LITTLE HARDER
THE ROLLING STONES
DECCA
DID NOT CHART

One of *the* great Rolling Stones singles is this version of the Stevie Wonder song, which far surpasses the original. 'I Don't Know Why' was cut in 1969, not long after Mick Taylor had replaced Brian Jones on guitar and, somewhat poignantly, on the very same night that they received news of Brian's death. The recording was finally released in 1975 as Decca trawled through their vaults for Stones material that they could profitably exploit. It is a general rule in such instances that recordings left on the shelf were, in truth, pretty substandard and should be left well alone… but not on this occasion because 'I Don't Know Why' is absolutely superb. This is the sound of the Stones getting it spot-on, taking somebody else's song and transforming it into something of their own; whereas Stevie Wonder's version had been somewhat gauche and flimsy, the Stones reading is mean and substantial. Jagger twists the lyrics all over the place, at one moment accusatory, the next pleading. Mick Taylor and Keith Richards create a wall of guitar and the rhythm is handled with dazzling aplomb. The only downside to this fantastic single is that it conclusively underlined just how great The Rolling Stones *had* been… and just how far they had slipped.

23
HOLD BACK THE NIGHT
TOM'S SONG
THE TRAMMPS
BUDDAH
5
When, in 1972, the Trammps had their first hit record with 'Zing Went the Strings of My Heart', they followed it up with 'Sixty Minute Man'. The B-side of this latter song was an instrumental called 'Scrub Board' that became a popular Northern Soul dance track and led to the idea of adding in a vocal track; this in due course became 'Hold Back the Night'. The Trammps were based in Philadelphia, and so leading lights from MFSB played on and produced their records, lending them the same sophisticated soul sound as acts like The O'Jays and Billy Paul. They also had, in lead singer Jimmy Ellis, a front-man who could instinctively transmit raw excitement

and joy, and it is the combination of all these ingredients which help to make 'Hold Back the Night' such a wonderful listening experience.

22
BORN TO RUN
MEETING ACROSS THE RIVER
BRUCE SPRINGSTEEN
COLUMBIA
DID NOT CHART (reached 98 in 2009 on download sales)
Massively over-hyped by Jon Landau – "I have seen the future of rock 'n' roll and his name is Bruce Springsteen" – this ludicrous quotation proved to be a significant millstone around Bruce's neck and he desperately needed to overcome suspicion and scepticism by delivering something that was quite a bit better than good… fortunately, with this single, he did just that. What we get here is a raging approximation of Phil Spector's "Wall of Sound" as well as a series of lyrical images that Springsteen sang with passion and authority, creating a word-picture that resolutely cried out for freedom… the freedom to escape, the freedom to chase a dream, the freedom to live and love. 'Born to Run' made Bruce Springsteen a star; it was a song that perfectly captured his essence, a pure distillation of what he was all about. Maybe this is the reason that following this record I neither needed, nor wanted, any more Bruce in my life – it was all here in this one song.

21
RED TEMPLE PRAYER
(TWO HEADED DOG)
STARRY EYES
R. ERICKSON AND BLEIB
ALIEN
MARS
DID NOT CHART

Roky Erickson, for it is he, was released from a State Mental Institution in 1972 after 3-years of electro-convulsive treatment and being dosed with Thorazine. Somehow, during his incarceration, he had found the will to work and wrote several songs and poems. In 1974 he put together a band, Bleib Alien (which translates roughly from German as Remain Alone) and recorded this single with Doug Sahm (of the Sir Douglas Quintet) in the producer's chair. 'Red Temple Prayer' was inspired by the grisly head-transplant experiments performed by Vladimir Demikhov in the Soviet Union during the 1950s. It is a blood-curdling, garage-rock exorcism of demons where, over crash-bang-wallop riffage, Roky sings "I'm in the Kremlin with a two-headed dog". This was stunning stuff and clearly a song that Erickson liked, since he re-recorded it on several other occasions.

20
LOOKIN' FOR A LOVE
SUGAR MOUNTAIN
NEIL YOUNG AND CRAZY
HORSE
REPRISE
DID NOT CHART

Finally Neil Young was moving away from the darkness that had engulfed him over the previous few years and 'Lookin' For a Love' was as optimistic as he had ever sounded. The song is written from the perspective of a man just out of a relationship and looking forward to meeting someone new – "She'll be nothing like I picture her to be", he says, but nevertheless his underlying feeling is that when he does get to meet her, it will bring happiness. Of course, this being Neil Young, his own faults are readily acknowledged as he sings "I hope I treat her kind, and don't mess with her mind, when she starts to see the darker side of me". The whole piece is played country-style and it could easily be passed-off as a lost classic by Hank Williams, although the delightful primitivism in the playing by Crazy Horse – who sound like they may have been enjoying one or two drinks – might not have gone down too well at the Grand Ole Opry...

19
STAND BY ME
MOVE OVER MRS L
JOHN LENNON
CAPITAL
30

In 1974 Lennon had twice tried to cut this song with his old Beatle buddy Paul McCartney on drums, but the recordings hadn't come up to scratch and were therefore shelved. Returning to it a third time, Lennon finally cooked-up one of the greatest cover versions in rock music history. Of course, the original version was already a classic as performed by Ben E. King (who had written the song along with Jerry Leiber and Mike Stoller) but Lennon increases the tempo just a touch, places his acoustic guitar right up-front in the mix and sings with tremendous fervour, adding bite where Ben E. King had purred. It proved to be the last Lennon single of his very patchy

1970s; at least he left us with a great one.

18
S.O.S.
MAN IN THE MIDDLE
ABBA
EPIC
6

Since 'Waterloo' had first catapulted Abba into the spotlight, they had floundered somewhat. In truth, they were releasing some pretty cheesy records but 'S.O.S.' changed that at a stroke. Not only was it a huge commercial hit but it also gave them a future template to work from and a sense of their own identity, whereas previously they always seemed to be trying to board somebody else's train. Put simply 'S.O.S.' was bathed in genius; a bravura construction and sung magnificently by Agnetha Fältskog who sounds as if she is on the brink of tears as she very movingly manifests the heartache in the lyric. Praised to high-heaven by venerated songwriters such as Ray Davies and Pete Townshend, and with a guitar riff that was later filched for Sex Pistols' 'Pretty Vacant', this had everything going for it – drama, pathos, melody and a crystal clear production of the brilliant singers and players. With this release Abba were elevated to the upper echelons in the pantheon of great pop-music makers.

17
JIVE TALKIN'
WIND OF CHANGE
THE BEE GEES
RSO
5

Residing in Miami, the Bee Gees soaked up influences that are fairly evident on this single, and it turned out to be the launch-pad for their second coming as an artistic and commercial force. For the rhythm they used the sound of their car crossing the Julia Tuttle Causeway as they travelled to the studio; for the riff they borrowed from Shirley and Co's 'Shame Shame Shame', and for the title and vocal hook – "Jive talkin', you're telling me lies" – they adopted black street-slang, which was certainly straight to the point. The scratchy guitar intro, played by Barry Gibb, was distinctive and seductive, and the pulsating bass-synth sound, provided by Blue Weaver, echoes the work of Stevie Wonder. I remember first hearing this record on a jukebox and marvelling at its brilliance; this was the sound of something big just around the corner... a tidal-wave of dance music. I pushed some more money in the slot to listen once again.

16
OLD MARCUS GARVEY
TRADITION
BURNING SPEAR
ISLAND
DID NOT CHART

The rise of roots and consciousness music in Jamaica reached its zenith with this radical sermon set to music – "No one remember old Marcus Garvey" chants Burning Spear. Full of fervent passion, fire and brimstone, he promotes the fallen prophet of Rasta culture while the cream of Jamaica's reggae players provide a suitable musical backdrop, creating a sound that is strongly suggestive of forward motion.

15
FAME
RIGHT
DAVID BOWIE
RCA
17
With the bulk of his *Young Americans* album in the can, recorded at Philadelphia's Sigma Sound Studio, David Bowie booked some time at the Record Plant to put down the finishing touches and along for the ride was John Lennon whom Bowie had befriended. Serendipitously Carlos Alomar began to play a guitar-riff he had worked out for a cover version of an old R&B hit called 'Footstompin'; Bowie felt it would be a waste to use it on a cover song and, as Alomar played, Lennon began to interject using the word "Aim". Bowie soon changed that to "Fame", and with a little bit of help from Lennon wrote a nasty lyric about the vacuous nature of the celebrity bubble that also served as a stinging rebuke to his manager, Tony Defries, and the Mainman Management Company who Bowie was fighting in court. The song then came together very quickly... and to great effect; Alomar's masterful funk-riff powering a superb, octave-jumping vocal performance from David Bowie.

14
MAKE ME SMILE
(COME UP AND SEE ME)
ANOTHER JOURNEY
STEVE HARLEY AND
COCKNEY REBEL
EMI
1
Cockney Rebel had been a great band, but like most great bands the enterprise was not run as a democracy;

democracy in a band is, by and large, very detrimental to quality. Consider The Beatles, The Kinks, T. Rex, The Wailers, Funkadelic and Kill Pretty – none of them had been democratic; if they had been, it would have diluted whatever it was that made each of them special. Milton Reame-James, Jean-Paul Crocker and Paul Jeffreys approached Steve Harley and insisted that they be allowed to write material for the next Cockney Rebel album. Harley pointed out to them that he had hired them in the first place and told them from the outset that he was the sole songwriter; he would not budge from that position and so they walked out. Feeling betrayed and deserted, Harley put his feelings into song. 'Make Me Smile' had originally been a blues dirge, full of vengeful, finger-pointing, lyrical bile however, for the studio version, the tempo increased, dead-stops and gaps were introduced, "Ooh la la las" were added and Jim Cregan played a fabulous, flamenco-influenced guitar solo. The lyric, though essentially unaltered, was disguised by the effervescence of the new arrangement, and so, from the depths of despair, Harley had his greatest ever triumph.

13
HURRICANE PART 1
HURRICANE PART 2
BOB DYLAN
CBS
DID NOT CHART
As Bob Dylan puts it in this song, "Ruben Carter was falsely tried", and throughout the rest of the track he tells the story of Ruben 'Hurricane' Carter's plight as he was arrested, tried and convicted for a double murder that he plainly did not commit. Carter was a contender

for the Middleweight world boxing title and he was framed, quite simply, because he was black, successful and didn't behave in a suitably humble manner which irked the white authorities who set out, and succeeded, to put him behind bars. Dylan had not written a protest song for many years and so 'Hurricane' came as something of a surprise. This was a hugely 'wordy' piece, and yet the infectious rhythm provided by Rob Rothstein's supple bass playing and the vivacity of Scarlet Rivera's frantically-played violin fills keep the track from ever lagging, as they support Dylan's word-flow, delivered with incredulous disgust at the justice system. Ruben Carter was certainly no saint; he had proven convictions of violence against his name... but he was innocent of the murders he was imprisoned for. He was finally freed in 1988 and all charges against him were dropped. Until his death in 2014, he worked as Executive Director of the Association in Defence of the Wrongly Convicted.

12
SHAME SHAME SHAME
MORE SHAME
SHIRLEY AND COMPANY
VIBRATION
6
This was written and concocted by the increasingly influential Sylvia Robinson but sung by Shirley Goodman who, as one half of Shirley and Lee, had last had a hit in 1956 with 'Let the Good Times Roll'. 'Shame Shame Shame' is built on a variant of the Bo Diddley beat, but discofied by the prominent hi-hat percussion and scratchy guitar, as well as the soulful vocal interplay between Shirley Goodman and the wild-voiced Jesus Alvarez. There's also a lyrical nod to William DeVaughn's 'Be Thankful For What You've Got' and a killer saxophone solo too. John Lennon proclaimed it as his favourite single which showed that, at the very least, the ex-Beatle still maintained his good taste.

11
LOVE IS THE DRUG
SULTANESQUE
ROXY MUSIC
ISLAND
2
This is the least cerebral, but the most accessible Roxy Music single. 'Love Is the Drug' is a joyous disco-romp where the bass-line, played by John Gustafson, carries the song in a slinky, hip-shaking direction out onto the dance floor, where Bryan Ferry re-enacts the mating ritual of the masses in his own inimitable style – "Face to face, toe to toe, heart to heart as we hit the floor", as he puts it both concisely and elegantly. Make no mistake, this is Roxy Music playing it funky; but of course, with the approach taken by Messrs MacKay, Manzanera, Thompson, Jobson and the aforementioned Gustafson, the way they use their instruments, it is funk played through the prism of European art-rock. With this release they finally got themselves a hit in the previously Roxy-resistant USA, where, in New York, listening very closely were Bernard Edwards and Nile Rogers, as they finalised the blueprint laid out for their new band, Chic, who would later be described as a black version of Roxy Music.

10

I'M NOT IN LOVE
GOOD NEWS
10CC
MERCURY
1

Working on tracks for their *Original Soundtrack* album, 10cc recorded a song written by Eric Stewart and Graham Gouldman called 'I'm Not In Love'. Using orthodox instrumentation and playing in a Bossa-nova style, a demo of the song was produced; at this point Kevin Godley and Lol Creme voiced their dissatisfaction. Godley was especially opposed describing it as "crap" and suggesting that they "chuck it". For a while they did just that as the band continued to work on other tunes but Stewart felt that the song could be salvaged and appealed to Godley to give it another chance. Godley agreed but only on the condition that they try an extremely radical approach and record without instruments and use voices only. They built-up layer by layer, recording each of their voices multiple times until they had a virtual choir, 48 members strong. Then they wished to keep the voice-track going for an extended length of time, so Creme suggested they use tape loops to achieve this. Doing all that in a pre-digital age was very laborious and arduous yet they persisted until, at the end of the process, they could form voice-chords to create accompaniment for the entire song; the effect was stunning… ethereal in fact.

The recording was completed with the addition of very subtle and minimal instrumentation – electric piano, guitar, a soft, synthesised heartbeat effect and a double-tracked toy music-box for the middle-eight. Eric Stewart sang the lead vocal with Creme and Godley doing harmonies. The lyric was quite brilliant and it concerned a man denying that he is in love but describing the day-to-day things in his life that make a mockery of the assertion. The final missing piece of this musical jigsaw was the insertion of the unconnected phrase "Be quiet, big boys don't cry" voiced in a whisper by reluctant studio receptionist Kathy Redfern.

At last it was done, and it was a masterpiece…

9

YOUNG AMERICANS
SUFFRAGETTE CITY
DAVID BOWIE
RCA
18

Bowie himself dubbed it "plastic soul", a pretty accurate description for a music that has all the trappings of authenticity, but no wish to *be* authentic, because it is, in reality, something very different, something dark and vampiric. Bowie was simply sucking all the goodness out of this musical genre in order to recycle and use it in a way that is, in part, a sincere and loving homage, but equally a sacrificial offering on a pagan altar; he saw soul music just as he saw rock – a means to an end and a corridor from one room to another. Bowie was clearly in a dark place at this time, and we are taken along with him on a strange ride as he displays, in full neon effect, vision after vision that reveals the sourness of the American dream. He sings spookily in a hammy, soulman voice, as if possessed simultaneously by the spirits of Jackie Wilson and Etta James. The backing vocalists, coached by Luther Vandross, deliver gospel-like support as Bowie executes his vocal tightrope-walk, referencing Watergate, McCarthyism, Barbie dolls, Cadillacs and Rosa Parks. All these images are drip-fed into the kaleidoscopic musical showreel that is the disturbing, but quite amazing, 'Young Americans'.

8

JOHANNESBURG
FELL TOGETHER
GIL SCOTT-HERON
ARISTA
DID NOT CHART

Robinson's Records was a dusty, giant-sized musical emporium, just over Blackfriars Bridge in Salford. It had racks and racks of records in no particular order, separated neither alphabetically or along genre lines; it could be a gruelling trawl if you didn't turn-up any gems (as was often the case) so even as an avid record collector I tended to give the place a wide-berth. Still, one autumnal Saturday afternoon in 1976 I found myself sifting through that shop's stock for several hours; I struck lucky – I picked up two Jackie Wilson and Count Basie singles and one by Gil Scott-Heron. The latter was a record I'd not heard before, but even in 1976 the 25p price tag was not off-putting. What I had bought was 'Johannesburg', an attack on South Africa's evil system of apartheid; but what it gave to me was an urgent prompt to investigate for myself what was happening out there, and to ask myself the question 'How do I like it?' The answer soon became clear: I didn't like it at all. In fact, I was incandescent with rage to discover what was going on, worst of all it went largely uncriticised and unreported in the UK. To the core of my soul, I despised and opposed that hateful system.

Gil Scott-Heron, along with Brian Jackson and The Midnight Band, had drawn my attention to the plight of people under this pernicious regime, and I found my feelings very much echoed in the lyrics "I hate it when the blood starts flowing, but I'm glad to see resistance growing". This proved to be a crucial record for me; it informed the way I looked out upon the world. In 1977 Steve Biko, a black South African student leader, was murdered by the authorities. This heinous act drew down a barrage of criticism upon the regime, although even into the 1980s American President Ronald Reagan was declaring the Nelson Mandela-led ANC to be a terrorist organisation, and he was supported in his assertion by Margaret Thatcher's racist Conservative Party. Pressure had to be exerted by artistic and sporting bodies rather than governments, and so increasingly artists spoke out against this evil… "You can blow out a candle, but you can't blow out a fire," sang Peter Gabriel as resistance grew. But for me, the lines that still resonated the most came from Scott-Heron himself, as he sang "What's happening in Johannesburg? Freedom ain't nothing but a word, in Johannesburg. What's the word? Johannesburg!"

7

LITTLE JOHNNY JEWEL PART ONE
LITTLE JOHNNY JEWEL PART TWO
TELEVISION
ORK
DID NOT CHART

Something was stirring in New York; it was whispered about, alluded to... something new and special emerging from the underground – the only problem was the total lack of evidence that any of these rumours were true. And then suddenly there was... 'Little Johnny Jewel' was released and it had no antecedents; it wasn't like the Velvets, Stooges or the Dolls as we had been led to believe. What we were presented with was spidery guitars, a rigid, unfunky rhythm-section and a weedy-voiced singer. They made a recognisable sound, but somehow things were all jumbled-up, as if a new language was in the process of being developed. The lyrics were poetic, but more in a William Blake, rather than a Bob Dylan style; they spoke of a man who could just "be", a man with no decisions to make, an alien in the modern world, a man out of time. This was pop-existentialism, it was rock-jazz, deeply enigmatic, cloaked in mystery and it was brilliant. Something was indeed happening in New York...

NB: Guitar player Richard Lloyd was so unimpressed with this record – feeling that something much more commercial should have been recorded – that he briefly left the band. He was replaced, equally briefly, by Peter Laughner who had quit Pere Ubu and Cleveland to try his luck in New York City. Laughner would very sadly die of pancreatic disease in 1977.

6

TANGLED UP IN BLUE
IF YOU SEE HER, SAY HELLO
BOB DYLAN
COLUMBIA
DID NOT CHART

A series of shifting images, time-lines defied, multiple perspectives on a blurred narrative, 'Tangled Up In Blue' was Dylan at his most secretive and vague, creating a haunting, beautiful and enigmatic song that only he could truly understand, that only he could truly explain; not that he ever would of course. Relationships are begun and swiftly abandoned, locations change in the blink of an eye, there is tenderness and there is pain in a jigsaw of fragmented pieces of memory – 'Tangled Up In Blue' is an album's worth of ideas within a five minute song. Dylan had certainly been no slouch in the intervening years, but this easily stood-out as his finest single since 'Like a Rolling Stone'.

5

ROADRUNNER
IT WILL STAND
JONATHAN RICHMAN
UNITED ARTISTS/BESERKLEY
DID NOT CHART
(Number 11 on re-release in 1977)

Velvet Underground obsessive Jonathan Richman first recorded this two-chord homage to that band's 'Sister Ray' with ex-Velvets member John Cale producing. This was followed by another version recorded with LA scenester Kim Fowley, and then a third effort produced by Beserkley Records boss Matthew King Kaufman. Each take had different lengths, slightly altered lyrics and modified instrumentation; Cale's version, made with Richman's band The Modern Lovers, was high-voltage, punk-energised and thrilling. This single version is played acoustically; it is ramshackle, charming and still absolutely thrilling. 'Roadrunner' is a driving song in which Jonathan cruises down route 28 looking at the power lines and pine trees; he is awed by their beauty and all the time he has "the radio on" which connects him to the modern world and makes him feel alive – it is both simple and extremely strange.

When John Peel played it on his radio show, my brother and I were struck dumb by the sheer audacious genius of the thing… by the mid-point of the record we were hypnotically singing along – "Radio on! Radio on!" Obviously we needed to hear more, and so, via Richard Branson's mail-order service, we secured a coveted import copy of *The Modern Lovers* LP for a rather hefty price. Happily, from start to finish, it comprised of genius songs that spoke immediately and directly to us. Thank you Jonathan for 'Roadrunner' – you made me feel happy and not quite so alone.

4

GOLDEN YEARS
CAN YOU HEAR ME?
DAVID BOWIE
RCA
8

There is a subtle and restrained grandeur about 'Golden Years', seemingly deliberate so as not to disturb its cool gracefulness… a statement of love viewed nostalgically through a lens. 'Golden Years' is a logical progression from 'Young Americans'; still recognisably based on black soul and funk, but much less overtly – there is a detachment from the form which allows room for manoeuvre and experimentation. The percussion track alone is a work of art, unobtrusive but endlessly inventive, and Bowie's vocal is a faultless masterclass in expressiveness. The song was offered to RCA labelmate Elvis Presley whose manager, Colonel Tom Parker, thought that Bowie should write something for his boy; Bowie was delighted and spoke of his adoration for Presley. Although, as it turned out, no collaboration ever took place, Presley did write a note to Bowie which said "All the best, and have a great tour"; this piece of paper was kept and treasured by the Englishman, right up until his own untimely death.

3

TAKE ME TO THE RIVER
COULD I BE FALLING IN LOVE
SYL JOHNSON
HI
DID NOT CHART

For some inexplicable reason, Hi Records chose not to release Al Green's self-composed song 'Take Me To The River' as a single, even though it had been the stand-out track on his superb album *Al Green Explores Your Mind*. The song examined the emotional landscape that hovers somewhere between the sacred and the earthly; it was not just fascinating as a revealing glimpse inside the author's head, but it really swung and grooved as well. Instead the song was handed to label-mate Syl Johnson, whose career had stagnated in the shadow of Green's success. Johnson had written and recorded the classic 'Is It Because I'm Black' in 1969, a record of huge power – speaking out against discrimination, its message was hard-hitting and plain-spoken. He was also much closer to the blues than the gospel-schooled Al Green, as well as being a mighty harmonica player. In any event, with the same producer in the chair (Willie Mitchell) and the same pool of musicians playing on the track, there are, of course, many similarities between the two versions, but Syl Johnson notably drops the spoken intro of the original and instead launches the song with a harmonica lick. The tempo is slightly quickened, the horns a tad punchier and Johnson sings in a more gritty, but no less impassioned style than Green, on what is undoubtedly one of the greatest soul records of all time.

2

30 SECONDS OVER TOKYO
HEART OF DARKNESS
PERE UBU
HEARTHAN
DID NOT CHART

Cleveland, Ohio? Where is that? I can't have been alone in my ignorance of American geography; in any case, I was soon checking a map after hearing Pere Ubu. '30 Seconds Over Tokyo' was their debut single written by leader David Thomas. Peter Laughner and Gene O'Connor, when Thomas and Laughner were still members of their previous band Rocket From the Tombs, and the song took its title from a film starring Spencer Tracy about the 1942 Doolittle air-raid by the USA on Tokyo. It is written in straight narrative style from the point of view of a pilot and reveals his emotional response to events that he is part of; on the one hand these seem to be a fantasy as he observes from the air and sees "toy city streets crawling through my sights, sprouting clumps of mushrooms in a world surreal", but on the other hand they are terrifyingly real – "no place to run, no place to hide, no turning back on a suicide ride". Thomas, credited as 'Crocus Behemoth', vocalises with frightening intensity; guitarist

Peter Laughner pulls harsh metallic noises from the guts of his instrument and synth player Allen Ravenstine provides a chilly wave of sound that ratchets the tension ever higher.

1

NO WOMAN NO CRY
KINKY REGGAE
BOB MARLEY AND THE WAILERS
ISLAND
22

'No Woman No Cry', a track on the 1974 Bob Marley and the Wailers album *Natty Dread*, was already recognised as a gem when, in July 1975, London's Lyceum Theatre hosted the band playing live for two consecutive nights; it was the hottest ticket in town. Marley had not had any hit records, his music was not played on the radio, his image was not ubiquitous, but his audience here in the UK had grown and for those with open ears and minds, he was already a star – the sheer quality of the music meant that Marley was already held in the same high regard as the likes of Stevie Wonder, Bob Dylan and John Lennon. Island Records head-honcho, Chris Blackwell, had arranged for The Rolling Stones' mobile recording unit to be in place at the Lyceum, and what it captured there was sublime... in particular the special alchemy between performers and audience.

Bob and the Wailers were pushed to a peak of performance by the crackling atmosphere; they rode a tidal wave of love and appreciation, and somehow this was translated onto tape. The resultant album, *Live,* was beyond compare and rightly hailed as an instant classic. 'No Woman No Cry' was released as a single and was impossible to ignore; it was play-listed by the radio stations and Marley finally achieved a small, but significant hit – for many people this was their first exposure to one of the most important musical voices of the 20th century. This particular version of 'No Woman No Cry' feels like a hymn; people commune and the voices of the audience are just as important as those on stage as they come together to sing "Everything's gonna be alright". It is also a spiritual folk song played reggae-style; the message is that no matter how tough life gets, love and sharing can overcome problems.

The song is nostalgic but unsentimental, and Bob speaks about real people. He remembers sitting in Tartar's tenement yard ("Tartar" being Vincent Ford, a man crippled by diabetes as a child, who had both legs amputated). Ford had overcome this severe handicap and he ran a soup kitchen for the deprived; he had befriended the young and destitute Marley, putting a roof over his head and food in his belly. Marley very touchingly gave the song-writing credit of 'No Woman No Cry' to Vincent Ford by way of a thank you. He speaks also of "Georgie" making the fire light – "Georgie" being George Headley Robinson, an older Rastafarian fisherman who would collect brushwood to build a fire as Bob and he discussed their faith throughout the night. In the morning, Robinson would cook up porridge for the hungry singer, whose principles and world-view were formed not just from the hardship endured, but also by the kindness and generosity shown to him by the good people he met. 'No Woman No Cry' was the sound of reality… but, just as importantly, it was also the sound of positivity. The song powerfully conveyed a message of love and hope, and it was a record of genius that has since touched many millions of people's souls.

1976

NOTABLE EVENTS

- Concorde makes its first commercial flight
- Harold Wilson resigns as Prime Minister; he is replaced by Jim Callaghan
- An Argentine military coup sees General Jorge Videla depose President Isabel Perón
- Body Shop opens its first store in Brighton
- Apple Computer Company is formed by Steve Jobs and Steve Wozniak
- The Soweto uprising begins in opposition to the system of apartheid which operates in South Africa
- Jeremy Thorpe, who is alleged to have attempted to have his former lover Norman Scott murdered, is replaced as leader of the Liberal Party by David Steel
- The "Son of Sam" murders begin in New York
- The Tangshan earthquake in China kills 242,769 people and injures a further 164,851
- *The Muppet Show* is screened for the first time
- Jimmy Carter becomes US President defeating Gerald Ford at the election
- Sex Pistols appear on a regional television programme hosted by Bill Grundy; the following day's *Daily Mirror* headline "The Filth and the Fury" propels them to notoriety the very next day
- Bob Marley and his manager Don Taylor are shot and wounded in an assassination attempt in Kingston, Jamaica
- Manchester United lose the FA Cup final to Second Division Southampton, Liverpool win the league title. Czech midfielder Antonin Panenka coolly chips the winning penalty to defeat West Germany and win the European Championships and in doing so immortalises himself

NOTABLE BIRTHS

Clarence Seedorf; Patrick Viera; Ruud Van Nistelrooy; Cristiano Ronaldo; Ryan Reynolds; Cillian Murphy; Benedict Cumberbatch

NOTABLE DEATHS

Howlin' Wolf; Agatha Christie; Paul Robeson; Sal Mineo; Florence Ballard; L.S. Lowry; Busby Berkeley; Luciano Visconti; Paul Kossoff; Howard Hughes; Ulrike Meinhof; Keith Relf; Fritz Lang; Jimmy Reed; Dalton Trumbo; Mao Zedong; Man Ray; Benjamin Britten

NOTABLE FILMS

The Omen; Carrie; All the President's Men; Marathon Man; Network; Taxi Driver; Rocky; The Outlaw Josey Wales; The Missouri Breaks; The Man Who Fell to Earth; Assault on Precinct 13

NOTABLE BOOKS

Roots – Alex Haley
The Boys From Brazil – Ira Levin
The Human Factor – Graham Greene
Kiss of The Spiderwoman – Manuel Puig
Slapstick, or Lonesome No More! – Kurt Vonnegut
The Fall and Rise of Reginald Perrin – David Nobbs
Coming Through Slaughter – Michael Ondaatje
Christopher and His Kind – Christopher Isherwood
Mother Ireland – Edna O Brian
In the Heart Of the Country – J.M. Coetzee

THE MUSIC

They didn't know it at the time, because they felt absolutely secure in their ivory towers, but the grown-up, "we know best" guardians of the music industry were about to be overthrown by upstart usurpers. On the face of it, all the strings were being pulled by be-suited, high-powered music executives who were sat in the comfortably furnished boardrooms of major record companies; but a new generation of street-level music lovers were sick to the back teeth of having terrible, predictable and dull music foisted upon them – and whether by design or not, they were instigating change by operating outside the system. If you were a teenager, you did not want to listen to the Bellamy Brothers or the Starland Vocal Band… or even look at them for that matter; and Brotherhood of Man did not exactly set the pulse racing either. The older generation of musicians such as The Who and The Rolling Stones, were undeniably past their best; Yes had released an album called *Tales From Topographic Oceans* which was so bloated and pretentious, that, although it sold millions, it was only listened to and endured once by any sane person. Black youth had their own soundtrack, the increasingly militant and socially-conscious sound of reggae, and disaffected white kids now wanted a music that spoke directly to their life experience.

Change in the UK had to come, and so the rootsy, but backward-looking pub-rock scene was superseded by a punk rock explosion, spearheaded by the Sex Pistols. For a brief period punk appeared to be a genuine threat to the system; in sound, look and attitude – for each of these three elements there was a real sense of freshness in the new and highly-confrontational approach. Of course, in the not too distant future, the system – in the form of major record labels – would rally together in attempt to co-opt the punks into a herd-like orthodoxy, turning them into just another product stream, but in these dizzying early days, as defences were being breached and foundations shaken, the establishment and the associated air of laid-back coolness, were caught off guard by the wind of change and left reeling in uncomprehending panic.

In the US the new bands faced a much more difficult task in shaking things up because the sheer size of the country worked against them; so, for example, The Ramones meant precisely zilch in Kansas or Milwaukee, even though they were stars of the New York scene based around CBGBs, a grotty dive on the Bowery. In America the punk scene would remain underground for several years to come, instead it was disco music that instigated change by attracting a mass audience consisting of a coalition of underdogs: the poor, blacks, latinos and gays who shared the experience of persecution everywhere else but found a home, and a voice, beneath the glitter balls of the disco clubs. Reggae, punk and disco were all kicking against the status quo, and whilst they did not, by any means, sweep away all of the establishment figures, they effected enough change to create cracks in the walls of a previously secure system, the arbiters of taste had been bypassed and through these cracks talented and creative new forces would creep, and have their voices heard for the very first time.

My 1976

I bought my first car, a 1963 Ford Anglia. I had no driving licence, no insurance, no tax and little knowledge of *The Highway Code*, but with these wheels I had a degree of freedom and could head off on a whim if I so chose. I felt change was coming and I looked for it constantly; I felt that whatever this indefinable thing would turn out to be, it was going to give my life a sense of purpose. Patti Smith and Dr Feelgood had captured something of what it was I was looking for, without quite being the real deal. I began to read about a group in London called Sex Pistols who were getting small and infrequent mentions in the music press. I gathered that they played a version of the Stooges song 'No Fun'; this was interesting because I knew of nobody outside my household who had ever even heard of 'No Fun', but these young musicians evidently not only knew the song, but related to it sufficiently to learn how to play and perform it.

In early June Sex Pistols performed at the hitherto unknown to me Lesser Free Trade Hall in Manchester. I was one of 28 people who bought a ticket and went to see them. It is no exaggeration to say that they changed my life and changed my perception of what could be done with music, and this in turn made me reassess my whole existence and thought processes. A week later I went to see The Who perform in Swansea; they played very well, played all their great songs and were rapturously received by a huge crowd yet somehow I was unmoved – I knew now that they were old hat... finished. I saw Sex Pistols once again in July and then twice more in December, accompanied by The Heartbreakers, The Clash and Buzzcocks. At this point I instinctively realised that I should form a band... but I didn't. There was nobody whose mind was similarly attuned; I decided I would rather wait until I had the right people, instead of compromising and being part of a band that I didn't believe in...

100
COCAINE
HEY BABY
JJ CALE
SHELTER
DID NOT CHART

In 1965 JJ Cale was a struggling musician looking for a foothold; he cut a demo-version of one of his songs – 'After Midnight' – but when this failed to attract any attention, he decided to quit music. Fast forward to 1970 and it was pointed out to him that Eric Clapton had covered the song on his first solo record. From the interest created by this endorsement, Cale secured a recording contract and returned to music. 'Cocaine' is a perfect example of his musical style, characterised by its deceptive subtlety; Cale sounds relaxed and laid back, his voice whisper-thin, his guitar playing a masterclass of economy... he doesn't hit many notes but he hits all the right ones. Neil Young, a unique guitar-stylist himself, once described JJ Cale as one of his two favourite guitarists, along with Jimi Hendrix – praise indeed! The lyric to 'Cocaine' is also the epitome of subtlety; if listened to on only a superficial level, it may sound ambiguous, or even be interpreted as a paean to the drug. However, closer examination reveals that it details the drugs pernicious nature and the lyric is, in fact, firmly anti-cocaine. Eric Clapton covered this song too, and his more mainstream effort yielded a hit for a great song that fully deserved recognition.

99
CITY LIGHTS
ST AMIE
DAVID ESSEX
CBS
24

Prominently featuring The Real Thing as backing vocalists, this is a piece of surrealistic funk masquerading as orthodox pop; it is 'Shaft' or 'Superfly' transported to London. With the ominous synths, jazz saxophone, heavy bass and swirling strings in a claustrophobic mix, the soundscape of 'City Lights' is a world away from the sparse neo-dub of Essex's early hits. This is giant-sized and it throws giant shadows, evoking the skyscrapers, speeding taxi cabs and, of course, the neon lights of the West End – 'City Lights' was the last great David Essex single. After this, presumably utterly perplexed and depressed by the lack of recognition from the music press, where on the totem pole of success he found himself looking upwards at the likes of Gary Glitter, Mud and Peter Frampton, he headed for safe, middle-of-the-road blandness. The horrific Andrew Lloyd Webber songs and 'Silver Dream Machines' were just around the corner...

98
CHELSEA KIDS
JACKIE THE LAD
HEAVY METAL KIDS
RAK
DID NOT CHART

This band named themselves after the street-gang in William Burroughs' novel *Nova Express*, which demonstrated fine taste and therefore piqued my interest. I got to see Heavy Metal Kids play as support act to Alice Cooper and found them to be highly entertaining as a live spectacle, mostly thanks to the charisma of front man Gary Holton who projected a deranged persona. The trouble was that the rest of the band looked, and played, as if they would rather be in some tedious hard-rock group – and indeed a pair of them did leave to join UFO and Uriah Heep respectively. Here, sensing what was coming, the hard-rock is played down and the brat angle is played up as they allude to amphetamine usage – "Wide-eyed sniffin', boys sniffin'", they chirrup like chorus-boys from Oliver! It has to be said that 'Chelsea Kids' was a rousing ditty and quite a lot of fun, but as a punk precursor (as it is sometimes described) this was closer to drama-school role-play than authentically insurrectionist.

97

A FIFTH OF BEETHOVEN
CALIFORNIA STRUT
WALTER MURPHY AND THE BIG APPLE BAND
PRIVATE STOCK
28

Walter Murphy was a classical music conductor who had an interest in pop – particularly pop that incorporated classical themes… 'A Lover's Concerto' by the Toys being a good example. He put together 'A Fifth of Beethoven', a disco treatment of the first movement from Beethoven's Symphony No. 5, and then he shopped the recording around to several record companies. Private Stock gave him a deal and issued the track, but they insisted that it be credited to the fictitious Big Apple Band, feeling that it stood much more chance of selling if the public believed it had been played by a group rather than just one man.

Wishing to avoid any accusation of understatement, I must nevertheless point out that 'A Fifth of Beethoven' is obviously a very good tune; in any case, it connected with the Zeitgeist and was a hit. Shortly afterwards, it was used as part of the Saturday Night Fever soundtrack, and for that reason this record has subsequently achieved disco immortality.

96

HEAVY MANNERS
HEAVY DISCIPLINE (Credited to the Mighty Two)
PRINCE FAR I
HEAVY DUTY
DID NOT CHART

A state of emergency had been declared by the Jamaican Government, restricting the freedoms of the people; in street-speak, it was known as living under 'Heavy Manners'. This recording was made with Errol Thompson and Joe Gibbs at the controls, and they produce a rocking rhythm over Naggo Morris's track 'Su Su Pon Rasta', whereupon Prince Far I proceeds to hold court as he philosophises – in 'stream of consciousness' style – about the state of the nation and the wider world, half-speaking and half-singing; "One of the noblest things a man can do, is try his best" he booms, in that unmistakable voice of thunder, that spoke of truth and justice.

95

SLIP KID
DREAMING FROM THE WAIST
THE WHO
POLYDOR
DID NOT CHART

The Who were, by this stage, no longer significant. Pete Townshend had lost the plot; their most recent

LP, *The Who by Numbers*, had been an exercise in tedious pontificating. The one exception was 'Slip Kid', yet another song from the abandoned Lifehouse project that had been resurrected to try and disguise the current lack of inspiration. 'Slip Kid' is excellent; there is a lightness of touch about the performance, particularly evident when compared to the lumpen thud that The Who were routinely serving up at that time. The song is a comment on the impossibility of always avoiding responsibility. It was originally written as a warning to young people thinking of entering the music industry, telling them they would be used and corrupted. 'Slip Kid' needn't be viewed through such a narrow prism though; there is a harsh, yet universal truth to its message.

94
BOOGIE ON THE STREET
CARAVAN MAN
LEW LEWIS AND HIS BAND
STIFF
DID NOT CHART

Lew Lewis was brought up on the same Canvey Island street as Dr Feelgood front-man Lee Brilleaux, who taught him how to play harmonica. Lewis was a member of Eddie and the Hotrods but quit due to disagreements with the band's management. Soon he reappeared on the fledgling Stiff label and 'Boogie On the Street' was its fifth release, backed by an uncredited Dr Feelgood. The single is, as one might expect, a harmonica-led blues shuffle in the style of Little Walter; pulled-off with a stylish and confident swagger, this was the highly acceptable face of pub-rock.

93
SHIPS IN THE NIGHT
CRYING TO THE SKY
BE BOP DELUXE
HARVEST
23

Be-Bop Deluxe struggled, in part, because they aspired to be accepted in the progressive rock sphere, but they looked, at least initially, like a bunch of tacky Bowie-clones; first impressions stick and the band's leader Bill Nelson was fuming. They had not been successful and now, on album number three, the record company told Nelson that he needed to come up with a hit single to help promote it. The problem was that Bill Nelson was not a singles kind of guy – in fact he hated singles and thought they were beneath him – but nevertheless he acquiesced and wrote a song to order. What he came up with was 'Ships in the Night', which he didn't like at all; sorry Bill, but I did like it and thought it was one of Be-Bop Deluxe's finest songs. It has a fabulous, spacey, electric piano motif, choppy guitar chords, a bizarre drop into a reggae-ish middle-eight, a coherent and clever lyric about the damage caused by the absence of love, and finally a splendid alto-sax solo. Excellent, job done, everybody happy… all except for Mr Nelson who got furious when people compared the single to Roxy Music or 10cc in a futile attempt to compliment him.

92
THE CHAMPION PART 1
THE CHAMPION PART 2
WILLIE MITCHELL
HI
47

As well as helming Hi Records and

producing the likes of Al Green, Ann Peebles and Syl Johnson, Mr Willie Mitchell had a long-standing career of his own. Specialising in instrumental dance tracks, he had a big sound on the UK Northern Soul scene with 'That Driving Beat', and 'The Champion' matched it by becoming a Wigan Casino classic as well as a bona fide hit. Here we have huge pounding drums (played by Al Jackson Jr from Booker T and the MGs) a stinging guitar part and horns that sound like they herald the charge... the charge onto the dance-floor, that is.

91
SPINNING ROCK BOOGIE
DON'T MESS WITH MY
DUCKTAIL
HANK C BURNETTE
SONET
21
Hank C Burnette was born Sven-Åke Högberg in the little town of Sveg in Sweden. In the late 1950s the tornado that was rock 'n' roll – and in particular Elvis Presley – took him and shook him, leaving the boy forever changed. By 1958 Sven had traded-in his previous musical instrument (the accordion) for a guitar, and aged 13 he began playing rockabilly... and never stopped. Somewhere along the journey he became Hank C Burnette, and when the music he loved came to be regarded as an anachronism, as new sounds came and went, Hank stayed true to his oeuvre and created, in Sweden, new and modern rockabilly sides. 'Spinning Rock Boogie' was a single dating from 1972, but this re-recording gave Burnette a well-deserved hit in 1976. It is greasy, trashy, loud and as vibrant as life

itself; this is the authentic sound of rockabilly transported through time and space, from Memphis in 1956 to Sweden in 1976.

90
X OFFENDER
IN THE SUN
BLONDIE
PRIVATE STOCK
DID NOT CHART
Blondie's first single came and went with little fanfare, causing barely a ripple of interest. This was odd because straight out of the box they sounded full-formed and focused; there is no sense at all of them tentatively feeling their way. 'X Offender' is great subversive punk-pop and one of the finest songs to emerge from CBGB, the club on New York's Bowery that was the proving ground for Television, The Ramones and Talking Heads, as well as Blondie and countless others. The song had originally been titled 'Sex Offender' by composer and bassist Gary Valentine; it was about an 18-year old boy being arrested for having sex with his younger girlfriend. Debbie Harry re-wrote the lyric, putting in a psychological spin by making it the story of an arrested prostitute who falls for the policeman who detained her. Producer Richard Gottehrer, who had a history of working with 1960s girl-groups, imbues the track with that sound and spirit, so when, at the record label's behest, "Sex" became "X", the iconic sound of Blondie was fully-formed and ready to be unleashed upon the world.

89

WE VIBRATE
WHIPS AND FURS
THE VIBRATORS
RAK
DID NOT CHART

As everybody knows the first British punk single was released by The Damned in October 1976, but often forgotten is the fact that, just a few weeks later, The Vibrators issued the second, which was 'We Vibrate' (as it happens, they also released the third as well – 'Pogo Dancing', a collaboration with Chris Spedding). 'We Vibrate' was written by bassist Pat Collier; it is a speedy, exciting romp that is tremendously fun and full of energy, and it showcases guitarist John Ellis's extraordinary prowess. The flip-side, 'Whips and Furs', was penned by front-man Knox Carnochan and it is another tuneful quick-step with sadomasochistic tendencies hinted at in the lyric.

88

DIRTY DEEDS
DONE DIRT CHEAP
R.I.P. (Rock in Peace)
AC/DC
ALBERT PRODUCTIONS
DID NOT CHART
(47 when re-issued 1980)

Informed by the TV viewing habits of the band, this song's title was provided by Angus Young via a television cartoon called Beany and Cecil in which a character called Dishonest John carries a business card that reads 'Dirty Deeds Done Dirt Cheap'. The song itself is a glorious blast of high-adrenaline rock which details the menu of services offered up by an extremely unsavoury individual to anyone willing to pay to extricate themselves from unhappy situations or relationships – "Concrete shoes, cyanide, TNT" are just some of the options customers can select. I saw AC/DC at Manchester's Electric Circus as they promoted this single and even the fact that I managed to set my own trousers on fire during the show didn't diminish my enjoyment at witnessing a great band at their hungry best. 'Dirty Deeds' has a guitar riff to die for and the fun the band were obviously having when performing this song is pleasingly transferred into the grooves of the vinyl. This record was truly a Technicolor tonic to combat the in-vogue brown and beige of mainstream tastes.

87

FOOL TO CRY
CRAZY MAMA
ROLLING STONES
ROLLING STONES RECORDS
6

The Rolling Stones were at something of a crossroads; lead guitarist Mick Taylor had bailed-out and the band were auditioning potential replacements as they recorded. Here American Wayne Perkins, who had contributed his guitar playing to The Wailers' Catch a Fire album, provides some reggae-tinged lead work that is an extra-texture to the soulful groove laid down by Keith Richards, Bill Wyman and Charlie Watts. The melodic base of the song is created by Mick Jagger's electric piano, and acoustic piano played by Nicky Hopkins, who also contributes a synthesiser part. Atop of all this, a bruised and vulnerable sounding Jagger sings softly of the melancholia that is affecting him; he tries to combat this by telling himself how lucky he really is. At this stage in their career, the Stones seemed to have lost the wherewithal to construct a coherent LP, but singles-wise they were still managing to conjure up some gems.

86
WHISPERING/
CHERCHEZ LA FEMME/
SE SI BON
SUNSHOWER
DR BUZZARD'S ORIGINAL
SAVANNAH BAND
RCA
DID NOT CHART
To link the sound of futuristic disco with big swing bands of the Busby Berkeley era was the ambitious modus operandi of Dr Buzzard's Original Savannah Band, and here, on 'Cherchez la Femme', they succeed brilliantly; it is stylish, funky, elegant and intelligent. The band was conceived by brothers Stony Browder Jr and August Darnell, and featured the light and airy voice of Cory Daye. Darnell would, along with Dr Buzzard's percussionist Coati Mundi, go on to form the highly successful Kid Creole and the Coconuts with what was a terrific take, albeit somewhat toned down, on the higher ambitions of the Savannah Band.

85
BIG BOY
FILL-ER-UP
SPARKS
ISLAND
DID NOT CHART
Sparks had moved back to the USA; recording in New York using American musicians, they were given a big, shiny, rock production and the results were generally poor, the power and gloss didn't suit the idiosyncratic songs that were Sparks' calling card. Fortunately the delightful 'Big Boy' was an exception to the rule because it definitely benefits from the muscular sound. The enormous, cavernous drums and power-chord guitar are a conceptual match for a tale of a 'Big Boy' who is looked up to in both the literal sense, and also because he is admired. But he is also feared – "The earth is shaking, so am I" sings Russ Mael at the bully's approach. The 'Big Boy' who "throws his weight around, throws our girls around" is a grotesque caricature worthy of Nikolai Gogol; it was a shame the record buying public chose this moment to abandon his creators.

84
BETWEEN THE LINES
SPOILING FOR A FIGHT
PINK FAIRIES
STIFF
DID NOT CHART
Rowdy psychedelia, acid punk or whatever name one chooses to label this noise from the returning counter-culture misfits, there was no denying the surging energy. Even though 'Between the Lines' is dreadfully recorded – which somehow adds to the charm – it still hits like a tidal wave against a ship's hull; this sounds like a ruckus in an adjacent room and it doesn't abate from start to finish. There is no intro, no middle-eight, no outro… just a slab of bone-jarring rock & roll, with Larry Wallis shouting his vocal and Duncan Sanderson strangling his guitar until it shrieks.

83
RHIANNON (Will You Ever Win)
SUGAR DADDY
FLEETWOOD MAC
REPRISE
46

After a 6-year absence from the UK chart 'Rhiannon' saw the return of Fleetwood Mac, although old fans of the Peter Green version of the band would have been forgiven for not recognising this highly Americanised incarnation. The arrival in their ranks of Stevie Nicks and her soon to be ex-boyfriend, Lindsey Buckingham, re-energised and rejuvenated; they brought with them fresh ideas, excellent songwriting skills and a youthful energy that would transform Fleetwood Mac from the status of has-beens, to that of the world's biggest band. 'Rhiannon' was written and sung by Stevie Nicks, inspired by a book which referenced a Welsh witch who bore that name. Nicks was evidently fascinated by the character and her empathy is obvious as she weaves the tale around a lean and sprightly piano-riff that Buckingham decorates with angular guitar fills; excellent, but a world away from the style that had originally been the Fleetwood Mac calling card.

82
LET'S STICK TOGETHER
SEA BREEZES
BRYAN FERRY
ISLAND
4

'Let's Stick Together' was a song by Wilburt Harrison, released as a single in 1962 to little appreciation. In 1969 Harrison re-worked the song, which had originally been about a close personal relationship, and gave it a more universal and social consciousness theme, as well as re-naming it 'Let's Work Together'. This second attempt was a minor hit for Harrison, but in the hands of Canned Heat it became a huge chart success. Bryan Ferry reverted to the original version and handles it mid-tempo with a horn-riffing introduction, a fantastically cutting saxophone solo courtesy of Chris Mercer, and exuberant squeals from a female backing vocalist, that add more than a touch of carnal excitement. Ferry, of course, is coolness personified and delivers a superbly well-judged vocal. On the flip-side, Ferry continues his excavation of old Roxy Music songs with a delicious re-make of 'Sea Breezes'.

81
MORE MORE MORE
MORE MORE MORE PART 2
ANDREA TRUE CONNECTION
BUDDAH
5

Andrea True was a porn-film actress hired to appear in TV adverts by a group of real estate businessmen in Jamaica. Job done, she found herself a victim of circumstance when the US imposed sanctions on Jamaica after the election of communist leaning Michael Manley; to return home, Andrea would have to either forfeit all of her earnings or spend the whole lot in Jamaica. Being somewhat disillusioned with the porn industry, Andrea now wanted to be a singer, and so she invested her money to make that dream happen; she recruited song-writing record producer Gregg Diamond to travel over to Jamaica to record a demo of 'More More More'. Although lacking a "good voice" in any traditional sense, disco, like punk, was more egalitarian in spirit than previous musical genres, and this meant that Andrea was more than capable of handling the simple lyrics, which, for an out-and-out dance track such as 'More More More', was just another component in the construction of the record, rather than being of prime importance.

80
I BELIEVE IN LOVE
SENSELESSLY CRUEL
LOU REED
ARISTA
DID NOT CHART
Here Lou presented the sweeter side of his nature; 'I Believe in Love' is tuneful, sprightly and optimistic sounding. Although Lou is in fine voice, there are, of course, indications that this is not the work of the most socially adept individual. Even as he sings about believing in "good times" and "good time rock 'n' roll", he can't resist declaring that he also believes in "the iron cross" – and although we don't really believe him, he remains reassuringly nasty and perverse enough to wish to shock and upset us.

79
STAR CHILD
(MOTHERSHIP
CONNECTION)
SUPERGROOVALISTIC-
PROSIFUNKSTICATION
PARLIAMENT
CASABLANCA
DID NOT CHART
Introducing 'Star Child', George Clinton's alter ego from outer space who, just like David Bowie's 'Starman', wants the children to boogie and break the chains of emotional imprisonment. 'Star Child' is a mixture of swinging funk horns and old-style spiritual jive sermonising, and it sees the P-Funk mob emerge from the mothership determined to blow our minds and move our feet.

78
YOU SHOULD BE DANCING
SUBWAY
BEE GEES
RSO
5
'You Should Be Dancing' is the moment when the Bee Gees unleashed their previously only hinted at secret weapon… the incredible falsetto of Barry Gibb. He had sung falsetto for the first time on the song 'Baby As You Turn Away' which had featured on the *Main Course* album; now, 10-months later, it returned on a single honed to perfection. The result was spectacular, irresistible and impressive; the voice was aligned to a wonderfully crafted and joyous dance track, on which every single element was spot-on. The guitars and keyboards practically sing, and the rhythm track – including a Stephen Stills contribution on percussion – is impeccably machine-like and acts as an alluring enticement to hit the dance floor with a vengeance.

77
PERSPECTIVE 1
PERSPECTIVE 4
HELDON
URUS
DID NOT CHART
Perspective 1 is a 10-minute, out-of-body-experience; as the droning and slowly pulsing analogue synthesisers do their work, I close my eyes and feel fully submerged in murky darkness. Some might attach the

"ambient" label to 'Perspective 1'… but this is not music to relax to; rather it chills and puts me in mind of floating, untethered, in endless space, lost and alone with only the certainty of death as some sort of comfort…

76
SOUL SHOES
WHITE HONEY
GRAHAM PARKER AND THE RUMOUR
VERTIGO
DID NOT CHART

I had previously seen Graham Parker performing a support set to some dull muso's at Salford University; he was raw, bristling with passion and had a definite hint of aggression … all rather wonderful! Now here was a single that made me want to jump for joy; this was pocket dynamite and much rawer than pretty much everything else that the major labels were releasing. Even though Parker was working in the same R&B seam that Van Morrison had been mining for years, he sounded fresh and new, somebody I could really relate to. I concluded that 'Soul Shoes' was great; there was a cockiness in the delivery from both band and vocalist and it was captured in full-on "right in your face" sound by the production of Nick Lowe. When Parker sneered "I feel like I've been living just to die, but when that rhythm plays I don't know how to cry", I felt as if he was speaking directly to me and my own sense that only the power of music was keeping me from throwing in the towel. In the same way that I hated the attitudes and opinions of nearly everybody older than me, I also loathed the conservatism that was peddled as a high ideal. I needed excitement – in fact I needed extreme excitement – unreasonable, "I couldn't give a toss" excitement. Graham Parker did not quite fulfil that need… but he was definitely heading in the right direction.

75
HEAVEN MUST BE MISSING AN ANGEL PART 1
HEAVEN MUST BE MISSING AN ANGEL PART 2
TAVARES
CAPITOL
4

Tavares had been performing as a soul/R&B act since the late 1950s, originally under the name The Turnpikes, and past members included future P-Funk keyboard wizard Bernie Worrell, and future Aerosmith drummer Joey Kramer. They had a classy and smooth style that had begun to yield hits when they covered the Hall and Oates song 'She's Gone' in 1973; now, as the disco movement was gathering pace, they moved seamlessly into this new genre. Freddie Perren, who as a Motown backroom man had guided The Jackson 5, as well as writing 'Love Machine' for The Miracles and 'I Will Survive' for Gloria Gaynor, now began to collaborate with Tavares, and he wrote and produced 'Heaven Must be Missing An Angel' which was handled with incredible panache by the band. This is what jubilation sounds like; the lead vocal is in ecstasy and the backing vocals from the brothers blend sweetly as the music moves between incessant disco beats and mellow, melodious breaks.

74
LEAVING HERE
WHITE LINE FEVER
MOTÖRHEAD
STIFF
DID NOT CHART

'Leaving Here' was a song written by the legendary Motown writing team of Holland-Dozier-Holland and it was issued as a single by Eddie Holland himself. Then The Birds (an English band featuring a young Ronnie Wood) covered it for a single in 1965. Ex-Hawkwind man Lemmy was a big fan of The Birds and so the song was chosen as the debut single by his new band Motörhead. Lemmy was still signed to Hawkwind's record label United Artists, but completely ignoring that fact, he struck a deal with Jake Riviera of Stiff Records for the release. The track was recorded in typically bone-rattling style by the three-piece Motörhead lineup, in which "Philthy Animal" Taylor and "Fast" Eddie Clark joined Lemmy with absolutely everything turned up to maximum volume. They created a fabulous racket, but barely had one copy of 'Leaving Here' actually left Stiff HQ when United Artists got wind of what was happening and demanded distribution of the single cease immediately.

73
YOU NEARLY DID ME IN
LETTER TO BRITANNIA
FROM THE UNION JACK
IAN HUNTER
CBS
DID NOT CHART

"You Nearly Did Me In" is a fine single; it prominently features a jazzy saxophone alongside the rolling piano style that Hunter was adept at utilising for his quieter, more reflective material. This is a something of a slow burner – dealing as it does with the emotional fall-out at the end of a relationship – but as the choruses approach it shifts gear and the entry of a female choir signals a lift in intensity, before Hunter is joined by the unmistakable sound of Queen on backing vocals, as the sax wails and the anguish reaches a fever pitch.

72
WRITING ON THE WALL
CRUISIN' (IN THE LINCOLN)
EDDIE AND THE HOT RODS
ISLAND
DID NOT CHART

Eddie and the Hot Rods were a young R&B band from Southend who moved up to London and secured themselves a residency at a pub called The Kensington, playing with another R&B band called the 101ers. They played loud and fast and there was very quickly a buzz about them. The music press seemed to salivate over the band hailing them as "the new thing" – which, of course, they never were – and soon enough they were signed by Island Records and out came this debut single. On it they sound like a slightly younger, a slightly rawer and a slightly inferior version of Dr Feelgood, but in the context of the time that was no bad thing. The record was urgent and energetic with Lew Lewis's harmonica high-up in the mix. The downside was that despite the speedy charm and adrenaline rush, 'Writing on the Wall' was, at best, a functional rather than inspiring song, and singer Barrie Masters sang in a fake American accent. The Hot Rods would soon be exposed and called-out as "punk phoneys" by Sex Pistols, even though, to be fair, they had never identified themselves as having anything to do with punk. Their champions in the press dropped them like hot potatoes, frightened that were they to be associated with the pariahs, they themselves would be tainted with the "un-punk" slur as the winds of cultural change swept across the land. There was still optimism in the Hot Rods camp, and some success did lie ahead – but by the end of the year they would look hopelessly passé and old-fashioned.

71
MPLA
MPLA VERSION
TAPPER ZUKIE
KLIK
DID NOT CHART
The troublesome Tapper Zukie had fallen out with his musical mentor Bunny Lee but in an act of reconciliation Lee armed him with rhythms and arranged for a session in King Tubby's studio. Over a rhythm by The Revolutionaries – a version of Little Richard's 'Freedom Blues' – Tapper cooked up this tribute to the Angolan MPLA who had, in 1975, freed themselves from Portuguese colonial rule. Star on the rise Patti Smith was so smitten with this record that she took Tapper Zukie out on tour as her support act, thus introducing his music to an international audience.

70
SILVER CLOUD
LA DÜSSELDORF
LA DÜSSELDORF
TELDEC
DID NOT CHART
Following the disbandment of Neu, Klaus Dinger began work on material for La Düsseldorf, a band he had

formed with his brother Thomas and Hans Lampe. Conny Plank produces this debut single and, as usual, he does it impeccably. 'Silver Cloud' is an instrumental which flows steadily along, but there are dramatic changes of mood throughout as we go from pastoral passages to sections of dark, brutal guitar noise. In short, this superb single takes us on a thrilling journey and sound is the mode of transport; it was highly regarded by the likes of Brian Eno and David Bowie – the latter even went so far as to describe the music of La Düsseldorf as the sound of the 1980s.

69
SAY YOU LOVE ME
MONDAY MORNING
FLEETWOOD MAC
REPRISE
40
Written by keyboardist Christine McVie, 'Say You Love Me' is one of those uplifting songs that somehow defy analysis. There is nothing particularly original about the structure or arrangement; it is a fairly straightforward, piano-led love song that moves along at quite a jaunty pace, and it is enhanced enormously by McVie's magnificent bluesy voice, which always carried the stamp of authenticity because her inherent English intonation was never changed or tampered with.

68
FALLING IN LOVE AGAIN
EVERYONE KNOWS THE SONG
KEVIN AYERS
ISLAND
DID NOT CHART
The Marlene Dietrich anthem 'Falling in Love Again' fitted Kevin

Ayers like a glove. I remember watching him perform the song at Manchester's Free Trade Hall, to great acclaim from the gathering of the faithful few that made up the small audience. However, on that occasion Kevin had re-purposed the tune as 'Falling Asleep Again', and he sang it in highly exaggerated, soporific style. It was such a delight, therefore I was an eager purchaser when this single slipped-out, unheralded and unnoticed, as his last release for Island Records. Transported musically to some tropical idyll, Ayers croons in a distracted but attractive manner, quite possibly sipping fine wine between verses, before eventually ambling away, seemingly bored by it all, in order just to soak up the sunshine.

67
ENJOY YOURSELF
STYLE OF LIFE
THE JACKSONS
PHILADELPHIA INTERNATIONAL
42
The hits had dried up for The Jackson 5; they didn't like the material Motown was giving them to record and they were reduced to playing in front of cabaret crowds. The final straw came when they realised just how small a royalty-rate they were receiving. The whole group, apart from Jermaine, decided to quit Motown and join-up instead with the new number 1 soul label, Philadelphia International. They were unable to call themselves The Jackson 5, because the rights to that name were owned by Motown, so they opted for the more succinct The Jacksons. Their first single was 'Enjoy Yourself', produced and written (with the considerable help of uncredited

MFSB guitarist TJ Tindall) by the ubiquitous Gamble and Huff. This was something of a half-way house for The Jacksons, and wisely the sophisticated, string-laden sound that is associated with Philadelphia soul was not utilised. Instead, the skeletal guitar riff dominates in a manner similar to the 1960s southern funk records of The Meters. Horns are used rather sparingly and the lead vocals are handled with aplomb by Michael and Jackie Jackson, who sound joyous and exuberant. There were still a few bumps in the road to come, but the rise of the Jacksons, and particularly Michael, as major artistic forces had begun anew.

66
WONDERING
MEURGLYS III
VAN DER GRAAF GENERATOR
CHARISMA
DID NOT CHART
Heroically individualistic and, by this point, completely out of step with prevailing trends, VDGG excised all frippery in an attempt at achieving some kind of commercial cohesion. Despite the grandiosity of Hugh Banton's keyboards, magnificent and cathedral-like in their imposing hugeness, the overall sound became leaner. Then, of course, there is Peter Hammill's near operatic vocal delivery, which terrified casual listeners due to its piercing, ice-pick sharpness, though here there is a hint of uncertainty introduced too, which only adds to the sense of darkening, Gothic dread. 'Wondering' is a hymn-like rumination on the pain of self doubt, which turns into hope that a degree of peaceful closure can be reached. Unsurprisingly, its

commercial aims were unrealised, but the very fact of its existence made the world an infinitely more interesting and a slightly better place.

65
HOT WIRE MY HEART/
BABY YOU'RE SO REPULSIVE
CRIME
CRIME MUSIC
DID NOT CHART

Hailing from San Francisco, with this double A-sided release Crime became the first band from America's West Coast to release a punk single; very good it is too, and notable for the fact that it doesn't conform to the 100mph approach that would become the defining sound of so many copycat acts. Having said that, Crime were undoubtedly noisy – their basic sound is a low rumble from the bass and drums, with slashes of angular guitar noise splattered, Jackson Pollock like, over anything that moves. They were obviously in thrall to The New York Dolls… but doubly-bratty. The guitar playing singers, Frankie Fix and Johnny Strike, both capture the whining obnoxiousness that was initially a refreshing change – but as it became *de rigueur* for a succession of punk wannabes it soon became incredibly boring.

64
ROAST FISH
AND CORN BREAD
CORN FISH DUB
LEE PERRY
ISLAND
DID NOT CHART

"Clip, Clop, Cloppity Cloppity" sings Lee Perry by way of introduction, which leads us into a walking pace skank, while he plucks more stream-of-consciousness phrases from the ether and delivers them up from the place where his mischievous inner-child resides. 'Roast Fish and Corn Bread' is trance like, unhurried and beautiful; Island Records disapproved, and a hostility between artist and label thus ensued.

63
BOSTON TEA PARTY
SULTAN'S CHOICE
SENSATIONAL ALEX HARVEY
BAND
MOUNTAIN
13

The Sensational Alex Harvey Band were always expressive and unafraid to tackle subjects that were beyond the imagination of most of their peers. Here, they play along to a martial drum beat reinforced by Hugh McKenna's simpatico piano, while Zal Cleminson plays long, sustained guitar notes, building up the atmosphere, as Alex half-sings and half-talks us through a history lesson about how repressive tea taxes, imposed by the British Crown, acted as a catalyst for the American War of Independence. There is even a reference made to the interesting fact that George Washington wore wooden false teeth; surely the only time that this particular piece of information has been referenced in a hit single!

62
GUESS WHO'S COMING FOR
DINNER
STRAIGHT TO ROD'S HEAD
(billed as the Morpheus Players)
MICHAEL ROSE
MORPHEUS
DID NOT CHART

Named after, and inspired by, the

1967 American movie starring Sydney Poitier, this was a brilliant piece of roots reggae that has since become a staple of many collections of classic tracks. Michael Rose would subsequently go on to join Black Uhuru; he took this song with him and it became a giant hit for them, solidly underlining their dread consciousness. Theirs was a fine record, though it was inferior to this original, solo version; here, the song is uncluttered and benefits hugely from the simple production given to it by Niney the Observer – the unaccompanied sweet voice and the taut rhythm combine to terrific effect.

61
BLINDED BY THE LIGHT
STARBIRD NO 2
MANFRED MANN'S EARTH BAND
BRONZE
6
Having scored big hits with Bob Dylan songs in the 1960s, in the 1970s Manfred Mann turned instead to the songs of Bruce Springsteen. 'Blinded By the Light' came from Springsteen's 1973 album *Greetings from Asbury Park* where it had been a flop for the composer. Unsurprising because Springsteen's version is far too long, much too wordy, over-cluttered and not very good at all; yet somehow, from this unpromising material, Manfred Mann transformed the song into a lean, sleek and fabulous piece of pop. Electronics replace the messy saxophone and guitars that Springsteen employed, and whereas The Boss bulldozed his way through the lyrics, trying (and failing) to invest them with some importance, here they are handled with a lightness

of touch that makes a virtue of how clumsy and ridiculously silly they are in actuality.

60
POLITICIANS IN MY EYES
KEEP ON KNOCKIN'
DEATH
TRYANGLE
DID NOT CHART
3 black brothers in Detroit: Bobby, Dannis and David Hackney, had a funk band called Rock Fire Funk Express, but after listening to Alice Cooper and seeing a concert performance by The Who, they decided to change both the band name and musical style; their father had recently died, and in attempting to make a positive from this huge negative, they became Death. Clive Davis (head of Columbia Records) gave them enough funds to record some demos, but their refusal to countenance a change of name made him lose interest. As a result, the band took a DIY approach with two of the seven tracks they had recorded, and had a run of 500 singles pressed-up. What any astute purchaser got was fabulous, well recorded, well played, angry and incendiary politicised songs in a style owing something to the MC5 and The Stooges; what they got was "punk" before the bandwagon rolled up.

59
DON'T TRY 'N' CHANGE MY MIND
WELL WELL HELLO (THE PARTY)
RONNIE LANE
ISLAND
DID NOT CHART
Ronnie Lane was a spent force as a commercial entity despite the fact

that at this time he was making some of the best music of his storied career. 'Don't Try 'n' Change My Mind' was the opening track on his superb album *One For the Road* and an obvious choice for a single. It is a good-natured, philosophical romp, with Ronnie musing on the wisdom of living as full a life as possible before the inevitable end comes – "When you come all alone, and you go on your own, out that door" is how he finishes up this jaunty number. Flipping the record over revealed a re-titled, but quite delightful, cocktail lounge retread of The Faces song 'Last Orders Please', unavailable anywhere else in Ronnie Lane's discography.

58
COULDN'T GET IT RIGHT
FAT MAYBELLENE
CLIMAX BLUES BAND
RCA
10
The Climax Blues Band were well-respected perennials; at this point they were on their eighth album and they existed in a bubble of gruelling touring that conspired to keep them running on the spot. Their manager, Miles Copeland, asked them to come up with something that might garner some radio exposure; he suggested that they try recording an Elvis Presley cover version… Instead they simply sat down and wrote 'Couldn't Get It Right'. The song detailed their life on the road without resorting to cliché; there is a fabulous, easy groove to it and the lead vocal nestles snugly on top of great harmonies. It goes without saying that the musicianship was top notch, and all-in-all, this record was a concise gem.

57
PUMPING MY HEART
ASK THE ANGELS
PATTI SMITH
ARISTA
DID NOT CHART
Already on her second album 'beat poet' Patti was now confident enough to go for a full rock 'n' roll assault with this single; subtle it is not – the drums sound as if they are being hit by shovels and the heavy metal guitars squeal. As for Patti she works herself up into a lather, wailing about her pumping heart and fists as she experiences something akin to total abandon. She had done better work before, and she would do better work again, but utilising the primal scream technique made famous by John and Yoko, 'Pumping My Heart' sounds like the exorcism of a demon that needed to be released. Though the A-side proved to be too much for listeners of a nervous disposition, there was the consolation that the outstanding 'Ask the Angels' was on the B-side.

56
JAH LIVE
CONCRETE
BOB MARLEY AND THE
WAILERS
ISLAND
DID NOT CHART
With news reports coming in from Ethiopia claiming that Haile Selassie had died; the supposition appeared to be that, without the figurehead, Rastafarianism would die too. Bob Marley was having none of this: "Yuh cyant kill god" he said, and to further underline his belief, he recorded this non-album single with Lee Perry. "Fools say in their heart, Rasta your god is dead, but I and I know, Jah,

Jah Dread" – this was chanted by Bob with unshakable certainty. The song was a reaffirmation of Marley's faith, and he delivered it in a solemn, spiritual tone.

55
CHERRY BOMB
BLACKMAIL
THE RUNAWAYS
MERCURY
DID NOT CHART

Five attractive young females, dressed provocatively in just their underwear and managed by sinister, creepy LA scenester, Kim Fowley – the whole thing stank to high-heaven of hype; but then, when this debut single appeared and we actually got to hear them, oh boy was it great! At just over two minutes long, this was concise and packed to the rafters with hooks – it also boasted a chorus that was pure bad attitude. The song was written by Joan Jett and Fowley, and played by the band themselves – this at a time when it was far from acceptable for women to wield such power over their musical output – though Nigel Harrison of Blondie did appear as a guest to contribute some bass guitar. This latter fact I present merely as an interesting detail, because The Runaways really were an inspiration and precursors for lots of women who decided that they also fancied being in a band, playing their own instruments and creating their own sound, completely free of any suggestion of male dominion.

54
LOWDOWN
HARBOUR LIGHTS
BOZ SCAGGS
COLUMBIA
32

Boz Scaggs was the singer in The Steve Miller Band when they recorded their excellent album *Sailor*; beyond that he was pretty much an unknown quantity in the UK, although in America he had forged a reputation as a fine purveyor of so-called blue eyed soul. Then 'Lowdown' came along, as alluring as it was subtle. Improbably constructed for both the disco dance floor and for comfortably lounging around, the lush sound just washes over you – this is a record that epitomized all that was cool and stylish. The producers of *Saturday Night Fever* enquired about using the song in the film; they were turned down and so they approached the Bee Gees instead…

53
DISCO BOY
MS PINKY
FRANK ZAPPA
WARNER BROTHERS
DID NOT CHART

Performed in satirical pop style, 'Disco Boy' is similar in its antagonism towards the new breed of vain, style-obsessed fakes as the early Mothers of Invention records were in their mockery of hippies. Using a dark rock guitar backing, Frank lets rip at the superficiality of 'Disco Boy' who believes that he is "outa sight" and who loves to be worshipped, "Leave his hair alone, but you can kiss his comb". Unfortunately for him, no disco girls want to go home with him, and 'Disco Boy' is left thankful that he has hands to "blot out his disco sorrow". This was Zappa at his most vindictive and sadistic but he was also saying things that needed to be said.

52
KEYS TO YOUR HEART
5 STAR ROCK & ROLL
PETROL
THE 101ers
CHISWICK
DID NOT CHART

John "Woody" Mellor, aka Joe Strummer, was a big Bruce Springsteen and Van Morrison fan. He was also the lead singer of the 101ers, who were a big noise on the London pub rock scene, playing perennial fare such as 'Gloria' and 'Route 66', as well as a sprinkling of original songs that Strummer had written following encouragement from his girlfriend Palmolive (later of The Slits). Ted Carroll, who ran the 'Rock On' record stall at Camden, was starting up his own record label called Chiswick, and he paid for the 101ers to go into a studio to record their complete repertoire. 'Keys To Your Heart' was the best track and thus it was selected to be a single.

In April the 101ers played a gig at a pub called The Elgin where they were supported by a young group called the Sex Pistols. Strummer immediately fell in love with them and out of love with his own band – he played his last gig with the 101ers in May and joined a group called The Clash instead. No doubt his sanity was seriously questioned because he was leaving a gigging band, with good, friendly and creative people in it, in order to join a group who could barely play their instruments and, as their earliest demos reveal, were absolutely hopeless but epiphanies

are always wasted on people who never act upon them and Joe's seized his epiphany by the scruff of the neck. So in June, 'Keys To Your Heart' was released and it was, and is, a good record. In July, The Clash played their first ever gig supporting Sex Pistols in Sheffield, a pub-rock stronghold which warmly welcomed Strummer... but not his new band, who were completely pathetic. Still, the die was cast and Strummer was determined to make The Clash work. Seeking inspiration, they went to see The Ramones play their first UK date at The Roundhouse; a lesson was learned... It was another light bulb moment. The band proceeded to double the speed of what had previously been rather lacklustre songs with great lyrics – things suddenly clicked into place and by December The Clash were the opening act on the infamous Sex Pistols' *Anarchy* tour. At a stroke they were transformed into a brilliant band and the rest is history. Meanwhile, 101ers drummer Richard Dudanski would, before too long, find himself playing with Public Image Ltd, the Raincoats and Basement 5 – but that's another story...

51
TEENAGE DEPRESSION
SHAKE
EDDIE AND THE HOT RODS
ISLAND
43

Style wise things were moving fast between the beginning of the year and the October release of this single. The Hot Rods had attempted to surf the wave of the impending coming of punk, without letting go of their pub-rock R&B roots. It wasn't always a comfortable fit, but with

'Teenage Depression' they managed to capture the Zeitgeist as this speedy and choppy hard-hitter expressed alienation and dissatisfaction in such a cartoonish angry fashion that the line between punk and pub-rock was momentarily blurred.

50

KEEP ME CRYING
THERE IS LOVE
AL GREEN
HI
DID NOT CHART

Al Green had just bought a church and he was about to abandon the secular world to fully embrace his faith; huge changes were afoot and 'Keep Me Crying' comes from the final collection of songs he recorded with Willie Mitchell. In view of this it might be considered somewhat surprising that 'Keep Me Crying' is one of the most joyful and eccentric of all Al Green's singles. It is more up-tempo than most of the great man's work, with horns very much to the fore, and he sings with a joyous frenzy as he playfully runs through a list of situations which leave him frustrated – e.g. being made to turn his music down, being told how to handle his own affairs – until it gets to the point when he just keeps on crying...

49

LET 'EM IN
BEWARE MY LOVE
WINGS
CAPITOL
5

By now Paul McCartney had little left to say; there would not be another 'Yesterday' or 'Let It Be'. He was no longer mining his emotions, and even if he had pretended to do that, the result would have been offensive. Instead McCartney simply utilised his song-craft and gift for melody to create this sherbet-dip of a single. This is a record which is effervescent and fizzing, lyrically slight but sweet and good natured – it is full of lovely moments and employs much less obvious instrumentation than the average popster might do. If McCartney was coasting, at least he was doing it on the crest of a wave.

48

CHANT DOWN BABYLON
VERSION
(credited to Ja-man All Stars)
JUNIOR BYLES AND RUPERT REID
BLACK WAX
DID NOT CHART

Junior Byles was a gentle singer; his voice was soft with an air of vulnerability that seemed to match his persona. On the other hand his material was concerned with struggle and the oppression of the poor, in which the soulfulness of his sad voice lent expressiveness to the sentiments. Here he was paired with Rupert Reid and they delivered a roots classic in what was a period of high productivity. Unfortunately this came to an end when, unable to reconcile himself to the death of Emperor Haile Selassie, he suffered deep depression and acute mental health issues.

47

RAIN
YOU LOST THE LOVE
STATUS QUO
VERTIGO
7

Quo had enjoyed a run of quite extraordinary singles throughout the decade, but soon the quality would diminish substantially as they adopted a more populist, keyboard-led approach, that admittedly yielded great success and turned them into a British institution to rival *Carry On* films and warm beer. 'Rain', along with 'Mystery Song' which followed, was therefore something of a last hurrah. Written by Rick Parfitt this is more understated than the majority of the band's hits lacking, as it does, a truly anthemic feel. Nonetheless it hits the spot once again with the relentless drive, as guitars are hammered unmercifully, creating a wonderful maelstrom of fantastic noise.

46
CAR WASH
WATER
ROSE ROYCE
MCA
9

Former Motown writer/producer Norman Whitfield was offered the job of writing the soundtrack for a comedy film to be called *Car Wash*. Initially reluctant, Whitfield was persuaded to take the commission because it would give exposure to Rose Royce, a funk band he had signed. This, the title track to the film, was the group's first single and it immediately grabs the listener with its combination of nimble bass and subtle horn riff. The light and cheerful lyric is handled by Rose Norwalt and Kenny Copeland and it tells a story of the easy-going carefree atmosphere among a team of carwash workers. Whilst we can safely take those sentiments with a large pinch of salt, this was a slice of pure dance-floor gold and it was a whole lot of fun.

45
MORE THAN A FEELING
SMOKIN'
BOSTON
EPIC
22

'More Than A Feeling' was the first single by Boston; it tells the tale of a man who hears an old song on the radio, and the way in which this sends a surge of emotion through his body because he associates the song with a lost love. This is hard rock performed with a soft edge; the sound is sleek and the soaring vocals are sumptuous. The main riff – copied by Kurt Cobain for Nirvana's 'Smells Like Teen Spirit' – is quite unforgettable, and the guitar solo induces men of a certain vintage to involuntarily play the air guitar to this very day.

44
YOU SEE THE TROUBLE WITH ME
I'M SO BLUE AND YOU ARE TOO
BARRY WHITE
20TH CENTURY FOX
2

Co-written by Barry White and Ray Parker Jr (an associate of Stevie Wonder and future *Ghostbusters* hitmaker) who didn't take too many liberties with the tried and trusted formula that had already made White a veritable one-man hit factory, yet 'You See The Trouble With Me' has one or two idiosyncrasies all of its own. There is a see-saw rhythm that is hard not to respond to and a drum sound, right at the front of the mix, alongside the unmistakable voice. Strings are employed as a sound-bed for the other instruments, and the guitar-effects used toward the end of the song are brilliantly bizarre. White was a master composer, under-rated and hiding in plain sight. "Always different, always the same", said John Peel of The Fall – a remark equally true of this musical colossus.

43
KID CHARLEMAGNE
GREEN EARRINGS
STEELY DAN
ABC
DID NOT CHART
Truly subversive, Steely Dan were operating from within the system but under their own terms and with their own agenda; insulated by success, they could pretty much do as they pleased. Here, they offer-up a single based upon the activities of Owsley Stanley, famed LSD chemist and 1960s counter-culture figure – they zero in on the fading psychedelic dream in favour of a new, more authoritarian and consumerist age. As ever the lyrics are astute and cutting: "Now your patrons have all left you in the red, your low-rent friends are dead, this life can be very strange, all those Day-Glo freaks who used to paint their face, they've joined the human race", sings Donald Fagan, enunciating each and every word with crystal clarity, while Larry Carlton plays jazz guitar from outer space over a funky rumba rhythm… remarkable!

42
SATISFACTION
LOSER = WEED
THE RESIDENTS
RALPH
DID NOT CHART
The Residents take on one of the sacred cows of rock mythology, tear it open and reveal it to be sick to the core; they twist it around until all the misty-eyed nostalgia has fallen away, and then, finally, they kick-over the pedestal it has been placed upon before a process of reconstruction begins. Stripped of all pomposity and self-reverence, the song is then performed nakedly, without the smoke and mirrors utilised by the accountants who had claimed it for themselves. The unmanageable weight that this slim song has laboured beneath is revealed; bloated and ugly, it crawls, slug-like, towards the edge of a cliff, where its suffering will mercifully end…

41
PLAY THAT FUNKY MUSIC
THE LADY WANTS YOUR
MONEY
WILD CHERRY
EPIC
7
Ohio band Wild Cherry were a regular gigging outfit and, by the mid-1970s as disco dominated the airwaves and clubs, they were increasingly being asked by audiences to play more dance music. At one gig, somebody shouted "Are you white boys gonna play some funky music?" – this serendipitous heckle gave singer/guitarist Rob Parissi the idea for a song. The song was titled 'Play That Funky Music' and when recorded it became a full-frontal assault on the senses. There is a turbo-charged guitar riff – sounding like a cousin to the one featured in David Bowie's 'Fame' – and a wild, exuberant vocal akin to some of Stevie Wonder's more uninhibited performances; in a nutshell, the song certainly didn't lack for excitement. There was also, in what were often segregationist times, a message of inclusiveness conveyed by the "Play

that funky music, white boy" refrain. The icing-on-the-cake of this mini-masterpiece was a quite incendiary guitar solo; the final, vital ingredient that helped to make this such an extraordinary and iconic record.

40

THE KILLING OF GEORGIE
PART 1 and 2
FOOL FOR YOU
ROD STEWART
RIVA
2

With his commerciality at a peak – following the gigantic success of a bland, middle-of-the-road cover of the Sutherland Brothers' song 'Sailing' – Rod Stewart's credibility rating had, conversely, never been so low; it was a little bit odd then that he chose this moment to release what was for the time a very brave single – the gay subject matter could easily have derailed the singer's burgeoning career, particularly in uptight middle-America. The song concerned a young gay man from New York who had been a fan of The Faces; his tale is told candidly, and with sensitivity, from the day he was thrown out of the family home by a father offended by his son's sexuality, right up to his murder by "queer bashers" as he was walking home from the theatre. The effective arrangement adopts a hybrid folk/disco style and a female "da da duh" backing vocal (similar to the one Lou Reed had employed for 'Walk on the Wild Side') added to the ambiance. In short, it was a superb single from Rod Stewart when expectations were very much at rock bottom.

39

WHAT A WAY TO END IT ALL
GET SET READY GO
DEAF SCHOOL
WARNER BROTHERS
DID NOT CHART

It seemed as if Liverpool had produced The Beatles but nothing else since of any note; that is until the arrival of Deaf School, who not only made eccentric and inspired music themselves, but just as importantly acted as a catalyst for the city's bohemian types to create a vibrant new music scene. Deaf School's considerable influence didn't just stop at the city limits – acts of the calibre of Madness and Dexy's Midnight Runners would later cite them as an inspiration. This was their debut single – a dark, comedic look at a would-be suicide, who is waiting for the telephone to ring so that he can be talked out of his plan. Played on banjo in a sort of art house/vaudeville style, 'What A Way To End It All' was clearly brilliant and Deaf School were obviously top notch performers. As an extra bonus, they had, in Clive Langer, a highly gifted songwriter. Sadly, as a commercial entity, Deaf School arrived at precisely the wrong time; stuck between glam and punk was no-man's land… and that was exactly where they stood.

38

ONE STEP FORWARD
ONE STEP DUB
MAX ROMEO AND THE
UPSETTERS
ISLAND
DID NOT CHART

In 1976 Max Romeo (whose former stock-in-trade had been the lewd and lustful) released a clutch of singles concerned with the growing consciousness and striving for self-determination that were central tenets of the Rastafarian faith. He worked at the Black Ark with the prolific and prodigious Lee Perry – along with his studio band The Upsetters – and together they produced some of the best reggae music ever recorded. 'One Step Forward' is one of those classic tracks; it harnesses The Upsetters rhythmic groove, Perry's trickery and studio mastery and a wholly convincing vocal by Max Romeo, ruminating upon the challenging journey to righteousness.

37
THE SOUL OF MY SUIT
ALL ALONE
T.REX
T. REX WAX CO
42
Easily the best T. Rex single in 3-years, 'The Soul of My Suit' sounded effortless, as if Marc Bolan had suddenly re-discovered his groove and managed to once again focus on what he was great at… sharp, snappy and melodic guitar pop. This is written in Marc's inimitable style and it is delivered in a clear voice, containing just the hint of a giggle – clearly he was wearing a smile again and seemed to be relaxed. There was huge affection for Marc; for many, he had been their first introduction to music and this single seemed to herald the end of his drink, drug and ego problems. It was heart-warming to see him re-emerge with such a fantastic record.

36
BALLISTIC AFFAIR
BALLISTIC DUB
LEROY SMART
ISLAND
DID NOT CHART
Producer Jo Jo Hoo Kim and his studio band, The Revolutionaries, were well ahead of the curve, and the sound they produced for Leroy Smart's 'Ballistic Affair' is rapidly moving towards "dancehall style", with a brisk rhythm that perfectly complements the agitated mood of the song. Smart speaks about the schism that has emerged in Jamaican society due to warring between two political parties (the JLP and PNP). His flamboyant and forceful vocal ensures that the song's message is heard loud and clear: "Throw 'way your gun, throw 'way your knife, let us all unite, everyone is living in fear, just through this ballistic affair" – bold, unambiguous and brilliant.

35
SOMEBODY TO LOVE
WHITE MAN
QUEEN
EMI
2
Queen had left the run-of-the-mill behind and were now hobnobbing in the upper echelons of the chart firmament; as a pop group, they had proven that they were special. After all they had four excellent songwriters, they harmonised brilliantly and they had their own unique guitar sound thanks to Brian May's homemade "Red Special". In addition the singer was spectacularly good, and as a front-man he was even better. In the previous 12-months they had reaped the bountiful rewards of the overblown extravaganza that was

'Bohemian Rhapsody', consolidated with the sweetly low-key 'You're My Best Friend' (penned by bassist extraordinaire John Deacon) and now they followed-up with another epic in Freddie Mercury's 'Somebody to Love'. This soul-searching faith song is delivered in the form of a rocking gospel tune, full of intricate harmonies. There is a glorious guitar solo and a stupendous vocal, pitched somewhere in the rarefied space between Aretha Franklin and Russ Mael. Without doubt, one of Queen's finest moments in a career littered with fine moments.

34
I'M MANDY FLY ME
HOW DARE YOU
10CC
MERCURY
6
Four-headed democracy within a band is not an easy thing to maintain – and by this point 10cc were not functioning with a great deal of team-spirit – but 'I'm Mandy Fly Me' shows how strong a unit they could be when able to summon-up a spirit of co-operation. Eric Stewart and Graham Gouldman had co-written the song, inspired by a billboard advertising holiday flights which featured a good-looking air-hostess. Letting their imaginations run riot, the song turned into a tale about a down-and-out character who was booking a flight in order to be near the girl. After hearing the first attempt Kevin Godley argued that it was too bland and safe – a good kick up the backside was required. The song went back to the drawing board; the tempo changed, two guitar solos were inserted and there was now a dreamy middle-eight in which

the aeroplane has crashed into the sea and Mandy, the stewardess, saves the life of her admirer. All pretty fanciful stuff... but it was supreme pop as well.

33
LOVE HANGOVER
KISS ME NOW
DIANA ROSS
TAMLA MOTOWN
10
Repositioning was the name of the game with the release of this single; the aim was to change the public perception of Diana Ross from old-fashioned entertainer to disco diva. To that end producer Hal Davis installed a strobe light in the studio as Diana recorded her vocal – this was a smart move. With a backing track that borrowed heavily from the sound Donna Summer was getting (courtesy of Georgio Moroder) the stage was set. Diana was clearly in the zone; she was having fun and her delightful performance is full of giggles, sighs and even an impersonation of Billie Holiday at one point. The record was a complete triumph and she once again sounded not just contemporary but streets ahead of the pack.

32
THE BOYS ARE BACK IN TOWN
EMERALD
THIN LIZZY
PHONOGRAM
8
Phil Lynott's mother ran a drinking-den in Manchester that was a favourite meeting place-cum-watering hole for criminals associated with the notorious Quality Street Gang. With members of her clientele often facing spells of incarceration,

there were regular occasions when glasses would be raised upon their release, and a typical salutation would be "the boys are back in town again". Lynott took inspiration from this colourful environment; he loved the tall tales told and wrote them up as a kind of Punch and Judy style romp… the result was this anthem to hard-drinking, womanising and hedonism. Lynott manages to write eloquently of such low-life places and imbue them with an edgy sheen of glamour, made all the more effective because even in a hard-rock outfit such as Thin Lizzy, melody was never sacrificed for power. This was the record that truly broke through for Lizzy; it made them huge stars and some very big-selling records followed. Unfortunately, nothing subsequently ever bettered this – 'The Boys Are Back In Town' will forever be this band's glorious peak.

31
RUBBERBAND MAN
NOW THAT WE'RE
TOGETHER
THE SPINNERS
ATLANTIC
16
I have never, ever, come close to being tired of this absolutely glorious and outrageously funky record; I find it enormously uplifting and it always puts a spring in my step and a smile on my face. The song was written and produced by Thom Bell and Linda Creed, and Bell once explained that it had been concocted in an effort to improve his overweight son's self-image, because he was being bullied. The titular 'Rubberband Man' replaced the original "Fat Man", but the attitude to inclusivity and being judgemental remained exactly the same. Lead vocalist Philippé Wynne perfectly captures the spirit of the song, and his performance is both expressive and celebratory. Backed by the musicians from MFSB, with bass playing "Funk Brother" Bob Babbitt moonlighting from Motown, something very special and magical was created here.

30
LIVIN' THING
FIRE ON HIGH
ELECTRIC LIGHT
ORCHESTRA
JET
4
This opens with a Mediterranean-flavoured orchestral flourish, and then the song settles into a mid-tempo groove powered by acoustic guitars, before rising upward to a chorus in which the string-section is highly prominent. Jeff Lynne sings and seems to capture a sense of pain as his voice rises towards falsetto, at which point Patti Quatro enters and adds her voice to this fabulously conceived and highly accomplished record. The song itself – though sometimes interpreted to be about drugs, abortion, suicide and other dark subjects – is clearly about love and the loss of love; it is concise and clever in its use of allegory. At this moment ELO were making some quite brilliant pop music, and this was a superb example.

29
CRIMINAL WORLD
PRECIOUS
METRO
TRANSATLANTIC
DID NOT CHART
Metro provided one last glorious gasp of glam before the door was

firmly slammed shut on the fanciful in favour of the furious. 'Criminal World' crept out of the speakers, infecting rooms with velvet-wrapped sleaziness; it was all very tempting, oozing with delicious decadence as Peter Godwin, all doe-eyes and glacial cheekbones, whispered the secrets he had to impart, joined by Duncan Browne for stern choruses of "Oh oh, what a criminal world, the boys are like baby-faced girls", only to be followed by yet more dark, poetic innuendo. The moral guardians at the BBC moved swiftly to ban this filth from the nation's air-waves. In so doing they banished Metro into harsh obscurity until, a full half-decade later, interest was piqued by David Bowie, who in the midst of treacherously, and calculatingly, denouncing his bi-sexual past, recorded a de-homosexualised version of the song for his *Let's Dance* album.

28
I WANNA BE
YOUR BOYFRIEND
CALIFORNIA SUN
THE RAMONES
SIRE
DID NOT CHART
Written by Tommy Ramone, this was a brilliantly simple subversion of the way in which masculinity was commonly portrayed. Standing orthodoxy on its head, the song parodies the girl-group pop that so often portrayed the female of the species as weak and needy, and it flips the genders around. The fact that this is also a lovely, sweet, melodic tune and that Joey gives a wonderfully in-character vocal is another huge bonus, and with Dee Dee and Johnny playing in their own inimitable styles,

everything adds up to making this a fabulous record.

27
(DON'T FEAR) THE REAPER
TATTOO VAMPIRE
BLUE OYSTER CULT
COLUMBIA
DID NOT CHART
(number 16 re-release 1978)
With one of the most distinctive and memorable of all guitar riffs, impressive use of the cowbell, a magnificent chorus and a sadly poetic lyric, this has "classic" stamped all the way through it like a stick of rock. Blue Oyster Cult were the metal band that it was acceptable to like; Patti Smith and Jim Carroll both contributed lyrics to their songs, which amply demonstrates their hipster pedigree. But this track, '(Don't Fear) The Reaper', was written solely by guitarist and vocalist Buck Dharma; it deliberates on the pointlessness of fearing death, and the way in which love is eternal, although it was often mis-interpreted as a song that glorified suicide.

26
ANOTHER WORLD
BLANK GENERATION/
YOU GOTTA LOSE
RICHARD HELL
STIFF
DID NOT CHART
Licensed from Ork Records in New York, Stiff provided us with our first taste of the much discussed Richard Hell. Having been the co-founder of both Television and The Heartbreakers, and then finding himself thrown out of both in turn, Hell put together his own group featuring the incredibly exciting guitar playing of Robert Quine.

Hell was steeped in poetry and literature and a huge admirer of Bob Dylan which shaped his own creativity. 'Another World' is a fine piece of writing, concerning (I think) the impact that one night of casual sex can have on a sensitive, romantic soul. The guitars, used in a most unconventional fashion and indiscriminately spraying shards of notes all over the place, are a perfect match for Hell's spat-out, rather than sung, vocal. 'Another World' validated a completely new way to make music, avoiding the clichéd sounds of so many in the mainstream rock genre.

25
GO YOUR OWN WAY
SILVER SPRINGS
FLEETWOOD MAC
WARNER BROTHERS
38
Lindsey Buckingham's vengeful invective concerning the relationship break-up with Stevie Nicks (his long-term lover and band-mate) is made public in song; what drama! What emotion! It can't have been pleasant for either party but it did make for brilliant music. Mick Fleetwood's drumming is extraordinary and John McVie powers-up the song with a propulsive bass track. As for Buckingham's contribution, the acoustic guitar assault is relentless and hard, the electric guitar absolutely breath-taking and his lead vocal perfectly judged, betraying both hurt and anger in the verses, before the chorus simply explodes as Stevie Nicks and Christine McVie join in, wailing like the proverbial banshees.

24
I WANT MORE
AND MORE
CAN
VIRGIN
26
Noel Edmonds quipped that he wanted Can to be the first act on the show, until he realised that he couldn't have a "can opener" – yes, amazingly, Can were on *Top of the Pops*. They achieved this feat by dint of 'I Want More', a repetitive minimalistic disco-ditty with a one-line lyric that they all chanted in unison. The record had obviously sneaked into the hit-parade on novelty value alone, and yet it was great; it grooved and contained a knowing humour, demonstrated even further when one flipped the record over to discover that you were being treated to 'and more'…

23
SO IT GOES/
HEART OF THE CITY
NICK LOWE
STIFF
DID NOT CHART
Stiff Records first release was Nick Lowe's double A-sided solo debut, and it was absolutely stupendous. Recorded for £40 with Steve Goulding on drums, Lowe played all the other instruments, as well as singing and producing. Two sides of loud catchy, guitar-driven pop were cooked up; 'So It Goes' is a big-hearted friendly take on the inevitability of death inspired by Kurt Vonnegut's *Slaughterhouse-Five* where every time a fatality occurs, the phrase "So it goes" is used. On the flip side, 'Heart of the City' is a glorious slab of rock 'n' roll, played and sung with brash charm.

22

GET UP OFFA THAT THING
RELEASE THE PRESSURE
JAMES BROWN
POLYDOR
DID NOT CHART

James Brown claimed that this song originated at a gig he was doing where the audience sat cross-legged, just listening, rather than responding to the music. Feeling energy being sucked from the stage because nothing was being reciprocated, he began to exhort the crowd to "Get up offa that thing, and release the pressure". Recording was done with the full band playing together, rather than each instrumentalist doing an individual take; this may or may not be the reason that this record packs such a wallop, but what is certain is that this was the most urgent and vital James Brown had sounded in several years.

21

STREET WAVES
MY DARK AGES
(I DON'T GET AROUND)
PERE UBU
HEARTHEN
DID NOT CHART

The third Pere Ubu single – and first without Peter Laughner – took a stranger, a more startling turn than either of the previous two. The sound is denser, with a distinctly Beefheartian flavour, as the instruments, all seemingly playing different songs, somehow mesh into a unified aural assault while David Thomas, clearly happily experimenting with his voice, careers across the resultant gleeful noise.

20

DANCING QUEEN
THAT'S ME
ABBA
EPIC
1

Whilst this is basically just a celebration of dancing and the enjoyment to be found on the dance floor there is a bitter-sweet quality to 'Dancing Queen' because it is sung from the point of view of an older woman looking back nostalgically to a time when she herself was "only seventeen"; of course, because this is Abba, the song is sung beautifully and the pathos comfortably co-exists with the joy. Musically, this is disco transported from the USA (via George McCrea's 'Rock Your Baby') but given a European make-over and laden with hooks, particularly the glistening piano fills which are heart-stoppingly dramatic. As inspired as 'Dancing Queen' is musically, it is matched by the care and craft that was put into the actual recording; every part is carefully considered and perfectly complements the song – as was often said of Phil Spector's best work, this is a 'pocket symphony'. Finally, if imitation is indeed the greatest form of flattery, then it wasn't very long before Abba were royally flattered by Elvis Costello – who borrowed the piano-line for his own song 'Oliver's Army' – and by Blondie, whose 'Dreaming' was a virtual retread of 'Dancing Queen'.

19
JOHNNY WAS (WOMAN HOLD
HER HEAD AND CRY)
CRY TO ME
BOB MARLEY AND THE
WAILERS
ISLAND
DID NOT CHART

'Johnny Was' is a slow blues lament to the tragedy of lost life; "Johnny" has been shot down because of the system reflecting the danger on the streets of Kingston as politically-sponsored gang-warfare left a trail of dead. Marley humanises the story, invoking the tears of a woman who cries over her dead son's body. It is by no means easy to chronicle a subject such as this without making it mawkish and overly sentimental, but Bob Marley speaks with sincerity and displays deep empathy; in short, he is a highly convincing commentator on events that were all too real for himself and his Trenchtown brethren.

18
YOUNG HEARTS RUN FREE
I KNOW
CANDI STATON
WARNER BROTHERS
2

The timelessness of this record is displayed by the fact that it was a UK hit single for Candi Staton not just in 1976, but once again in1986, and then for a third time in 1999. The song was written by David Crawford after a conversation he had with her in which she told him that she was in a bad and abusive marriage and struggling to escape. Recorded in one solitary take, with the hurt and emotion evident in Staton's singing, the song manages to be both uplifting and cautionary. This was a brilliant disco single – a guaranteed floor filler

– but it is disco with deep soul, and a message that means it transcends the boundaries of all musical genres.

17
I WISH
YOU AND I
STEVIE WONDER
TAMLA MOTOWN
5

Stevie is at his funkiest on 'I Wish'. Lyrically, he looks back on his childhood in the 1950s and recalls his misbehaviour and happiness in equal measure, as he wishes that those days could return. The tune is horn heavy, up-tempo and highly exuberant, almost seeming to leap out of the speakers as the record spins.

16
LET'S TAKE IT TO THE STAGE
BIOLOGICAL SPECULATION
FUNKADELIC
WESTBOUND
DID NOT CHART

Sinuous riffs, nursery rhymes and lyrics which throw down the gauntlet to the likes of Sly Stone, James Brown and Rufus; it could only be George Clinton and the P-Funk crew enjoying a playful musical romp, having mile-wide grins and defying listeners not to giggle as they groove.

15
LOVE AND AFFECTION
HELP YOURSELF
JOAN ARMATRADING
A&M
10

A hauntingly beautiful song, full of vulnerability and questioning, it is sung magnificently and soulfully by Joan Armatrading, and intriguingly we also hear a male baritone voice – does this perhaps suggest some element of coercion and/or manipulation? Armatrading plays acoustic guitar in an almost percussive style, and she is backed by ex-Fairport Convention members Jerry Donahue and Dave Mattacks, with Gallagher and Lyle side-man Jimmy Jewel contributing a splendidly inventive saxophone part. I remember hearing this being played on the radio one day and the sense of awe it gave me; that night, on my way home from work, I stopped in at a record shop in Ashton-under-Lyne to buy the single and went home to play it repeatedly, feeling almost dumbstruck by the grace and artistry of this talented woman.

14
HARVEST FOR THE WORLD
HARVEST FOR THE WORLD
(INSTRUMENTAL)
THE ISLEY BROTHERS
EPIC
10
Many protest songs inevitably serve a cause at a particular moment in time, and then afterwards cease to have any further merit... but 'Harvest For The World' has a timelessness that unfortunately makes it just as sadly relevant today as it was back in 1976. This is a furious song and yet it is delivered with no trace of anger; instead, there is a smooth groove and Ronald Isley's vocal, though not lacking passion, is easy on the ear as he questions the greed of the powers that be who take more than they need whilst spreading war and famine, and exploiting the poorest and most needy.

13
ARMAGIDEON
(ARMAGEDON)
BLACKHEART MAN
BUNNY WAILER
ISLAND
DID NOT CHART
A stately horn fanfare leads us elegantly into this extraordinary single by Bunny Wailer. Over a chattering percussive rhythm and piano trills, we hear melodica, which adds a little touch of lightness, as Bunny half-speaks and half-sings his warning to a world that is heading to hell in a handcart – a world of war, setting father against son. Heavily biblical in content, this is a powerful and persuasive call for sanity to prevail, for goodness to triumph over evil, for justice and equality for all people...

12
COCAINE IN MY BRAIN
BUCKINGHAM PALACE
DILLINGER
BLACK SWAN
DID NOT CHART
Here we have Dillinger (clearly under the influence of something quite stimulating) serving up a proto-rap slice of funky reggae over a rhythm based on Gamble and Huff's Philly soul track 'Do It Anyway You Wanna', originally recorded by People's Choice. The chorus of "Cocaine running around my brain" is borrowed from 'Cocaine Blues' by blues singer Reverend Gary Davis but the rest of the piece consists of Dillinger amusingly voicing the words of two characters, Jim and John, as they converse in nonsensical drug-related jive – Dillinger claimed that the lyric sprang from listening to American and English tourists, who

were all crazy for the white powder. Whatever the genesis might be, this is a highly original, pretty strange and utterly beguiling record.

11
SHAKE SOME ACTION
TEENAGE CONFIDENTIAL
FLAMIN GROOVIES
SIRE
DID NOT CHART

The Groovies had never been afraid to proudly wear their influences on their sleeves; when Roy Loney had fronted the band that influence had often been The Rolling Stones – now, with Chris Wilson at the microphone, the band were be suited and sported mid-1960s bowl-cut mops of hair so *Revolver*-era Beatles was the template now being used as their heavy-duty instrumentation were replaced with 12-string Rickenbacker guitars. 'Shake Some Action' was recorded at Rockfield Studios, with Dave Edmunds at the controls, and this was one of those rare occasions when magic was somehow caught and bottled before being transferred to vinyl. The shimmering riff is outstanding and the song rides along on a quick fingered bass-line and huge sounding drums. Wilson, describing a state of turmoil, sings it like he means it; he is bruised and has had enough. The song quite simply explodes into each chorus, unleashing all of the pent-up emotion and tension in an exquisite eruption of blessed relief.

TOP 50 - 4TH SEPT 1976

1	1	DON'T GO BREAKING MY HEART, Elton
2	5	LET 'EM IN, Wings
3	2	A LITTLE BIT MORE, Dr. Hook
4	3	JEANS ON, David Dundas
5	4	IN ZAIRE, Johnny Wakelin
6	9	YOU SHOULD BE DANCING, Bee Gees
7	6	HEAVEN MUST BE MISSING AN ANGEL
8	8	DR. KISS KISS, 5000 Volts
9	17	YOU DON'T HAVE TO GO, Chi-Lites
10	7	NOW IS THE TIME, Jimmy James & The
11	18	YOU'LL NEVER FIND, Lou Rawls
12	19	16 BARS, Stylistics
13	11	WHAT I'VE GOT IN MIND, Billie Jo Spear
14	14	EXTENDED PLAY, Bryan Ferry
15	10	HERE COMES THE SUN, Steve Harley & (
16	23	DANCING QUEEN, Abba
17	13	MYSTERY SONG, Status Quo
18	22	THE KILLING OF GEORGIE, Rod Stewart
19	12	MISTY BLUE, Dorothy Moore
20	16	THE ROUSSOS PHENOMENON, Demis F
21	41	DOINA DE JALE, Gheorghe Zamfir
22	25	NICE AND SLOW, Jesse Green
23	29	TRY TO GET IT TOGETHER, Barry White
24	36	HERE I GO AGAIN, Twiggy
25	26	AFTERNOON DELIGHT, Starland Vocal B
26	46	I CAN'T ASK FOR ANYTHING MORE, Cli
27	28	MORNING GLORY, James & Bobby Purif
28	15	HARVEST FOR THE WORLD, Isley Broth
29	21	KISS AND SAY GOODBYE, Manhattans
30	–	Y VIVA SUSPENDERS, Judge Dread
31	20	LOVE ON DELIVERY, Billy Ocean
32	43	DANCE LITTLE LADY DANCE, Tina Char
33	32	JAILBREAK, Thin Lizzy
34	44	ARIA, Acker Bilk
35	47	MAKE YOURS A HAPPY HOME, Gladys
36	24	SHAKE YOUR BOOTY, K. C. & The Suns
37	50	HEAVEN IS IN THE BACK SEAT OF MY (
38	38	NIGHT FEVER, Fatback Band
39	39	LOVING ON THE LOSING SIDE, Tommy
40	33	A FIFTH OF BEETHOVEN, Walter Murphy
41	–	BLINDED BY THE LIGHT, Manfred Mann
42	35	IF YOU KNOW WHAT I MEAN, Neil Diam
43	48	SATIN SHEETS, Bellamy Brothers
44	45	IT'S SO NICE, New Seekers
45	42	LULLABYE OF BROADWAY, Winifred S
46	–	WORK ALL DAY, Barry Biggs
47	–	SHANNON, Henry Gross
48	–	MISSISSIPPI, Pussycat
49	–	I NEED IT, Johnny Guitar Watson
50	–	I WANT MORE, Can

10

GLORIA
MY GENERATION
PATTI SMITH
ARISTA
DID NOT CHART

"Jesus died for somebody's sins, but not mine" is a strong candidate for best-ever opening line to a song; that in itself would make this single stand-out in a crowd, but the conviction and intensity with which it is delivered does never relents. This is a battle cry of a record – it positively screams for the shackles to be removed. Ostensibly a cover version of Van Morrison's 1960s classic, in truth it is only loosely related to it because Patti takes huge liberties with both lyric and structure. The B-side, a live rampage through Pete Townshend's 'My Generation' (with John Cale on thunderous bass) culminates in Patti declaiming "We created it, let's take it over!", signifying a line being defiantly drawn in the sand.

9

RADIOACTIVITY
ANTENNA
KRAFTWERK
CAPITOL
DID NOT CHART

Opening with Morse code signalling that spells out the word 'Radioactivity', this original version of the song offered no value judgment on the subject matter, simply acknowledging its power and omnipresence in our lives – later versions would be explicitly anti-nuclear. This was Kraftwerk's first all-electronic record, but that did not mean any loss of melodic content and 'Radioactivity' is strangely and hauntingly beautiful.

8

WAR INNA BABYLON
REVELATION
MAX ROMEO AND THE UPSETTERS
ISLAND
DID NOT CHART

Recorded at the Black Ark by Lee 'Scratch' Perry and given his customary heavy dread sound, this is one of the most remarkable sides cut by the great producer. The Upsetters were a well-oiled, intuitive groove-machine and they provide supple support for what is a brilliant vocal by Max Romeo as he excitedly recounts the persecution of 'Rastas' by policemen and, more generally, conventional society... but in the end he believes that he will see Babylon burning. The chanted chorus of "War Inna Babylon" had such power and resonance that ultimately it came to exist as a completely separate entity from the song.

7

TVC15
WE ARE THE DEAD
DAVID BOWIE
RCA
33

This was the strangest single David Bowie had released up to this point in time. Inspired by a hallucinating and drug-fuelled Iggy Pop (who was convinced that Bowie's television set had swallowed-up his girlfriend) Bowie re-worked the tale whereby the song's narrator watches his girlfriend crawl into the television set and he wants to follow her. The song has a disjointed, mutant-disco feel – played alternately on tinkling piano and heavily fuzzed guitar – and there is a disturbing, manic cheerfulness in the execution, almost as if we are sat inside a Bavarian beer-hall, with Bowie at the head of the table leading a madcap sing-a-long.

6

FINAL SOLUTION
CLOUD 149
PERE UBU
HEARTHEN
DID NOT CHART

'Final Solution' is an Absurdist look at alienation – think Eddie
Cochran's 'Summertime Blues' with the angst turned-up to the
max, twisted out of shape and then played on ray-guns. This is
an incredible record; accessible, but still extreme in the use of
sonics, it sounds just like a war-zone. When you add in singer
David Thomas's yelped vocals, along with the allusion to suicide
in the form of a warped sing-a-long chorus, you are left with a
classic pop record that was genuinely capable of terrorising the
average pop-music fan.

5

POLICE AND THIEVES
GRUMBLING DUB
JUNIOR MURVIN
ISLAND
DID NOT CHART
(number 23 re-release 1980)

Junior Murvin, with his Curtis Mayfield-influenced falsetto, was
something of a peripheral figure in the Kingston music scene.
After a previous rejection he approached Lee 'Scratch' Perry
to audition his song 'Police and Thief'. Upon hearing it Perry
decided to record the track that very afternoon, using the stellar
talents of Boris Gardiner on bass, Sly Dunbar on drums, the
legendary Ernest Ranglin on guitar, Keith Sterling on keyboards
and Barry Llewellyn and Earl Morgan from The Heptones as
backing vocalists. The lyric was a condemnation of the violence
and brutality used by police and gangs, making them both
equally feared; it was straight to the point, and although written
specifically about Kingston, it resonated way beyond that to
places such as London, Manchester, New York and Detroit. The
song was picked-up by The Clash and included on their debut
album; although theirs was a crude, sledgehammer version, their

heart was in the right place and it helped spread the word about this fantastic single.

4

BLITZKRIEG BOP
HAVANA AFFAIR
THE RAMONES
SIRE
DID NOT CHART

The first opportunity to hear The Ramones came with the release of this single; it did not disappoint. Opening with a chanted "Hey ho, let's go", we are then hit with a wondrous whirlwind, a wall of noise as Johnny on guitar and Dee Dee on bass attack the strings of their instruments; playing constantly on the down-stroke, they sound like a swarm of angry hornets. Tommy holds down the beat on drums and Joey delivers the hand-grenade lines in a snivelling, nasal whine. 'Blitzkrieg Bop' sounded exactly like the rallying cry we had been waiting for, and a rallying cry it certainly proved to be. It was fast and loud and dumb in a smart way; utterly incendiary, this was a meaningful strike against the boring predictability of the mainstream.

3

ANARCHY IN THE UK
I WANNA BE ME
SEX PISTOLS
EMI
38

Having twice seen Sex Pistols in the summer, and having been convinced of their greatness with immediate and lasting effect, the release of their debut single could not have been awaited with a greater degree of anticipation; I paid my money for what I hoped was a slice of vinyl dynamite and hurried home. Onto the turntable it went, and I listened intently… it was good… very good… perhaps even great… and yet I felt a sense of disappointment. Had I been expecting too much? Had the Pistols' fire been dampened in EMI's swanky studios? Probably a bit of both. I had certainly never related to, or believed in, any other band like I had the Pistols; I thought they were capable of changing everything, and part of what I loved was the ragged glory of their "don't care" live sound which Chris Thomas had neutered with his shiny production. I knew how the Pistols should sound; it wasn't like this. They had been made to seem more 'ordinary' than they actually were – a bit like Alice Cooper, a bit like Hawkwind, a recognisable, comforting, acceptable noise for a wider 'rock' audience whom the record label didn't want to frighten.

Of course the song was great; a slap across the chops for the establishment. This was the gauntlet being thrown down, a challenge to the safe and mediocre. Credit must go to the band's manager, Malcolm McClaren, who had lobbied for a more honest, less professional recording to be issued; he had partially won the day with the inclusion of 'I Wanna Be Me' on the B-side recorded by Dave Goodman, the Pistol's live soundman; it wasn't half-as-good a song as 'Anarchy'… but it sounded twice as good.

2

I'M STRANDED
NO TIME
THE SAINTS
POWER EXCHANGE
DID NOT CHART

The Saints came out of nowhere – or Brisbane, Australia to be precise. Their brand of music was not embraced in their homeland; indeed, they were viewed as some sort of disease to be stamped out, and frequently the police would break up any shows they managed to play and make token arrests. They were, as this song attests, "stranded on their own". They self-released 'I'm Stranded' as a 500-copy pressing, and mailed-out copies overseas where, in contrast to their homeland, it was received with much enthusiasm; the record was a barely contained blast of energy, frustration and anger. The Saints were soon labelled as "punks" – a description they rejected. Instead, they described themselves as "gritty realists", and this record is most certainly gritty; the honesty and reality were unquestionably sincere too… there was no plastic posing at all. The record leapt out of the traps, a huge slab of noise with no concessions whatsoever made to politeness or convention. Singer Chris Bailey's vocal is similarly impressive; spat out without artifice or any attempt to impress. This was a "take it or leave it" performance for a "take it or leave it" song. Nor can it be said that The Saints were a flash in the pan; they proved themselves to be one of the greatest guitar bands ever to plug-in and play. Their stance, reflected in their music, was highly principled; they would not dress-up and pretend to be something they were not; they would not hangout in cool places with the in-crowd. They remained apart, unloved and criminally underrated… forever stranded.

1

NEW ROSE
HELP
THE DAMNED
STIFF
DID NOT CHART

Pop this single onto the turntable, and as Dave Vanian deadpans "Is she really going out with him?" (lifted from the Shangri-las) it feels as if The Damned are in the room with you. Nick Lowe's primitive lo-fi production gives the record massive impact and immediacy, which is just one of the reasons that 'New Rose' is so special… but only one… The band's performance is startling but then The Damned were (whisper it!) very good musicians. What separated them from contemporary instrumentalists of similar ability is that The Damned didn't use their prowess to show off – the ego was suppressed; there were no superfluous notes played, no unnecessary drum fills, they served the song and kept it lean and mean. As for the song itself, it is absolutely wonderful, open-hearted and celebratory; a salute to the new sound breaking out of rehearsal rooms and grotty clubs demanding to be heard. Disguised as a simple love song, 'New Rose' has no cynicism – it has a pure heart, it's quick as a whippet, the drums are like bombs, the guitars like jet engines and the vocal is assured and quite delicious. This single is as near to perfection as Elvis Presley's 'Heartbreak Hotel' or the Kinks' 'You Really Got Me'; in short, we are talking about a classic. The Damned would soon be caught-up in political machinations that were aimed at ensuring primacy of Sex Pistols as undisputed leaders of this new

thing – The Damned's reputation was tarnished and they were trivialised. It is doubtless true that they were a significant threat to this narrative of the new order hierarchy, and so the threat was ruthlessly eliminated – but 'New Rose' remains magnificent, untarnished by time and all attempts at revisionist re-writing of music history.

Photo booth, 1977

1977

- Snow falls in Miami for the only time in the United States' existence
- The rings of Uranus are discovered
- A collision between two Boeing 747s at Tenerife Airport kills 583 people; the deadliest accident in aviation history
- David Berkowitz (aka "Son of Sam") is apprehended in Yonkers, New York
- Hamida Djandoubi is executed by guillotine in Marseille, France – the last legally-sanctioned beheading in the western world
- Imprisoned Red Army Faction members Andreas Baader, Jan-Carl Raspe and Gudrun Ensslin commit suicide in Stammheim prison, West Germany
- Gay activist Harvey Milk is elected City Supervisor of San Francisco
- Egyptian President Anwar Sadat, seeking a permanent peace settlement, makes an official visit to Israel to meet Prime Minister Menachem Begin; he is the first Arab leader to do so
- Manchester United defeat league champions Liverpool to win the FA Cup, weeks later manager Tommy Docherty is dismissed

NOTABLE BIRTHS

Shakira; Floyd Mayweather Jr; Chris Martin; Kanye West; Raul; Edward Furlong; Thierry Henry; Andrew Flintoff

NOTABLE DEATHS

Erroll Garner; Anthony Eden; Anais Nin; Joan Crawford; Olave Baden Powell; Vladimir Nabokov; Elvis Presley; Groucho Marx; Steve Biko; Marc Bolan; Maria Callas; Bing Crosby; Ronnie Van Zandt; Cassie Gaines; Steve Gaines; Charlie Chaplin

NOTABLE FILMS

Saturday Night Fever; Close Encounters of the Third Kind; Annie Hall; Star Wars; The Island Of Dr Moreau; Der Amerikanische Freund; The Last Wave; Suspiria; Stroszek; Eraserhead

NOTABLE BOOKS

The Shining - Stephen King
A Scanner Darkly - Philip K Dick
In Patagonia - Bruce Chatwin
The Book Of Merlyn - T H White
The Flounder - Günter Grass
Dispatches - Michael Herr
Success - Martin Amis
Johnny I Hardly Knew You - Edna O'Brien

THE MUSIC

This was a wonderful year for music. It seemed as if the cork that had been stuck in the neck of the bottle for so long had finally been extracted, and what had been steadily building beneath suddenly erupted in a rush of fizzing energy. Tired establishment acts retreated to darkened rooms to escape the possibility of being swept away by the tide of youthful euphoria; their absence left room for true creativity to flourish and fill the gap. In the UK, small independent record labels proliferated and brought freshness with them – this was an involuntary spring clean for the music industry. Songs got shorter, snappier and they ceased to be simply spring-boards for extended musical masturbation, which had, increasingly, been the prevailing trend. For the major labels there was a frenzied and desperate policy of signing-up anything that remotely resembled 'punk' as they realised that they needed to get in on the act. Inevitably, this meant that a lot of signed acts were of little worth and much that was released was absolute rubbish… but if one was discerning with one's choices, there was also some quite remarkable music to be heard.

In America, the CBGB bands had gained both acceptance *and* record deals, and so we were treated to some of the best music we had ever heard from acts such as Talking Heads, Blondie, Richard Hell and the Voidoids, Mink DeVille and the

The Sex Pistols hijack the Queen's Silver Jubilee

Dead Boys – alongside the already listened to semi-established Television and Ramones. Stirrings from the West Coast were noted too, and from Ohio the remarkable Devo were revealed to be revolutionary conceptualists who were as funny as The Marx Brothers but had a barrier-pushing musical sound of sheer genius. Also pushing the envelope was propulsive electronica that came out of Munich, courtesy of Giorgio Moroder; when matched with the breathy vocals of Donna Summer this was stunning and it revolutionised music at a single stroke.

Despite all this rock 'n' roll activity it was disco that was the pre-eminent genre of the year as the film *Saturday Night Fever* (and superb attendant soundtrack album) sent people off in search of dance-floor thrills and a joyous escape from 9 to 5 tedium. Reggae, too, in the year of *Two Sevens Clash*, was at its zenith both artistically and commercially; long regarded as being little more than a novelty sound by the colonialist music media, it now commanded, and was afforded the respect it was due. However, I don't wish to give the impression that new genres and new acts were totally dominating proceedings because that would not be correct. Burning just as brightly as ever, and issuing music that was challenging, contemporary, and in some cases ground-breaking, were well-known figures such as Stevie Wonder, Bob Marley, Abba, T. Rex, Parliament/Funkadelic, Kraftwerk and inevitably David Bowie, who, as ever, still had his finger on the pulse of the cultural Zeitgeist.

MY 1977

My year was filled with too much drinking, too many drugs and a suicide attempt; it felt like heartbreak, but in hindsight I realise it was simply a bad case of teenage angst. Interwoven within that mess was the happiness that seemingly only music could instil within me. Records were eagerly anticipated and rarely did they disappoint – the debut Damned LP, Sex Pistols singles, The Saints, Iggy Pop, Television, Devo, Culture, Dillinger, Al Green and James Brown – it all seemed so endlessly brilliant. Gigs also regularly put a smile on my face, with the likes of The Fall, The Modern Lovers, X-Ray Spex and Elvis Costello all filling my heart with joy. I had a drunken night with Sex Pistols Cook and Jones that saw me get in for work 4 hours late the next day; naturally enough, this exposed some serious fault-lines between my bosses and I. The year ended with me adrift in Torquay, replete with stitches from a razor-slashed wrist that was seeping blood and pus. A puke-stained t-shirt was my only protection against the biting cold wind as I stood atop a cliff, wondering whether to jump. Instead, I took my death-wish to a biker-bar in order to antagonise an axe-toting Hells Angel; I was not in good shape…

100
RIVERSONG
FAREWELL MY FRIEND
DENNIS WILSON
CARIBOU
DID NOT CHART

Dennis was perceived to be the playboy of the Beach Boys, and indeed, he did live a hedonistic life to the full and had never publicly shown anywhere near the same level of creativity as his brothers Brian and Carl. However, 'Riversong' was written primarily by Dennis (with some help from Carl) and had been played live by The Beach Boys in the early 1970s, although never recorded. When Dennis belatedly got around to making a solo album, *Pacific Ocean Blue*, this was the opening track and first single release. 'Riversong' is stunningly beautiful and captures the glory of nature, as Dennis – his voice a bruised rasp as a result of lifestyle excesses – sings tenderly and soulfully about rejecting the fast-paced and polluted city in order to embrace country living with its clean water and fresh air. He accompanies himself on piano, and his voice is surrounded, with great effect, by a full Baptist choir which lends grandeur to the track and perfectly complements its subject.

99
IN THE CITY
TAKIN' MY LOVE
THE JAM
POLYDOR
40

The Jam were heavily touted as the next big thing which placed a somewhat unhelpful weight of expectation upon their very young shoulders. They had transformed themselves from a Dr Feelgood style R&B group into a hybrid punk/mod revival act, they had, like many others, jumped aboard the passing bandwagon. During this formative period The Jam were an unpleasantly strange act; their three stylistic influences did not always fit together seamlessly, and with their scrubbed-up schoolboy looks and silly matching suits attracted much derision. Their debut album revealed the most glaring problem – despite the undoubted explosive musical edge, they had a stodgy, low-quality repertoire that contained only one good song; fortunately, that one song, 'In the City' was chosen to be the single that would introduce them to the wider world. With its jagged, Who-style riffage, Rotten-esque anger and palpable energy, further enhanced by Paul Weller's passionate vocal performance, this couldn't be easily dismissed. The Jam had announced themselves in fine style, and in so doing earned themselves the time and space to go away, assess their strengths and weaknesses to come back even stronger.

98
MOONDANCE
COLD WIND IN AUGUST
VAN MORRISON
WARNER BROTHERS
DID NOT CHART

Amazingly it had been seven-and-a-half years this first appeared as the title track of Van Morrison's third album before it was issued as a single. Although it is now considered to be a standard and a radio staple, this belated release was not the success it deserved to be. 'Moondance' is an acoustic piece, played with jazz timings, given thrust by a very nimble bass line and embellished by prominent flute and saxophone parts. Morrison sings of a romantic tryst beneath an autumnal night sky; he expresses, with simple elegance, awed wonder at the beauty that surrounds him and he sings from the soul. This is a sophisticated and melodic piece of work that wouldn't have felt out of place on a Frank Sinatra album… as Van himself astutely observed.

97
HOW MUCH LONGER
YOU BASTARD
ATV
DEPTFORD FUN CITY
DID NOT CHART
Mark Perry saw Sex Pistols perform and following that transformative moment he quit his job in a bank, began to write and distribute a fanzine that was adopted as the punk bible *Sniffin' Glue*, and also formed a band called Alternative TV. The group were reasonably well-placed to go onto fame and fortune if they so chose… but Mark Perry had an inner dilemma; although he clearly loved a lot of the music and the rhetoric of revolutionary thought, at the same time he could see through the lies and insincerity of many of its purveyors. He perceived that much of the growing audience were simply hero-worshippers who lacked a mind of their own, and he saw the nightmare evolving in real-time for exactly what it was. This was the thought process that produced 'How Much Longer' where, over a brutal riff, he compares the attitudes of punks (who wear Nazi armbands and dye their hair) to that of hippies ("You make your peace signs… man") and 'straights' who "spray their Ford Cortinas". The depressing conclusion is that there is no difference: they are all conformists

who "know nothing, and don't really care".

96
CRANKED UP REALLY HIGH
THE BITCH
SLAUGHTER AND THE DOGS
RABID
DID NOT CHART
Slaughter and the Dogs are the worst group I have ever seen in my life… and I've seen plenty of bloody awful groups; they were dull as ditchwater, idiotic, despicable and more. They had been operating at the fag-end of glam rock, a sort of sub-metal cabaret band, dressed in blouses and playing painful versions of Stones and Bowie hits. Then they lucked out with a gig supporting the Pistols; they were a complete embarrassment to themselves on the night of the gig when the highlight of their set was the singer's graceless primadonna temper-tantrum after being struck by a jelly-baby. Slaughter and the Dogs had no pride and no shame, and therefore they seized the opportunity, grabbed onto the Pistols' coat-tails and refused to let go. They decided to try and re-invent themselves as a punk band – a terrible punk band – because although they cut their hair, changed their outfits and sped-up their songs, they were undeniably clueless… or, to put it another way, absolutely crap. Then they released this single where, thankfully, the pathetic lyrics are inaudible – "Getting high on glue and cocaine, jabbing things into my vein, a Lucifer lord, holding my hand, pushing pills to a rock 'n' roll band". The mind-boggling truth though is that the sound was incredible; the drums and bass were thunderous, the guitar loud and full of attack – they could have been mistaken for a young

untutored MC5. Overall this was fast, ragged, and sounded like it might just crash on every corner… in fact it was excellent. Not quite excellent enough to make me eat humble pie in my assessment of them as a band, but certainly good enough to make me realise that my prejudices needed to take a temporary back-seat while I sat-up and enjoyed the noise.

95
AMERICAN GIRL
THE WILD ONE, FOREVER
SHELTER
TOM PETTY AND THE
HEARTBREAKERS
40

Byrds-like jangling guitars playing a high-speed Bo Diddley riff, a quote plucked from Francis Ford Coppola's 1963 movie *Dementia 13* and an impassioned vocal redolent of Bob Dylan; 'American Girl' was packed with all the ingredients to succeed, which it deservedly did – initially on a small scale, but eventually this came to be regarded as Petty's best-ever song and a much-loved classic of American rock music.

94
WAY DOWN
PLEDGING MY LOVE
ELVIS PRESLEY
RCA
1

This was the final single release by Presley during his lifetime, a surging piece of up-tempo rock 'n' roll with a playfully flirtatious Elvis, evidently having fun and accompanied by his close friend gospel singer J.D. Sumner, whose incredibly low bass voice is a stand-out element of the recording. Presley's untimely demise no doubt helped propel 'Way Down' to the very top of the chart, but it wasn't just sympathy and grief that made this a hit; 'Way Down' was genuinely excellent and a worthy follow-up to 'Moody Blue', which earlier in the year had reached number 6 entirely on its own merits.

93
DO THE STANDING STILL
(CLASSICS ILLUSTRATED)
THE MAGICAL MELON OF
THE TROPICS
THE TABLE
VIRGIN
DID NOT CHART

Hailing from Cardiff, The Table had recorded a demo version of 'Do the Standing Still' in 1975 – in their words, "Virgin (Records) had a little nibble"; now, as punk broke, Virgin decided to bite. The Table were given a deal for the single and it was released to acclaim in the music press, as well as receiving airplay on John Peel's late-night radio program. This is a fantastically odd record where, over a propulsive rhythm, the singer yells phrases from comic books before we hear deadpan choruses of "Do the standing still, do the standing still" which act as punctuation marks before the track kicks-in again. The Table were not punks and nor did they pretend to be – they were, in fact, a bunch of long-haired Captain Beefheart fans – and correspondingly 'Do the Standing Still' is not a punk record… but it did share a similar feeling of irreverence, and its lack of pomposity allowed it to be embraced by the ever growing spike-haired tribe.

92
YOUNG SAVAGE
SLIP AWAY
ULTRAVOX
ISLAND
DID NOT CHART

Moving away from the glam sound of their previous release, 'Young Savage' saw Ultravox incorporate a blistering staccato riff for this stripped-to-the-bone single that has a violent energy, further enhanced by the clipped, almost shouted, vocal from John Foxx. As a psychedelic keyboard part and wailing lead guitar are introduced, the sound becomes ever more frenzied and more extreme, offering no respite from the maelstrom until the record comes to a startling jarring halt.

91
OXYGENE PART IV
OXYGENE PART VI
JEAN-MICHAEL JARRE
POLYDOR
4

Constructed from a short musical phrase borrowed from 'Popcorn' (which Jarre had previously covered) 'Oxygene IV' is one man armed with an array of analogue synthesisers, creating a sound that would help to shape and influence the future of electronic music. Loved by the record-buying public – but derided by the punk-obsessed music press – 'Oxygene IV' worked equally well on the dance-floor or as head-music; it was stylish, memorable, melodic and undoubtedly most enjoyable.

90
QUARK STRANGENESS
AND CHARM
THE FORGE OF VULCAN
HAWKWIND
CHRYSALIS
DID NOT CHART

A much-changed Hawkwind line-up – featuring a much-changed Hawkwind sound – released this eccentric and charming single with a lyric from vocalist Robert Calvert that references subatomic particles and nuclear physics, while jokingly mocking the lack of romantic prowess displayed by the likes of Albert Einstein and Galileo. Only a jammed space-rock instrumental passage hints at the band's former glories, because the new sound resides somewhere between Chas & Dave and The Stranglers, with Viv Stanshall on vocals – which, of course, is a very good thing indeed...

89
HOTEL CALIFORNIA
PRETTY MAIDS ALL IN A ROW
THE EAGLES
ASYLUM
8

The Eagles were a band I did not like. I found their smug, laid-back, easy-listening anthems absolutely insulting and nausea inducing but 'Hotel California' is the opposite of that. This is an inspired piece of work, a complex and ambitious soundscape that clearly demanded a lot of effort to piece together. The song presents a good deal of (perhaps sub-conscious?) self-awareness too; the lyric paint a Gothic picture of innocence lost, decadence, hedonism, self-destructive greed and madness. Musically, the band stretch out with a Latin-flavoured phrase that carries a rather sinister undercurrent, and this leads into the famous twin-guitar coda of exquisitely good taste.

88
DO ANYTHING YOU WANNA DO
SCHOOLGIRL LOVE
THE RODS
ISLAND
9

Eddie and the Hot Rods had slimmed their name down to the more punchy The Rods for this single, but conversely they had beefed-up and widened the parameters of their sound by recruiting guitarist/songwriter Graeme Douglas from the Kursaal Flyers; out went the spidery R&B of yore and in came wide-screen, breezy power-pop. This release also benefited hugely from a clear and bright production, courtesy of Steve Lillywhite, with a hand-clap rhythm and jangling guitars to the fore. Lyrically the verses detail the wrongs done to the young by the old and powerful, who "don't like to see you grow", and there is an anthemic, shout-along and punch-the-air chorus. All-in-all, it's a great slice of guitar pop.

87
COMIN' ROUND THE MOUNTAIN
IF YOU GOT FUNK, YOU GOT STYLE
FUNKADELIC
WARNER BROTHERS
DID NOT CHART

'Comin' Round the Mountain' is a simple, nursery-style chant, with no meaning other than get your ass onto the dance-floor; but this functions as the perfect excuse for an absolutely mind-spinning guitar wig-out, the

like of which no black act since Jimi Hendrix had performed.

86
GO BUDDY GO/PEACHES
THE STRANGLERS
UNITED ARTISTS
8

Punk went top-10 with this release, mostly because 'Peaches', with its high-level smut content, seemed to excite lots of teenage boys during their pubescent fantasy stage of development. The Stranglers were, quite deliberately, setting themselves up as bad-boy sexual predators, baiting those they perceived to be hypocritical, fake liberals. At the same time, they were also strapping themselves into a straight-jacket from which they never quite managed to free themselves, as they were forevermore compelled to continually use derogatory and violent imagery in their portrayal of women. That said, beyond the lyrical content, 'Peaches' was excellent, rebelling, as it did, against the "play it fast" conformity; they created a still dangerous-sounding, but snail-paced piece of music that was quite compelling. On the flip-side, 'Go Buddy Go' exhibited no such musical adroitness; it was simply a return to the band's pub-rock roots as it bounced along frantically. The lyrics were a paean to street-level hedonism and the music crackled, fizzed and was easy to love. In that sense this was something of an aberration for The Stranglers who were usually intent on displaying a dark, vicious, hard and uncaring image – personally, I always imagined that Norman Tebbit, Margaret Thatcher's hatchet-man, must be a Stranglers fan.

85
SCIENCE FRICTION
SHE'S SO SQUARE/DANCE BAND
XTC
VIRGIN
DID NOT CHART

The UK was not one homogeneous mass in 1977; towns and regions had distinct features and flavours all of their own. Therefore it was completely natural that a band hailing from Swindon would sound nothing whatsoever like a band from Manchester or London – even though they might operate under the umbrella term of 'punk', their sensibilities would be quite different, as would be the differing voices and sounds. So it was with XTC, who had their own unique take on what was happening; they were as sharp, abrasive and angular as anyone, but they combined this with a pop sensibility often suppressed by others. There were even 'prog' influences – especially displayed in Barry Andrews' keyboard playing – and "clever" lyrics, courtesy of the constantly punning Andy Partridge. All of these contrasting elements were manifested on this single, which set the tone for their unorthodox career.

84
RIO
LIFE, THE UNSUSPECTING CAPTIVE
MIKE NESMITH
ISLAND
28

As the Monkees-era came to an end, Mike Nesmith launched a solo career and helped to pioneer "country rock" – 'Rio' was a track taken from his ninth solo album and it was a charming delight. We, the listeners, are privy to the thoughts and flights-of-fancy of the song's narrator, as he day-dreams and muses on the possibility of an imminent flight to Rio; the beach, sunshine and cocktails are all conjured-up in the imagination. This is blissful escapist fantasy, as even Nesmith himself admits… "It's only a whimsical notion, to fly down to Rio tonight, and I probably won't fly down to Rio, but then again, I just might".

83
READ ABOUT SEYMOUR
RIPPED AND TORN/ BLACK VELVET
SWELL MAPS
RATHER RECORDS
DID NOT CHART

Solihull teenage brothers Epic Soundtracks and Nikki Sudden, along with their pal Jowe Head (not their real names!) formed Swell Maps as early as 1972, but the birth of punk was their gateway out of bedrooms and onto the national stage. 'Read About Seymour' was their first release; it was a knowing, witty discourse in coded language, over a bass riff and spluttering guitar, which also featured a section of unstructured noise – happily ramshackle, this was a world away from the 1-2-3-4 of Pistols and Damned copyists. Swell Maps had located a window through which they nimbly clambered in order to escape the stultifying orthodoxy; they opened up a vista of new possibilities through their radical re-imagining of rock 'n' roll. Later, many others would follow them down the rabbit-hole and find inspiration in that landscape first populated by Swell Maps.

82
BIRDLAND
THE JUGGLER
WEATHER REPORT
CBS
DID NOT CHART
'Birdland' was written by keyboardist Joe Zawinul as a tribute to the jazz club in New York where he first saw acts of the calibre of Louis Armstrong, Duke Ellington and Miles Davis perform; it was also the place he met his wife, so it definitely deserved to be commemorated! Weather Report was the jazz-fusion band Zawinul had founded and co-led with saxophonist Wayne Shorter, with whom he had played in Miles Davis' late-1960s band. Here new bass player Jaco Pastorius is featured and a magical alchemy occurs – from the opening bass figure, the tune opens out. There is a wonderful groove and Shorter plays breathtaking sax with a beautiful, yearning quality. This is the kind of jazz that even people who profess not to like jazz can dig on, because it transcends dumb genre classifications and exists purely in the space of blissful and brilliant pieces of music.

81
BLACK BETTY
I SHOULD HAVE KNOWN
RAM JAM
EPIC
7
Although credited to Huddie Ledbetter (aka Leadbelly) who popularized the song in the 1930s, 'Black Betty' is widely regarded to have originated in the 1800s. There are several theories as to what exactly is a 'Black Betty' – plausible reasons exist to suggest that it could be either a bullwhip, whisky bottle or a musket. Whatever the truth may be, this arrangement was by ex-1960s popstar Bill Bartlett, once of the Lemon Pipers, but here performing with southern American hard-rock band Ram Jam, who play a dynamic, stomping version of the song, characterised by its staggered, powerful guitar riff, skittish drums and urgent vocal.

80
STAR
THE OWL
KEVIN AYERS
HARVEST
DID NOT CHART
Kevin Ayers last single of the 1970s was plucked from his *Yes We Have No Mañanas* album and is a soaring piece of classic Ayers magic, with a wise and wonderful lyric concerning aspiration and ambition versus leisurely contentment. As ever Kevin sings in his lugubrious, world-weary way, while over a glorious melody, Ollie Halsall serves up a tasteful, yet still emotionally-charged, guitar masterclass.

79
SCREWED UP
OUTRAGEOUS–
CONTAGIOUS/LET'S LOOT
THE SUPERMARKET AGAIN
LIKE WE DID LAST SUMMER/
SHOCK HORROR
MICK FARREN & THE
DEVIANTS
STIFF
DID NOT CHART
Stiff had released a Pink Fairies single, and now Mick Farren, another old hero of the counter-culture, was offered the opportunity to record one as well. And so, with Farren in charge, the Pink Fairies became The

Deviants for the purpose of this record, to which Larry Wallis applied his decidedly lo-fi production values. 'Screwed Up' is a testimonial to amphetamine use, and is afforded a suitably scuzzy sound featuring a fuzz-drenched guitar and one of Paul Rudolph's insane out-on-the-edge solos, while elderly delinquent Farren rasps out the vocal… It is fabulous.

78
BOP GUN
(ENDANGERED SPECIES)
I'VE BEEN WATCHING YOU
PARLIAMENT
CASABLANCA
DID NOT CHART

Stone-cold genius here from George Clinton and company; just as Funkadelic's sound was dominated by guitar, Parliament utilised the horn section and 'Bop Gun' has a mighty horn riff that plays out alongside a brilliant piano track and the customary elasticated bass line. The 'Bop Gun' is part of P-Funk's self-written mythology – a weapon used for protection against threatening enemies, which infects them with funkiness – and here it is employed to great effect with splatter-squelch sound-effects added to the rhythm, while Glen Goins sings soulfully on what turned out to be his last P-Funk record.

77
EGYPTIAN REGGAE
ROLLER COASTER BY THE SEA
JONATHAN RICHMAN AND
THE MODERN LOVERS
BESERKLEY
5

Having re-moulded The Modern Lovers sound from loud and electric to quiet and acoustic, in order to enhance the emotional impact of his songs, Jonathan Richman's next startling move was to release an instrumental cover version as a single. 'Egyptian Reggae' began life as a song called 'None Shall Escape the Judgment' when issued by its writer, Earl Zero, and it was then popularised in Jamaica by Johnny Clarke. Richman's version, a delightful oddity, was refreshing and fun as he plays spritely guitar whilst percussion maestro D. Sharpe excelled with his playful utilisation of sticks, cymbals and shakers.

76
ROCK AND ROLL HEART
SENSELESSLY CRUEL
LOU REED
ARISTA
DID NOT CHART

Lou was rescued from impending bankruptcy by Clive Davis, the head of Arista, who gave him a record contract when he was being shunned by others. By way of a thank you, Lou seemed to genuinely work hard so as to give his new label some accessible songs to try and sell; 'Rock and Roll Heart' is a great example of this effort. Here we have Lou adopting an everyman persona as he regales us with lines about not liking opera or ballet – of course, in reality Reed was highly-cultured and very open minded. "I guess that I'm dumb, Lord knows I'm not smart, but deep down inside I've got a rock and roll heart" he deadpans through the chorus. , all this masquerading happens atop a riff that is monumental and brutal; all-in-all, a beautiful, relentless piece of noise.

1977

75
DON'T DICTATE
MONEY TALKS
PENETRATION
VIRGIN
DID NOT CHART

Penetration (named after a track on Iggy and the Stooges *Raw Power* album) were led by Pauline Murray, an early punk convert after seeing and meeting Sex Pistols in Northallerton in the spring of 1976. 'Don't Dictate' was the band's first and best release. Over a churning rhythm and power-chord guitar, Pauline, her voice urgent and soaring, sang this anti-authoritarian declaration with total belief; it was defiant, articulate and liberating to hear a female voice from the grim industrial North be possessed of such conviction. Sadly, Penetration did not improve; instead, due to the presence of backward-thinking and rock-fixated members within the band, they soon sounded past their sell by date.

74
LESS THAN ZERO
RADIO SWEETHEART
ELVIS COSTELLO
STIFF
DID NOT CHART

At this point every release on Stiff Records was worthy of attention, and so this debut single by the unknown Elvis Costello was snapped-up in the first week of release and quickly revealed itself to be a genius slice of almost – but not quite – reggae, with a rather sinister edge. The song unleashed a vicious attack on Oswald Mosley, the infamous leader of the British Union of Fascists. At the same time the underhand seduction of the uneducated and vulnerable by racist organisations is represented in the song as covert and coercive sexual coupling with teenagers as a weapon of control. Mr Costello had announced himself as a stellar talent in one song; I could hardly wait to hear more…

73
STAYIN' ALIVE
IF I CAN'T HAVE YOU
THE BEE GEES
RSO
4

From the *Saturday Night Fever* soundtrack, this was disco with a heart and disco as high-art. Lyrically the song concerns itself with the daily struggles we all endure and the refusal to buckle under the weight of our problems; its sentiments certainly struck a universal chord. The song has an upbeat feel and adopts a proud, indomitable strut. Sung in glorious falsetto by Barry Gibb, the track utilises synthesisers, horns, "chikka-chikka" scratch guitar and a looped drum-beat. 'Stayin' Alive' was a veritable tour-de-force; disco music, which was showing signs of decline, also received a shot-in-the-arm, and this was almost completely down to the work produced by the Bee Gees at this time.

72
THIS IS TOMORROW
AS THE WORLD TURNS
BRYAN FERRY
POLYDOR
9

Inspired by the title of a pop-art exhibition featuring the work of Richard Hamilton (Ferry's former teacher) 'This Is Tomorrow' was the assured and confident sound of an optimistic Bryan Ferry viewing a future he was keen to embrace.

The song is given the soul-review treatment, with a core band of Roxy Music's Paul Thompson and John Wetton – on drums and bass respectively – along with Chris Spedding who plays tasteful guitar; they are supplemented by keyboards, a brass section and female backing vocalists. Whilst the chugging rhythm never quite takes flight, it nonetheless moves at a steady and pleasing pace, arriving at its destination, most agreeably, in its own good time.

71
TELEPHONE LINE
POOR BOY (THE GREENWOOD)/
KING OF THE UNIVERSE
ELECTRIC LIGHT ORCHESTRA
JET
8
Taking as a song's starting-point the somewhat clichéd lyrical device of a man trying to get through to a lost lover who will not pick-up the phone does not augur well; and yet the skill and craft lavished on this record, allied to Jeff Lynne's impeccable melodic sensibility, make this a wonderful trip into a camp, symphonic, pop-nirvana. With a doo-wop chorus, romantically yearning strings and Jeff Lynne's mournful vocal, there is a distinct 1950s feel to 'Telephone Line'; somehow it feels as if we are gently spinning through time and space and could easily end up in the land of Oz, somewhere on the yellow brick road.

70
PROVE IT
VENUS DI MILO
TELEVISION
ELECTRA
25
The bookish Tom Verlaine was quite rightly acclaimed for his idiosyncratic guitar-playing prowess, but he was also a brilliant lyricist and with 'Prove It'… well, he proved it! Seemingly inspired by a Raymond Chandler detective story, Verlaine's words are concise and to the point – almost forensic one might say. Musically the sound of the verses is clipped and angular before the chorus opens out into a crescendo of notes that brings to mind the *Liege and Leaf*-era sound of fellow virtuoso guitarist Richard Thompson.

69
FADE AWAY
FADING DUB
JUNIOR BYLES
EAGLE
DID NOT CHART
In the year that 'Fade Away' got a UK release, Junior Byles remained a long-term patient at Bellevue Hospital due to his mental health problems so this was an excellent reminder of his supreme talent as both writer and performer. The track was recorded at Channel 1 with "Jo Jo" Hoo Kim producing and it is a wonderfully wise song that gives a warning to the greedy and avaricious of the fate that awaits them – "He who checks for only wealth, and not for his physical health, shall fade away". The backing is sparse but Junior Byles, with his keening voice, carries the song magnificently. It is true that 'Fade Away' is perhaps this artist's greatest achievement… but even more than

that, it is also one of the finest records in the entire history of reggae.

68
GOIN' THROUGH THE MOTIONS
SEARCHIN' FOR CELINE
BLUE OYSTER CULT
CBS
DID NOT CHART

Written by Eric Bloom with ex-Mott the Hoople front-man Ian Hunter, 'Goin' Through the Motions' is a song about the emotionally empty sexual relationships between male musicians and female fans of the 1970s, where for one night they would hook-up and pretend to genuinely care for each other before moving on to pastures new with the dawning of a new day; here, the rock-star flatters his own ego by leaving a signed photograph of himself as a souvenir, imagining that it will somehow give the encounter a degree of meaning. The song has all the stylistic hallmarks of a Mott the Hoople number, with its chugging piano-riff and pastiche 1950s middle eight, but set against the sleek, restrained power of Blue Oyster Cult's polished performance, it made for an excellent single.

67
GOT TO GIVE IT UP PART 1
GOT TO GIVE IT UP PART 2
MARVIN GAYE
TAMLA MOTOWN
7

Teetering close to bankruptcy, Marvin was encouraged to record a disco record, which he strongly resisted as he felt that the genre lacked real substance; eventually he decided to record a kind of funk parody of the disco sound. Gathering people together in a party atmosphere, their chatter was recorded as an element of the backing track, which is a sinuous, snaking groove, heavy on percussion with saxophone floating over the mix. Marvin sings about going to a club where his initial shyness about dancing evaporates due to the power of the music, and then the evening progresses from that point onward. Ironically, this reluctantly recorded dance track was the biggest hit that Gaye had enjoyed in several years and it was also a huge influence on the direction that Michael Jackson's songwriting would take, being a virtual blueprint for The Jacksons 'Shake Your Body (Down to the Ground)' and Michael Jackson's own 'Don't Stop 'Til You Get Enough'.

66
THE FOOL
ENDLESS SLEEP
ROBERT GORDON
WITH LINK WRAY
PRIVATE STOCK
DID NOT CHART

Written by Lee Hazelwood and originally a hit in the US for Sanford Clark, 'The Fool' was much covered by a variety of rock 'n' roll and country singers including Elvis Presley and Johnny Kidd and the Pirates. On this fantastic rockabilly version of the song, ex-Tuff Darts singer Robert Gordon is teamed with guitar playing legend Link Wray… it's fair to say that sparks fly. Gordon sings in a hiccupping baritone the like of which hadn't been heard for nearly two decades and Wray puts down a relentless, fidgeting lick on guitar; no frills, no tricks, just a great song well sung with a rockabilly beat that sounded as fresh as the proverbial daisy.

65
DOWN DOWN DOWN
OVER AND OVER
SYLVESTER
FANTASY
DID NOT CHART

After two rock albums as Sylvester and the Hot Band, Sylvester James Jr transitioned into a soul/disco solo act and the results were immediately exciting. This was his first single and it defined his career for the next few years, with an up-tempo rhythm and Morse code style horns to keep the sound sharp. Sylvester unleashes his glorious soulful falsetto and the lyrics, as always, reflect compassion and empathy – an outlook that helped make him the champion for a host of persecuted groups of people, and a star who was genuinely loved and admired.

64
CELEBRATE SUMMER
RIDE MY WHEELS
T. REX
EMI
DID NOT CHART

Whereas the emergence of punk spelt redundancy for many acts of his generation (and hence they railed against it, affronted by the perceived lack of musicianship of their usurpers) Marc Bolan embraced the spirit of the young bands – and what's more, he found that they liked him too, since for many of them T. Rex had been their gateway drug into music in the first place. Marc took The Damned out on tour with him and, as someone who was there, I can promise you it was a well-matched bill. Bolan was putting his demons to bed; he looked healthy again and his happiness was plain to see. All of this energised his music and gave him fresh impetus, and so this final single of his lifetime found him in brilliant form. Buzzsaw guitar riffs and drop-dead stops are the order of the day and he sings with that familiar hint of lovable impishness in his voice. The single oozes positivity and reflects a man back on track and looking optimistically toward the future…

63
SHEENA IS A PUNK ROCKER
I DON'T CARE
THE RAMONES
SIRE
22

Joey Ramone was a brilliant, walking and talking manifestation of what punk really stood for; he was the anti-rock star – too tall, too thin, sickly and nasal sounding. He was also decidedly non-macho, never afraid to display his sensitivity and he had an ingeniously abstract thought process which he employed in his songwriting. Here, from a cartoon comic book, *Sheena the Queen of the Jungle* is transported into a modern day urban environment where the primal sound of punk rock is the one thing that she can relate to. Played in the surf-rock style that Joey loved, this proved to be irresistible to even the most prejudiced ears and it put The Ramones in the charts.

62
I'VE GOT THE GROOVE
OPPORTUNITY
GEORGE FAITH
ISLAND
DID NOT CHART

George Earl began cutting a collection of soul cover versions with Lee Perry at the Black Ark; progress was slow with each track taking up to a month to complete and so Perry commented that Earl had a lot of faith and maybe he should use the word as a name… and so George Faith was born. 'I've Got the Groove' is a re-make of a track released by The O'Jays in 1969 although it has undergone a complete transformation; to begin with, it is taken at a far slower pace, and whereas The O'Jays' arrangement is filled with horns and lavish orchestration, Perry provides a minimal and idiosyncratically brilliant rhythm with discreet backing vocals to support Faith's sweet voice. Overall, it is far superior to the source material, 'I've Got the Groove' displayed rare artistry and supreme talent.

61
DISCO INFERNO
YOU TOUCH MY HOTLINE
TRAMMPS
ATLANTIC
16
A spicy riff immediately bursts out of the speakers and, after a few bars, horns and vocals are added; the effect is incendiary and the track does not let up. It rides its elastic groove until the horns and guitars drive each chorus to successively higher and wilder peaks as the vocal becomes ever more urgent and electrifying. This record really scorched and 'Disco Inferno' was indeed a highly appropriate title.

60
SUCCESS
THE PASSENGER
IGGY POP
RCA
DID NOT CHART
Iggy Pop had been through the hell of drug addiction and mental hospitals but now, with the aid of his friend David Bowie, he was seemingly out on the other side of despondency and looking forward to an upward trajectory and 'Success'. Confident enough to junk much of Bowie's input on this song, Iggy trusted his instinct and simplified the arrangement until it became a repetitive pounding riff without chorus or middle-eight. Over the top of this Iggy indulges himself in a gonzo-style listing of all the material things that success will bring him – a car and a Chinese rug being just two examples. His brutal rhythm section of Hunt and Tony Sales proceed, unrehearsed, to chant back each line to Iggy, becoming ever wilder and eventually cracking each other up. It was a delicious, madcap single – and the B-side was pretty good too…

59
MAGIC FLY
BALLAD FOR SPACE LOVERS
SPACE
PYE
2
Space were a French electronic band who came into being when Didier Marouani presented 'Magic Fly' to his record label (Polydor) who promptly rejected it as sub-standard. Marouani persuaded another label to release it but they couldn't use his name under the terms of his contract with Polydor; to solve the problem, Space was formed, with Marouani using the pseudonym "Ecama" and the band dressing themselves in space suits, replete with helmets, as a cunningly effective disguise. The track itself was fantastic – there is a propulsive drum beat, a haunting melody and the synthesisers combine to give a very futuristic feel that echoes through various dance tracks right up to the present day.

58
GRIP
LONDON LADY
THE STRANGLERS
UNITED ARTISTS
44

'(Get a) Grip (on Yourself)' was The Stranglers first single and it was most pleasing on the ear. Produced by Martin Rushent, who added a sprinkling of fairy dust to the band's aggressive sound, 'Grip' was an up-tempo song about life at the bottom of the rock 'n' roll food chain – the condition of being penniless and desperate, with only a belief in music for sustenance. It features a saxophone introduction (played by a Welsh miner) along with what would later become staples of the band's sound: Hugh Cornwell's barked vocal, the loping bass of Jean-Jaques Burnel, Dave Greenfield's odd boogie-woogie organ sound, snarling guitar licks and some excellently nimble drumming courtesy of Jet Black.

57
TWO SEVENS CLASH
TWO SEVENS CLASH
VERSION/PROPHESY
CULTURE
JOE GIBBS
DID NOT CHART

As a fervent religious disbeliever, I do not empathise with the sentiments in this song – or indeed with many others in the Rasta-dominated reggae canon – but much as I can still appreciate gospel music, I cannot fail to be moved by the conviction of the performers and I greatly appreciate the integrity of their belief; ultimately, the end result is fantastic music that simply transcends its subject. Here, Joseph Hill's starting-point is the prophecy by Marcus Garvey that on July 7th 1977 there would come a day of reckoning; this notion is fleshed-out to create a picture of impending disaster, a coming apocalypse. The track was recorded and released by Joe Gibbs and it utilised stellar performers such as Sly Dunbar and Robbie Shakespeare to create an immediately recognisable roots track of beguiling beauty which made a platform for Hill to breathe blood and fire into his words, while his band-mates harmonise sweetly. The record was an instant classic and such was its power and influence that on the 7th July that year, many people in Kingston shuttered themselves up away from harm, businesses did not open and the streets were eerily silent...

56
SHOW YOU THE WAY TO GO
BLUES AWAY
THE JACKSONS
EPIC
1

Gamble and Huff wrote and produced this single for The Jacksons. Recorded at Sigma Sound in Philadelphia, it contains all the familiar Philly Soul features of sophisticated strings and a hi-hat heavy disco groove but the magic ingredient here is the remarkable voice of Michael Jackson who, as he matured, was able to invest real character into his singing. He captures every nuance of the lyric and totally inhabits the song as he handles the lead vocal, getting sterling background support from his brothers along the way. Of note too was the B-side of the single; this was the first song written entirely by the increasingly precocious Michael.

55
BLANK GENERATION
LOVE COMES IN SPURTS
RICHARD HELL AND THE
VOIDOIDS
SIRE
DID NOT CHART

'Blank Generation' was a newly recorded version of the song that had been on Hell's little heard Stiff Records release a year earlier but on this revved-up version the sparks really begin to fly. The track has a tough heart which acts as a springboard for the guitars to thrillingly slash around like demented razor blades as Hell, in an adrenalised yelp, gets passionately philosophical about existence being nothing more than a blank canvas, his prose as sharp as needles and laced with disgust. The B-side, 'Love Comes In Spurts', is every bit as good and equally stirring as the agony of teenage love and sex is examined in a sub-two minute experience that is jam-packed with poetry and cascading guitar noise.

54
DON'T STOP
GOLD DUST WOMAN
FLEETWOOD MAC
WARNER BROTHERS
32

Written by Christine McVie following the break up of her marriage to John McVie (the band's bass player) 'Don't Stop' is decisively *not* a song of recrimination; instead, it is all about moving on with positive thoughts and – very wisely and impartially – it could equally apply to either party in the split. The track is taken at a brisk tempo and there is a jaunty feel to the piano playing as the rhythm section provides a dynamic sense of forward motion. Sung with complete conviction by Christine McVie and Lindsey Buckingham (with Buckingham also supplying an electrifying guitar break) this was sublime, breezy pop music from a grown-up perspective.

53
MOTÖRHEAD
CITY KIDS
MOTÖRHEAD
CHISWICK
DID NOT CHART

No trace of the Hawkwind-era "space rock" sound was evident in Lemmy's new band. Motörhead played bone-shaking, furious, hard and fast no-frills rock 'n' roll and sung in a wild, neo-primitive style. Sounding dangerous, looking menacing and unapologetically singing a song extolling the delights of amphetamine sulphate, Motörhead seemed set for outlaw status and outsiderdom. That they became so loved that "national treasure" status was bestowed upon them speaks volumes for the no bullshit attitude that managed to endear them to the mass of people who consciously rejected 'acceptable' consumer trends.

52
BEAUTY AND THE BEAST
SENSE OF DOUBT
DAVID BOWIE
RCA
39

After an ominous musical opening in which the tension steadily rises, Bowie launches into a song that can be interpreted in several ways, though the general theme is certainly the juxtaposition between good and evil, whether that be drugs, marital relationships or Berlin divided by the wall – all of these have been mentioned as sources of inspiration. Whatever the song's provenance, there is a dark hue and a jagged edge provided by Robert Fripp's extreme guitar part, Eno's treatment of the sound, the grinding and crashing rhythm and Bowie's incredible use of his voice to convey a feeling of dissoluteness and decadence.

51
POLICE CAR
ON PAROLE
LARRY WALLIS
STIFF
DID NOT CHART
Larry Wallis, like former bandmate Lemmy, was one of those unrepentant rockers who it was difficult not to love; fate constantly conspired against him, but he was a fine writer and guitar player. Having cut 'Between the Lines' for Stiff (as a member of The Pink Fairies) he was offered the opportunity to release a solo single and so, with the Fairies laid to rest, he entered the studio with Eddie and the Hotrods rhythm section as his studio band, along with Nick Lowe who was producing... they cut 'Police Car'. There is a circular riff that exudes bad attitude and a guitar sound that simply demands attention, redolent as it is of a key scratching against a car door as the Hotrods dutifully and gleefully pound away while Larry sings about prowling the dark and dangerous city streets in his titular vehicle and coming down hard whenever and wherever he sniffs out trouble. This could almost be "Dirty Harry – the Musical"... and it is great, great fun.

50
LOVE (GOES TO) BUILDING ON FIRE
NEW FEELING
TALKING HEADS
SIRE
DID NOT CHART
Talking Heads announced themselves to the world with the release of 'Love (Goes to) Building On Fire', which features the original three-piece line-up of David Byrne, Tina Weymouth and Chris Frantz, for the only time on record. Detractors would focus on the pretentiousness and deliberately twee quirkiness, but what they were missing was the fact that Talking Heads were twisting music into radically different shapes, and they were attempting to merge the physical and the cerebral. Here, although producer Tony Bongiovi clearly gets his way by introducing some clichéd rock orthodoxy, there are still enough elements of what became Talking Heads trademarks to make this a special record – Byrne's clipped vocal style and impressionistic lyricism, the sharp, angular guitar playing and the rock-solid yet supple rhythm provided by Weymouth and Frantz. In addition, the very un-Talking Heads Stax-style horn riffing works wonderfully well; more was eagerly anticipated.

49
MANNEQUIN
FEELING CALLED LOVE/ 12XU
WIRE
HARVEST
DID NOT CHART
'Mannequin' was a conceptual masterclass by Wire – using a simple chord structure they take umbrage with the fickle followers of fashion.

Vocals are without artifice, matter-of-fact and concise; backing vocals come from Dave Oberlé, a former member of hippy prog band Gryphon. There is a traditional rock middle-eight and the song is completed by a coda of yobbish "La, la, las", a slyly funny parody of the empty-headed brand new punks that Wire were so cleverly undermining by virtue of their very existence.

48
JAMMING/PUNKY REGGAE PARTY
BOB MARLEY AND THE WAILERS
ISLAND
9

Jamaica was in violent turmoil; in 1976 Bob Marley had been shot in the chest in an assassination attempt – his musical response was to write the celebratory 'Jamming'. Although 'Jamming' functions brilliantly as a party record, with its insistent rhythm and catchy chorus, it was certainly no cry for empty hedonism, instead it was a call for unity and for people to stay strong amidst the crisis: "No bullet can stop us now, we neither beg nor we won't bow" he sang, in defiance of the gunmen and their political masters who wished to silence him. Double A-side 'Punky Reggae Party' was recorded in London with English reggae band Aswad providing the backing. It was a gesture of friendly reciprocal recognition to the punk scene which had adopted reggae as a soundtrack of the times.

47
BOOGIE NIGHTS
ALL YOU DO IS DIAL
HEATWAVE
GTO
2

Keyboardist Rod Temperton wrote a clutch of hits for this British funk/disco act with 'Boogie Nights' being the pick of them; it is a hymn to hedonism, a paean to dancing and feeling good. This is a brilliantly constructed record with its imaginative use of cello and synthesiser as well as a fantastic deep backing vocal which underpins the general exuberance of the song. It was such a stand-out track in the way that it could make people dance and feel happy that it soon caught the ear of Quincy Jones who would invite Rod Temperton to work on material with Michael Jackson, for whom he would write *Off The Wall* and *Thriller* amongst others.

46
KING'S LEAD HAT
RAF
ENO
POLYDOR
DID NOT CHART

'King's Lead Hat' is an anagram of Talking Heads, a band that Eno first encountered supporting The Ramones and whom he would go on to produce; B-side 'RAF' is a collaboration with female band Snatch. It seems fairly clear that Eno was expressing his approval of – and enthusiasm for – the new wave of musicians, and here he adopts some of their direct, stripped-back approach to great effect. 'King's Lead Hat' is a galloping wilfully obscure song with Eno's rapid delivery of the bewildering lyric riding upon a bubbling back-beat of treated guitar, funky bass and insistent drumming, the latter courtesy of former Free bass player Andy Fraser.

45
SONIC REDUCER
DOWN IN FLAMES
THE DEAD BOYS
SIRE
DID NOT CHART
As the title of their debut album proclaimed, the Dead Boys were *Young, Loud and Snotty*; however, they were not dumb, so in a sense they were a bit like Slaughter and the Dogs, but with brains. 'Sonic Reducer' was a song written by Cheetah Crome and David Thomas while they were band-mates in Rocket From the Tombs; with lyrics re-written by Stiv Bators, it was presented here as a gloriously noisy message delivered from the gutter. There are scorching Stooges-style guitars, a rattling bass and Stiv Bators howls out his defiance at a world he doesn't much care for, and that, in return, doesn't care much about him.

44
GARY GILMORE'S EYES
BORED TEENAGERS
THE ADVERTS
ANCHOR
18
Double murderer Gary Gilmore was due to be executed by firing squad in Utah; he had chosen to leave his eyes to science and so a team of surgeons were waiting for his death, ready to remove his corneas and transplant them into another person. T.V. Smith's song is sung from the perspective of the person who has received the transplant and comes to realise that he is, quite literally, "Looking through Gary Gilmore's Eyes". This is modern Gothic horror worthy of Edgar Allan Poe, and delivered in a speedy two minutes and 13 seconds – delightfully sick and twisted musical drama, it was a brilliant record.

43
NAME OF THE GAME
I WONDER (DEPARTURE)
ABBA
EPIC
1
With the synthesised opening borrowing stylistically from Stevie Wonder, before more European influences are revealed, 'Name of the Game' is a complex song both musically and lyrically. It is sung from the point of view of a woman in love with a psychiatrist; she opens up emotionally to him, wanting to know if his interest in her is purely professional, or does their bond run deeper. This does sound like a somewhat unwieldy subject for a song, but by this stage Abba were imperial – there was very little beyond their capabilities and so they turn this dark tale, with its yearning, desperate edge, into highly sophisticated and melodic pop gold.

42
SPANISH STROLL
GUNSLINGER
MINK DEVILLE
CAPITOL
20
Written by the pencil-thin (and equally sharp) Willie DeVille, this record was adopted by the new-wave crowd who had seen the band when they were CBGBs regulars. In truth Mink DeVille were rooted in tradition; they were classicists and 'Spanish Stroll' was a Latin-flavoured,

ice-cool swaggering blues. Willie sings with huge style and assurance and we are introduced to a litany of colourful street characters, while bass player Rubén Sigüenza interjects with an unforgettable Spanish segment during the middle eight. Fingers are clicked, Cuban-heels are stamped and smooth backing vocals work like magic on a brilliantly evocative record.

41
WHITE RIOT
1977
THE CLASH
CBS
38

I saw The Clash a couple of times in 1976 before they had released a record – they were fierce and fiery. They impressed me with their passion and clearly there was an intelligence about them that many other sound-a-likes lacked (although, in the maelstrom of noise, this intellect was quite difficult to pinpoint, one had to sometimes rely on intuition about these things). Fast forward a little while and The Clash – despite much revolutionary rhetoric – signed a big bucks contract with the giant CBS label. They were accused of being sell-outs; maybe they were… but even if they weren't they were certainly hypocrites.

What though of the music? Thankfully, that did not disappoint; produced by their live-sound engineer Mickey Foote, their authentic punk sound was replicated in the studio. With wailing police sirens announcing the intro, the band wade in as if their lives depend upon it accusing the white British populace of being mere spectators of their own subjugation. It goes on to encourage revolt in the same manner

as the oppressed black youth who had rioted at the 1976 Notting Hill Carnival. This song signalled an end to passivity and the acceptance of the status quo; it ignited feelings of justice and equality, and set off thought processes that found their ultimate expression in the *Rock Against Racism* movement which ultimately won the argument against the rising fascist organisation, The National Front.

40
SHOWROOM DUMMIES
EUROPE ENDLESS
KRAFTWERK
CAPITOL
DID NOT CHART

By this point Kraftwerk had refined their sound and image into a single homogenous entity, and they were wholly unmistakable. Far from being austere and po-faced, despite the deadpan persona they habitually projected, here they are having fun with the count-in of "Eins, zwei, drei, vier" parodying the equally unmistakable "One, two, three, four" introductions of The Ramones. The source material for the song (another sly wink) comes from a negative concert review in which Wolfgang Flür and Karl Bartos are described as looking like 'Showroom Dummies' being controlled by Ralf Hütter and Florian Schneider.

39
(I CAN'T GET NO)
SATISFACTION
SLOPPY
(I SAW MY BABY GETTIN')
DEVO
BOOJI BOY
41

This fidgety, fractured assault on The Rolling Stones standard takes the feeling of alienation to an absolute extreme. The singing is yelped, paranoid and jumpy; the music abandons the song's traditional groove in favour of an ants-in-your-pants squirming discomfort that caused apoplexy within the trad-rock fraternity.

38

LOVE LIES LIMP
(THIS WAS A ONE SIDED FLEXI DISC)
ALTERNATIVE TV
S.G. RECORDS
DID NOT CHART

The final edition of the *Sniffin' Glue* fanzine (Issue 12) came with a free flexi-disc which marked the recorded debut of ATV; it featured a song written by Mark Perry and Alex Fergusson, the latter of whom had already left the band. Over a slow twisting rock/reggae rhythm, Perry addresses gender roles and the often sad disappointment of sex. It is a self-lacerating look at dysfunction through the prism of the emasculating effect of impotence. This difficult subject matter, along with a palpable sense of self-loathing, makes for very uncomfortable listening – but it was exactly this brave and thought-provoking approach that made ATV one of the absolute must-hear bands of the era.

37

LIKE A HURRICANE
HOLD BACK THE TEARS
NEIL YOUNG AND CRAZY HORSE
REPRISE
DID NOT CHART

Nobody plays a guitar like Neil Young; nobody sings like Neil Young and nobody writes songs like Neil Young. 'Like a Hurricane' is one of his greatest songs; sung in that pained, yearning and world-weary voice that touches my soul, and performed as an epic, spacey guitar workout that reaches upward toward the sky, only remaining tethered to Earth by the sheer solidity of Crazy Horse's rugged backing.

36

SIR DUKE
TUESDAY HEARTBREAK
STEVIE WONDER
TAMLA MOTOWN
2

Stevie's swing-era musical heroes were dying off, and culturally they were being ignored. So, when Duke Ellington passed away in 1974, Stevie wrote 'Sir Duke' as a eulogy and a reminder of the talent and influence that Ellington and others of his generation possessed. Stevie sings of the joy that music can bring us and he points out its colour blindness, saluting not just Ellington, but Count Basie, Ella Fitzgerald, Louis Armstrong and Glenn Miller too. The song is frisky and exuberant; it is neither R&B nor jazz, but some unusual combination of the two wherein Stevie displays his love for both forms without being constrained by undue reverence. Huge jazzy horns are utilised and they add real punch, but equally effective are the little pop flourishes that are thrown into the pot on this marvellous, celebratory record.

35

CHINESE ROCKS
BORN TO LOSE
THE HEARTBREAKERS
TRACK
DID NOT CHART

What a wonderful band The

Heartbreakers were – this was apparent from the first moment I saw and heard them on the *Anarchy* tour, which Malcolm McLaren had reluctantly invited them to join simply to make up the numbers. There was nothing gauche about The Heartbreakers: they were men, their musicianship was excellent and they knew they had the songs to leave a strong impression in pretty much any company. They were composed of ex-New York Dolls Johnny Thunders and Jerry "Needles" Nolan, along with Walter Lure and Billy Raith. This single, hamstrung by Speedy Keen's atrocious production, was their UK introduction. 'Chinese Rocks' does have shared writer credits, but in fact it was composed entirely by Dee Dee Ramone. It is a song about heroin addiction, and since it was written by a junkie and performed by junkies, the authenticity is disturbingly conspicuous. Once The Ramones had decided the song wasn't for them it became, despite the murky sound, an anthem for The Heartbreakers. Although intense, this record was buoyed-up by a defiant swagger which gave us a real taste of the New York underbelly from which The Heartbreakers had emerged to take on the world… and to where they would ultimately return, sadly broken by a drug that both defined and controlled them.

34
LOVELY DAY
IT AIN'T BECAUSE OF ME
BABY
BILL WITHERS
COLUMBIA
7 (92 in 1987 / 4 in 1998)
The music of Bill Withers often has a quality of simple truth about it; I feel almost cleansed by its purity and 'Lovely Day' is a glorious record with the power to heal a damaged soul. Over a gentle rhythm sweetened by muted horns, Bill sings in praise of a lover whose presence gives him strength and transforms any kind of mundane day into one that is sublime, special and… yes indeed, lovely.

33
PANIK
LADY COCA COLA
METAL URBAIN
COBRA
DID NOT CHART
Influenced equally by Sex Pistols and Lou Reed's *Metal Machine Music*, this forward-thinking Parisian four-piece created a magnificent wall of noise using synthesiser, guitar, bass and, distinctively, a drum-machine that was seemingly set to "primitive". Amidst the ensuing cacophony singer Clode Panik shouts out unintelligible lyrics in French whilst periodically the whole ensemble shouts out the word "Panik"! What's more, in the middle of this breathless piece, a guitar solo pops up like a migraine attack and then, all too soon, the track comes to an end. All-in-all it was brilliant, and without doubt a huge influence on the likes of D.A.F., Big Black and the Jesus and Mary Chain, who would all follow in Metal Urbain's footsteps

32
SOLSBURY HILL
MORIBUND THE
BURGERMEISTER
PETER GABRIEL
CHARISMA
13
'Solsbury Hill' was the first solo single by Gabriel and it addressed his feelings about, and motivation

for, the split from Genesis: "I was feeling part of the scenery, I walked right out of the machinery" he sings, expressing his need to move on – something that was complicated by his friendship with the band's members. The song is played in the unusual 7/4 time signature which gives it a see-sawing effect that adds tension. Beautifully arranged by producer Bob Ezrin, his perceptive removal of an electric guitar part, replaced by Steve Hunter multi-tracking on acoustic, adds a rustic folky element to the track, though the whole still manages to maintain an ominous, uncertain ambiance, perfect for Gabriel's ruminations in the beguiling lyric.

31
WHOLE WIDE WORLD
SEMAPHORE SIGNALS
WRECKLESS ERIC
STIFF
DID NOT CHART
Eric Goulden was another of the genius misfits to whom Stiff Records gave an opportunity. With Ian Dury trying his hand at producing, Goulden was re-christened Wreckless Eric and sent into the studio with Nick Lowe and drummer Steve Goulding acting as his band. He dished-up this pop gem which is full of naive, wide-eyed charm and sung with a knowing chuckle that lingers just beneath the surface. 'Whole Wide World' was one of those songs that somehow seemed to make life on planet Earth a happier prospect, and it should have propelled Eric toward pop stardom, because everybody who heard it loved it… even my mum! Sadly, not enough people did get to hear it as the radio programmers rigidly stuck to promoting the same old tried and trusted has-beens who had toothlesly managed to suck all of the joy out of music.

30
ONE CHORD WONDERS
QUICK STEP
THE ADVERTS
STIFF
DID NOT CHART
The musical proficiency of the Adverts might generously be described as limited; being less generous it was fair to say they were pretty ropey. Having said that, surely it's better by far to be a band of poor musicians with brilliant songs and ideas, than a band of brilliant musicians playing awful songs. In leader and singer Tim "T.V." Smith, the Adverts were blessed with a genius songwriter – his work was topical, sharp and literate. Here, on 'One Chord Wonders', it was wonderfully self-deprecating too; the band's inability as players is laid bare in the lyric when the nightmare scenario unfolds as they "look up and the audience is gone". Meanwhile, the band give their instruments a damn good thrashing, producing a thrilling and liberated racket over which they sing in unison "The wonders don't care, we don't give a damn". By making a strength from perceived weakness they were striking a blow against the smug, lazy fretboard-wanking snobs who were sneering at the Adverts and other bands like them.

29
WAITING IN VAIN
ROOTS
BOB MARLEY AND THE WAILERS
ISLAND
27

Bob Marley was a rebel for sure, but when it came to his music he was not a one-dimensional man and his softer love songs were often exceedingly beautiful. This is the case with 'Waiting in Vain', which casts him in the guise of a man struggling with a case of unreciprocated love; he is growing tired and wishes to know where he stands. Marley delivers a superbly nuanced and soulful performance whilst The Wailers, as usual, provide an outstanding backing of pulsating rhythm and intricate guitar work. The B-side is also noteworthy; unusually for one of the band's singles on Island Records, it is a non-album track. 'Roots' was a song cut in 1976 during the sessions for *Rastaman Vibration*; it is curious that it was omitted from that album because, quite simply, it is excellent.

28
ROCKAWAY BEACH
LOCKET LOVE
THE RAMONES
SIRE
DID NOT CHART

Beach Boys-style harmonies and surf-rock played at 100mph, atop a blur of scuzzy guitar. This was written by Dee Dee about a beach in Queens where he liked to hang-out, and it was also where Joey lived. The song is a hook-laden celebration of sunshine, transistor radios and discotheques; bright, breezy and impossibly catchy, this was just a brilliant pop single.

27
BELLE
TO SIR WITH LOVE
AL GREEN
CREAM
DID NOT CHART

Ever since a horrific incident in 1974 when his girlfriend had poured scalding hot grits over his back before shooting herself dead, Al Green had wrestled with his conscience in a battle between the sensual and the spiritual. 'Belle' took us into the confessional and this song was where the singer declared a life-changing new direction in both his music and his future career. Producing himself for the first time, he conclusively severed the connection between Al Green, the snake-hipped soul superstar, and Al Green the man of faith. With 'Belle' he did this quite beautifully; we hear a hymn-like ballad of aching sincerity where he makes plain to a lover his reaffirmed calling – a spiritual reawakening – "It's you that I want, but it's Him that I need" he explains definitively.

26
COMPLETE CONTROL
CITY OF THE DEAD
THE CLASH
CBS
28

Were The Clash so stupid? They'd signed to CBS and now they were whinging about corporate interference. DJ John Peel, for one, was unimpressed: "Surely they must have realised CBS were not a foundation for the arts", he opined. Still, at least the puppies were showing their teeth and beginning to growl at their masters, rather than rolling over to have their tummies tickled. Megalomaniac manager

Bernie Rhodes was also attacked in the song; indeed he gave the track its title, after calling a band meeting to announce, to the great astonishment of Strummer and Co., that he wanted 'Complete Control'. On the musical front this was the first single that genius drummer Topper Headon played on, and he provided a solidity they had previously lacked. The overall sound here is much more powerful than on their first recordings, and Joe Strummer sounds magisterially commanding as he expresses his indignation at the position the band were in. One might be tempted to thank Lee Perry for this, since he receives the nominal production credit; but the finished product that the great Jamaican provided was far too radical for The Clash. So they tampered with his mixes and pushed the guitars up in trad-rock style, and also eliminated the heavy, echoing bass in favour of a sound that – ironic, due to the subject matter of the song – would be much more acceptable to the men in suits at CBS.

25
WATCHING THE DETECTIVES
BLAME IT ON CAIN/
MYSTERY DANCE (credited
to ELVIS COSTELLO & THE
ATTRACTIONS)
ELVIS COSTELLO
STIFF
15
Costello is at his most cynical and cutting on this. What, on the face of it, is a simple song about a girl more interested in TV than his amorous attentions, takes on a new layer of intrigue as Costello weaves into the lyric elements of the detective film plot that is airing. The whole piece

is played in cod-reggae style that emphasises the artificiality of the situation and his own pretence that he really cares for her. The tension is ratcheted-up by keyboard player Steve Nieve attempting to replicate Bernard Herrmann-style dramatic orchestral stabs, while Costello sings sneeringly, adding a chilling quality to this twilight-zone noir classic.

24
KNOWING ME,
KNOWING YOU
HAPPY HAWAII
ABBA
EPIC
1
The real-life splits and divorces between the couples who made up Abba hadn't yet occurred when this prescient single was released, but clearly all was not well within the group. 'Knowing Me Knowing You' is as melodic as Abba had ever been but the fun-factor has somehow been sucked out of the tune and replaced with some serious grown-up sadness. The dramatic chord progression is highly melancholic, and the lyrics paint a picture of a barren, loveless landscape, sung with great conviction by Anni-Frid Lyngstad with Agnetha Fältskog's supporting vocal displaying equal hurt. In a few short years Abba had transitioned from lightweight pop act to emotional heavyweights – but at great personal cost...

23
LOVERS OF TODAY
PETER AND THE PETS
THE ONLY ONES
VENGEANCE
DID NOT CHART
I remember reading the music press about this record and taking the bus

into Manchester and buying it from "Rare Records" on John Dalton Street; I also recall looking at the cover photograph and knowing it was for me. When I got home I placed it on the turntable and heard The Only Ones for the very first time. I was well and truly smitten; they were immediately installed as my favourite band and I played both sides of the single over and over again… it was wonderful. 'Lovers of Today' announces itself with a lovely lead guitar figure, before singer Peter Perrett enters, laconic and slightly shambling, with a voice that was defiantly anti-macho, singing words that were wise, but enigmatic, on the nature of bruised love. This reminded me a bit of Syd Barrett, and Bob Dylan– unique talents whom I had placed upon a pedestal; I immediately decided to make some room next to them… there was definitely a place at the top table for The Only Ones.

22
PSYCHO KILLER
PSYCHO KILLER
(ACOUSTIC VERSION)/
I WISH YOU WOULDN'T SAY
THAT
TALKING HEADS
SIRE
DID NOT CHART
With the addition of ex-Modern Lovers guitar player Jerry Harrison, Talking Heads were now fully-formed, and having acquired some studio experience they were better able to impose their will on proceedings and capture on vinyl a true representation of their sound. 'Psycho Killer' had been written by David Byrne in 1974, to be performed in ballad style; as Byrne himself put it, "Kind of like Alice Cooper sings

Randy Newman". It was a first-person account of the thoughts of a serial killer. This released version had somehow morphed into edgy, neo-funk territory; it has a pulverising bass-line and jittery guitars, while Byrne sings in a bugged-out style – his voice rises and falls but never settles into a predictable pattern. A section in French then detaches the character even further from the orthodox man on the street, and as a whole, the song leaves a quite astonishing and indelible impression.

21
SOUND AND VISION
A NEW CAREER IN A NEW
TOWN
DAVID BOWIE
RCA
3
David Bowie recognised that he was a mess; he was heavily into cocaine, alcohol and the occult. In order to purge himself of these handicaps, and rediscover good health and contentment, he decided to remove himself from his self-imposed exile in Los Angeles and head back to Europe. In France he busied himself working on "lab rat" Iggy Pop's album *The Idiot*, with its radical, mechanised funk sound. Happy with the result he was emboldened to begin recording his own album, *Low*, in similar style. RCA were horrified; Bowie was essentially the label's only golden egg laying goose and now he was jeopardizing his commercial appeal by making "weird art music". 'Sound and Vision' was the first single release – it was beautifully other-worldly and, in an understated and unobtrusive way, extremely progressive. The first half of the song is instrumental (apart from some

wordless backing vocals by Brian Eno and Mary Hopkin) as a lively guitar figure is juxtaposed against a more stately synthesiser backing, and then, with minimal expression, Bowie begins to sing about retreating into a room of cool blue, a place of tranquillity, where he can conquer his demons and re-discover himself. That was his inner world; but in the outside world Bowie was changing the musical landscape… yet again.

20
ORGASM ADDICT
WHATEVER HAPPENED TO
BUZZCOCKS
UNITED ARTISTS
DID NOT CHART
Buzzcocks had lost singer, lyricist and figurehead Howard Devoto, who was sickened by his very first sight of punk orthodoxy. Here though, his influence lives on in the single that bridged the gap between the old "art" Buzzcocks and the new "pop" Buzzcocks. This was plucked from the repertoire of the original band and it features Devoto's acidly humorous lyric, detailing sex as an empty mechanical compulsion rather than the culmination of a romantic ideal or overwhelming eroticism. Musically it fizzes and bangs quite wonderfully and is notable for being the only record on which bassist Garth appeared before, as legend has it, he spontaneously combusted. Sung ever so sweetly and disarmingly by Pete Shelley – who came to be embarrassed by the song (he shouldn't have been) – this was marvellous stuff.

19
HOLIDAYS IN THE SUN
SATELLITE
THE SEX PISTOLS
VIRGIN
8
The last of the four 'proper' Sex Pistols singles was also the first one that original band member Glen Matlock did not contribute to as a writer… and it showed. The rest of the band may not have liked him and positively welcomed his departure, but his melodic sensibility was sorely missed. The onus was now placed on the shoulders of Steve Jones to come up with the goods, and though his belligerent and aggressive guitar style often defined the band's sound, it was somewhat of a blunt and brutal instrument as a song-writing tool. Because of this, 'Holidays in the Sun' is high on power and savage riffing, but lower on tunefulness. Still, it is a mighty and meaty sounding song, and Johnny Rotten had come armed with a superb lyric about exploitative tourism which he cackled out quite wickedly – "A cheap holiday in other people's misery!"; it was not a slogan that Thomas Cook picked up on.

18
DON'T LEAVE ME THIS WAY
TO BE FREE TO BE WHO WE
ARE
HAROLD MELVIN AND THE
BLUENOTES
PHILADELPHIA
INTERNATIONAL
5
Bizarre as it may seem this stone-cold classic was not recognised as single material by Philadelphia International Records; it was seen as just another track on the Bluenotes album *Wake up Everybody* released

in 1975. However in 1976, Motown had Thelma Houston record a string-laden, disco version of the song which was, quite deservedly, a big hit. Belatedly Harold Melvin and the Bluenotes original was then issued; it was grittier and more soulful than the Motown interpretation, featuring an exquisite vocal by Teddy Pendergrass, full of an aching hurt that finds release in the explosive chorus, which is a dizzying exultation of powerful love.

17
NEAT NEAT NEAT
STAB YOUR BACK/
SINGALONG WITH SCABIES
THE DAMNED
STIFF
DID NOT CHART
With Captain Sensible serving up one of the most earth-shaking bass rumbles ever (maintained throughout the song), Dave Vanian absolutely snarling the vocal like a vampire with the scent of blood in his nostrils, Brian James's guitar roaming through the mix, seemingly intent on filling every single nook and cranny, and Rat Scabies' power-house drumming remaining right on the beat, this has all the incendiary excitement that made The Damned such a vital band at this time. Lyrically the song is very obscure; maybe it could be perceived to be vaguely political… but no matter. The verses are simply there to be crashed through so we can get into the shouted, high-speed chorus of Ramones-like simple genius.

16
EXODUS
EXODUS (INSTRUMENTAL)
BOB MARLEY AND THE
WAILERS
ISLAND
14
A re-telling of the biblical story of Moses leading the Israelites out of exile tied into the hope that Jah would deliver the Rastafarians out of Babylon and back to Africa. Somehow this radical and revolutionary parable is turned into a hugely celebratory single by the inspired craftsmanship of Bob Marley. The track is a churning mix of reggae and disco, with the addition of uplifting horn flourishes. The mood is unceasingly positive, albeit deadly serious in intent, with the group chant of "Movement of Jah people" indicating unity and strength.

15
THE MODERN DANCE
HEAVEN
PERE UBU
HEARTHEN
DID NOT CHART
On one level 'The Modern Dance' seems almost conventional; there is a propulsive bass riff that one can actually dance to; there is not really a chorus but at least we have a vocal hook to cling to. Beyond that Pere Ubu were still writing their own musical language –a harsh, brutal noise was definitely an element, along with guitars and synthesisers that were used to create decidedly non-textbook sounds. They were taking us way out of the comfort zone, challenging preconceptions and ungluing orthodoxy, before reassembling it in novel and thrilling ways that opened up a whole new vista of possibility.

14
PRETTY VACANT
NO FUN
THE SEX PISTOLS
VIRGIN
6

Written almost entirely by Glen Matlock – Johnny Rotten added the second verse – 'Pretty Vacant' was inspired by Matlock seeing one of Richard Hell's set-lists that Malcolm McLaren had brought back from New York. Amongst the song titles was 'Blank Generation'; this captured the imagination of the bassist, despite him never having heard the song (at that time it was still un-recorded) and he decided to write something with a similarly dramatic title. Filching the guitar riff from Abba's 'S.O.S.' he wrote 'Pretty Vacant' in the style of The Who's 'My Generation'. Toughened up and stripped of unnecessary frills by Steve Jones and Paul Cook, it soon became the early-Pistols' live anthem. This studio version crackles with unrestrained energy; Jones' guitar sounds as big as a jumbo jet and Rotten has glorious fun providing a seemingly demented vocal… notable is his pronunciation of the word "vacant" which he turns into something threatening with more than just a hint of the obscene.

13

NO MORE HEROES
IN THE SHADOWS
THE STRANGLERS
UNITED ARTISTS
8

Perfectly capturing the mood of the times – since heroic characters seemed to be somewhat thin on the ground – The Stranglers evoke a litany of historical figures who were demonised within polite society, and they reposition them as true heroes: among them Leon Trotsky (murdered by Stalin's agents), Lenny Bruce (murdered by the sanctimonious American justice system), master art forger Elmyr de Hory and the literary figure Sancho Panza (Don Quixote's trusting and kindly helper). With their keyboard-led sound honed to perfection by producer Martin Rushent, the song galloped along at quick tempo, and its sloganeering chorus managed to lodge itself firmly into the Nation's collective consciousness.

12

I GOTTA RIGHT
GIMME SOME SKIN
IGGY POP AND JAMES WILLIAMSON
SIAMESE
DID NOT CHART

"I've saved something for you", said my friend Mark Reeder – and from beneath the counter of the Lever Street branch of Virgin Records he pulled out 'I Gotta Right'. One might be forgiven for thinking that this was an out-take from the *Kill City* sessions that Iggy and James did in Los Angeles during 1975 but that would be incorrect. The two tracks on this single were in fact cut in London in 1972 prior to the recording of *Raw Power* and feature Ron and Scott Asheton on bass and drums respectively. What we have here is Iggy and the Stooges at their wildest and most powerful; this is a powder-keg of a single that explodes from the speakers. High-voltage is a phrase that pretty much sums up 'I Gotta Right' perfectly; every single thing is turned up to maximum and played with absolutely evil intent, while Iggy howls out his refusal to be anything other than what he chooses to be. This record is so fast and so intense that you think there can't possibly be more than what you hear within the first thirty-seconds; but incredibly James Williamson then sets his guitar to "stun" and delivers a ridiculously nerve-shredding solo, before the band somehow manage to go up yet another gear before this majestic single finally comes to an end.

11
FISHERMAN
FISHERMAN DUB (Credited to The Upsetters)
THE CONGOS
UPSETTER
DID NOT CHART

The Congos were a vocal trio composed of "Ashanti" Roy Johnson, Watty Burnett and Cedric Myton. Here they are magnificently recorded by Lee Perry at the Black Ark using high-calibre musicians such as Boris Gardiner (bass) and Ernest Ranglin (guitar) to back them, before adding his own brand of inventive studio magic to create this cultural roots masterpiece of gently rocking, transcendent wonder. Myton takes the lead vocal with his clear falsetto, while Johnson and Burnett provide gentle ballast in what is a wondrous, meditative hymn to the tradition and nobility of the 'Fisherman'.

TOP 40 – 4TH JUNE 1977

1	1	I DON'T WANT TO TALK ABOUT IT, Rod Stewart
2	4	LUCILLE, Kenny Rogers
3	2	AIN'T GONNA BUMP NO MORE, Joe Tex
4	3	A STAR IS BORN / EVERGEEN, Barbra Streisand
5	6	THE SHUFFLE, Van McCoy
6	5	GOOD MORNING JUDGE, 10cc
7	9	GOT TO GIVE IT UP, Marvin Gaye
8	24	HALFWAY DOWN THE STAIRS, Muppets
9	8	MAH NA MAH NA, Piero Umiliani
10	13	OK, Rock Follies
11	--	GOD SAVE THE QUEEN, Sex Pistols
12	10	HOTEL CALIFORNIA, Eagles
13	17	LIDO SHUFFLE, Boz Scaggs
14	41	SPOT THE PIGEON, Genesis
15	23	TOO HOT TO HANDLE / SLIP YOUR DISC TO THIS, Heatv
16	15	WE CAN DO IT, Liverpool Football Team
17	45	YOU'RE MOVING OUT TODAY, Carole Bayer Sager
18	28	TELEPHONE LINE, Electric Light Orchestra
19	7	FREE, Deniece Williams
20	12	WHODUNIT, Tavares
21	14	SOLSBURY HILL, Peter Gabriel
22	33	BABY DON'T CHANGE YOUR MIND, Gladys Knight & the
23	--	SHOW YOU THE WAY TO GO, The Jacksons
24	16	IT'S A GAME, Bay City Rollers
25	18	DISCO INFERNO, Trammps
26	20	TOKYO JOE, Bryan Ferry
27	36	PEACHES GO STEADY, The Stranglers
28	19	GONNA CAPTURE YOUR HEART, Blue
29	22	SHEENA IS A PUNK ROCKA, Ramones
30	26	NAUGHTY NAUGHTY NAUGHTY, Joy Sarney
31	43	JOIN THE PARTY, Honkey
32	30	UPTOWN FESTIVAL, Shalamar
33	11	SIR DUKE, Stevie Wonder
34	37	CALANDAR SONG, Trinidad Oil Company
35	42	FEEL LIKE CALLING HOME, Mr Big
36	--	GOOD OLD FASHIONED LOVERBOY, Queen
37	27	RENDEZVOUS, Tina Charles
38	50	DON'T LET GO, Manhattan Transfer
39	31	HELLO STRANGER, Yvonne Elliman
40	47	IN THE CITY, The Jam

10

THIS PERFECT DAY
L.I.E.S.
THE SAINTS
HARVEST
34

An admittedly lowly chart position saw The Saints appear on the BBC's *Top of The Pops* to deliver the most nihilistic and ferocious performance ever to be aired on that light-entertainment vehicle; it was sensational. The Saints looked greasy, unkempt and delinquent; they were anti-fashion and anti-showbiz; they were the types who get labelled as "bad influences" because they might end up tempting impressionable sons and daughters to go "off the rails". Here they were blasting out a monolithic wall of terrifying noise over which the singer spat-out undiluted negative bile. The Saints were making a statement; it was short and sharp and aimed at everybody who put them down, from the Melbourne police force, to the UK's punk-poseurs... their message was "Fuck You!"

9

SEX & DRUGS & ROCK & ROLL
RAZZLE IN MY POCKET
IAN DURY
STIFF
DID NOT CHART

Ian Dury, ex-Kilburn and the Highroads vocalist extraordinaire, turned up as Stiff Records next signing with the quite wonderful and anthemic 'Sex & Drugs & Rock & Roll'. Dury was signed as a solo act, although he was backed on the track by future members of his band (The Blockheads) in the form of bassist Norman Watt-Roy, drummer Charlie Charles and guitarist and co-songwriter Chaz Jankel. Although not the author of the titular phrase, Dury certainly populised its usage. The single was, of course, immediately and dutifully banned by the BBC, and it sold a very modest 19,000 copies before being deleted; however, none of this prevented the song from becoming very widely loved. It concerns itself with championing alternative lifestyle choices, and a rejection of what is expected; orthodoxy is the enemy seems to be the message, or, as Dury puts it, "They will try their tricky device, trap you with the ordinary, get your teeth into a small slice, the cake of liberty". This was served up on a bass-riff nicked from an Ornette Coleman track named 'Ramblin'. Dury was at pains to apologise to both Ornette and original bass player Charlie Haden for 'borrowing' it, but both assured him it was fine because they in turn had appropriated it from an old Cajun tune.

8

OH BONDAGE UP YOURS
I AM A CLICHÉ
X RAY SPEX
VIRGIN
DID NOT CHART

When Sex Pistol Johnny Rotten claimed that he would like to see "loads of groups like us", he didn't mean the idiotic sound-alikes who, within months, had reduced punk to a pointless, dull thud. He meant instead that he wanted to hear groups who dared to be different, who had ideas and opinions, and who had a world-view that offered a challenge to complacency. In other words, he meant groups like X-Ray Spex, led by the incredible Poly Styrene, who expressed herself over a soundscape dominated by free-form saxophone player 16-year old Laura Logic. Once again the moral watchdogs at the BBC issued a banning order on the record, whilst turning a blind-eye to the evil doings of their cheery ambassador Jimmy Savile. "Some people think little girls should be seen and not heard", announced Poly, as, with scalpel-like sharpness, she chastised and mocked the consumer society and railed against the objectification and subjugation of women, before neatly tying these themes together and identifying them as being both driven by the profit motive. These observations are shared with us in a voice full of simultaneous glee and anger; she shrieks out the words ignoring all rules and boundaries – she is crying out for freedom! She is shouting "Oh bondage up yours, oh bondage no more!"

7

UPTOWN TOP RANKING
CALICO SUITE
ALTHEA AND DONNA
LIGHTNING
1

Produced by Joe Gibbs as a musical riposte to Trinity's 'Three Piece Suit', this used the rhythm of Alton Ellis's 1967 single 'I'm Still in Love'. What was intended to be merely a novelty record took on a life of its own thanks to the cheeky spirit of teenage singers Althea (Forrest) and Donna (Reid) being captured on record, as they ad-lib their way through the track using, to European ears, some extremely bewildering expressions. The girls are obviously and audibly having a great time as they record the song, and their effervescent joy is utterly contagious.

6

MARQUEE MOON PART 1
MARQUEE MOON PART 2
TELEVISION
ELEKTRA
30

All the instruments mesh together brilliantly, but in particular the guitars intertwine to weave a soundscape that draws listeners into its very heart; this was a truly radical sound – no rock power-chords anywhere to be heard – and in fact Television were much more of a jazz than a rock band. Completely rejecting all musical cliché, they employed a loose, minimal structure that is, nevertheless, absolutely hypnotic. Listening to *Marquee Moon* is akin to being taken on a journey by the band with Tom Verlaine narrating, as we survey the emotional interior of the song in a coded language patently influenced by the poet philosophers of France. Richard Lloyd plays an illuminating guitar solo, and later there is another one, this time by Verlaine, that is dazzlingly inventive. The song was recorded with the band playing live in the studio; there was only one take; there were no overdubs, no drop-ins, no fix in the mix… just sheer genius captured on tape and pressed into vinyl grooves.

5

I FEEL LOVE
CAN'T WE JUST SIT DOWN
AND TALK IT OVER
DONNA SUMMER
CASABLANCA
1

In Munich Georgio Moroder, Pete Bellotte and Donna Summer came together with the intention of creating a futuristic disco record, using a synthesiser rather than conventional instrumentation. What they achieved was truly ground-breaking and highly influential, a sound that changed what was possible for musicians on a global scale; it influenced the post-punk electronic acts; it informed techno, house and many more genres. The pulsing sound and programmed rhythm gave the track an exciting space-age feel, while Donna Summer provided the human element in the song's recipe as her purrs grew in intensity until they were expressions of pure ecstasy. Underneath strobe-lit dance floors all around the world people were captivated and they danced – and in rehearsal rooms all around the world guitars were laid to rest and replaced by machines.

4

GOD SAVE THE QUEEN
DID YOU NO WRONG
THE SEX PISTOLS
VIRGIN
2

Premiered as 'No Future' during the *Anarchy* Tour in 1976, the song that we came to know as 'God Save the Queen' was clearly outstanding; it was as rousing and passionate as an alternative national anthem should be. The circumstances created by Sex Pistols being sacked by both EMI and A&M Records meant that the scheduled release date was pushed backwards – and so it was that, for better or worse, the single was finally made available in the build-up to the Silver Jubilee pageant to commemorate the coronation of Queen Elizabeth II. The storm that ensued was wholly predictable; the BBC banned the record (of course)

and although it sold more than enough copies to be number one on the hit-parade figures were manipulated to prevent that intolerable event from occurring. As for the record itself, it was the Pistols' crowning glory – their finest moment – melodic, but vicious, with Steve Jones' guitar sounding enormous and punishing. Meanwhile Johnny Rotten had written a lyric utilising unlikely imagery and metaphor to attack the way in which the hierarchical system of monarchy was used to propagate a class-based society where those at the bottom – "the flowers in the dustbin" – are trampled on and crushed. The entire state-apparatus was attacked – "There is no future in England's dreaming", he stated truthfully, and with so much conviction that the pillars on which the structure of society had been erected began to tremble and shake.

3

TRANS-EUROPE EXPRESS
FRANZ SCHUBERT
KRAFTWERK
CAPITOL
DID NOT CHART

'Trans-Europe Express' is a celebration of the sleekly engineered train of the title but also movement itself, and the idea of Europe being but a single entity, rather than a collection of separate nations. The sweeping grandiosity of the synthesiser lines suggest the great classical concert halls of Paris or Vienna. It is a haunting and awe-inspiring piece in which the rhythms echo the movement of the train. Emotionless voices chant out the vocal, conjuring up the detached and deadpan announcements on the train's intercom. Within the lyric a highly consequential meeting is evoked, when Ralf Hütter and Florian Schneider connect with Iggy Pop and David Bowie; what has been discussed we wonder? Onwards we travel, and we hear the sound of metal on metal as the wheels turn on the train tracks; we look through the windows at towns and countryside as the scenery constantly changes. By the time we reach the end of the line we have travelled with Kraftwerk on a journey of sonic possibility, and we are forever indebted to them for taking us along for such an unforgettable ride.

2

JOCKO HOMO
MONGOLOID
DEVO
BOOJI BOY/STIFF
62

'Jocko Homo' grabbed us by the throat and simply demanded attention. The ascending/descending riff, played in an awkward 7/8 time signature, caused it to lurch about ape-like, as synths gurgled and a crisp drum kept time; somehow it sounded like futuristic music played in a primitive style. In addition to the amazing soundscape, 'Jocko Homo' was crammed full of serious ideas, albeit humorously presented, that kept us wondering if we were actually in on the joke, or if Devo were just putting us on? The basic premise seems to be that the human race is not evolving anymore but devolving; this was enigmatic and unsettling stuff indeed. The lyric takes inspiration from both the movie adaptation of HG Wells's *Island of Lost Souls* and an anti-evolution tract named *Jocko-Homo Heavenbound*, mixing up various ideas inside absurdist lyrical riddles that poke fun at humankind's supposed superiority over all other species: "God made Man, but he used a monkey to do it, God made man, but a monkey supplied the glue", sings Mark Mothersbaugh, before the song enters into an elongated call and response coda of "Are we not men? We are Devo", chanted in the manner of the "We accept you, you are one of us" scene, from Todd Browning's film *Freaks*. This was, and it remains to this day, a quite astounding record.

1

HEROES
V2 SCHNEIDER
DAVID BOWIE
RCA
24 (12 following Bowie's death in 2016)

Written in Berlin by David Bowie and Brian Eno, 'Heroes' is a profoundly moving record about love and optimism triumphing in the face of oppression and adversity. It started life as an instrumental track; the title was a nod to 'Hero' by Neu, and the rhythmic base was inspired by the Velvet Underground song 'I'm Waiting for the Man'. Bowie decided to include a lyric after looking through the window of Hansa Studios and seeing producer Tony Visconti embracing vocalist Antonia Maass beneath a Berlin Wall watchtower; this inspired Bowie to write words that are an uplifting celebration of the human spirit. 'Heroes' is a wonderful song, of that there is no doubt; but what makes this such an iconic single is the way in which the pieces of the puzzle are put together by Visconti and the transcendent performances that were captured on tape. In the 1970s Bowie was never really given much credit for his brilliant singing; his style was under-appreciated and it was much more showy vocalists who received the highest accolades.

It seems ludicrous now but at the time the likes of Robert Plant and Ian Gillan were considered to be exceptional, whereas Bowie was thought to be merely adequate. Here he makes an absolute mockery of that assessment; his vocal on 'Heroes' is magnificent – it soars as he pushes his voice to capture all the longing, hope and, ultimately, the sense of triumph that his words convey. Brian Eno too plays his part by laying down the incredible sonic-bed of low frequency drone that is a bedrock of the recording, while Robert Fripp (recruited after RCA sabotaged Bowie's plan to work with Michael Rother) provides an amazing guitar track of pitch-shifting feedback and prolonged sustain that required great skill, ingenuity and imagination. Bowie clearly believed in this record; he promoted it much more than any single he had released in years, performing it on Marc Bolan's TV show and also making his first appearance on *Top of the Pops* since 1973. Sadly the critics were underwhelmed, radio stations unsupportive and the public indifferent. Only the passage of time would eventually change people's perceptions, and 'Heroes' is now justifiably recognised as one of the greatest singles ever released.

*1978 - Despite the culture clash a happy lodger (me)
with my landlords Lynne and Tony.*

*1978 - WITH THE OTHER HAMSTERS IN DENTON
From left: Steve Mardy, Bobby Williams, Steve Middlehurst, myself
and Derek Howarth (looking remarkably like Andre Previn).*

1978

NOTABLE EVENTS

- Workers in Mexico City discover the remains of the Great Pyramid of Tenochtitlan beneath the heart of the city
- The soap opera *Dallas* makes its TV debut
- The *One Love Peace Concert* takes place in Kingston, Jamaica where Bob Marley brings together opposing politicians Michael Manley and Edward Seaga in a gesture of unity
- In a military coup President Daoud Khan and his family are murdered, triggering the beginning of the Afghanistan Civil War which has not yet ended
- Louise Brown, the World's first "test-tube baby", is born in Oldham
- In Tehran demonstrators come under fire from Iranian troops; 122 people are murdered and 4,000 others injured
- Jim Jones leads his Peoples' Temple cult into a mass murder/suicide at Jonestown, Guyana – 918 people die
- Chicago serial killer John Wayne Gacy, who has murdered 33 men and boys, is arrested
- Home-brewing of beer is legalised in the USA
- The first successful trans-Atlantic balloon flight is completed from Maine, USA to Miserey, France
- New Manchester United manager Dave Sexton signs Joe Jordan and Gordon McQueen from Leeds but his first season at United is not successful. Bobby Robson's Ipswich win the FA Cup while Brian Clough leads newly-promoted Nottingham Forest to the club's first league title. Argentina beat The Netherlands in the World Cup Final in Buenos Aires under the watchful eye of the military junta

NOTABLE BIRTHS

Ashton Kutcher; Gianluigi Buffon; Carles Puyol; Ariel Pink; Panda Bear; Kobe Bryant; Jake Shears; Julian Casablancas

NOTABLE DEATHS

Sandy Denny; Keith Moon; Jacques Brel; Harvey Milk; Ed Wood ; Golda Meir; Chris Bell; Aldo Moro; Jack Warner; Hubert Humphrey

NOTABLE FILMS

Days of Heaven; The Deer Hunter; Midnight Express; Superman; Dawn of the Dead; Coming Home; In a Year of 13 Moons; La Cage aux Folles; I Spit on Your Grave

NOTABLE BOOKS

The World According to Garp – John Irving
The Cement Garden – Ian McEwan
Rumpole of the Bailey – John Mortimer
The Sea, the Sea – Iris Murdoch
1985 – Anthony Burgess
Requiem for a Dream – Hubert Selby Jr.
The Human Factor – Graham Greene
Young Adolf – Beryl Bainbridge
Mommie Dearest – Christina Crawford
Crónicas y Reportajes – Gabriel Garcia Marquez

THE MUSIC

This was a year in which lots of high-quality music was released. Out of the mid-decade slump the punk movement had re-invigorated the slumbering muse within musicians and those who did not succumb to a "punk by numbers" conformity often had thought-provoking methods of framing interesting ideas. The opening up of record companies to these new concepts was long overdue but now the moment had finally arrived... what we heard was a genuine progression. It would have been impossible, for example, for acts such as Siouxsie and the Banshees or X-Ray Spex to have been signed to a major record label in 1974 or 1975, let alone have hits with what were often challenging and intelligent material that owed nothing whatsoever to traditional styles. It must also be noted that both these named acts were fronted by women with strong opinions who created and controlled their own images which were a world away from the manner in which their sex had previously been portrayed by the music business. So, there *was* forward momentum and it was undeniably exciting to be swept up on the wave of change.

Johnny Rotten and Howard Devoto were owed a special debt of gratitude for manoeuvring themselves out of the cul-de-sac they were being steered toward within Sex Pistols and Buzzcocks respectively, and once extricated they tore up the script to do something radically different, re-invigorating themselves and others too; figures with the influence of these two daring to be unorthodox really was something of a revelation. Also apparent this year was the explosion of electronic music inspired by the likes of Kraftwerk and Georgio Moroder, synthesiser acts such as Suicide, The Normal and The Human League made an indelible mark on the landscape. Not that the synthesiser was unique to the post-punk scene; in disco it powered musical classics by Cerrone and Sylvester while on its way to becoming the dominant tool for engineering dance-floor hits. Oldsters Bob Dylan, Lou Reed, The Walker Brothers and Johnny "Guitar" Watson all released great records and remained relevant, proving that talent and attitude were not determined solely by the date on one's birth-certificate. At the other end of the spectrum, the precocious talent of the teenage Kate Bush was showcased when her 'Wuthering Heights' single emerged, announcing the first flowering of a substantial and original talent.

MY 1978

I had a topsy-turvy year; I attempted to take my own life with a drug overdose but failed miserably. I therefore resolved to try and make the most of this second chance and at the same time I came to realise how much hurt and damage I was loading onto my parents. I did some drawing and painting and I tried my hand at writing lyrics. I also read a prodigious number of books and I moved into a shared flat. The flat was nothing short of horrific; it had holes in the floor through which feral cats used to pay us unwelcome visits. According to his birth-certificate my flat-mate was an adult... but unfortunately he had the mind of a child and that inevitably invited trouble. I lived with him for 8-months and in that time, two stabbings and an alleged rape took place on the premises, experiences which stand-out conspicuously even amid the everyday chaos and disorder. I quit my job after undergoing an LSD-induced epiphany at a Patti Smith concert. I also sang on stage again – an opportunity afforded by the fact that my brother had formed a band called the Frantic Elevators who gifted me a support slot. With my friend Bobby and the borrowed Elevators' rhythm section, we performed a version of Sam the Sham's wonderful song 'Wooly Bully', along with a self-written Yoko Ono-style piece called 'You!' – I really enjoyed myself, and the singer from my brother's group encouraged me to continue and called me a star. Gigs I saw this year included Iggy Pop, David Bowie, Wire, Bob Dylan, Suicide and The Fall. Records were bought whenever I had any money in my pocket, and, as always, they provided me with both comfort and inspiration.

100
RECONNEZ CHERIE
RAGS AND TATTERS
WRECKLESS ERIC
STIFF
DID NOT CHART

Eric was a formidable talent but unfortunately he was presented as a novelty act by Stiff Records – he was poorly served by them and, it must be said, by his own self-destructive urges. Here, on his second single, he demonstrates his gift for writing idiosyncratic little gems that are heartfelt and deeply romantic snapshots of the everyday life of ordinary people, a similar talent to that of Ray Davies at his finest. 'Reconnez Cherie' was completely out of step with the times – and all the better for it – with a meandering rhythm, saxophone solo and passages sung in French… it was quite divine.

99
BORSTAL BREAKOUT
HEY LITTLE RICH BOY
SHAM 69
POLYDOR
DID NOT CHART

In Jimmy Pursey Sham 69 had a front man who was genuinely charismatic… and he wore his heart very much on his sleeve. He saw in punk the possibility to give young, disenfranchised working-class kids a voice – Pursey was hopelessly naive but at least he was honest. Inadvertently though Sham became a magnet for violent mobs of racist skinheads; rather than come out and condemn them, Pursey tried to understand and reason with them; of course, he failed dismally in this endeavour and a lot of innocent bystanders were hurt as a result. These errors of judgment, along with the embarrassingly hideous pop-punk sing-a-longs which turned Sham 69 into chart regulars, mean that the band are now regarded, quite correctly, as stupid and abhorrent. The shame though is that, albeit briefly, they were an exciting alternative to the more art-fixated outfits and on this first major-label single they sound full of righteousness and fury. It is unsubtle but undeniably powerful; a head-long rush of adrenaline with a bad-boy chorus that expressed ideas of insurrection and escape. This was a moment of inspiration that Sham 69 would never come close to emulating again – the great potential of this fleeting moment was never firmly grasped and it somehow slipped through their fingers like water down the drain.

98
HEARTS IN EXILE
SOFT SOUTH AFRICANS
THE HOMOSEXUALS
LORELEI NO 1
DID NOT CHART

Bruno Wizard joined a band called The Rejects as a drummer; shortly thereafter he installed himself as front-man and leader. They played several times at The Roxy in Covent Garden and were highly confrontational. Wizard, tired of punk conformity, changed the band's name to The Homosexuals and they stopped performing at recognised venues. At the same time the sound of the band changed significantly, and, in order to document this, they recorded and self-released 'Hearts in Exile'. The song was inventive and tuneful, with an unorthodox structure and unconventional mix. In essence, like Swell Maps and Pere Ubu for example, they were utilising the energy of punk, but moving far beyond its limitations and providing a much welcome and refreshing alternative for what were already becoming somewhat jaded palates.

97
SIGN OF THE TIMES
FOUR LETTER LOVE
BRYAN FERRY
POLYDOR
37

After a very public break-up with model Jerry Hall, the lovelorn and angry Bryan Ferry took the unusual step (for such a quintessentially English artist) of heading off to Los Angeles to record with American musicians; the move invigorated him and 'Sign of the Times' bristles with barely suppressed passion. The swinging, finger-clicking riffs of Roxy Music are evoked, but the playful lyrical couplets are dropped in favour of more vivid imagery, and Ferry all but abandons his delicious croon in favour of a hard-edged delivery that perfectly suits his subject matter of betrayal. Atypically for Ferry the character adopted to sing the song here is very much a flesh and blood creation who happens to bear a striking resemblance to the composer and performer himself.

96
NICE 'N' SLEAZY
SHUT UP
THE STRANGLERS
UNITED ARTISTS
18

With a whizzing synthesiser high in the mix and a wonderful bass-line providing the musical backbone, The Stranglers defiantly display their prog-rock leanings. The lyrics allude to overseas touring where the band attracted and bonded with gangs of Hells Angels, sharing some rather exotic and unsavoury tastes. By mixing these elements together on 'Nice 'N' Sleazy', The Stranglers created a pop record that boys and girls in discos could actually dance to. In doing this they transcended their core audience and managed to both infiltrate and gently subvert the mainstream.

95
SANDWICHES OF YOU
FOREIGN ACCENTS
GODLEY & CREME
POLYDOR
DID NOT CHART

'Sandwiches of You' is a love song – a bizarre, but quite brilliant love song. The title is an odd metaphor for carnal desire and the track has what I can only describe as an art-rock dub backing, which uses manic guitar playing and percussion that sounds as though it has been borrowed from a *Tarzan* film score. The song scrutinises a sly seduction in which, even at the moment when he can take what he desires, the narrator backs away from responsibility and commitment as he states "Shame, shame on you, I want to keep this friendship platonic". As always with Godley & Creme, every detail of the song is honed to meticulous perfection, from the glorious backing vocals to the spacious, high-definition production.

94
LITTLE QUEENIE
HARD LOVIN' MAN
JOHNNY MOPED
CHISWICK
DID NOT CHART

Like Alice Cooper before them, Johnny Moped were a band whose singer shared the band's name. They had been making a gloriously anarchic racket since 1974, playing in parks and people's back gardens, but in 1976, when punk caught-up with them, they actually got a record contract with Ted Carroll's Chiswick label and in 1977 they released the diabolically brilliant 'Incendiary Device'. This was the band's second outing and, by pro-musician standards, they deliver a quite atrocious version of Chuck Berry's 'Little Queenie'. It is untidy, it plods along wearily, it is not at all reverential… and yet it is absolutely fantastic! Johnny (the singer) tackles the song in an unlovely and unnatural falsetto, and then, out of nowhere and completely out of context, a hard-rocking guitar solo appears – tremendous stuff, human, funny and a brilliant dismantling of orthodoxy. If The Residents or Devo had released this it would have been hailed as conceptual genius – in Johnny Moped's hands it was still genius but as natural as the breeze.

93

SOLITARY CONFINEMENT
RAT UP A DRAINPIPE
THE MEMBERS
STIFF
DID NOT CHART

Too tongue-in-cheek to be truly moving, but nevertheless 'Solitary Confinement' did tackle a serious and important issue – the loneliness and emptiness that can be felt by displaced people. Here, the narrator is a young man who has moved to London because that's where he feels excitement lies. However, the reality is that he lives in a bedsit, travels to work on the tube, has no friends and stays in all the time watching TV. From his window he spies a girl in an adjacent flat and observes that her life is a mirror-image of his own. The whole shebang is played as crash, bang, wallop punk rock, with rowdy shouted vocals and a splendidly haphazard production by Larry Wallis. The Members were a great exemplar of what was going on in the music business; they had a couple of excellent songs and on the back of this single they were signed to a major label. The next step was to put them into an expensive recording studio to make an album; the album, despite being polished and professional, would then expose the band's huge limitations – not enough ideas and/or quality material. Still, this was a flash of genius, as was the follow-up 'Sound of the Suburbs'; as for the rest… forget about it.

92

BABY, STOP CRYING
NEW PONY
BOB DYLAN
COLUMBIA
13

In 1978 the UK was in thrall to Dylan when, after an absence of more than a decade, he returned to a British stage playing a week-long residency at the cavernous Earls Court Arena. I, for one, was caught-up in the excitement, and, if not scrutinised too critically, the concerts were fabulous events. The interest and goodwill also swept 'Baby, Stop Crying' into the pop charts – after a long absence for Dylan – and, if judged on its own merits rather than compared with previous classics, it deserved its success. There is a big, full-band sound, with prominent use of saxophone and a cascading guitar riff intro that gives way to an electric organ accompaniment. The track also features a trio of female backing vocalists that give the song an R&B flavour, while lyrically Dylan takes on the role of consoler to a distraught woman – possibly borrowing a little inspiration from bluesman Robert Johnson's similarly themed 'Stop Breaking Down'.

91
KILLING AN ARAB
10.15 SATURDAY NIGHT
THE CURE
SMALL WONDER
DID NOT CHART

The Cure's first single was fabulous; though the title was an obvious provocation, once the record was listened to, it became apparent that the song was an ingenious re-telling of Albert Camus's novel *The Stranger*, replete with eastern-flavoured backing – an existential treatise on contrition (or, more precisely, the lack thereof) and it carried no racist overtones whatsoever. Sadly, the world has changed since 1978 and more recently the song has been used by people to cause offence and division, meaning that it is seldom heard these days. That, however, is not reason enough for its exclusion from this book – 'Killing an Arab' is a superb record.

90
THIS IS POP
HEATWAVE
XTC
VIRGIN
DID NOT CHART

Swindon's XTC were another band resentful of the punk label that was pinned upon them. On 'This is Pop' writer Andy Partridge rejects the whole bandwagon of talentless oafs, and instead aligns XTC with The Beatles by using the instantly recognised opening chord from 'A Hard Day's Night' as a signifier of what he perceived his band to be. This track is as wriggling and jittery a piece of music as early XTC ever recorded, adorned with lovely inventive flourishes even as the vocal is spat-out with venomous disdain towards a fashion-based movement that XTC quite rightly refused to be press-ganged into.

89
SUSPECT DEVICE
WASTED LIFE
STIFF LITTLE FINGERS
RIGID DIGITS
DID NOT CHART

Highway Star were a heavy-rock covers band, but after hearing punk they changed their name to Stiff Little Fingers after a track on the Vibrators' album *Pure Mania*. A journalist by the name of Gordon Ogilvie then became their lyricist; he wrote about "The troubles" – a euphemism for the bloody civil war that was raging in Ireland. Stiff Little Fingers took Ogilvie's words and married them to unrelenting buzzsaw guitar riffs, pounding drums and the abrasive vocals of Jake Burns. Musically they were totally unoriginal – indeed 'Suspect Device' owes the entirety of its tune to 'Space Station #5' by American metal band Montrose. In this case, however, the band's limitations were less important than the message they delivered with great fury and passion. There could be no doubt that Stiff Little Fingers were telling the truth; they vented their anger at the way their own and others lives were negatively affected by the violence and the attendant suppression of freedom. By the end of the song, as the rage and sense of injustice spirals ever upward, Burns is portraying himself as a 'Suspect Device' ready to explode.

87
RADIO RADIO
TINY STEPS
ELVIS COSTELLO AND THE ATTRACTIONS
RADAR
29

Costello now had his own band… but not just any band… The Attractions were superb – tight as a nut and red-hot and they added a new dimension to his sound; he was now able to play, not just loudly, but with controlled power. With 'Radio Radio', Costello re-worked a song he had first written in 1975, and turned it into a stinging rebuke of radio formatting, following the BBC's attempts to suppress Sex Pistols' 'God Save the Queen'. It is bold and unequivocal in its condemnation of the blandness of radio programming, and, of course, The Attractions play magnificently with Costello riding their wave of energy as he delivers savage lines about wanting to bite the hand that feeds him, culminating in the brutal put-down "Radio is in the hands of such a lot of fools, trying to anaesthetise the way that you feel". Unsurprisingly, the BBC didn't offer much in support of this single, but its message was delivered loud and clear.

88
GANGSTER OF LOVE
YOU STAY BUT THE NOISE MUST GO
JOHNNY "GUITAR" WATSON
DJM
DID NOT CHART

Johnny "Guitar" Watson was a flamboyant singer and blues guitar player in the vein of T-Bone Walker. His recording career began in the early 1950s, and he cut his first version of 'Gangster of Love' in 1955 as a blues shuffle. The song came to define him and it was one that he returned to and re-recorded several times. By the 1970s, he was releasing a potent brand of sassy guitar-led funk, and this version of 'Gangster of Love' is in that style. His singing voice is thin and raspy but there is, nonetheless, a classy, assured elegance about his understated style, as he details why Jesse James and Billy the Kid hung up their guns in his presence and how, ultimately, he rides out of town taking the Sheriff's wife along with him. One of the old-style troubadours who made the stage his home, he died in 1996 while performing in Yokohama, Japan. It seems somehow fitting that the 'Gangster of Love' died with his boots on, and with a guitar in his hands.

86
BOXCARS
HONKY TONK MASQUERADE
JOE ELY
MCA
DID NOT CHART

In the beginning were The Flatlanders, featuring the song-writing talents of Joe Ely, Butch Hancock and Jimmie Dale Gilmore, along with a host of other musician friends. Plain bad luck saw the band fall apart, and so the three principal members each became a solo act, whereupon Joe Ely, initially the most popular, recorded some well-regarded albums and toured as support act to The Clash. Though no slouch at penning original material, Ely peppered his albums with songs by his friends, and naturally this added a variety of different styles to his repertoire. 'Boxcars' is a brilliant song, written by Butch Hancock, and Ely performs it quite wonderfully. There is a haunted, introspective quality, as we are told the (depression era?) tale of a man who loses his home when the bank calls in his loan; he sits outside the church, where the automobiles of the conspicuously wealthy congregation are parked, before heading off to the railroad tracks, to watch the boxcars passing as he ponders his bleak and lonely life. Joe Ely sings with a sense of weary resignation in his voice, and the track draws to a suitably sorrowful conclusion with a moving and melancholic violin coda.

85
ALL I WANT
WHEN I'M BORED
SNATCH
LIGHTNING
54
Snatch were American exiles Judy Nylon and Patti Palladin; they had recorded 'RAF' with Eno as the B-side of 'King's Lead Hat' and Judy had also sung on John Cale's 'The Man Who Couldn't Afford to Orgy'. As punk erupted they took the opportunity to record and sporadically tour – fortunately I saw them and was mightily impressed. In truth, they were not really a band at all; it was actually just Judy and Patti plus whoever else was around. They operated in a connected orbit with

Sex Pistols and The Heartbreakers, and indeed, on this very record, Jerry Nolan beats out the rhythm to a catchy, incessant guitar riff, and the girls sing together sounding like the Shangri-Las on amphetamine sulphate. This was top-notch stuff that they showed no particular urgency in following up; indeed it was obvious that this pair were not remotely interested in being marketed as cute, sexy punkettes – they would do exactly as they pleased. Judy went on, in the 1980s, to record for Adrian Sherwood's pioneering On-U Sound label, and Patti cut an album of duets with Johnny Thunders. They continue their artistic endeavours to this day, as strong, independent women.

84
HONG KONG GARDEN
VOICES
SIOUXSIE AND THE BANSHEES
POLYDOR
7
Siouxsie and the Banshees had been in existence since the summer of 1976 and there had been no shortage of record company interest in signing them. Tempting though that may have been, they held-out for a deal that gave them control over their releases and marketing. This meant that 'Hong Kong Garden' belatedly became their first release in the summer of 1978 and it was worth the wait. They sounded unlike any of their contemporaries; the guitar playing was determinedly anti-rock – no power chords, no residue of the blues – instead the sound had a glacial, icy sheen with a distinctly European sensibility. Not to be outdone, the rhythm section utilised a motorik beat, similar to Can and Neu, and

Siouxsie herself adopted a strident vocal style, strong and noticeably unsentimental. Here, on 'Hong Kong Garden', a xylophone motif features as a very un-rock 'n' roll hook, and the song itself references a Chinese restaurant that the band had frequented, often witnessing the staff suffer hateful and racist abuse from mindless local thugs.

83
FUNKY BUT CHIC
THE ROPE (THE LET GO SONG)
DAVID JOHANSEN
BLUE SKY
DAVID JOHANSEN

Four years after the demise of The New York Dolls we were treated to the welcome return of singer David Johansen with the added bonus of Syl Sylvain joining him as guitarist and co-songwriter. Via their work with The Heartbreakers, Johnny Thunders and Jerry Nolan had already displayed that they were the rock 'n' roll heart of the Dolls but here Johansen and Sylvain prove equally convincingly that they were the architects of the Dolls' decadent, theatrical style. 'Funky but Chic' exhibits the same carnival feel as Dolls' classics such as 'Frankenstein' or 'Who are the Mystery Girls', along with an equivalent degree of swagger. Johansen declaims his street-smart, bohemian credentials as he states "I don't wear nothin' not too fussy or neat", while Sylvain plays peacock-strutting guitar and Nona Hendryx wails along on backing vocals.

82
FOXHOLE
CAREFUL
TELEVISION
ELEKTRA
36

After 1977's masterpiece *Marquee Moon*, Television returned with *Adventure*, a very good album that was damned for not being the equal of its predecessor. Perhaps one reason for this was the fact that the former was full of songs that the band had honed over a long period of time, whereas the latter contained newer, less practised material. Also, a change of producer gave *Adventure* a much softer and warmer sound than the abrasive *Marquee Moon*. Whatever the truth of the matter, 'Foxhole', the single plucked from the follow-up album, was superb; lyrically, it is much more straightforward than we had previously heard from Tom Verlaine – the poetic symbolism is replaced with a pretty straightforward criticism of the Vietnam War in particular, and war in general. The narrator is dug into a 'Foxhole' awaiting orders, whilst questioning the purpose of being there, and simultaneously being aware of the danger all around him. Of course, the playing is excellent; it is taut and tense with the twin guitars acting like flares shooting up into the night sky, and spectacularly illuminating the distressing scene that we picture in our minds.

81
YMCA
THE WOMEN
VILLAGE PEOPLE
CASABLANCA
1

If one takes 'YMCA' at face value it is a tribute to the wholesomeness of the "Young Men's Christian Association" and the undoubted good work done under their roof. If one looks a little deeper, 'YMCA' is really about the opportunity to cruise for sex which young gay men were afforded by the intimate contact that can be initiated in the communal showering and changing areas. But irrespective of any of this analysis 'YMCA' is, of course, a genius disco record, from the triumphal horn fanfares, the irrepressible beat and the celebratory lyrics and delivery. When one considers it's extraordinary success it would be difficult to argue a case against The Village People being the most subversive act of all time, and 'YMCA' certainly the most subversive record.

80
IT'S THE NEW THING
VARIOUS TIMES
THE FALL
STEP FORWARD
DID NOT CHART

This is an attack on the music business – hardly original – but what distinguishes this song is the way in which it is written, switching the narrative from one perspective to another, and the nuanced referencing of Eliot Ness and the Untouchables, Gene Vincent and The Electric Circus punks, the Worst. On a musical note, Yvonne Pawlett's bold but untutored electric keyboard playing, and Karl Burns's brilliant, propulsive drumming carry the track, while Mark Smith's sarcastic and sardonic vocal is nothing short of revolutionary in its anti-cliché, anti-style unorthodoxy. Of particular note too was B-side 'Various Times', where long-form repetition and dark storytelling are combined to create a

true masterpiece.

79
CAN YOU FEEL THE FORCE?
CHILDREN OF THE GHETTO
THE REAL THING
PYE
5

The Real Thing were a black soul band from Liverpool. As well as touring and recording with David Essex, between 1976 and 1980 they had a good run of success of their own, including the number one hit 'You To Me Are Everything'. Many of their releases were excellent, but if you had to choose just one, it has to be this because here we have not just one, but *two* sides of aural gold. 'Can You Feel the Force?' is a pile-driving slice of funky disco distinction, with a chanted refrain and a monumental horn riff while 'Children of the Ghetto' is the group's absolute pinnacle. Written about the Toxteth streets they grew up in, this aching song addresses social concerns about discrimination and deprivation but preaches unity and positivity. It has a slow, deep, soulful groove, similar in sound to Curtis Mayfield or Donny Hathaway, and it is an absolute classic by anybody's standards.

78
ACTION TIME VISION
ANOTHER COKE
ALTERNATIVE TV
DEPTFORD FUN CITY
DID NOT CHART

This single had been recorded by a line-up of Alternative TV that no longer existed, featuring Alex Fergusson on guitar; it was, by far, the most orthodox song the band had written up to that point in time. With a dynamic, all-action sound, insistent, barked-out vocal and shout-a-long chorus, it called attention to another string in the band's musical bow – ATV as a pop/punk group seemed to work very well indeed. The other side, 'Another Coke', was a live, improvised piece of dark, psychosexual self-analysis, and it was devastatingly brilliant.

77

TEENAGE KICKS
TRUE CONFESSIONS
THE UNDERTONES
GOOD VIBRATIONS / SIRE
31

With 'Teenage Kicks', which was this young band's debut release, Northern Ireland's Undertones immediately charmed pretty much everyone who had a love of guitar-driven pop. Written originally as a masturbatory fantasy about a desirable girl, for the recording that aspect was heavily toned down and turned into a sweeter, and much more innocent longing. The Undertones were clearly indebted to the sound of The Ramones, and accordingly their guitars buzzed in melodic tribute; they also had a secret weapon in singer Feargal Sharkey whose quivering voice was quite remarkable, and he magically made main writer John O'Neill's songs sound especially vivid and lifelike.

76

ALOHA STEVE AND DANNO
ANGLO GIRL DESIRE
RADIO BIRDMAN
TRAFALGAR
DID NOT CHART

Deniz Tek was a teenager from Michigan whose family emigrated to Australia. Soon after he formed a band called Radio Birdman, named

after a Stooges lyric. The group were inspired by the Detroit rock sound of the MC5 and the aforementioned Stooges, and so Radio Birdman set about trying to achieve a similar level of intensity as their role models. 'Aloha Steve and Danno' was a high-energy recording with a surf-rock style, and it was a tribute to the TV series *Hawaii Five-O* and its two central characters – the lyric basically describes an episode in which they hunt down a KGB agent. Tek plays a brilliantly fiery guitar solo that incorporated the theme of the TV series; most regrettably, this got them into copyright trouble, and by the end of the year the band had split.

75

MR BLUE SKY
ONE SUMMER DREAM
ELECTRIC LIGHT
ORCHESTRA
JET
6

Celebrating the joy of living, 'Mr Blue Sky' is absolutely gorgeous and chock-full of memorable moments: Bev Bevan's cowbell percussion, the vocoder-heavy vocal sections, sawing cellos, Jeff Lynne's wonky guitar solo and the insanely over-the-top backing vocals. This is a trip through a happy land, where Beatlesque flourishes abound and the warmth and brightness of the sun eases our sagging spirits.

74
(I'M ALWAYS TOUCHED BY YOUR) PRESENCE, DEAR
POETS PROBLEM / DETROIT 442
BLONDIE
CHRYSALIS
10

Although bassist Gary Valentine had already left Blondie, drummer Clem Burke lobbied the band to record Valentine's song '(I'm always touched by your) Presence, Dear'. It was duly included on the album *Plastic Letters* and – following Blondie's success with their cover of Randy and the Rainbows 'Denis' – was then issued as a single which proved to be a smart move. The song concerns telepathic communication between lovers separated by thousands of miles; it treads a fine line between the absurd and the sincere, but, due to the outstanding performances, manages to stay resolutely onside. Debbie Harry was much, much more than just a pretty face to front the band, and her ice-cool vocal is marvellous as the band fills-up the track with an exquisite, swirling pop noise of keyboards and guitar, while Clem Burke performs what amounts to a drumming masterclass.

73
NOBODY'S SCARED
DON'T SPLIT IT
SUBWAY SECT
BRAIK
DID NOT CHART

Subway Sect were one of those bands with whom my instincts were more important than my ears. I saw them a couple of times before they released 'Nobody's Scared' as their first single – it would be polite to say that they were a bit ramshackle – but in truth they sounded worse than that… they were sloppy and lacking any sort of cohesion. Still, I was determined to like them: by virtue of their ordinariness, they looked stunningly original – surely this could be no accident… there must be something going on. It turned out, when one heard their record, that much of their amateurish sound was a deliberately provocative anti-orthodox rock music stance, aimed not just at the Eric Clapton's of this world, but equally intentionally at their punk peers. 'Nobody's Scared' unashamedly nailed their colours to the mast, once its lyrical genius was deciphered; "Everyone is a prostitute" was Vic Godard's opening line, as he took careful aim at the get-rich-quick mentality of the supposedly radical scene, where "talking the talk" rather than "walking the walk" was the hypocritical convention. "We shout publicity hand-outs" was another line, laying bare the tsunami of empty sloganeering that was going on; it turned out that Mr Godard was a bit of a genius… I was glad I trusted my intuition.

72
TAKE THE CASH
GIRLFRIEND
WRECKLESS ERIC
STIFF
DID NOT CHART

Was this tongue-in-cheek? – or a wry recognition that, in the music business, money doesn't always reach the artist? Whatever the motivation, it was a funny and clever song, played and sung with a raucous edge. "Where's all the good times in a pocket full of I.O.U.s?" Eric demanded to know, while my mum danced around the ironing board and joined him in singing the choruses… happy memories.

71
I LOVE THE SOUND OF BREAKING GLASS
THEY CALLED IT ROCK
NICK LOWE
RADAR
7

As Nick Lowe said himself his song 'I Love the Sound of Breaking Glass' is nothing; simply a studio idea that he followed-up on with Steve Goulding and Andrew Bodnar (drums and bass respectively) – a nonsense lyric was attached, and that was that. All of which just goes to show that you don't necessarily need a great song to make a great record, because this is a fabulous track. It has a distinctly funky feel adorned with a deliciously madcap piano part, and although the vocal is deadpan and restrained, the overall sound is crisp and welcoming.

70
EVERYBODY DANCE
YOU CAN GET BY
CHIC
ATLANTIC
9

Chic relied not just on the outstanding individual playing of their members, but also the way in which each individual musician melded into one unstoppable, rhythmic entity. Nile Rogers' clipped guitar sound was unique, and quite understandably it became one of the band's signature sounds while the playing of ex-Labelle drummer Tony Thompson is supremely accomplished – but on 'Everybody Dance' it is the bass playing of Bernard Edwards that leads. Lead vocals come courtesy of Norma Jean Wright, backed-up by

Luther Vandross and Robin Clark, who had both performed the same chore on David Bowie's *Young Americans*. Set-up to emulate the style and sophistication of Roxy Music – but positioned within a black music setting – Chic succeeded beyond their wildest expectations.

69
NIGHT FEVER
DOWN THE ROAD
THE BEE GEES
RSO
1

The mixture of beautiful melody, shuffling rhythm and the smooth falsetto of Barry Gibb reaches its apex with 'Night Fever'; in fact, so good was this track that the film it was written for changed its title from *Saturday Night* to become *Saturday Night Fever*. We have here a brilliantly crafted, fabulous and slinky record with feline grace – and although Barry Gibb is the star of the show, the harmony work of his brothers Maurice and Robin is worthy of recognition too.

68
DO YOU WANNA DANCE?
CRETIN HOP / IT'S A LONG WAY BACK TO GERMANY
THE RAMONES
SIRE
DID NOT CHART

The last single by the original Ramones; after this record Tommy hung up his drumsticks because he was tired of the grind of striving for a commercial success that continued to elude them and he was equally tired of the overtly right-wing Johnny's abrasive dictatorship. Here, "da bruddahs" romp through the much-covered Bobby Freeman surf-anthem, with customary unrestrained glee. The magic and energy are all present and correct as they rattle the bones of this chestnut; but by the time their fourth album, *Road to Ruin*, was released later in the year, the band would be in terminal decline as they began to sound like only a pale imitation of their former selves.

67
MISS YOU
FAR AWAY EYES
THE ROLLING STONES
ROLLING STONE RECORDS
3
The Rolling Stones of the mid-1970s had been mostly lacklustre but in 1978, spurred-on by the emergence of punk and disco, they briefly re-vitalised themselves before falling once again into an almost fatal torpor. A very good album called *Some Girls* was recorded but it was preceded by 'Miss You', which was excellent from start to finish. The song was written during a jam by Mick Jagger and the uncredited Billy Preston, and was then crucially steered in a disco direction by Charlie Watts's Phillysound-influenced drumming and Bill Wyman's glorious bass line. Guitars are prominent, but they are used to pepper the groove rather than lead it, while Ian McLagen plays a subtle organ part that adds to the funky vibe, as ex-King Crimson man Mel Collins (saxophone) and street musician Sugar Blue (harmonica) add colourful solos. Finally, as was often the case, Mick Jagger delivers a highly mannered and theatrical vocal that reeks of high-camp, but is, undeniably, very effective.

66
SURFIN' BIRD
THE WAY I WALK
THE CRAMPS
VENGEANCE
DID NOT CHART
The Cramps debut single aimed to "out-trash" The Trashmen's original version of 'Surfin' Bird'; it succeeded with ease because few bands in history have sounded so thrillingly unhinged as The Cramps. Every component of the group was perfect – Nick Knox played straight, simple and primitive drums; Bryan Gregory ripped-up the script on how to play guitar and he simply made a howling, rhythmic noise; the bass from Poison Ivy throbbed and singer Lux Interior yelped, crooned, hiccupped and bawled, re-shaping vowels as he went. The first-half of 'Surfin' Bird' is a fairly faithful, if manic, reading of the song, whereas the second-half is pure psychedelic garage thuggery… and quite brilliant it is too.

65
WHERE WERE YOU/
I'll HAVE TO DANCE THEN
(ON MY OWN)
THE MEKONS
FAST
DID NOT CHART
'Where Were You' opens with a drum roll, winding up to a crescendo, this signals a change in tempo with a repetitive two-chord guitar pattern; then the song proper crashes in and a see-saw rhythm ensues. Over this, the narrator, in simplistic and straightforward terms, addresses a woman he is obsessed with… but he isn't talking *to* her – instead, we hear the dialogue he has with himself. Our first feeling is one of sympathy at his desperate plight, but in the next verse

we understand that he is stalking the woman and we now realise that he is dangerous. He goes on to reveal that his obsession is with a total stranger – "Would you like me?" his internal voice asks. We already suspect that the answer would be a definitive 'No! Leave me alone!'. Suddenly, the self-deception fades, leaving the narrator alone, frustrated and vulnerable; mirroring this, the music simply breaks down and this incredible record comes to an end.

64
BOOTZILLA
VANISH IN OUR SLEEP
BOOTSY'S RUBBER BAND
WARNER BROTHERS
DID NOT CHART
Bootsy introduces his alter-ego with this single – 'Bootzilla' is a wind-up toy with funky moves which provides the subject matter for this fun single. Bootsy plays his usual elasticated bass lines, as well as doing the drumming, while the presence of mentor George Clinton is felt as both co-writer and producer. 'Bootzilla' is a great example of P-Funk at its best; based on a sinuous groove, with an attitude that could only be described as "not dull", absurdity reigns and wears a smiling face… no bad thing at all.

63
CITY SLANG
CITY SLANG
SONIC'S RENDEZVOUS BAND
ORCHIDE RECORDS
DID NOT CHART
The world wasn't listening to what was happening in Detroit; the wild antics and resultant bad reputation garnered by MC5 and the Stooges meant that record companies paid no heed to MC5 guitarist Fred "Sonic"

Smith's band, featuring ex-Stooge Rock Action (Scott Asheton), as well as Gary Rasmussen of The Up and Scott Morgan from The Rationals – a veritable Motor City supergroup… but sadly, hardly heard outside the Midwest, as in six-years together, only this solitary, one-song single was released. 'City Slang' appeared on both sides of the record, marked as being mono and stereo versions – in fact both sides were exactly the same. The band could only afford to mix one track from their repertoire and happily Smith's masterpiece was selected. 'City Slang' is a high-intensity, high-speed express train of a record; it hurtles along, rattling and shaking. The guitar screams, the bass and drums thunder and the vocal is a bad attitude whine; in short, a thrilling record with a rock 'n' roll heartbeat and a racing pulse.

62
FIRE
IF THIS IS WRONG
ROBERT GORDON
AND LINK WRAY
PRIVATE STOCK
DID NOT CHART
Bruce Springsteen wrote 'Fire' with Elvis Presley in mind; he sent off a demo to Presley offering him the song, but Elvis died shortly thereafter. Then, after seeing a gig by Robert Gordon and Link Wray, the song was offered to them instead… and it was readily accepted. Cut with Springsteen himself guesting on piano, 'Fire' perfectly suited Robert Gordon's neo-rockabilly style – the romanticism inherent in the song was explicitly emphasized by Gordon's emotional vocal delivery, and the uncluttered backing helped in this regard too. Unfortunately, this wasn't

the hit single that it deserved to be, but on the strength of this record, and much to his delight, Robert Gordon was signed to RCA records, where Elvis Presley had recorded for so many years.

61
IS THIS LOVE
CRISIS (VERSION)
BOB MARLEY AND THE WAILERS
ISLAND
9

'Is This Love' was one of the seemingly effortless love songs that Bob Marley created; like Paul McCartney before him, Marley quite simply had the innate musicality that made commercial success seem easy and inevitable – of course, such musicality needs to be wedded to solid technique and an artistic sensibility that can sort the good ideas from the bad. 'Is This Love' has an easy-on-the-ear lightness, a memorable yet simple lyric and hooks galore. It grooves too, and the almost bluesy guitar lick that is such a feature of the record is a delight, along with the superb harmonies provided by the I-Threes. Because of his success, there was jealousy and resentment aimed at Bob Marley; this was, in part, down to a kind of twisted and inverted snobbery, where it is felt that certain artists should somehow remain poor because they are defined more by the poverty they have risen from than by their talent. It became, in some circles, hip to dismiss Bob Marley as reggae-lite – this was not only ludicrous but also ignored the fact that his genius should be allowed to roam wherever he chose to look for inspiration. Besides – though no further vindication is required

– it was the success of Bob Marley that completely changed Western perceptions of reggae music and placed a spotlight on many other Jamaican artists who had previously gone unnoticed and ignored.

60
THE MAN WITH
THE CHILD IN HIS EYES
MOVING
KATE BUSH
EMI
6

Written when she was 13-years old, and recorded at the age of sixteen, 'The Man with the Child in his Eyes' is an astonishing song – irrespective of the age of its composer – full of insight and wisdom. It is also performed with absolute mastery and an admirable restraint that allows the delicacy of the orchestrated music to combine with the sublime lyric, creating a piece that borders on the realm of mystifying magic.

59
ROCKERS
THEME FROM ROCKERS
BUNNY WAILER
SOLOMONIC
DID NOT CHART

'Rockers' is a fabulously grooving record, and although its horn riff packs a hefty punch, harmonica and melodica sweeten the track, and with his lyrics Bunny celebrates the reggae sound that can lift people's spirits. With Errol Thompson at the desk and a crop of Jamaica's finest musicians supporting, Bunny Wailer remained at the forefront of the evolution – and revolution – in reggae music.

58

WHERE'S BILL GRUNDY
NOW?/PART TIME PUNKS
HAPPY FAMILIES/POSING AT
THE ROUNDHOUSE
TELEVISION PERSONALITIES
KINGS ROAD
DID NOT CHART

Pertinent, topical, funny, cynical and highly satirical, this was recorded in a lo-fi, naive, amateurish and slightly out-of-tune style which was a welcome relief, announcing to the world, without any pomposity whatsoever, the talent of songwriter and singer Dan Treacy. As their 1982 album title attested, *They Could Have Been Bigger than the Beatles...* what a delicious thought that is!

57

IDENTITY
LET'S SUBMERGE
X RAY SPEX
VIRGIN
24

'Identity' was written by Poly Styrene after she witnessed one of the female faces of the punk scene slash her wrists backstage at The Roxy Club. Poly ties this conspicuous public self-harming into a discourse on consumerist magazine images which alter people's perceptions of themselves. She sees them chasing after an unobtainable image, becoming delusional and prone to radical attention-seeking behaviour. Fittingly, since the song is dealing with extreme ideas and actions, the performances reflect this; Poly Styrene's vocal is a visceral, glass-shattering shriek, while the band hammer out a primal and unrelenting saxophone-led riff.

56

OUTDOOR MINER
PRACTICE MAKES PERFECT
WIRE
HARVEST
51

A song that details the life-cycle of the Serpentine Leaf Miner – an insect that songwriter Graham Lewis was fascinated by – seems an unlikely candidate to trouble the chart compilers, but because Harvest felt that Wire's beautiful 'Outdoor Miner' (a track on their *Chairs Missing* album) had enormous hit potential, they took the unusual step of asking the band for a longer version of the song in order to release it as a single. Another verse was duly added and producer Mike Thorne added a piano break; these amendments gave the song an extra minute's duration. Wire were always rhythmic but 'Outdoor Miner' was also dream-like; with its delicious harmonies and sensuous delivery, this great single was redolent of being kissed by velvet lips...

55

NOW THAT WE'VE FOUND
LOVE
ONE COLD VIBE (COULDN'T
STOP DIS YA BOOGIE)
THIRD WORLD
ISLAND
10

'Now That We've Found Love' was a Philly soul song written by the prolific Kenny Gamble/Leon Huff partnership and issued as a track on The O'Jays superb *Ship Ahoy* album. Third World, though nominally a roots reggae band, created this version of the song as a soul/reggae hybrid, stripping away the strings that adorned The O'Jays original. The tempo is increased and a funky rhythm introduced giving the song an energetic buoyancy that complements the message of universal love. With its energy and earworm of a chorus, this found favour far and wide and made Third World an act of international acclaim.

54
I WANNA BE AN ANGLEPOISE
LAMP
FATMAN'S SON
THE SOFT BOYS
RADAR
DID NOT CHART

Led by Robyn Hitchcock, The Soft Boys provided a whimsical take on the sort of British psychedelic music popularised in the 1960s by the likes of The Move and Syd Barrett. Here though, on 'I Wanna Be an Anglepoise Lamp', they are informed by the spirit of the age and turn in a snappy, punkish confection to accompany the surreal and Absurdist vocal juxtapositions of Hitchcock.

53
FLASHLIGHT
SWING DOWN SWEET
CHARIOT
PARLIAMENT
CASABLANCA
DID NOT CHART

George Clinton sings and incorporates a "Ha Da Da Dee Da Hada Hada Da Da" chant into the song, taken from a dance heard at a Bar Mitzvah party. Bass maestro Bootsy plays no bass at all, but he does drum up a storm while his brother Catfish plays nerve-jangling rhythm guitar. However, the real star of this particular track is keyboardist Bernie Worrell, who creates a swaggering bass-line with a dirty tone by playing through a series of connected mini-

Moog synthesisers – a technique that would be widely imitated. The whole thing joined together is a riot of joyous invention and yet another slice of P-Funk genius.

52
KU KLUX KLAN
KU KLUX KLAN DUB
STEEL PULSE
ISLAND
41

British reggae bands were proliferating and being given a stage as rebel reggae music was taken up by the punk crowd, and it was not uncommon to see bands from these two genres playing on bills together. Aswad, Merger, Harlem Spirit and the Tribesmen all played on that circuit, and producer Dennis Bovell from Matumbi gained huge respect for his work with The Slits and others. However, my favourite British reggae band were Steel Pulse from Handsworth in Birmingham. They were disciples of Bob Marley and the Wailers and their sound owed much to the Jamaican act, but the lyrics to their songs were written from a very black British perspective. 'Ku Klux Klan' was written when that vile American group's so-called "Grand Wizard", David Duke, was invited to the UK to forge links with the equally foul National Front. The song is an emotional and visceral response to the very real possibility of being attacked by white supremacist thugs – "One nigger the less, the better the show" sing the band, articulating the thoughts of the racists. The song concludes with black people rising-up to fight back against oppression and refusing to be treated as second-class citizens anymore. In 1981 the streets of Handsworth burned, as did other inner-city ghettos of the UK: Moss Side, Toxteth, St Paul's and Brixton all witnessed rioting aimed at ending racist persecution. This record was both a warning and a prophesy.

51
AEROSOL BURNS
WORD FRICTION
ESSENTIAL LOGIC
CELLS
DID NOT CHART

After leaving X-Ray Spex, following the release of 'Oh Bondage Up Yours', Laura Logic finished her schooling and then formed the band Essential Logic, prominently featuring her avant-garde saxophone playing and wild, untutored singing. 'Aerosol Burns' was the band's first release and it is an unrestrained release of energy with very sharp edges, thus avoiding contamination by even the merest hint of conformity; this was an exercise in aural free flight, where the chance of crashing was just as great as the chance of soaring – 'Aerosol Burns' soared.

50
DAMAGED GOODS
ARMALITE RIFLE/
LOVE LIKE ANTHRAX
GANG OF FOUR
FAST
DID NOT CHART

Neither preachy nor didactic, 'Damaged Goods' was radical but still accessible. Deadly serious in its damning message on the topic of sexual politics, and yet danceable, abrasive and funky; this was a route map out of punk orthodoxy. The bass line is punishing, the guitar cuts, the drums are crisp and the vocal impassioned. What's more, the songs on the B-side were of equal quality;

this was a must have release.

49
GERM FREE ADOLESCENTS
AGE
X-RAY SPEX
VIRGIN
19

'Germ Free Adolescents' is a kind of artificial reggae waltz, and over its magnificently odd soundscape Poly Styrene sings, absolutely beautifully, a magnificently odd love song. It concerns a girl who is obsessed with cleanliness; she cleans her teeth ten-times a day ("the SR way"), her compulsive behaviour encouraged by advertising strategies and slogans which trap her within a world of empty-headed acceptance of what the advertisers are selling. She meets a boy but judges him solely on his cleanliness... deeply disturbing and very sad. Once again, X-Ray Spex were making pertinent and valuable comments on society via infiltration of the very mainstream that they attacked.

48
BLAME IT ON THE BOOGIE
DO WHAT YOU WANNA
THE JACKSONS
EPIC
8

Confusingly, 'Blame It On The Boogie' was written and recorded by British singer Mick Jackson, before being picked-up by the American Jacksons, whose version featured Michael Jackson on lead vocals. The records were issued almost simultaneously and Mick Jackson managed to achieve a number fifteen hit. The version by The Jacksons though was undeniably superior; it is the one with the wow factor in the form of Michael's uninhibited vocal performance, full of little magical moments where the sheer joy in his singing becomes infectious. This, combined with a monster disco beat, the backing vocals of the brothers and a killer chorus, made this an irresistible dance-floor filler.

47

HANGING ON THE
TELEPHONE
WILL ANYTHING HAPPEN
BLONDIE
CHARISMA
5

The Nerves were a San Francisco power-pop band, fronted by one Jack Lee, who wrote 'Hanging on the Telephone' which his group released to overwhelming apathy in 1976. Jeffrey Lee Pierce, later the front man for seminal punk blues act The Gun Club, was the President of Blondie's fan club and he sent them the Nerves single to listen to and possibly record... which, of course, they did. In the studio producer Mike Chapman persuaded the band – against their initial misgivings – to use the sound effect of a ringing telephone as an introduction, and then a double backbeat rhythm was employed, giving the song an up-tempo feeling of breathless urgency. Debbie Harry yet again excels vocally, her tone going from controlled to desperate as the lyric unfolds. In short, this is a mini-epic of an everyday drama that we can all relate to – a brilliant version of a brilliant song.

46
REALITY ASYLUM
SHAVED WOMAN
CRASS
CRASS RECORDS
DID NOT CHART

'Reality Asylum' is a spoken-word polemic against the use of religion as a tool to control believers; highly articulate and intelligent, it is superbly delivered by Eve Libertine over a sound collage assembled by Penny Rimbaud. Penny had written the lyric in 1977 as part of his book of the same name, in the same period when Crass were first put together. This record was somewhat unusual – possibly unique? – in that it attracted a visit from the Vice Squad along with a threat of prosecution! It also sold for 45p when the cost of a single was usually £1 – the band had failed to factor VAT into their expense calculations and consequently they lost money on each and every sale. Crass were a fascinating group – apart from the music, their ideals and ideas were most worthy of consideration – 'Reality Asylum' is a brilliant record.

45
NATIVE NEW YORKER
EVER LOVIN' SAM
ODYSSEY
RCA
5

Sandy Linzer and Denny Randell were a songwriting team who supplied Frankie Valli and the Four Seasons with several hits. They wrote 'Native New Yorker' and Valli was the first to record it on his 1977 album *Lady Put the Light Out*. The song was picked-up by Odyssey – who were, at least, based in New York, albeit not natives – and when given a sumptuous production and disco treatment it evoked a feeling of the urban big city full of glitz and glamour, covering up the hurt and heartbreak that lies beneath. The lyric comes from the perspective of a friend offering advice and pointing out that love can be as artificial as a Broadway show; it is a gritty and realistic song that resonated with people who lived their lives underneath the mirror balls of discotheques, all the way from Manhattan to Manchester.

44
CAIRO
CAIRO DUB
JOYELLA BLADE
VIRGIN FRONTLINE
DID NOT CHART

I know absolutely nothing about Joyella Blade or the circumstances of this recording, which seems to have been her only recorded release. What I do know is that it is superior, eastern-tinged reggae, and it has an effervescent quality and an uplifting sound; a single that has lightened my life ever since I first heard it.

43
DOWN IN THE TUBE STATION AT MIDNIGHT
SO SAD ABOUT US /
THE NIGHT
THE JAM
POLYDOR
15

In 1978, singles wise, The Jam had released the atrocity that was 'News of the World', written by bassist Bruce Foxton, followed by a cover version of The Kinks' 'David Watts'; which suggested that maybe Paul Weller was struggling to pen any quality songs himself. That theory was thoroughly debunked by 'Down in the Tube Station at Midnight', which showed an enormous flowering in Weller's songwriting potential. Gone was the ham-fisted sloganeering, replaced by a perceptive and empathetic tale of a man randomly attacked on the London Underground. It twists from reportage of the assault to his internalised thought processes of where the violence could ultimately lead; this is tense and sickening stuff because we recognise what is, unfortunately, a familiar everyday occurrence that could just as easily happen to us as to the narrator of the song. With a syncopated beat, train sound-effects and strained vocal, 'Down in the Tube Station at Midnight' paints an ugly and bleak picture of society and it marked out The Jam as being a little bit more than just silly pseudo-mods or fake punks.

42
BEING BOILED
CIRCUS OF DEATH
HUMAN LEAGUE
FAST
DID NOT CHART
(No. 6 when re-released in 1982)

Reviewing this single for *New Musical Express*, John Lydon dismissed it as being the work of "trendy hippies"; of course, he was wrong. This was a music forged in the post-industrial landscape of Sheffield, by very working-class sonic pioneers – indeed, the original recording of 'Being Boiled' was made in an abandoned factory and recorded directly onto cassette, all for the princely sum of £2.50. The band used only synthesisers – something which was quite revolutionary in the UK – and they created a hissing, ominous soundscape that nodded toward film-noir and P-Funk, while singer Phil Oakey deadpans a most confusing lyric which references silk farming and bell ringing (the voice of Buddha) to create a quite unique and compelling single.

41
HIT ME WITH YOUR
RHYTHM STICK
THERE AIN'T HALF BEEN
SOME CLEVER BASTARDS
IAN DURY AND THE
BLOCKHEADS
STIFF
1

By all accounts Ian Dury already had the basic lyric written for several years when he and Chaz Jankel convened in the garage at Dury's Toad Hall residence in Kent to work on it. Jankel, inspired by his own funky piano part on the earlier song 'Wake Up and Make Love With Me', provided the music, and Dury the fascinating and entertaining lyric that name-checks various exotic worldwide locations, uses phrases in French and German and, of course, uses the attention grabbing "Hit me, hit me, hit me!" as a compelling hook. In the studio Norman Watt-Roy's complex bass-line was added and Davey Payne's free-jazz saxophone excursions blazed across the rhythm like a blow torch. All-in-all, one never tires of being pummelled by this record.

40
BE STIFF
SOCIAL FOOLS
DEVO
STIFF
71

'Be Stiff' became an anthem for Stiff Records who managed to persuade various artists from their roster to record versions of the song and go out on the *Be Stiff* Tour together. But Devo's original was actually a reaction against the complacent sound of soft-rock that was poisoning the radio airwaves; to that end, 'Be Stiff' is jerky and restless – it stops and starts, stops and starts and then stops and starts again. The abrasive-sounding guitar is very up-front in the mix while the lyrics are barked out. For the chorus there is more than a hint of something rude and sexual, which adds a further layer of assault and insult to the bland, conformist mainstream; put simply, there are no soft edges on this record whatsoever.

39
TOMMY GUN
1-2 CRUSH ON YOU
THE CLASH
CBS
19

From The Clash album *Give 'Em Enough Rope*, which was indeed, er… ropey, apart from two excellent tracks, both of which were thankfully released as singles. The first of these was 'Tommy Gun', a song reflective of a time when peaceful protest was being abandoned and the shooting of bullets was perceived to be the best way to make a point. Joe Strummer, as the songs narrator, adopts the position of a gunman reading his own press with all the satisfaction of an actor perusing a flattering review; he is sarcastic and sardonic and echoes the stance and sentiments of The Beatles on their song 'Revolution' – something of an irony considering Strummer's "No Elvis, Beatles or Rolling Stones" pronouncement in 1977. Still, one could not doubt his sincerity as he hoarsely spat-out his invective over buzzing, over-loaded guitars and rapid-fire snare drum flurries from the highly impressive Topper Headon.

38
BALTIMORE
FORGET
NINA SIMONE
CTI
DID NOT CHART

'Baltimore' was written by Randy Newman, without him ever having set foot in the city; instead, his inspiration came entirely from a magazine article. Because of this unusual provenance, 'Baltimore' could just as easily be replaced by Birmingham, Middlesbrough, Cardiff, Glasgow or any other multitude of places that, in the 1970s, offered little opportunity for their citizens and where poverty was plentiful. Nina Simone offered up her version one year after Newman's original appeared. It was the title-track of an album that she hated and publicly disavowed, feeling that the arrangements foisted upon her by producer Creed Taylor were gimmicky and over-the-top; she did have a point, but taken in isolation, 'Baltimore' is a fabulous single. This is a snail-paced jazz / reggae concoction with a sympathetic and unobtrusive string arrangement which provides a perfect base for Nina to give pained expression to the lyric, bestowing it with sadness and soul, even though she apparently practically phoned-in her vocal.

37
DOT DASH
OPTIONS R
WIRE
HARVEST
DID NOT CHART

I suppose 'Dot Dash' is about a car crash – either literally or metaphorically. Although up-tempo and rhythmically relentless, this is a dark-sounding single, full of foreboding. Perhaps because the song owed something to J.G. Ballard in the use of lyrical imagery, it seems to play more to the head than the feet, but be that as it may, this was a stark and disturbing single that continues to fascinate to this day.

36
FREE AFRICA
SPECIAL BREW
TWINKLE BROTHERS
VIRGIN FRONTLINE
DID NOT CHART

The Twinkle Brothers were formed in 1962 and they are still active today, playing a curious hybrid of reggae and górale (a traditional music of the Northern Carpathians) in collaboration with Polish group Trebunie-Tutki. Few would disagree that their heyday came in the mid-to late-1970s, and that 'Free Africa' captures them in all their glory as they advocate freedom from colonial rule and self-determination for all African nations. 'Free Africa' is roots reggae at its finest; graceful and hypnotic, the voices are calm but steadfast, possessed of spirit and dignity. On this record the sound of the Twinkle Brothers is captured superbly, and this song is an exemplar of the roots movement.

35
I'M EVERY WOMAN
A WOMAN IN A MAN'S
WORLD
CHAKA KHAN
WARNER BROTHERS
11

Chaka Khan's solo career was

launched with this single, even as she was still fronting Rufus. Much care and attention went into the release, which was written by the formidable Ashford and Simpson partnership and produced by the legendary Arif Mardin; together they crafted a quite brilliant record. The song, which emphasises women's strength, is sensational; set to a high-class disco groove, it is adorned by sumptuous orchestration and horns. All that was then required was a half-decent vocal and it would be great – but what Chaka Khan actually provided was not simply good … it was superb. She employed her deeply soulful voice with enormous power and 'I'm Every Woman' justly became her theme-song and an instant classic.

34
JET BOY JET GIRL
POGO POGO
ELTON MOTELLO
LIGHTNING
DID NOT CHART

Alan Ward, formerly of mid-1970s proto-punk band Bastard (who boasted Brian James, later of The Damned, as another member) had relocated to Belgium, along with Mike Butcher, where they worked as studio engineers; during this period they recorded 'Jet Boy Jet Girl'. They were then approached by a Belgian producer who wanted to release a French language punk single, so they gave him the backing tracks for both 'Jet Boy Jet Girl' and 'Pogo Pogo', whereupon a Belgian gentleman named Roger Jouret (otherwise known as Plastic Bertrand) recorded what became 'Ça Plane Pour Moi'. Before that record was released though, using a different mix of the exact same track – with Alan as Elton

Motello and Mike as Jet Staxx – 'Jet Boy Jet Girl' was released. It had a riotous riff that drilled itself into one's consciousness and a highly risqué lyric about a fifteen-year-old boy in a sexual relationship with a man who abandons the boy for a girl. The song was so catchy that were it not for the "deviant" lyric it would surely have been a hit… but alas, it was of course banned, although, one year later, Plastic Bertrand's more radio-friendly French version did hit the chart.

33
WHAT DO I GET?
OH SHIT
BUZZCOCKS
UNITED ARTISTS
37

Any thoughts that Buzzcocks might flounder without Howard Devoto's writing input were immediately dismissed by the first all Peter Shelley written single; 'What do I Get?' was noisy and melodic at the same time, albeit less spiky and angular than before. At a stroke Buzzcocks became a completely separate and very different entity than they had been with Devoto, but crucially, they achieved this without losing any of their potency. Lyrically Shelley revealed himself to be a romantic soul, and this was the first of the lovelorn classics that came, seemingly effortlessly, from his pen. Deceptively simple sounding, 'What Do I Get?' was a song that people could relate to; it was sung with sincere vulnerability, over a barrage of guitar, and it made for a thrilling pop noise full of wonderful hooks and harmony.

32
I AM THE COSMOS
YOU AND YOUR SISTER
CHRIS BELL
CAR RECORDS
DID NOT CHART

After leaving Big Star in 1974, Chris Bell continued to make music but this single was the only product released before his untimely death in a car accident in December 1978. Bell was a man who suffered with deep depression and he had a very unhealthy relationship with drugs. This fragility bleeds into his music, but although 'I Am the Cosmos' is drenched in melancholia, it remains ethereal and soulful; it is though a sense of beauty that is conveyed rather than any maudlin sickness. 'I Am the Cosmos' echoes the sound of – and arguably surpasses – Chris Bell's work as a member of Big Star… by stating that point of view, this means that I personally place it very high in the pantheon. When Gram Parsons coined the phrase "Cosmic American music", he may very well have been describing this record.

31
(I DON'T WANT TO GO TO)
CHELSEA
YOU BELONG TO ME
ELVIS COSTELLO AND THE
ATTRACTIONS
RADAR
16

Influenced by a run of 1960s "set in London" films that he saw on TV, Costello came up with 'Chelsea'; it is a song tinged with sinister intent and sexual menace that he and The Attractions turned into a tour-de-force. It has the choppy, stop-start riffing lifted from the early hits of The Kinks and The Who – but that

is merely the starting point. High-up in the mix, Bruce Thomas plays a bass part with power and precision that is absolutely fundamental to the song; Pete Thomas is tricky and inventive on the drums while Steve Nieve selected an out of tune Vox organ for his part, which Costello described as sounding "thin and evil". As for Costello himself, he sings superbly, lacing his words with venom and contempt. On this form Elvis Costello and the Attractions were a veritable juggernaut and they seemed to be pretty much unstoppable.

30
HYSTERIE CONNECTIVE
PAS POUBELLE
METAL URBAIN
RADAR
DID NOT CHART

Think of a speeded-up Kraftwerk singing in French, along with Steve Jones of the Sex Pistols playing power-chord guitar amid a wall of feedback; now throw in a dentist drilling teeth in the corner and finally imagine Hank Marvin wandering in to play some Shadows-style lead guitar breaks. If you can conjure-up that sound in your head you will have some approximation to the sound of 'Hysterie Connective'. The only two things left to add to that description are the gloriously slinky rhythm and a very Parisian sensibility that is genuinely chic.

29
UNITED
ZYKLON B ZOMBIE
THROBBING GRISTLE
INDUSTRIAL
DID NOT CHART

The first single from art terrorists Throbbing Gristle was the surprisingly pleasant sounding 'United'. It is minimal in both conception and execution, featuring just a simple drum loop and synthesiser pattern, as Genesis P-Orridge hypnotically recites a lyric which is remarkable for its positivity... even though ' the great beast', Aleister Crowley, is referenced via the use of his "Love is the law" phrase.

28
SUPERNATURE
GIVE ME LOVE
CERRONE
ATLANTIC
8
French drummer and disco producer Cerrone was noted for his combination of lush orchestration and synthesizers, but, perhaps influenced by Georgio Moroder's innovations in Munich, 'Supernature' is stripped-back to lean and clean synthesiser with a machine-generated propulsive pulse. This is a remarkable piece of music; urgent, but with no loss of melody, and it boasts a lyric written by Lene Lovich that describes a mutated species of gigantic creatures, created by chemical waste who turn upon mankind in retaliation for the damage that we inflict upon the earth. 'Supernature' was the sound of the future... now! Minds were well and truly blown and dance-floors reverberated to the sound of this disco monster.

27
SATISFY MY SOUL
SMILE JAMAICA
BOB MARLEY AND THE WAILERS
ISLAND
21
'Satisfy my Soul' was a re-working of the earlier Wailers' track 'Don't Rock My Boat' which had employed a rocksteady rhythm. This re-visitation saw the song slowed down and delivered as a soul/reggae hybrid with heavy use made of the I-Threes supporting the main vocal, along with prominent use of horns. Marley uses the metaphor of a boat to represent a relationship in which he asks for calm seas where harmony and love can flourish. This record was yet another example of the genius Bob Marley possessed in marrying a winning melody to a lyric of universal appeal, full of hooks and optimism – in essence, simply brilliant pop music.

26
THE ELECTRICIAN
DEN HAAGUE
THE WALKER BROTHERS
GTO
DID NOT CHART
General Augusto Pinochet was Margaret Thatcher's friend and favourite dictator; he presided over 1,300 prison camps and torture chambers that were very extensively used. How Thatcher must have wished she could have had the same facilities over here in order to deal with the UK's miners, gays, travelling communities and Northerners. Here, The Walker Brothers – or, more specifically, Scott Walker – redefined what a pop single could be, pushing at the boundaries both sonically and lyrically. Over a low drone of synthesizer and strings, with a stark bass punctuating the hum, John Walker softly harmonises while Scott half-sings, half-speaks, in the voice of one of Pinochet's torturers, addressing the victim of his sadistic work... "There is no help, no", he repeats, underlining the fact that,

for his victim, there is no hope of salvation; they are quite alone and he can inflict as much pain as he likes. The torture is slow and the music matches the pace – despite the horror, or perhaps because if it, this remains a compelling and highly memorable single .

25
AMBITION
DIFFERENT STORY
SUBWAY SECT
ROUGH TRADE
DID NOT CHART

Subway Sect had recorded an album but just prior to release manager Bernie Rhodes sacked the entire band with the exception of Vic Godard. The album was shelved but 'Ambition' and 'Different Story' were re-mixed and issued as a single. 'Ambition' is a breathtakingly brilliant song featuring a bouncing organ riff played over chorded guitar and chattering drums. Atop the backing track Vic Godard, with his totally unaffected and unique vocal style, sings a lyric of existential questioning before concluding the song with some of my favourite ever lyrics – the emphatic "And I won't be tempted by vile evils, because vile evils are vile evils".

24
YOU CAN'T PUT YOUR ARMS AROUND A MEMORY
HURTIN'
JOHNNY THUNDERS
REAL
DID NOT CHART

The Heartbreakers broke-up and the pieces were scattered but Johnny Thunders remained in London and cut a solo album – aptly titled *So Alone* – which contained 'You Can't Put Your Arms Around a Memory', a beautiful song about the aching sadness of loneliness. With soul-mate Peter Perrett of The Only Ones featured heavily on rhythm guitar and vocals, this is played as a wistful rock & roll ballad; Thunders turns-in a bruised vocal performance and peels off howling lead guitar licks as the track that became his signature song lurches towards its bitter-sweet conclusion.

23
COME BACK JONEE
SOCIAL FOOLS
DEVO
VIRGIN
60

Here Devo produce an inimitable interpretation of groovy, swinging-1960s guitar rock & roll, as they sing about John F. Kennedy re-imagined as a rock star. Kennedy is unfaithful to his wife – no surprises there – and he makes her cry; he jumps into his Datsun and drives off down the freeway where he crashes and dies… once again, his wife cries. this is Devo as pointed and provocative as ever, poking fun at the mythologising of dead heroes and America's pining for a heroic and fabled past, whilst, at the same time, making some really exciting music too.

22
LE FREAK
YOU CAN GET BY /
SAVOIR FAIRE
CHIC
ATLANTIC
7

Invited to Studio 54 by Grace Jones, the Chic main men Bernard Edwards and Nile Rogers were refused admission; the door was closed in their faces accompanied by a curt "Fuck off!". The pair decided to expend their energy by writing a song, so, inspired by the evening's events, they put down a ridiculously catchy groove with a chanted "fuck off" refrain. When they came to record the song properly, radio play became an obvious consideration and so "fuck off" morphed into "freak out". Once the track was completed they found that every single component part locked together perfectly; the rhythm was crisp and funky, the bass line was as monstrous as Godzilla, and when the vocals were added, the whole piece was hugely celebratory. They had made a brilliant record that has since gone on to achieve much merited disco immortality.

21
BECAUSE THE NIGHT
GODSPEED
PATTI SMITH
ARISTA
5

In the beginning Bruce Springsteen had a song without any verses; there was no need to finish it because he was in a legal dispute that prevented him from doing any recording – an unpleasant situation which lasted for three years. Jimmy Iovine, who had worked on Springsteen's *Born to Run* album, was now producing Patti Smith, and he persuaded Springsteen to give the song to Patti... so a cassette copy was duly delivered to her door. One night, as she was waiting in her New York apartment for a telephone call from her Detroit-based lover, Fred "Sonic" Smith, she decided to play the demo of 'Because the Night' which Springsteen had sent. She wrote the verses on the spot about her yearning love, being

extremely specific in the line "Love is a ring, the telephone". However, Patti was strangely unconvinced of the song's worth – though eventually she was persuaded by Jimmy Iovine and her band members to give it a go. This proved to be a very wise choice; 'Because the Night' simply roars out of the speakers with full-on power, poetry and passion. It transformed Patti Smith's career and it has gone on to become the song that she is most associated with.

20
MAN NEXT DOOR
GET AWAY (VERSION)
DENNIS BROWN
D.E.B. MUSIC
DID NOT CHART

John Holt's original take of 'Man Next Door', cut with The Paragons in 1968, was sensational; an utterly brilliant song with universal appeal (who *doesn't* fear the nightmare of a bad neighbour?). The song has attracted many cover versions and, with such great source material, many of these have been truly excellent – for example, those by The Slits and the Horace Andy-voiced Massive Attack. My personal favourite though is this magnificent take by Dennis Brown, who was dubbed (by no less an authority than Bob Marley) "The Crown Prince of reggae". Self-produced and utilising a reggae-flavoured disco beat, Brown glides ever so smoothly over the top with his silky and soulful voice.

19
KILL CITY
I GOT NOTHIN'
IGGY POP
& JAMES WILLIAMSON
RADAR
DID NOT CHART
This was recorded in 1975 when Iggy Pop was allowed weekend leave to go and record vocals, by the mental hospital in which he was being treated. Intended as a demo to try and stir-up record company interest, it failed miserably. Iggy was tainted, damaged goods... but after the David Bowie assisted re-birth with *The Idiot*, we finally got to hear the masterpiece that is 'Kill City'. It is a statement song, and the statement that Iggy is making is, yes, he recognises that he is down... but he is most certainly not knocked out – "If I have to die here, first I'm going to make some noise" he defiantly screams. Lyrically, the song is quite brilliant; the words are vivid and frighteningly real, and they are matched by the slashing, dangerous noise that James Williamson somehow manages to wrangle from his guitar. Music recorded in such circumstances has no right to be good – and yet, full of venom and determination, 'Kill City' was a complete triumph.

18
HUMAN FLY
DOMINO
THE CRAMPS
VENGEANCE
DID NOT CHART
Dirty and fuzz-drenched, 'Human Fly' is a mid-tempo crawl through filth, over a brutally simplistic beat, with Lux Interior at his most vocally deranged as he inhabits the insect's body, crawling and buzzing with gleeful relish. No other band was ever like The Cramps; they were amusing, but disturbing too... one-part Addams Family and one-part *Texas Chain Saw Massacre*. 'Human Fly' was a moment of genius and producer Alex Chilton deserved a big thumbs-up for the empathetic way in which he captured The Cramps' inimitable sound.

17
ONE NATION UNDER A GROOVE
ONE NATION UNDER A GROOVE PART 2
FUNKADELIC
WARNER BROTHERS
9
A manifesto of positivity and unity is contained within the grooves of this P-Funk anthem. Simultaneously targeted at both the feet and the mind – "Here is a chance to dance our way out of our constrictions" is one choice line – the funk bubbles and the rhythm simmers with a rich spiciness; all the ingredients mix together magnificently to cook up a dish of tasty excellence.

16
ANOTHER GIRL, ANOTHER PLANET
SPECIAL VIEW
THE ONLY ONES
CBS
57
It inexorably winds itself up, before the guitar blazes into life... and thus was created one of the most astonishing introductions to a song that I have ever heard. After this, singer Peter Perrett sounds remarkably nonchalant as he deadpans the immortal opening lines, "I always flirt with death, I look ill but I don't care about it". Following

this statement the song proceeds, never losing momentum (no mean feat!) because fascinating Dylanesque couplets continue to tumble from Perrett's mouth, and guitarist John Perry persists in unleashing hell-fire from his instrument. Was this an ode to heroin, as has been suggested? Or, somewhat less salaciously, merely an impressionistic love song? Actually, it matters little either way, because the overall impression left by this amazing record is one of awed wonderment and incredulity.

15
THE DAY THE WORLD
TURNED DAYGLO
I AM A POSEUR
X RAY SPEX
VIRGIN
23
Eco-consciousness expressed in a furious blast of beautiful noise, decades before ecological concerns began to surface in the mainstream. Poly Styrene is unrelenting as she throws grotesque image upon grotesque image of a world choking itself to death on plastic and Styrofoam. X-Ray Spex sound enormous on this single – it is a tidal wave of energy and intelligence, smashing its way into our hearts and minds; impossible to ignore, even if anyone was foolish enough to want to.

14
CHEREE
I REMEMBER
SUICIDE
BRONZE DID NOT CHART
Suicide comprised of Martin Rev, a man who extracted astonishing noises out a cheap, battered keyboard, and Alan Vega, who mined his soul in order to add vocals to the blissful cacophony; in fact, so deep did Vega dig, that to me he often sounded like Elvis Presley in an electric chair. I saw them perform on a bill with The Clash; they played to a constant backdrop of booing and whistling, as objects were hurled from the audience toward them. I saw them perform on a bill with Joy Division at The Factory; they survived for twenty minutes before the audience swarmed the stage to physically attack them and prevent them from continuing. I loved Suicide; they were brilliant. Amongst all the noise and the confrontational pieces there were also some beautiful songs, and 'Cheree' was one of those. Rev creates a one-man facsimile of Phil Spector's famous "Wall of Sound" as Vega pours out his love in a rockabilly croon. On this record, the two combine perfectly to create something astonishing and unmistakable – the gloriously unique sound of Suicide.

13
EVER FALLEN IN LOVE
(WITH SOMEONE YOU
SHOUDN'T'VE)
JUST LUST
BUZZCOCKS
UNITED ARTISTS
12
Inspired to write after hearing a line of dialogue from a Marlon Brando film on television, Peter Shelley came up with this highly personal song about a love that is hamstrung by attendant baggage. It is a sad and wistful tale, full of regrets, not just about the failure of the relationship as such, but also the wasted time spent in coming to that hurtful realisation. The lyric was aligned to a glorious melody, played with a blur of guitar, and the song was choc-full of dynamic moments, along

with a chorus of succinct genius that Shelley sang with magnificent clarity. Last, but definitely not least, Martin Rushent's patented production technique enhances this fabulous recording to the status of a classic.

12
KNOW YOUR PRODUCT
RUN DOWN
THE SAINTS
HARVEST
DID NOT CHART
If 'Know Your Product' isn't the greatest ever Australian single, then surely it is only bettered by the Saints' very own 'This Perfect Day' or 'I'm Stranded'. Lyrically, this is a cousin of '(I Can't Get No) Satisfaction' with the disdainful lampooning of advertising and consumerism… although the vocal by Chris Bailey is far more virulent and acidic than Mick Jagger's ever was. Of course, The Saints were a band who conjured up titanic sounding riffs – and this is no exception – but here the guitars are bolstered even further by a hard-hitting horn section who sound as if they've just dropped-in from the middle of a Sam & Dave or Otis Redding session. As ever, Ed Kuepper supplies a barrage of vicious guitar during this rampage through a smart-thinking, bad-attitude, sonic wonder.

11
BINGO MASTER
REPETITION/
PSYCHO MAFIA
THE FALL
STEP FORWARD
DID NOT CHART
This was the only release by the original line-up of The Fall; before their next recordings, crucial members Una Baines and Tony Friel would depart. In fact, Una is credited as the composer of 'Bingo Master' and she was clearly an excellent foil for Mark Smith's word-play. The song itself is more straightforward than what we would later come to expect from The Fall, but it still contains much of what made them a uniquely uncompromising prospect. Lyrically, Smith spins the tale of a bingo-caller going crazy due to the inane repetition of his job, but it was the way in which Mark Smith combined a northern working-class sensibility with darkly comic surrealism that was totally ground-breaking – as was his completely unaffected anti-rock vocal style. Musically, things are pretty radical; the sound is defiantly unorthodox – it is untidy, thin, verging on amateurish and slightly out-of-tune… and yet, it is also spiky, vibrant and a spit-in-the-eye for complacent, conformist pro-musos.

10

THE ROBOTS
SPACELAB
KRAFTWERK
CAPITOL
DID NOT CHART
(Number 20 on 1991 re-release)

A not-unpleasant machine-driven introduction leads to the opening lines; sung through a Vocoder, Kraftwerk state "We're charging our battery, and now we're full of energy", before the song continues on the theme of robotics and mankind's use for this technology. The phrase – in Russian language – "I am your servant, I am your worker", is used for a bridge, as the clean, rhythmic sound constructed by Kraftwerk suggests unceasing automation along a conveyor belt. If Kraftwerk and Fritz Lang had co-existed in pre-Nazi Germany, 'The Robots' would surely have soundtracked Lang's masterpiece *Metropolis*.

9

I AM THE FLY
EX-LION TAMER
WIRE
HARVEST
DID NOT CHART

On 'I Am the Fly', which preceded its parent album (*Chairs Missing*), Wire sounded somewhat bigger than before, though no less artful and darkly humorous. Over a brisk, hand-clapped rhythm, guitars churn and a keyboard plays merrily, evocative of a fairground. However, this is no House of Fun; indeed, it is much closer to a House of Horrors that we are trapped inside. The music swirls and spins dizzyingly, while an evil-sounding chanted vocal (concerning a malevolent fly intent on spreading disease) hammers home the message "I am the fly in the ointment". Certainly this is a metaphor for something; it could be something personal or quite general, though my own pet theory, given the period it originates from, is that it may be the "punk-rock industry" selling itself in the shop window, and Wire have chosen to contaminate the goods via their ever so delightful subversion.

8

(WHITE MAN)
IN HAMMERSMITH PALAIS
THE PRISONER
THE CLASH
CBS
32

This was the almighty leap that The Clash needed to make in order to separate themselves from the constantly growing "all sound the same" punk-rock pack. Although 'White Man' is nowadays routinely cited as the band's finest record, at the time it was seen as a weird aberration and it was certainly not universally loved. Starting with a fanfare of guitar, the song moves into something similar to a grooving ska-rhythm, a perfect backing for Joe Strummer to expound his thoughts, in what is a far-reaching and outstanding lyric. The scene is set for us when Strummer describes attending a reggae gig at Hammersmith Palais which featured Delroy Wilson, Leroy Smart and Dillinger. He is disappointed by the way in which the artists embrace showbiz protocol, when he expected to be enthused by a rebel spirit. After this, his thoughts turn to the disillusionment he feels with the new "power-pop" groups whom he considers to be in it solely for the money, and he rails against the sheer stupidity and ignorance of the punk rockers who are too self-obsessed with their petty squabbles to notice that the establishment is completely corrupt and has no moral compass. Angrily, he makes the point that even Adolf Hitler would be welcomed by the Government if that happened to be expedient. This burgeoning maturity suited The Clash; they had removed their own self-imposed shackles and could now move forward free of any baggage.

7

WUTHERING HEIGHTS
KITE
KATE BUSH
EMI
1

Having fought – and won – against her record company's intention to release the track 'James and the Cold Gun' as a single, Kate Bush audaciously and brilliantly announced herself to the world with this debut single which was stunning in its outright uniqueness. The arrangement, though sumptuous and arresting, is never overpowering, and this allows Kate to employ her crystalline operatic range to inhabit the persona of Cathy, the doomed heroine from Emily Brontë's novel. She stands outside the window of her lover, Heathcliffe, and implores him to let her in for she is so cold. It is not made explicit in the song, but those who have read the book realise that she is a ghost, which only magnifies the chilly, Gothic atmosphere of a song that startled a whole new generation of music lovers, and heralded the arrival of a wondrous talent to be appreciated and enjoyed for many years to come.

6

WARM LEATHERETTE/
T.V.O.D.
THE NORMAL
MUTE
DID NOT CHART

Daniel Miller worked on a film script of J.G. Ballard's 1973 novel *Crash*, together with a college friend. The project did not come to fruition but Miller decided to write a two-and-a-half minute song that would encapsulate the unorthodox subject matter of the enterprise i.e. the sexual thrill of finding mutilated bodies in a car wreckage. 'Warm Leatherette' succeeded as a synopsis… but it also achieved much more. It featured a punishing brutal Korg synthesiser pattern and very little else, apart from Miller's deadpan voice repeating the title over and over again, occasionally adding snippets of disturbing imagery. The piece was brilliantly executed and was years ahead of its time; science-fiction mixed with electronics and a sleazy, punky edge. To get the record released Miller adopted the nom-de-plume of The Normal and also founded Mute Records, which would become a hugely influential label that would go on to release many brilliant records – but this one was the first, the template for all that followed. Initially issued with the excellent T.V.O.D. as the A-side, it was ground-breaking – and even better – 'Warm Leatherette' picked up the plaudits and airplay; and so it was that after the initial pressing of 2,000 records had sold-out, 'Warm Leatherette' was installed as the A-side for all future pressings.

5

YOU MAKE ME FEEL (MIGHTY REAL)
GRATEFUL
SYLVESTER
FANTASY
8

Sylvester had led quite an interesting life by the time he came to write and record 'Mighty Real'. In the late 1960s he had been a member of The Disquotays, a fierce group of black teenage drag queens in LA that openly flouted a Californian law that prohibited public transvestitism and who threw lavish, hedonistic parties. Next, he moved to San Francisco to become a member of The Cockettes, a cross-dressing theatre troupe in which, during the LSD-fuelled anarchy of their shows, Sylvester would perform blues and jazz standards with his extraordinary gospel-trained voice. Early in the 1970s he aimed for crossover appeal by fronting a rock band called The Hot Band, but even though David Bowie was a fan (and publicly endorsed them) a black drag-queen singing Neil Young songs both terrified and repulsed mainstream America in equal measure. Then Sylvester went solo; he was fabulous but now, aged thirty, he still didn't have a hit to his name.

At this point, he heard guitarist James Wirrick working on what would become 'Mighty Real'; the song was completed, but somehow it was still missing the magic ingredient that would make it truly special. Enter Patrick Cowley, who had been inspired by Wendy Carlos and Tomita; he introduced a relentless and highly propulsive electronic throb, similar to the sound that Georgio Moroder had given to Donna Summer. Cowley happened to be gay, and his sound reflected that sensibility; it was gritty and dirty it was the sound of a speeding man in a bathhouse. Sylvester's words were then added, concerning going out, dancing, cruising and going home to have sex – all of which makes him "Feel mighty real", like he is not just pretending. This is an ecstatic celebration of life and chosen lifestyle, full of pride in individual choice and identity; it is dance-floor heaven, and with the special ingredient of Sylvester's soaring and soulful voice, this is a record that has every right to be described as great.

4

SHOT BY BOTH SIDES
MY MIND AIN'T SO OPEN
MAGAZINE
VIRGIN
41

With a riff gifted him by Peter Shelley, his one-time partner in Buzzcocks, Howard Devoto launched his more ambitious new band, Magazine, with 'Shot By Both Sides'. Self-consciously more expansive, having shed his punk rock ball and chain, Devoto sings of his realisation that enemies may wear different uniforms, but their motives are always pretty much the same, and he is therefore imperilled at every turn. The previously unknown John McGeoch proves to be a new-style guitar hero for a new age; the blues-infused likes of Eric Clapton and Rory Gallagher were, at a stroke, made to sound like dinosaurs, as McGeoch fills the song with imaginative and abstract strokes and flourishes, playing neither strictly lead or rhythm, simply relying on taste, instinct and disregard for convention in order to create something stunningly different. 'Shot By Both Sides' introduced Magazine to the world and immediately marked them out for greatness.

3

STREET HASSLE
WAITING FOR THE MAN/
VENUS IN FURS
LOU REED
ARISTA
DID NOT CHART

With a playing time of nearly eleven-minutes, 'Street Hassle' would have previously been impossible to release as a single but the rise in popularity of the 12-inch single facilitated the existence of this towering song in a non-album format. 'Street Hassle' is a suite composed of three separate segments, all linked by a narrative written in the "noir-style" of some of Reed's favourite authors, such as Nelson Algren and Hubert Selby Jr. The piece came together at the end of Reed's three-year relationship with a trans-woman called Rachel, and it appears to be somewhat symbolic of the ending of this association. Part One ("Waltzing Matilda"), sees a woman picking up a male prostitute and it concludes with "Neither one regretted a thing". This segment is played in neo-classical style, with violins sawing away like shredded nerves. Part Two ("Street Hassle"), takes on a very dark and menacing hue; it is voiced by a drug-dealer who has just had a young woman unhappily die of an overdose in his apartment, and he is matter-of-factly advising her paramour of how best to dispose of the body. Reed's voice is notably non-judgmental as he inhabits the characters of the song in a very accomplished and actorish fashion. The final section ("Slipaway"), is a jagged musical re-visiting of "Waltzing Matilda", though this time the muted violins sound as if they are being played by mittened fingers, while guitars are churning like an upset stomach. We hear Bruce Springsteen – in a Bukowskiesque drawl – voicing this part, before Reed returns and concludes tenderly, transforming the song into a lament for the death of hope and dreams.

2

ARMAGIDEON TIME
ARMAGIDEON VERSION
WILLIE WILLIAMS
STUDIO 1
DID NOT CHART

'Real Rock' was a single by a Jamaican act, The Soul Vendors released in 1968. It was produced by Coxsone Dodd and featured a three-note Hammond organ figure, played by Jackie Mittoo. 'Real Rock' was not a chart hit but it was significant because it gave rise to a rhythm that has proved to be possibly the most popular in all of reggae history; it has been utilised hundreds of times. A decade after The Soul Vendors recording, Willie Williams was at Studio 1 to cut 'Armagideon Time' with Coxsone Dodd and Jackie Mittoo and 'Real Rock' provides the rhythm – this is a militant song about the need for suffering people to stand up and fight. Williams sings in a most understated fashion which, by some mysterious alchemy, allows the power of the music and lyrics to really resonate with the listener; his quiet, steely performance is perfectly judged.

1

PUBLIC IMAGE
THE COWBOY SONG
PUBLIC IMAGE LIMITED
VIRGIN
9

By now John was an ex-Pistol; he had ceased to be Rotten and was once more being referred to by his birth name of Lydon. He had suffered – he was very young but had found himself in the invidious position of being simultaneously the most vilified figure in the UK *and* the totem for a movement that he wanted absolutely nothing to do with. He felt cheated, betrayed, misunderstood and used. Richard Branson hatched a crackpot scheme to install Lydon as the singer in Devo – an idea which thankfully came to nothing. Instead Lydon approached one of his oldest friends, John Wardle, to form a band, since they shared eclectic tastes and had a particular love of reggae music. This was a repetition of the behaviour that had seen Sid Vicious join the Sex Pistols when, despite Lydon's confidence that his friend would master the bass guitar, he had remained utterly clueless right up to the bitter end. Wardle, however, was a natural, and he took to the instrument like a duck to water; he became Jah Wobble. Also into the band came one-time Clash guitarist Keith Levine who Lydon knew from the gigs that the Pistols and Clash had played together, when the pair realised that each was a stranger within their own band. The final piece in the jigsaw was Canadian student and drummer Jim Walker, known as Donut. The band was named after Muriel Spark's 1968 novel *The Public Image*, and a central point of the group's manifesto was the aim to be devoutly anti-rock.

PiL's opening salvo, and debut single, fully delivered on this intention; it was incredibly uncompromising and sounded unlike anything else that had gone before. The prominent bass-line was astonishing, owing more to Boris Gardiner than Dee Dee Ramone; it was supple, nimble and played with power and assurance. Levine's guitar sound was equally radical; he created sheets of noise that he would then proceed to shatter so that his notes could cut like shards of glass. Donut was the rock-solid base for all these explorations while John's voice was masterfully controlled as his venomous tongue spat-out pointed and cutting words about the way in which he had been (mis)treated within the Sex Pistols. His ex-bandmates and manager are savaged for their neglect, and for their obsession with superficiality. The press, both musical and mainstream, are firmly in his sights too, as are record companies with their presumptions as to who he is and how he should be portrayed; as Lydon states, he is his "own creation" – his public image belongs to him. So, in conclusion, 'Public Image' by Public Image Limited set a new standard; it showed a new way of doing things and it was a total triumph. Lydon had ignored what the music industry wanted and expected from him; he risked alienating his Sex Pistols audience and by presenting himself as he wished to be presented, he could feel at peace with himself... for a little while at least.

1979

NOTABLE EVENTS

- The People's Army of Vietnam take Phnom Penh ending the rule of Pol Pot and his Khmer Rouge forces
- The Shah of Iran flees the country and is replaced by Ayatollah Khomeini who returns to the country following 15 years in exile to form the Council of Islamic Revolution
- In New York, to combat a tide of violent crime, a group of young, unarmed vigilantes, the "Guardian Angels", is formed.
- Snow falls in the Sahara desert
- The Conservative Party, led by Margaret Thatcher, defeats Jim Callaghan's Labour Party at the UK general election
- In Uganda, Kampala falls to Tanzanian troops; dictator Idi Amin flees
- In a power-sharing deal the first black government in 90-years takes power in Rhodesia, replacing Ian Smith's government
- The Sony "Walkman" goes on sale in Japan
- The Sandinista Liberation Front defeats the American-backed Somoza dynasty in Nicaragua
- Iraqi President Saddam Hussein orders the arrest and killing of 70 members of his ruling Ba'ath party
- Manchester United reach the final of the FA Cup but lose 3–2 to Arsenal, who score a last-minute winner. Liverpool win the league… again

NOTABLE BIRTHS

Valentino Rossi; Pete Doherty; Heath Ledger; Avey Tare; Diego Forlán; Ladyhawke; Jonny Wilkinson

NOTABLE DEATHS

Charles Mingus; Donny Hathaway; Sid Vicious; Josef Mengele; Jean Renoir; Richard Beckinsale; Zulfikar Ali Bhutto; Blair Peach; John Wayne; Lowell George; Van McCoy; Minnie Riperton ; Louis Mountbatten; Gracie Fields; Jimmy McCulloch; Barnes

Wallis; Judee Sill; Darryl F. Zanuck

NOTABLE FILMS

Apocalypse Now; Alien; Mad Max; The Warriors; Life of Brian; Being There; Quadrophenia; Scum; Driller Killer; The Marriage of Maria Braun; Nosferatu the Vampyre; Tess; The Tin Drum

NOTABLE BOOKS

The Executioner's Song – Norman Mailer
The Hitchhiker's Guide to the Galaxy – Douglas Adams
Smiley's People – John Le Carre
Field Work – Seamus Heaney
Jailbird – Kurt Vonnegut Jr.
Prick Up Your Ears – John Lahr

THE MUSIC

In many ways, this final year of the decade could be viewed as just a continuation of the previous year; post-punk, disco and reggae continued to flourish, but a closer look reveals that change was afoot. Noticeable was the heavy incorporation of funk into the music of white post-punk bands, as the crude, heavy guitar sound, reeking of machismo, that had come to define punk was increasingly discarded in favour of supple bass lines that returned some sensuality to the music. The influence that reggae had exerted on British youth was again felt as the multi-racial and highly political Specials were in the vanguard of a clutch of bands on their own 2-Tone record label who leaned heavily on the sounds of Jamaican ska and rocksteady in order to colour their songs and project an anti-racist agenda. Meanwhile, in Jamaica, digital technology was changing the shape of reggae and the roots style was being superseded by a busier, more insistent rhythm that would yield dancehall.

Between them P.I.L. and The Pop Group incorporated dub, funk, rock, jazz and even classical influences in their sonic experiments, and in so doing helped rip-up the rule book of what is allowed to be present in a pop record. Disco too embraced the possibilities afforded by improved equipment and became, as a result, ever more sophisticated. The highly influential Fall and Joy Division began making a mark that was hugely disproportionate to their very modest record sales. Prince, who would go on to become a dominant cultural figure of the next decade, released his first UK single, and it was a minor classic. Synthesisers were seriously threatening the position of the guitar as the pre-eminent instrument of choice, but perhaps most importantly of all, hip hop came crashing into the mainstream, giving a voice to coming generations of youth who had an axe to grind, and thereby altering the culture and musical landscape in a radical fashion.

MY 1979

I moved out of the squalor of my shared flat into a place that was even worse; I rented a house for £1-50 per week (the rent on the flat had been £8 per week) that was adjacent to an animal by-products factory and the whole area stank to high-heaven. The house was stone-floored and uncarpeted; there was neither bath nor shower, there was only an outside toilet, but in what was a long, harsh winter, the pipes froze and split, rendering even this unusable. I had no bed or mattress and so I slept on a hard floor wrapped-up in a blanket. My next-door neighbour was an army man and he took an immediate dislike to me; this manifested itself in random assaults incorporating extreme violence. My benefit payments were spent on going to gigs; I couldn't afford to buy any records and I quite often went without food for a day or two, such was my penniless state. Nor did I have a television set, though I wasn't too bothered about that because at least I still had my records, and it was these that fed my need for entertainment and enlightenment. I did get out-and-about to see the likes of P.I.L., Pere Ubu, The Pop Group and Human League, but most notably I formed a band called The Hamsters, along with two non-musician friends. We played our first gig less than 24 hours after forming, which the police came along and stopped. Thus began a career that was defined by clashes with authority figures, right-wing skinheads who had infiltrated the landscape, and snobby scenesters who populated the music environment and sniped at us for being – as they saw it – crude and untalented. I was 22-years-old as the 1970s ended and the eighties began. It felt like a long, strange trip… but the accompanying soundtrack had been glorious.

100
WHITE ROOM
LOSERS IN A LOST LAND
HUGH CORNWELL AND
ROBERT WILLIAMS
UNITED ARTISTS
DID NOT CHART
Head Strangler Hugh and Magic Band drummer Robert combined to record an album that was an imaginary score to F.W. Murnau's 1922 film *Nosferatu*. The single extracted from the album was a cover version of the Jack Bruce and Pete Brown classic 'White Room', originally recorded by power-trio superstars Cream; Cornwell and Williams produce a version that is crunching, gothic and full of dramatic tension. Hugh Cornwell snarls out the vocal and Williams hammers on the huge sounding drums. With Ian Underwood (from Frank Zappa's band) guesting on synthesiser and adding further dark textures to the titanic riff, this was something rather special.

99
THE PRINCE/MADNESS
MADNESS
TWO TONE
16
This mob from North London were just as much influenced by Deaf School and Ian Dury's Kilburn and the Highroads as they were by the more obvious late-1960s ska sound of Jamaica. Here, on their debut single, they pay tribute to ska legend Prince Buster in a highly energetic and fun-filled fashion that owes as much to the tradition of English music-hall entertainment as it does to Jamaican sound systems. They create a fusion of two sounds and cultures that felt like a jolt of electricity; it was irresistible, and Madness were quite irrepressible and brought fun to the fore.

98
IT'S TOO FUNKY IN HERE
ARE WE REALLY DANCING?
JAMES BROWN
POLYDOR
DID NOT CHART
Since the early part of the decade James Brown had been out-of-step with the times; there had been sporadic moments of inspiration, but generally his work had been laboured and frankly sub-standard. 'It's too Funky in Here' was therefore a very welcome return to form; the groove had been happily re-located in a way that sounded natural and effortless but Brown wasn't trying to re-invent the wheel; 'It's too Funky in Here' didn't try to chase after contemporary and fashionable sounds – it simply relied on the tight-as-a-nut rhythm section and the power of the horns, along with female backing vocals and Brown himself at the very centre of the piece, calling the shots on this dance-floor gem.

97
FIVE FOOT ONE
PRETTY FLAMINGO
IGGY POP
ARISTA
DID NOT CHART
Perhaps Iggy's last truly great record was 'Five Foot One' – it is lusty and good-humoured, quick-witted and intelligent. The song concerns a short of stature guy who is working at an amusement park; he is shunned by the big folks that he wishes to connect with and he has a giant-sized libido, meaning that he is left unsatisfied and alone – "I wish life could be Swedish magazines", he

declares. All his concepts are abstract and distorted by the frustrating life that he is leading. The song is rocking and up-tempo and features live-wire guitar playing and punchy horns. Produced by one-time Stooge James Williamson and boasting a significant musical contribution from Scott Thurston (another ex-Stooge), this was a confident and assured single from the legendary Iggy Pop.

96
BORN TO BE ALIVE
I GIVE YOU RENDEZVOUS
PATRICK HERNANDEZ
GEM
10
Frenchman Patrick Hernandez wrote 'Born to be Alive' ostensibly as a rock track; but in the studio, with producer Jean Vanloo, the song was transformed into the uplifting, celebratory disco monster that was released. It was an immediate success all over Europe before hitting the dance-floors and charts in the UK and the USA, where, incidentally, a young Madonna was recruited as a dancer for Hernandez's live performances.

95
CONTACT
DON'T WASTE YOUR TIME
EDWIN STARR
20TH CENTURY FOX
6
Over an electronic Moroder-style rhythmic structure, replete with synchronised handclaps, emerges the unmistakable voice of Edwin Starr. Urgent and impassioned, the soul-man was making a seamless transition into disco territory. Something of an unsung artist, Edwin had adapted to the changing scene in order to survive. He worked hard and was a

dynamite live performer with a big personality that exuded warmth. Surely nobody with a beating heart could begrudge him this little taste of success…

94
CONFUSION/
LAST TRAIN TO LONDON
ELECTRIC LIGHT
ORCHESTRA
JET
8
This double A-side release was excellent value; 'Last Train to London' was a fine, funky, almost electro piece – but it was on 'Confusion' where the true alchemy was achieved. This song has a Phil Spector-ish wall of sweet sound at its core, but it re-routes itself via strident Abba-esque piano chords into beautiful harmony and fabulous chorus. Chock-full of hooks and honed in the studio to near-perfection, this was meticulous craftsmanship being touched by something approaching genius.

93
JUMPING SOMEONE ELSE'S
TRAIN
I'M COLD
THE CURE
FICTION
DID NOT CHART
Released as a stand-alone non-album single, with Siouxsie Sioux assisting on the flip side, the title of the A-side, 'Jumping Someone Else's Train', is a derisive swipe at the copyists and scenesters who wear the right clothes, get the proper haircuts and steal other people's ideas in an attempt to appear with-it and relevant. Set to a rhythmical, jangling musical backing, the train is again evoked to excellent effect and The Cure, at this

early point of career development, were definitely standing-out from the crowd and travelling very much under their own steam.

92

DANCING FOOL
BABY SNAKES
FRANK ZAPPA
CBS
DID NOT CHART

Zappa once again looks toward disco music as a vehicle for his song satire. Although the earlier 'Disco Boy' had been a mean-spirited attack on the perceived vacuous content of the genre, 'Dancing Fool' is aimed squarely at the people who can't dance but still insist upon filling the dance-floor in a horribly uncoordinated mass of arms and legs. Zappa does include himself in the ranks of the "dancing fools", making lyrical reference to the leg injury he suffered when he was pushed off the stage in London, leaving him with one limb shorter than the other. Coke-spooned lotharios are lampooned in bar-style dialogue that is both accurate and funny. The music is fizzing and frenzied and the vocals are warm and witty. 'Baby Snakes' on the flip-side of the record was equally excellent.

91

I WANT YOU TO WANT ME
CLOCK STRIKES TEN
CHEAP TRICK
EPIC
29

'I Want You to Want Me' was released in its studio form in 1977; it was a great song, but somewhere something was lacking and it duly flopped. This live version, recorded in Japan, was taken from the *Cheap Trick at Budokan* album and it proved to be much more satisfying and successful. Speedier, and more solid, it dispensed with the studio version's piano solo and intricate niceties and relied instead on the atmosphere created by the live audience who act as impromptu harmony vocalists. Anyone who loved the early Beatles, Big Star or Badfinger couldn't help but be smitten, for this was guitar pop of the very highest order.

90

AQUA BOOGIE
YOU'RE A FISH
(AND I'M A WATER SIGN)
PARLIAMENT
CASABLANCA
DID NOT CHART

The P-Funk era was coming to an end, and 'Aqua Boogie' was one of the last tracks that key trio George Clinton, Bernie Worrell and Bootsy Collins would write together. It came from the album *Motor Booty Affair* and it is a delight of squelching synths, loose-limbed bass, cartoon voices and chanting. Superficially the song seems to be about an underwater party, but beneath that surface-layer the lyrics address the sad truth that in the impoverished neighbourhoods of the USA, people are made to jump through hoops just to try and survive.

89

EXTRACT 1
EXTRACT 4
FAUST
RECOMMENDED
DID NOT CHART

As was my habit I was perusing the wares of city-centre music vendors one Saturday morning when a new Faust single was presented to me; this was a purchase that could not be declined and so I handed over the requisite coinage. Once the record was actually in my possession, I could feel my palms begin to sweat and my pulse begin to race – I couldn't wait to hear it. Had Faust, one of my all-time favourite groups, reformed? The red sleeve offered no clues at all as to the record's provenance. One side played at 33rpm and the other at 45rpm. This seemed to indicate that 'Extract I' was a longish track whereas 'Extract 4' would be somewhat shorter… Indeed, this did prove to be the case. But what of the music itself? When the needle hit the record it was clearly the sound of the band from the early-1970s, and it held me in thrall just as Faust's music had always done before. It was melodic, but odd; a little wonky – the sheer unorthodoxy kept you off-balance. Of course, I loved it. It was only much later in the Internet age that I finally discovered its origin was from the almost mythological *Faust Party Tapes* of 1971.

88
BOOGIE WONDERLAND
BOOGIE WONDERLAND INSTRUMENTAL
EARTH WIND AND FIRE WITH THE EMOTIONS
CBS
4

The biggest and most successful funk band on the planet were Earth Wind and Fire; they took the form by the scruff-of-the-neck and injected a new-found freshness into it. Maurice White oversaw every aspect of their sleek and meticulously produced sound. The horn arrangements on Earth Wind and Fire records were always magnificent; they added a punchy and fiery counterpoint to the overall smoothness of the sound. Here, augmented by vocal group The Emotions, every aspect of the band's sound is magnified to create a disco record of symphonic grandeur, similar to the way in which Duke Ellington had earlier infused jazz music with melodic sophistication. In 1979 Earth Wind and Fire also released 'September' – again, it was quite superb; only the sheer number of brilliant records from this year prevents me from including that one as well.

87
UP THE JUNCTION
IT'S SO DIRTY
SQUEEZE
A&M
2

Earlier in the year Squeeze had hit the charts with the extraordinarily good 'Cool for Cats', an amusing recollection of hanging around the streets in their early teenage years; to follow it up, they released 'Up the Junction' inspired by the gritty, realist British films of the early 1960s that portrayed the harsh dramas of working-class life. Here, over a muted but melodic backing, a tale is told – in straight-to-the-heart rhyming couplets – of a young couple meeting, falling in love, having a baby, his problem drinking before they separate. The intense sadness and deep regret, expressed by the male narrator, leaves not a dry eye in the house. It was an astonishingly mature song for such a young band, and it marked them out as very gifted songsmiths.

86
GENERAL PENITENTIARY
GENERAL PENITENTIARY
VERSION
BLACK UHURU
TAXI
DID NOT CHART
Teamed-up with the Taxi Gang, a group of musicians who included rhythm aces Sly and Robbie, Black Uhuru were thrust towards the cusp of international stardom following a series of single releases. 'General Penitentiary' – written by lead vocalist Michael Rose – is an almost meditative treatise on the soul-sapping brutality dished out in the Jamaican penal system to the incarcerated. 'General Penitentiary' was militant dread consciousness sweetly served-up to reach the ears of the many and not just the few.

85
POP MUZIK
M FACTOR
M
MCA
2
According to Robin Scott, the 'M' mastermind, "Rock 'n' roll had created a generation gap". In order to compensate for this, he wanted to embrace the disco ethos of making a simple but unifying statement; from such a train of thought emerged 'Pop Muzik'. Though it was banal, it was also as catchy as measles, and therefore it spread rapidly to a point where the entire populace seemed to be parroting "New York, London, Paris, Munich". Originally the song had been conceived as a funk-style workout but the suggestion of using synthesiser was crucial to its success. 'Pop Muzik' had a very modern feel, but the incorporation of robotically performed 1950s-style "Shooby doo" female backing vocals was knowingly kitsch and most effective.

84
TIME GOES BY SO SLOW
PILLOW FIGHT
THE DISTRACTIONS
FACTORY
DID NOT CHART
The Distractions were a very superior pop group who wrote and performed love songs that didn't have happy endings and were laced with a degree of sexual tension. Their first EP had been cheaply produced but that fact couldn't disguise the quality of the songs or the quality of their performance. 'Time Goes By So Slow' was written by guitarist Adrian Wright, and although it is a sad lament it is taken at a brisk pace, name-checking Manchester's Albert Square in a surreal lyric where the author imagines the object of his desire to be a statue. Singer Mike Finney was well-blessed in the vocal department, and he sounded utterly convincing as he relayed the lyric while the rhythm section of Pip Nichols and Alec Sidebottom are tight as a nut while Wright and Steve Perrin provide Byrds-like guitar, harmony vocals and organ, in a display of exactly what it was that made The Distractions rather special.

83
SHAKE YOUR BODY
(DOWN TO THE GROUND)
THAT'S WHAT YOU GET FOR
BEING POLITE
THE JACKSONS
EPIC
4
In 1978 The Jacksons renewed their contract with Epic where they had

been moderately successful. In the new contract they gained "complete artistic control" and for the first time they could follow their own instincts. 'Shake Your Body' was written by Michael and Randy Jackson, and although they borrowed from Marvin Gaye's 'Got to Give it Up' and Teddy Pendergrass 'Get Up, Get Down, Get Funky, Get Loose', there was still plenty of room for their individual stamp. With 'Shake Your Body' they concocted a highly effective mix of rhythm and melody, with enough space for Michael to sing the lead vocal in his unique style, full of playful hiccups and ad libs. His brothers, meanwhile, were no vocal slouches themselves, and their parts offered a good deal of imaginative support and intuitive rapport.

82
HORRORSHOW
ADULTERY
SCARS
FAST
DID NOT CHART
Scars emerged from Edinburgh; their sound, inescapable and ominous, is a bit like a nail being scratched down a car door. The guitar circles, wasp-like and malevolent; the singer doesn't actually sing, but simply emotes… a wound-up, snarling menace conveyed through growls and shouts. Meanwhile the drums and bass chatter and clatter from another corner of the weirdly thin, empty mix. Scars were creating a quite remarkable sound – it was awkward and abstract but had a distinct pop sensibility about it. For whatever reason, things didn't work out for them, but without too much tweaking, one could easily imagine these boys having the hit records that their originality deserved.

81
ANGEL EYES
MY LITTLE GIRL
ROXY MUSIC
POLYDOR
4
Bryan Ferry was nothing if not smart and he didn't hide away from the fact that sales of his solo material didn't match-up to those of the now defunct Roxy Music. So, cynically but cleverly, Roxy were re-formed as a brand as much as a band, although the creative interplay between Manzanera, MacKay and Thompson nevertheless brought out the best from Ferry. 'Angel Eyes' was a re-make of a track from Roxy Music comeback album *Manifesto*, where it had a quirky, rock feel. The single version was much more lavish and it was aimed squarely at the nightclub dancefloor. The song's languid melody and easy pace were perfect for MacKay's smoky saxophone lines, which added the appropriate atmospherics to Ferry's delightful croon.

80
MAKING PLANS FOR NIGEL
BUSHMAN PRESIDENT/
PULSING PULSING
XTC
VIRGIN
UNKNOWN★
Most of XTCs best known material was written by Andy Partridge, but 'Making Plans For Nigel' came from the pen of bassist Colin Moulding and it clearly displays just how much songwriting talent there was within the band. 'Nigel' is about a boy on the cusp of adulthood who is having

★ *A computer error meant the precise position was unknown although it was undoubtedly in the top 17.*

his dreams stolen by over-controlling parents who have his future mapped-out for him with a job at British Steel. Soundwise the band consciously aped Devo and they construct the song on a juddering rhythm that suggests industrial machine presses, while a guitar adds to the feel with chopping, syncopated chords which allows Partridge to play a little two-note counterpoint pattern while he also supports the lead vocal by high-pitched yelping and whooping.

79

GYPSY BLOOD
LOSE MYSELF
DOLL BY DOLL
AUTOMATIC
DID NOT CHART

By dint of arriving at approximately the same time, Doll By Doll were categorized as a punk band and although they did share a similar manic intensity, the truth is that they had very little else in common. Doll By Doll were men and not boys – and hard-looking men at that – albeit with sensitive souls. They had emerged from the London squatting community and their fuel was alcohol, drugs and poetry. Led by Jackie Leven, who possessed a voice that could soar into the heavens, 'Gypsy Blood', like much of their material, borders on the psychotic. It is a confessional of sorts – a psychodrama played-out over a cascading guitar figure and a solid rhythm. It is full-sounding to an almost claustrophobic degree, and although it does contain great beauty, there is also discernible brutality as well. Doll By Doll were a totally unique proposition, and this single captured them at their finest.

78

THE KID WITH THE REPLACEABLE HEAD
I'M YOUR MAN
RICHARD HELL AND THE VOIDOIDS
RADAR
DID NOT CHART

'The Kid With The Replaceable Head' is fizzing, speedy pop, replete with a "bop bop bop" middle-eight and ice-pick guitar played sharp and angularly by Robert Quine while Richard Hell entertains us with the tale of somebody whose chameleon-like changes make him appear to have a shelf that is full of replaceable heads – "He's my three best friends" states Hell, in the chorus of what would turn out to be his last single for many years.

77

GOLDEN LOCKS
TRIBULATION
BIM SHERMAN
SAVANNAH
DID NOT CHART

Clocking in at 8 minutes, Bim Sherman's 'Golden Locks' contains the exquisitely-voiced singer's most iconic song. Transportive, meditative and soothing; a thing of wonder as his smooth-as-silk but still highly expressive vocal, glides atop a gentle, skanking rhythm before giving way to a dissection of the song in dub that is so good that when the needle hits the run-out groove, you are compelled to play it over again.

76
I WANT YOUR LOVE
(FUNNY) BONE
CHIC
ATLANTIC
4

Chic lowered the tempo for 'I Want Your Love' but the result was still the same... another disco masterpiece. The rhythmic mesh of guitar, bass and drum act as a springboard for striking use of horns and synthesised strings; it is lush and elegant, and with Alfa Anderson providing a yearning lead vocal (along with fabulous harmonies from Sister Sledge) we have the icing on a most efficacious confection.

75
IN A RUT
H-EYES
THE RUTS
PEOPLE UNITE
DID NOT CHART

The Ruts were real musicians; they had previously used the name Aslan but they were inspired by punk to drop their jazz/funk/fusion thing in favour of short, sharp, shocks of reality. They solidly aligned themselves with the *Rock Against Racism* movement, and their commitment to opposing injustice won them respect and real street-level support. This, their debut single, tackles the lethargy and apathy that we must all conquer, to some degree, in order to instigate change and betterment in our lives. It is aggressively played and sung as the highly dynamic arrangement twists and turns, surging from a whisper to a scream. The flip-side of the single, 'H-Eyes', is a tirade against the destructiveness of heroin; the sad irony is that only a few short years later singer Malcolm Owen would lose his life in the grip of an addiction

to this most pernicious of drugs.

74
THE PICTURES ON MY WALL
READ IT IN BOOKS
ECHO AND THE BUNNYMEN
ZOO
DID NOT CHART

Three young men and a drum machine; in thrall to the West Coast sounds of 1960s icons such as The Doors and Love, the fledgling Echo and the Bunnymen ambitiously set about emulating the high-quality work of their musical predecessors. 'The Pictures on My Wall' was, as a consequence, a fabulous collision of ambition and naivety; crystalline guitars shimmered while Ian McCullough – who was yet to perfect his croon – sang his poetic lyric with an uncertain vulnerability that is plainly discernible in his delivery... the overall effect was quite magical.

73
BUSTIN' LOOSE PART 1
BUSTIN' LOOSE PART 2
CHUCK BROWN
& THE SOUL SEARCHERS
SOURCE
DID NOT CHART

"Go-go" was a genre of music highly popular in Washington DC from the late 1960s onwards. In 1978/79, it threatened to spill-out of the regional scene and become a worldwide phenomenon – only for the rise of hip-hop to supplant it in both column inches and radio airplay. Chuck Brown was the arch-exponent of Go-go and 'Bustin' Loose' was a seminal record for him. It is a highly-charged funk piece with James Brown-style horns and a shouted call and response vocal. The real power-source though is delivered by the pounding, incessant, up-tempo rhythm; truly raw and exciting, 'Bustin' Loose' captures a moment in time when Go-go really did look set to conquer the world.

72

THE STAIRCASE (MYSTERY)
20TH CENTURY BOY
SIOUXSIE AND THE BANSHEES
POLYDOR
24

This particular staircase spirals upward and then descends into a frightening, sinister place that we can only imagine in the darkest recesses of our minds. 'The Staircase (Mystery)' is compelling and mesmerising, multi-layered and cloaked in darkness, akin to the most disturbing films of Alfred Hitchcock. Strident and rhythmically strong, with a quite astonishing guitar sound augmented by chilly piano notes towards the end, Siouxsie matches the adventurousness of the music with a remarkable singing performance as she treats the song like a demented nursery rhyme. The Banshees were still in their infancy – this being only the band's second single – and yet they were confident and assured enough to create an eerie world of great imagination.

71

DA YA THINK I'M SEXY
DIRTY WEEKEND
ROD STEWART
RIVA
1

Disco was dominant and rock 'n' roll lotharios such as Rod Stewart were suddenly feeling a trifle neglected and out-of-vogue. Acting on the old maxim that "If you can't beat 'em, join 'em", Rod decided to have some fun with the disco form and

wrote a song about a lounge-lizard type with insecurity issues. For the music he plagiarized 'Taj Mahal' by Brazilian musician Jorge Ben Jor and the distinctive synth melody that adds a lot to the song's flavour was lifted directly from Bobby Womack's '(If You Want My Love) Put Something Down On It'. These infringements were settled financially and so they don't count for much when coming to judge 'Da Ya Think I'm Sexy' which showed Rod Stewart – for the first time since his Faces days – having a bit of a spring in his step, a smile on his face and not taking himself too seriously. Oh, and it was also a superb record.

70

THE DAY MY BABY
GAVE ME A SURPRISE
PENETRATION IN THE
CENTREFOLD
DEVO
VIRGIN
DID NOT CHART

Sweet tenderness delivered Devo-style; amidst jerky, angular guitars and keyboards and underpinned by severe but considered drumming, this song, about a man sitting at the hospital bedside of his lover as she begins to awaken from a coma conveys his palpable joy and delight when his baby gives him a most pleasant surprise.

69

EMPIRE STATE HUMAN
INTRODUCING
HUMAN LEAGUE
VIRGIN
DID NOT CHART
(62 when re-released in 1980)

'Empire State Human', with its chanted "Tall, tall, tall" chorus, has been interpreted by some to be Phil Oakey expressing his ambition to become a "big" pop star; personally, I get no sense of that whatsoever. The Human League were inspired and informed by science-fiction and I perceive this song to be just a straightforward excursion into that genre. However, what cannot be disputed is that this was brilliant pop music in terms of its sound structure, which alternates between sombre and gleeful, with Oakey's vocal capturing an optimistic wonderment that is pleasingly infectious.

68

I WANNA BE YOUR LOVER
JUST AS LONG AS WE'RE
TOGETHER
PRINCE
WARNER BROTHERS
41

'Soft and Wet' had been the debut single for Prince in his homeland; that single however had merely hinted at his potential. On this, his first UK single, the talent was captured in full-bloom. 'I Wanna Be Your Lover' was a slippery, daringly minimalistic funk number, sung in falsetto. It was arresting and there was a futuristic edge to the sound. It was indeed that sound (along with the photographs I had seen of this elfin figure who pushed at the barriers of conventional decency) that made it so fascinating for me. 'I Wanna Be Your Lover' is a fairly orthodox declaration-of-love song, although, this being Prince, even at this early point in his career, some of the lines − 'I wanna be the only one you come for' is a good example − were delivered with deliberate ambiguity. The singer Patrice Rushen, who had done some work on his first album,

was the object of Prince's affections here; indeed, he was so smitten with her that she was offered not only this song, but 'I Feel For You' as well... both were declined.

67

STRANGE TOWN
THE BUTTERFLY
COLLECTOR
THE JAM
POLYDOR
15 (42 when re-issued in 1983)

The Jam were maturing into a superb singles act and 'Strange Town' was further evidence of what a fine songwriter Paul Weller was becoming. 'Strange Town' is a cousin to David Bowie's 'London Boys' and The Members 'Solitary Confinement' in that it is about somebody moving to the big city and trying to fit in, only to be met by unfriendly and unwelcoming indifference from people who are too wound-up in their own lives to show any kindness to strangers. Weller's lyric though is more deep-reaching and infected by hurt than either of the two other songs − "You can't be weird in a strange town" he sings perceptively, understanding full-well how one must conform in order to gain acceptance. The song is taken at mid-pace in the manner of a folk-song, allowing each and every word the space in which to be heard. In addition, there is a clever breakdown in which a sense of isolation is intensely conveyed, and the backing vocals are also exemplary and atmospheric.

66
LUCKY NUMBER
HOME
LENE LOVICH
STIFF
3

Detroit-born Lene moved to the UK aged 13. She became involved in theatre, recorded screams for horror films, was a go-go dancer at Radio 1 roadshows and was part of the singing audience on Chuck Berry's horrible number one single 'My Ding-a-Ling'. She also wrote the lyrics for Cerrone's superlative 'Supernature' and eventually signed as a solo act to Stiff Records. 'Lucky Number' was originally the B-side of her debut single, which was a cover of Tommy James and the Shondells 'I Think We're Alone Now". That record flopped but 'Lucky Number' was released once again, this time as an A-side. Quirky is the only really adequate description of what was on offer; during the verses, 'Lucky Number' has a bouncing-ball quality which Lena delivers in staccato fashion. The chorus was just pure genius; Lene vocally emulates a four-note synthesiser part and her partner, Les Chappell, follows-up with a simple guitar figure that hooked-in listeners instantaneously… absolutely inspired stuff!

65
BOUNCING BABIES
ALL I AM IS LOVING YOU
THE TEARDROP EXPLODES
ZOO
DID NOT CHART

Julian Cope was a trainee teacher and an aspiring musician in a band called The Crucial Three, alongside future Bunnyman Ian McCulloch and future Wah Heat front-man Pete Wylie.

Those three gigantic egos couldn't be contained in one band and so The Crucial Three bit the dust before they had even played a gig. Cope's next move was another band with Wylie called The Nova Mob, and after that followed two more bands with McCulloch, called Uh! and finally A Shallow Madness… but fed-up with the constant bickering, McCulloch eventually departed and formed Echo and The Bunnymen. Now, with Gary Dwyer as McCulloch's replacement, Cope re-branded A Shallow Madness as The Teardrop Explodes, a name taken from a caption in a Marvel comic. Their name earned them a deal with fledgling Liverpool label Zoo and they issued a dreamy single called 'Sleeping Gas', rich in promise and possibility. 'Bouncing Babies' followed and it was devastatingly good. There is a heavy psychedelic feel to it, provided by a reedy organ sound (borrowed from The Fall) and a drum-pattern that suggests nails being hammered into a coffin lid. Meanwhile, Cope sings about the poisoning effect that life has had upon him, and he states that the bouncing baby he once was is now a dangerously ticking bouncing bomb.

64
BELA LUGOSI'S DEAD
BOYS
BAUHAUS
SMALL WONDER
DID NOT CHART

A gloomy, unchanging bass-line anchors the sound, which also contains a skittish drum pattern, echoing dub effects and scything squeals of guitar noise. On top of that we hear an extremely mannered and theatrical vocal which paints an impressionistic word-portrait of the funeral of famed horror actor Bela Lugosi, in which the bats have left the bell tower and dead flowers are strewn across the coffin. This was a strikingly original single; in fact it was so good that it spawned a whole movement of Gothic rockers to rise up. Of course, the trouble with movements is that they strangle originality, and Goth was as dull and predictable as any other gathering of imitators. Bauhaus were not to blame for that, and 'Bela Lugosi's Dead' should be seen as the individualistic piece of musical genius it undoubtedly was, rather than merely a harbinger of miserable tastelessness.

63
SPACER
DON'T GO
SHEILA AND B. DEVOTION
CARRERE
18
French disco-act, Sheila and B. Devotion, put themselves in the hands of The Chic Organisation and were rewarded with this sci-fi themed floor-filler. All the usual Chic elements are present and correct, from Nile Rodgers's chattering guitar to Tony Thompson's machine-like drumming – but a camp European element is also incorporated, most obviously in the Abba-like use of a strident and dramatic piano. The final touch is the heavily-accented vocal from chanteuse Sheila; she glides effortlessly over the rhythm, expressing the lyrical inanities with a sincerity that is genuinely touching.

62
ELECTRICITY
ALMOST
ORCHESTRAL MANOEUVRES
IN THE DARK
FACTORY
DID NOT CHART
Taking Kraftwerk's 'Autobahn' as a starting point, teenagers Andy McCluskey and Paul Humphreys wrote a faster version, combining it lyrically with themes relating to our wastefulness in regard to energy usage, and advocating the use of solar power – pretty impressive forward-thinking for 1979! Interestingly though, McCluskey and Humphreys did not attempt to replicate Kraftwerk's chilly robotic perfection; instead, the pair sang the song in unison, giving it an almost jaunty and very flesh and blood feel.

61
STREET LIFE
THE HUSTLER
THE CRUSADERS
MCA
5
Veteran jazz fusion band The Crusaders had a song that had been written for them by Joe Sample and lyricist Will Jennings; it was about the hustle, bustle and non-stop drama of the streets. They recruited the respected Randy Crawford (who at that point was still unsuccessful) to sing the song… and this turned out to be an inspired choice – she takes the song away and owns every single line of it. Her performance was simply sensational; sassy, streetwise and gritty, she lived the song as she sang it. As for The Crusaders themselves, they were seasoned professionals and hence they were predictably tight, displaying great taste and economy as

they deployed their exceptional skills within the boundaries of the song and its horn-led arrangement.

60
OLIVER'S ARMY
MY FUNNY VALENTINE
ELVIS COSTELLO AND THE
ATTRACTIONS
RADAR
2

Great pop music needn't come with any profound message, but when somebody *does* marry a lyric of substance to an irresistible melody, it tends to add to my appreciation of the song. Elvis Costello was an expert in this regard, and 'Oliver's Army' was his master-stroke. The lyric commences by referencing the occupation of Northern Ireland by young troops who had little in the way of career options (other than joining the army) before further acts of colonialism are included. The titular "Oliver" is Oliver Cromwell, the puritan Lord Protector; as the effective ruler of Britain, he was intolerant and brutal, particularly to the Irish Catholic community when he ordered that acts of genocide be committed. The superlative lyric is integrated with a high-production piece of shining pop in the style of Abba's 'Dancing Queen' and there is even a sing-along chorus that enabled this thought-provoking piece to infiltrate the music mainstream. I must also mention Costello's second single of 1979, 'Accidents Will Happen', which again was quite outstanding; I must confess to feeling a trifle guilty about not including it in this collection, but such was the volume of great music in this particular year that it is, most regrettably, omitted.

59
WOW
FULLHOUSE
KATE BUSH
EMI
14

Superficially, 'Wow' may appear to be just a pretty and melodic piece with an uplifting chorus – which is undeniably the case – but a closer inspection of the lyric (and the way in which it is delivered) reveals this to be an extremely dark and deeply cynical song about the moral turpitude within the world of show-business. Shallow conceit, bullying, the massaging of egos and exploitative sex are all touched upon in a highly incisive manner. When one takes into account that this single was released at a time when evil, manipulative predators such as Gary Glitter and Jimmy Savile were allowed to get away with their predilections by an obsequious establishment, then the power of the song is magnified further. To cocoon this heavyweight and controversial material inside such a sweet concoction – thus enabling it to reach a mass audience – was a brilliant manoeuvre… but not really a surprise, because Kate Bush was indeed a brilliant artist.

58
GOOD TIMES
A WARM SUMMER NIGHT
CHIC
ATLANTIC
5

With its irrepressible funk groove, uncluttered yet still sophisticated production and brilliant individual musicians joyously expressing themselves, this showcased Chic as the absolute masters of music-making that they undoubtedly were.

Also very much on point lyrically, they capture the essence of what it means to live in the present and not squander any opportunity to enjoy "good times", although the references made to depression-era songs ('Happy Days are Here Again' and 'About a Quarter to Nine') are a deliberate way of drawing attention to the economic situation faced by so many of the underclass in the USA. Copied by Queen and sampled by thousands of hip hop acts, 'Good Times' has left an indelible mark within popular culture.

57
TUSK
NEVER MAKE ME CRY
FLEETWOOD MAC
WARNER BROTHERS
6
After the astronomical success of their singles and albums of 1976 and 1977, Fleetwood Mac had the world at their feet; however principal songwriter Lindsey Buckingham had no intention whatsoever of re-treading past glories... inspired by the punk and post-punk sounds that he was hearing, he wanted to do something more daring and experimental. He was supported in this endeavour by Mick Fleetwood in particular and 'Tusk' was created; an epic drum track with vocals during which Buckingham hit Kleenex tissue-boxes and Fleetwood slapped lamb chops with a spatula. In addition to this percussive madness the University of California's Trojan Marching Band were invited to play on the single and they were recorded at Dodger Stadium in Los Angeles. Their masses of drums and horns create a carnival-like atmosphere on the record, and, incidentally, their

astounding contribution set a record for being the highest number of individual musicians to perform on a pop single.

56
LIVING ON THE FRONTLINE
FRONTLINE SYMPHONY
EDDIE GRANT
ENSIGN
11
In the 1960s, The Equals had been a significant but unheralded act; the mixed ethnicity line-up, making records that included socio-political points – such as 'Black Skin Blue Eyed Boys' – was revolutionary in its day, but they found themselves swimming against a tide of passive-aggressive media apathy and it was this that caused their demise. The singer and writer of The Equals was the Guyanese-British Eddy Grant; away from the public-eye, he continued to make music that incorporated a heady mixture of reggae, calypso, soca and funk, but always with a pop sensibility. These were only released in Africa, where Nigerian sales in particular were quite exceptional... but then Grant found the rug pulled from beneath his feet when that country's government banned the importation of records and, as he was left with a mountain of vinyl to shift, Grant began selling his records to British shops and discotheques – it wasn't long before 'Living on the Frontline' began to get played in clubs, where its potent synthesiser lines and strident chorus strongly appealed to revellers who sought-out the track and thus created a healthy demand. Grant's independent label, "Ice", struck a distribution deal with Epic and the record began to sell enough copies to belatedly put Eddy

Grant back in the British charts.

55
MAP REF. 41N 93W
GO AHEAD
WIRE
HARVEST
DID NOT CHART

Wire continued to beguile, and 'Map Ref. 41N 93W' carried on a run of singles that were varied and dissimilar, even as they were still immediately identifiable as being by Wire. This single appears to be about categorization; the lyric is cryptic with the delicious announcement of the chorus's arrival making us ponder our perceptions of what constitutes a "proper song". Meanwhile, we could whistle or dance to the tune or simply smile at the pleasure of another slice of highly stimulating and thought-provoking pop.

54
YOU SAY YOU DON'T LOVE ME
RAISON D'ETRE
BUZZCOCKS
UNITED ARTISTS
DID NOT CHART

Another song of unrequited love from Buzzcocks and this one might well be the saddest of them all. Beautifully melodic, 'You Say You Don't Love Me' features a series of mini-swells that build-up to a surge before finally smashing on to the rocks. Pete Shelley sounds weary and heartbroken and the record carries a desperate edge of genuine despair. By this point Buzzcocks were beginning to fragment, and although this was one of their finest ever songs, the air of introspection and disappointment was surely an indication that for them, time really was up.

53
AIN'T YOU
HEDI'S HEAD
KLEENEX
ROUGH TRADE
DID NOT CHART

Kleenex were a noisy and exhilarating female punk band from Switzerland whose untutored musical primitivism was countered by their originality and verve. Ideas were allowed to flourish and grow, and when formed into songs they became glorious expressions of uninhibited free-thought. 'Ain't You' was a raucous, shouty wonder, and even though (to my ears) it is utterly unintelligible, it still sounds fabulous in every single aspect, from the scratchy guitar hooks, the simple repetitive tune and the toy-town drum sound. One more single followed this one, before Kleenex were forced to change their name under threat of legal action; they became LiLiPUT and remained a quite magical musical proposition.

52
DANCE AWAY
CRY CRY CRY
ROXY MUSIC
POLYDOR
2

'Dance Away' was written in 1977 but inexplicably omitted from Bryan Ferry's next two solo albums, before finally making an appearance on the Roxy Music comeback album *Manifesto*. After an extensive re-mix the track was extracted as a single; all of the arty elements were removed, and instead it was the groove that was emphasised... in particular the clever use of claves which added a distinctly Latin-flavour to the sumptuous and unhurried ballad. This was a very different Roxy Music; a world-away from the extreme sonic adventures of the early 1970s, with all the jagged edges removed, never to return. From this moment onwards their music would have a calm, luxurious sheen that eventually evolved into nothing more than sterile and shallow pointlessness.

51
DON'T STOP ME NOW
IN ONLY SEVEN DAYS
QUEEN
EMI
9

A valid criticism of Queen at this time was that they would often smother a perfectly good song beneath layers of studio trickery and heavyweight pomposity but 'Don't Stop Me Now' did not suffer from any of that negative over-indulgence. It is a driving, unpretentious song that builds-up nicely from Freddie Mercury's piano intro. There are flourishes of the band's trademark, multi-tracked harmonies, but here they are used sparingly and effectively; unfortunately, there still remains an ill-judged guitar solo but it is thankfully brief. However the reason that this song is such a triumph (and arguably Queen's finest ever single) is that Freddie Mercury delivers an unambiguous vocal of thrilling defiance to anyone who would dare reprimand him, along with a hedonistic celebration of his own sexuality and promiscuity. The man sounds proud and completely at ease with himself and his lifestyle choices, and this conviction bleeds into what is a glorious and triumphant single.

50
BACK TO NATURE
THE BOX
FAD GADGET
MUTE
DID NOT CHART

Fad Gadget's 'Back to Nature' was the second release on Daniel Miller's "Mute" label, following Miller's own 'Warm Leatherette', and it shared a similarly bleak and dystopian outlook – the theme seemingly being the aftermath of a nuclear catastrophe, with lyrics full of disturbing and arresting images. Recorded cheaply on a sparse assortment of relatively inexpensive electronic equipment, the sound is harsh and distorted, but the droning and a rumbling, menacing bass-line are off-set by a simple, almost pretty melody.

49
BOMBER
OVER THE TOP
MOTÖRHEAD
BRONZE
34

Earlier in the year Motörhead had released the excellent 'Overkill' and 'No Class' as singles, but this latest effort topped them both. Issued in good time to be an alternative to a nice Cliff Richard-style Christmas record, 'Bomber' is a furious 100mph explosion of relentless bass, thrashing drums and screeching guitar noise – of course Lemmy also lends his death-rattle of a voice to tell the tale of night-time flying raids through anti-aircraft flack, in order to unleash a fire-storm of napalm onto a target below. Full of ugly brutality, this was harsh reality delivered with a huge dollop of aggression. Motörhead were the perfect antidote to corporate slickness and escapism, and very worthy carriers of the rock 'n' roll flame.

48
ZEROX
WHIP MY VALISE
ADAM AND THE ANTS
DO IT
DID NOT CHART
(reached 45 in 1981)
The early Adam and the Ants line-ups had a devoted following, presumably attracted only by the image portrayed, because musically speaking, the band were desperately dull. However 'Zerox' was the exception that proved the rule. Adam Ant had latched onto a comment by David Bowie who had compared himself to a 'xerox machine' – a type of early photocopier. So Adam wrote a song about musical plagiarism, utilising the "Xerox" metaphor as a hook. It was unclear whether the song was being critical of Bowie or, conversely, expressing admiration for Bowie's utilisation of other people's innovations. What was clear however was that 'Zerox' was snappy, focussed and extremely good; an early indicator of the pop genius that would be revealed more fully in the early 1980s.

47
TURN TO RED
NERVOUS SYSTEM/ARE YOU RECEIVING?
KILLING JOKE
MALICIOUS DAMAGE
DID NOT CHART
Killing Joke appeared – seemingly from nowhere – with this astounding record; it was an amalgam of fascinating sounds set within a framework of deep and dark dub that carried traces of Middle-Eastern flavouring. In a pre-sampling world they were highly inventive, taking facets of musical language from around the globe and weaving them into a new creative tapestry of sound that encompassed the edgy and awkward dialects of the marginalised. This is exceedingly unorthodox stuff; uncompromising and thrilling.

46
GOTTA SERVE SOMEBODY
TROUBLE IN MIND
BOB DYLAN
COLUMBIA
DID NOT CHART
Apparently, Dylan had a religious epiphany and felt compelled to express his new-found faith and belief through his music. As was the case with my attitude regarding Rastafarian-infused reggae or soulful gospel music, I did not share any of the convictions but I was, nevertheless, more than happy to listen to him expressing his devotion. Many scoffed; for example John Lennon, who parodied Dylan in his satirical 'Serve Yourself'. What many people missed in the rush to condemn what they perceived to be betrayal – rather than simply an individual choice – was the fact that this was a record on which Dylan sounded absolutely convinced of his convictions, where each and every word seemed sincere. This was also a record that was full of warmth and built upon an infectious groove... even Dylan's famously nasal vocal is surrounded and supported by rich-voiced female gospel singers. Put simply, received wisdom had it that this was sub standard fare but received wisdom was wrong 'Gotta Serve Somebody' is a really splendid record.

45
WHITE MICE
MASOCHISTIC OPPOSITES
MO-DETTES
MODE
DID NOT CHART

Kate Korris (who had been an original member of The Slits) and Jane Crockford (from Bank of Dresden) formed the Mo-Dettes; they sparkled brightly for a short period of time but they did leave behind 'White Mice', which was an absolutely superb debut single. Lyrically we have a situation where the rules and conventions of the dating game are reversed – the female is empowered and she is enjoying having the upper-hand; the guitar is jumpy, the bass playing is sinuous and the vocal arch and playful.

44
CONTORT YOURSELF
(TROPICAL) HEATWAVE
JAMES CHANCE AND THE
CONTORTIONS
ZE
DID NOT CHART

James Chance took a mixture of free jazz, funk rhythm and punk attitude, and he mixed it all together. His shows would often degenerate into brawls as he provoked the audience but despite his shock tactics the music was never compromised – it was razor sharp, exciting and unpredictable. 'Contort Yourself' is a mutant dance track of funky rhythms that are constantly crashing before re-igniting and beginning over again; there are horns that squeal and squawk and could easily strip paint from the wall and a jittery, screamed vocal is the cherry on top of the pie. Highly invigorating and highly recommended too.

43
THE FABULOUS SEQUEL
(HAVE SHOES WILL WALK)
HUMOUR ME/
THE BOOK IS ON THE TABLE
PERE UBU
CHRYSALIS
DID NOT CHART

'It's me again!' shouts David Thomas by way of introduction, and then the band gallop-off into what sounds like the spontaneous exploration of a newly created riff. There is a discordant piano thrown in, funky rhythm guitar and drums that are gleefully pounded. Add to this handclaps that are suggestive of an extremely unruly party, a guitar solo of near deadly intent, and a vocal so unrestrained that it seems as if Thomas is allowing his inner-child to front-up the band, armed only with a lyric full of unconnected phrases. I used to attempt to figure-out 'The Fabulous Sequel'… but these days I just enjoy it.

42
SO MUCH TROUBLE IN THE WORLD
SO MUCH TROUBLE IN THE WORLD (INSTRUMENTAL)
BOB MARLEY AND THE WAILERS
ISLAND
56

Bob Marley received criticism in some quarters when he allowed his muse to settle on what people viewed as inconsequential issues; they wanted militancy in his message at all times. Effectively he was being treated in the same way that Bob Dylan had been by the folk-music mafia in the early-1960s, when they demanded nothing other than protest songs be allowed in his repertoire. To some extent 'So Much Trouble in the World' might have assuaged Marley's critics, because he does speak here about global problems – in particular the threat of nuclear war. However he is *not* preaching fire and brimstone but rather taking a quiet, meditative approach to the issues. Marley marries his words to a gloriously sunny melody, and imaginatively utilised percussion propels the track forwards as a sweet, melodic synthesiser-line adorns it.

41

I (WHO HAVE NOTHING)
I NEED SOMEBODY TO LOVE TONIGHT
SYLVESTER
FANTASY
DID NOT CHART

'I (Who Have Nothing)' is an English-language version of an Italian song called 'Uno Dei Tanti'; the English lyric was written by Jerry Lieber and Mike Stoller and it was first recorded by Ben E. King. The song soon became something of a standard, attracting covers by the likes of Shirley Bassey and Tom Jones… but my favourite version of the song is this disco epic by Sylvester, who drags every single shred of emotion from it in his dramatic performance. Building slowly over a percussion track, Sylvester and his backing singers trade verses in serene style before the piece develops further and Sylvester unleashes his devastating falsetto, pushing the intensity levels ever higher while Patrick Cowley, in his role as producer and musical director, ignores any temptation to steer the track towards an obvious high-energy conclusion, opting instead for tasteful restraint, allowing Sylvester the space to give free-reign

to his marvellously expressive voice.

40

LOST IN MUSIC
THINKING OF YOU
SISTER SLEDGE
ATLANTIC
17 (re-release 1984 reached 4)

Sister Sledge were a barely-known act when they were approached by Bernard Edwards and Nile Rogers of Chic, who went on to write and produce the *We are Family* album for them. From that superb hit-laden record came this single; 'Lost in Music' was a celebration of living life to the maximum, quitting the nine-to-five drudgery and forming a band. I guess that for many people this is just a harmless daydream… but having it voiced so sublimely in this record really seemed to strike a chord. With the rhythm section keeping the song firmly rooted to the dance-floor, and Rogers's "chaka chaka" guitar prominent in the mix, the strings and the voices of the Sledge sisters are allowed to aim resolutely skywards, way-up into the realm of dreams.

39

YOU'VE GOT TO PAY
THIS AIN'T ALL (IT'S MADE OUT TO BE)
THE ONLY ONES
CBS
DID NOT CHART

A jumping introduction that features a ringing cowbell leads into a wordy and wise discourse on the nature of failing love. Lyrical couplets of delicious quality drip from Peter Perrett's lip, his reedy voice a perfect vessel for this kind of soul-searching introspection, where the only conclusion to be drawn is that, as in life, so too in love… the pleasure comes mixed with the pain. Elegant guitar lines from John Perry adorn this slim, but very precious gem of a single.

38
SMASH IT UP
BURGLAR
THE DAMNED
CHISWICK
35

The Damned were a volatile band and their momentum had been significantly stymied by personnel changes, splits, reformations and tangential one-off projects; but here the ship was steadied and the in-fighting ceased. Free of unpleasant distractions, The Damned produced this incredible and incendiary rabble-rousing anthem to the power of the human spirit; they denounce all that they see as false – Krishna burgers, Glastonbury hippies and blow-dried hairdos are all gleefully dismissed, amidst a barrage of magnificent, anarchistic noise-making.

37
I GOT MY MIND MADE UP
(YOU CAN GET IT GIRL)
CRYING
INSTANT FUNK
SALSOUL
DID NOT CHART

Horns, wah wah pedal, cowbell, conga, handclaps and chanted vocals, all combine to create a seriously smoking disco groove; a synth part then gives way to heavy smooching sounds, before a rasping male voice implores his female partner to get physical with him. It wasn't going to win any awards for literary merit, but as an invitation to dance, this was impossible to refuse.

36
RING MY BELL
IF I COULD FEEL THAT OLD
FEELING AGAIN
ANITA WARD
TK RECORDS
1

'Ring my Bell' was a song written by Frederick Knight and it was all-set to be recorded by an 11-year old Stacy Lattisaw. With subject matter concerning the weighty matter of kids talking on the telephone, this was directly targeted at a young, teen audience. However that plan was scuppered when Lattisaw moved to a different record label; the lyrics of the song were then amended in order to suit an older performer, and now it was about a woman encouraging her partner to relax after a tough day at work. This new version was handed to Anita Ward whose ecstatic vocal performance – aligned to a prominent electronic drum sound – made it absolutely impossible to ignore. Although the lyric had deliberately been kept squeaky clean to protect the image of Ward, this is widely regarded as a come-on song with sexual undertones that were most certainly unintended.

35
DUCHESS
FOOLS RUSH OUT
THE STRANGLERS
UNITED ARTISTS
14

'Duchess' is a tender picture-portrait of a lonely woman played as a jittery, ornate dirge, with harpsichord being the predominant instrument. Structurally it is quite minimal; the song simply begins and ends with nothing much changing in the middle… nevertheless, it is wonderful.

Hugh Cornwell sings with endearing empathy for his subject — a woman allowing her life to go to waste as she sits in her decrepit dream-world, imagining that she is somehow special and that one day her prince will surely come.

34
LIFE DURING WARTIME
ELECTRIC GUITAR
TALKING HEADS
SIRE
DID NOT CHART

One of the greatest things that this great band ever recorded was this single; here, Talking Heads embrace funk — a twitchy and anxious funk admittedly, but still funk. 'Life During Wartime' sounds desperate and claustrophobic; the vocal conveys anxiety as if the singer is being hunted and fearful of what is waiting for him around the next corner. "This ain't no party, this ain't no disco, this ain't no fooling around", sings the increasingly spooked David Byrne, and we feel a shiver go down the spine just as if we have been parachuted unwillingly into a warzone.

33
WHERE'S CAPTAIN KIRK?
AMNESIA
SPIZZENERGI
ROUGH TRADE
DID NOT CHART

Spizz was a teenager from Solihull who seized on the possibilities afforded him by punk to express himself and have a bit of fun. He formed Spizz Oil, who then became Spizzenergi, before eventually becoming, in turn, Athletico Spizz 80 and The Spizzles. 'Where's Captain Kirk?' (with a sleeve designed by Spizz himself, using felt pens) was the ace-in-the-pack single; it boldly went where other records didn't dare — right to the bridge of the Starship Enterprise from famous sci-fi TV series *Star Trek*. It fizzed and banged excitedly while Spizz, barely able to contain himself, yelped and spluttered his words, each verse ending with the unanswered question… 'Where's Captain Kirk?'

32
AT HOME HE'S A TOURIST
IT'S HER FACTORY
GANG OF FOUR
EMI
58

'At Home He's a Tourist' is a ferocious single; anger and intent run through each and every line of the song, and every note is hammered out. The bass is a relentless funk rumble that underpins the song, while the guitar is slashed and lacerated until it bleeds noise. The lyric is about domestic alienation, examined from both the male and female perspective; the protagonists can find no escape, even in the disco as they dance and seek illicit sexual encounters, only to realise that the system is controlling them, using invisible strings to extract a profit in all possible situations.

31
VIDEO KILLED
THE RADIO STAR
KID DYNAMO
BUGGLES
ISLAND
1

'Video Killed the Radio Star' was written by Trevor Horn, Geoff Downes and Bruce Woolley; it was initially released by Bruce Woolley and the Camera Club… but it flopped. Meanwhile, Horn and Downes also recorded the song under the name Buggles. Whereas the synths in the Woolley version had been somewhat muted on the Buggles version they were as sharp as razors. The vocals were also harder, edgier and had a more cynical hue; in fact pretty much everything was leaner, cleaner and machine tightened. This record perfectly captured a particular moment in time when technology and attitudes toward it were rapidly changing. It was brilliant pop; a sweet confection that nonetheless conjured up visions of a frightening and impersonal dystopian future.

30

REBOP–ATTITUDES
RIEN A DIRE MEDLEY
MARIE ET LES GARÇONS
ZE
DID NOT CHART
John Cale produces and also plays piano and marimba on this record... and that is the totality of my knowledge about Marie et les Garçons. However, what I do know is that I bought the single simply because it was on the ZE label, which always signalled to me a certain sensibility and quality and this made shelling-out on completely unheard records much less of a risk than one might imagine, fortunately I made a very wise investment. 'Rebop / Attitudes' is a head-spinning, hip-shaking mix of Latin dance and New York disco with a punky sensibility – it's as catchy as a cold, but far more pleasing.

29

GIMME! GIMME! GIMME!
(A MAN AFTER MIDNIGHT)
THE KING HAS LOST HIS
CROWN
ABBA
EPIC
3
Recorded at the same time as their *Voulez-Vous* album, but issued as a stand-alone single, 'Gimme!' clearly displayed everything that was great about Abba. Musically it is titanic – muscular, but lithe it effortlessly combines disco and rock, and it burns with sexual tension. The sound is clean, the musicians are tight, and the voices are magnificently full of passion and character.

28

DANCE STANCE
I'M JUST LOOKING
DEXYS MIDNIGHT RUNNERS
ODDBALL
40
The Killjoys had been a theatrical punk band from the Midlands who folded after releasing just one inconsequential single. The band's singer, Kevin Rowland, teamed-up with Kevin Archer, and together they assembled Dexy's Midnight Runners as a forward-thinking soul band, replete with horn section and a dress-code modelled on characters from Martin Scorsese's film *Mean Streets*. Bernie Rhodes (the ex-Clash, Subway Sect and Specials manager) gave them the opportunity to release a single on his fledgling "Oddball" label and 'Dance Stance' was the result of the liaison. Opening with a jarring horn salvo, the song then settles down, allowing the bizarre but brilliantly voiced Rowland to deliver a lyric aimed at dismantling the anti-

Irish prejudice and stereotyping of the "thick Paddy" that was so commonplace at every level in English society; "Shut your fucking mouth until you know the truth" he spits-out venomously, before reciting a list of names of conspicuously "unthick" Irish literary figures. "Never heard about Oscar Wilde... Brendan Behan... Sean O'Casey... George Bernard Shaw?" he asks, before continuing with the list, making a highly valid point and launching Dexy's in exceptionally superb style.

27

TYPICAL GIRLS
I HEARD IT THROUGH THE GRAPEVINE
THE SLITS
ISLAND
DID NOT CHART

The Slits were one of the first – and best – of the British punk bands in 1976. They had a ferocious, untutored sound which was used as a base for screamed vocals, often lampooning and challenging sexist attitudes. As an all-female band, rejecting the traditional passivity and sweetness expected from them, The Slits asked uncomfortable but necessary questions of the music scene, and indeed of their own audience. They were also unafraid of musical change so by the time 'Typical Girls' was issued they had replaced original drummer Palmolive with ex-Big in Japan sticksman, Budgie. Also in was Neneh Cherry (as an additional vocalist) and producer Dennis Bovell who helped move the sound from the sharp and angular, to a more rounded, bass-led reggae-influenced re-imagining. 'Typical Girls' duly appeared in this pleasing new form,

mostly sung by the irrepressible Ari Up; it holds-up for inspection a list of the preconceptions of what constitutes a 'Typical Girl', and then proceeds to mock them, before gleefully ripping them up.

26

CALIFORNIA ÜBER ALLES
THE MAN WITH THE DOGS
DEAD KENNEDYS
FAST
DID NOT CHART

The debut single by San Francisco's Dead Kennedys was this stinging, satirical attack on California Governor Jerry Brown, drawing parallels between his agenda and that of Adolf Hitler's Nazis. The works of William Shakespeare and George Orwell are referenced in the lyric, as is the Nazi atrocity of making lampshades out of human flesh that had been stripped from their victims. The song plays out over a sinister militaristic drum beat and an ominous, doom-laden bass, while surf guitars add a healthy measure of incongruous madness. The pace drops and then speeds-up again, as singer Jello Biafra sneers contempt at the reprehensible Jerry Brown, while the band are locked in breathtaking unison during the thrillingly adrenalised chorus.

25

HEY HEY MY MY
(INTO THE BLACK)
HEY HEY MY MY
(OUT OF THE BLUE)
NEIL YOUNG AND CRAZY HORSE
REPRISE
DID NOT CHART

One of Neil Young's most forceful songs, 'Hey Hey My My', came from him questioning his own relevance in light of the upheaval brought about by the punk scene and the patchy nature of his most recent record releases. The track was originally recorded in collaboration with Devo – whose Mark Mothersbaugh gifted him the line "Rust never sleeps" – before being magnificently re-worked in the company of Crazy Horse. Containing, as it does, a crashing and brutal riff of huge potency, a lyric of intelligence and insight, and a fierce, fiery vocal, Neil Young was able to convincingly put his doubts to one side; he was a long, long way from being obsolete.

24
AIN'T NO STOPPING US NOW
I GOT THE LOVE
MCFADDEN & WHITEHEAD
PHILADELPHIA
INTERNATIONAL
5
McFadden & Whitehead were songwriters for Philadelphia International Records but they also aspired to perform and record their own material. Gamble and Huff, their bosses, did not like the idea and denied them the opportunity. Then the song-writing pair came up with 'Ain't No Stopping Us Now' by way of riposte; it was a sure-fire hit. The song is a fabulous, grooving piece that exudes positivity before leading into an irrepressible chorus of defiance and pride. Gamble and Huff lobbied for The O'Jays to record the song, but McFadden and Whitehead dug-in their heels and said no. Reluctantly, they were allowed to record their song themselves and were triumphantly vindicated when it became a worldwide best-seller, with the fully deserved label of "classic" appended to it.

23
CARS
ASYLUM
GARY NUMAN
BEGGARS BANQUET
1
Gary Numan had been the face and talent of Tubeway Army, who had crashed their way into the musical consciousness of the nation earlier in the year; this was Numan's first solo release as he decided to no longer hide behind the band name. 'Cars' came with an absolute killer synthesiser riff and it dealt with the alienation of individuals in society, locked inside their vehicles where they are lulled into an artificial sense of security as they travel through the streets, alone and untouched. Numan would go on to become hugely successful, but he was often sneered at by the cognoscenti; in the end he would have the last laugh because future generations from hip hop, electro and industrial genres, all willingly queued-up to freely acknowledge Numan's influence upon their own music.

22
NAG NAG NAG
IS THAT ME (FINDING
SOMEONE AT THE DOOR
AGAIN?)
CABARET VOLTAIRE
ROUGH TRADE
DID NOT CHART
After one EP and an appearance on the inaugural Factory Records release, this was Cabaret Voltaire's first single. It begins with a grinding noise, redolent of a cement-mixer, before the highly distorted riff takes over – a sheet of electric noise with hissing and pulsing underpinned by the rhythm of a primitive drum

machine. The voices are also heavily treated, but not enough to disguise the obvious disdain being articulated. Cabaret Voltaire had perfectly captured their home environment – a declining and decaying post-industrial Sheffield – just as surely as the Stooges had mirrored the noise of the car manufacturing plants in turn-of-the-decade Detroit...

21
FAIRYTALE IN THE SUPERMARKET
IN LOVE/ADVENTURES CLOSE TO HOME
THE RAINCOATS
ROUGH TRADE
DID NOT CHART

Before students Ana Da Silva and Gina Birch saw The Slits, the idea of being in a band seemed a ridiculous non-starter; but duly inspired they picked up guitar and bass respectively and as complete novices they formed The Raincoats where they created fascinating, intelligent music that was full of restless adventuring and sheer joy. By the time they came to record this debut single the line-up had expanded to include ex-Slit Palmolive on drums, and classically-trained violinist Vicky Aspinall. Their expressive music was thrilling – a mixture of enthusiastic amateurism married to skill and expertise; Palmolive drums in a totally unique style, driving the song along as if navigating traffic and Vicky Aspinall's violin style is reminiscent of John Cale's crucial contribution to The Velvet Underground. The lyric (which I read as being concerned with the suppression of female identity) is full of arresting imagery, and is sung in unison with commendable gusto.

20
FUNKYTOWN
ALL NIGHT DANCING
LIPPS INC.
CASABLANCA
2

'Funkytown' is an idealised, metaphorical place where everybody and everything is "movin' and groovin'". The song was written by musician/producer Steven Greenberg as the Minneapolis-based Lipps Inc. were daydreaming about relocating to New York. Disco, as a genre, was a waning musical force, but 'Funkytown' shot it through with new life. It is playfully robotic and futuristic, utilising a vocoder to great effect; this is combined with a stunningly simple synth line and some strident funk-guitar riffing on the chorus.

19
HEART OF GLASS
RIFLE RANGE
BLONDIE
CHRYSALIS
1

Blondie were stacking up hit record after hit record, but the biggest and best of all was 'Heart of Glass'. Debbie Harry and Chris Stein had written the first version of the song based on the Hues Corporation single, 'Rock Your Boat'. Somehow they never quite seemed to get it right, after trying the song out in ballad and reggae styles. But after hearing these failed attempts producer Mike Chapman recognised that there was something worth pursuing and he encouraged the band to keep working to get it right. Because both Harry and Stein were big disco fans (Blondie had performed both Labelle's 'Lady Marmalade' and

Donna Summer's 'I Feel Love' in concert) as well as appreciating the electronic sounds of Kraftwerk, they decided to try-out the troublesome track with a European disco arrangement. Keyboard player Jimmy Destri purchased a drum-machine and synthesiser and he set about programming them to create the finished record's distinctive pulsing sound. The rhythm was produced by combining the machine with Clem Burke's live drumming, and an extraordinarily propulsive beat was the result; and finally, Debbie Harry supplied a superlative vocal that is cool and controlled. Of course, the punk rock die-hards were sniffy about the band going disco, and the hardcore disco crew were equally sniffy for the reverse reason… but the rest of the world simply got on with the job of enjoying it.

18
TRANSMISSION
NOVELTY
JOY DIVISION
FACTORY
DID NOT CHART

I often saw Joy Division perform in their early days; they were so-so, struggling for focus and direction – in short, they were not a band that I expected to change the face of music. Then 'Transmission' and 'She's Lost Control' were added to their set-list; these were great songs, and so suddenly it became a pleasure to watch them perform. In some ways 'Transmission' belies Joy Division's gloomy reputation; it is a quick-tempo adrenalised track over which Ian Curtis emotes on a lyric that seems to be about the nasty and insidious nature of commercial radio and the way in which it deadens the soul. With a chorus of "Dance, dance, dance… to the radio" delivered with such pained desperation, this could never be perceived as being celebratory. I ran into Joy Division bassist Peter Hook about a week after the single's release and congratulated him, adding that I hoped it would be a success. "It's already a success", he replied, before explaining that "It doesn't matter if it sells or not – what matters is that we've made a record we are all proud of". I was very impressed by his words and the underlying attitude, and he was right to feel proud – 'Transmission' is a brilliant record.

17
I WILL SURVIVE
SUBSTITUTE
GLORIA GAYNOR
POLYDOR
6

Surprisingly, this was originally released with 'Substitute' as the A-side, but when 'I Will Survive' began to pick-up the plaudits, the record was reissued with the A- and B-sides reversed. Of course, 'I Will Survive' went on to become a disco anthem; its powerful message of finding strength and hope, even in the depths of adversity, saw it adopted as a symbolic representation of female empowerment. Similarly, at the height of the HIV/AIDS crisis, the gay community took the song to their hearts as the spectre of death loomed large. Remarkably, the record manages to shoulder this cultural baggage with ease, because it is undeniably brilliant, thrilling and hugely dramatic. The disco-balls may have been shining less brightly as the racist, conservative backlash began to hold sway, and in the intolerant USA, disco was deemed to be irrelevant and bonfires of disco records were lit across the country; but they couldn't silence records as good as 'I Will Survive', a song that has touched the hearts and minds of many ever since.

16
SONNY'S LETTAH
(ANTI-SUS POEM)
IRON BAR DUB
LINTON KWESI JOHNSON
ISLAND
DID NOT CHART
A piece of 19th-Century legislation was revived by the Government; initially part of the Vagrancy Act, it gave police the power of stop and search on suspicion, it targeted black youths disproportionately. It was a weapon of the state used against a minority community; they were harassed, arrested and jailed, often fitted-up for crimes they had not committed… understandably, anger was building. In 'Sonny's Lettah', Linton Kwesi Johnson recites a poem, over a reggae rhythm, that portrays a letter from Brixton Prison, telling the story of a black youth and his brother, Little Jim, who are stopped and mistreated by police who target Little Jim in particular. In the letter, Sonny explains to his mother that he couldn't stand by as this happened… and in the altercation that ensued as he tried to protect his brother, a policeman is accidentally killed – so as a result of going for an innocent walk, Sonny now finds himself incarcerated on a charge of murder. The story, although clearly a work of dramatic fiction, nonetheless conveyed the truth of what was happening on the streets; it was a powerful and potent message, performed with both passion and eloquence in equal measure.

15
LET IT BLURT
LIVE
LESTER BANGS
SPY
DID NOT CHART
Lester Bangs was a rock music critic famed for telling it as he saw or heard it; he was sacked by the esteemed *Rolling Stone* magazine for delivering a viciously scathing review of an album by Canned Heat. He wound up living in New York, working freelance and watching the CBGBs scene unfold. Bangs built-up various friendships and connections and in 1977 he went into the studio with, among others, Jay Dee Daugherty (from The Patti Smith Group) on drums, Robert Quine (of Voidoids fame) on guitar, and to cover production duties, no lesser personage than Velvet Underground legend John Cale. Out of that session 'Let it Blurt' was released as a single, and it is a record the like of which I'd never heard before. Musically it is wild, free-form and anarchic… but the lyric and unrestrained vocal are even more startling. We hear a blood-spattered diatribe concerning Bangs' girlfriend's decision to have an abortion, though even as he points an accusatory finger, he lays his own faults bare with lacerating self-loathing. There is no attempted cool about this whatsoever; absolutely nothing is held back – this is primal scream turned up to eleven… a journey into a tortured mind and without doubt one of the most extraordinary and visceral records that I have ever heard.

14
WE ARE FAMILY
EASIER TO LOVE
SISTER SLEDGE
ATLANTIC
8

'We Are Family' is a rallying cry for unification and solidarity. The genius of this record is in the succinct simplicity of its message, aligned to the uplifting dance-floor filling groove. It was the first song written by Bernard Nelson and Nile Rogers for an act other than Chic. The unknown Sister Sledge were chosen to be the recipients of the song, so that, if it were to be successful, the success would be earned on the intrinsic merit of the track, rather than the reputation and existing audience of an established act. The lead vocal by 19-year old Kathy Sledge was captured in one magical take, and her three sisters surround her with their own voices full of spirit and love.

13
ROCK LOBSTER
RUNNING AROUND
B-52s
ISLAND
37

'Rock Lobster' was recorded and released on DB records in 1978; it was fascinating and quirky, but this 1979 re-recording is far superior because all of the wit and charm of the original remain intact but now the track has developed big muscles... along with the air of confidence that goes with them. The astonishingly catchy riff, played on surf-style guitar, is supported by a synthesised bass, Farfisa organ and rattling drums. This provides the backing for Fred Schneider to execute a lyric describing a beach party scene, containing a parade of both real and imaginary marine creatures. Meanwhile Kate Pierson and Cindy Wilson (one singing high and the other low) approximate the noises of the various creatures, before reaching a crescendo of "Ah-Ah-Ahs", followed by Schneider's yelped phrase, 'Rock Lobster'. This was an "art band" who actually dared to smile.

12
DON'T STOP 'TIL YOU GET ENOUGH
I CAN'T HELP IT
MICHAEL JACKSON
EPIC
3

This first single taken from his stellar *Off the Wall* album marked the defining turning point in Michael Jackson's transformation from teen-idol to heavyweight musician. Jackson wrote the song, and then recruited the esteemed Quincy Jones to handle production duties; between them they served up a veritable epic that, despite being grandiose, never loses sight of the fact that it is, at heart, just a simple pop song. It proceeds at a brisk 120 bpm tempo but it remains melodic – and it is on this record that Jackson first utilises the vocal style that would later become his trademark... hiccups and ticks, squealing and James Brown-style grunts adorn the high-energy performance of a lyric which preaches positivity as a way to self-empowerment, with *Star Wars* references delightfully included too.

11
NUMBER ONE SONG IN HEAVEN
NUMBER ONE SONG IN HEAVEN (LONG VERSION)
SPARKS
VIRGIN
14

Somebody had a lightbulb moment… hey how about teaming up Sparks with Georgio Moroder? – it was a genius idea. Sparks, with their pop music nous, smart lyrics and Russell Mael's stunning falsetto, combined with Moroder's sequencers, machine rhythms and European disco sensibilities, it was a marriage made in heaven, and 'Number One Song in Heaven' was the absolute jewel in the crown of their collaboration. Starting gently, light as a soufflé, the power is only switched on at the midpoint, and the song then becomes a gushing torrent of euphoria; it pulses, surges and soars skywards, spinning wildly. By pushing conventional instruments to one side, and instead experimenting with synthesisers and sequencers, Sparks re-ignited their career both commercially and artistically, and as they did it, they influenced a whole raft of future electro-pop stars such as New Order and Soft Cell.

TOP 75 - 20TH OCT 1979

1	1	VIDEO KILLED THE RADIO STAR, Buggles	Islan
2	1	MESSAGE IN A BOTTLE, Police	A & M
3	4	DON'T STOP TIL YOU GET ENOUGH, Michael Jackson	Epi
4	3	DREAMING, Blondie	Chrysali
5	9	ONE DAY AT A TIME, Lena Martell	Py
6	11	EVERYDAY HURTS, Sad Cafe	RC
7	6	SINCE YOU'VE BEEN GONE, Rainbow	Polydc
8	5	WHATEVER YOU WANT, Status Quo	Vertig
9	26	WHEN YOU'RE IN LOVE, Dr Hook	Capit
10	16	CHOSEN FEW, Dooleys	GT
11	18	QUEEN OF HEARTS, Dave Edmunds	Swan Son
12	23	OK FRED, Erroll Dunkley	Scop
13	10	KATE BUSH LIVE ON STAGE, Kate Bush	EM
14	7	CARS, Gary Numan	Beggars Banqu
15	15	YOU CAN DO IT, Al Hudson and The Partners	MC
16	8	IF I SAID YOU HAD A BEAUTIFUL BODY, Bellamy Brothers	Warner Bro
17	28	BACK OF MY HAND, Jags	Islan
18	30	TUSK, Fleetwood Mac	Repris
19	14	CRUEL TO BE KIND, Nick Lowe	Rad
20	27	THE DEVIL WENT DOWN TO GEORGIA, Charlie Daniels Band	Ep
21	36	THE GREAT ROCK AND ROLL SWINDLE, Sex Pistols	Virgi
22	19	THE PRINCE, Madness	2 Ton
23	51	MY FORBIDDEN LOVER, Chic	Atlant
24	21	TIME FOR ACTION, Secret Affair	I Sp
25	34	STAR, Earth Wind and Fire	CB
26	12	LOVE'S GOT A HOLD ON ME, Dollar	Carre
27	47	GONNA GET ALONG WITHOUT YOU NOW, Viola Wills	Ariola/Hans
28	37	MAKING PLANS FOR NIGEL, XTC	Virgi
29	54	LUTON AIRPORT, Cats UK	WE
30	NEW	GIMME GIMME GIMME, Abba	Ep
31	42	CHARADE, Skids	Virgi
32	25	SLAP AND TICKLE, Squeeze	A &
33	NEW	CRAZY LITTLE THING CALLED LOVE, Queen	EM
34	17	STRUT YOUR FUNKY STUFF, Frantique	Phil I
35	40	SPIRIT BODY AND SOUL, Nolan Sisters	Ep
36	20	DON'T BRING ME DOWN, ELO	J
37	41	LET ME KNOW (I HAVE A RIGHT), Gloria Gaynor	Polyd
38	13	SAIL ON, Commodores	Tamla Motow
39	39	SING A HAPPY SONG, O'Jays	Phil I
40	NEW	NUCLEAR DEVICE (WIZARD OF AUS), Stranglers	United Artis
41	29	DIM ALL THE LIGHTS, Donna Summer	Casablan
42	33	DON'T BE A DUMMY, John Duncann	Verti
43	NEW	SMASH IT UP, Damned	Chiswi
44	63	I DON'T WANT TO BE A FREAK, Dynasty	Sol
45	52	THE SHAPE OF THINGS TO COME, Headboys	RS
46	NEW	SHE'S IN LOVE WITH YOU, Suzi Quatro	RA
47	64	ON MY RADIO, Selecter	2 Tor
48	35	POINT OF VIEW, Matumbi	Matum
49	24	STREET LIFE, Crusaders	MC
50	58	HEARTACHE TONIGHT, Eagles	Asylu
51	73	THE SPARROW, Ramblers	Dec
52	66	RISE, Herb Alpert	A &
53	32	THE LONELIEST MAN IN THE WORLD, Tourists	Lo
54	31	REGGAE FOR IT NOW, Bill Lovelady	Charisn
55	48	JUMP THE GUN, Three Degrees	Ario
56	45	SUMAHAMA, Beach Boys	Carib
57	44	STRAW DOGS, Still Little Fingers	Chrysal
58	NEW	SARAH, Thin Lizzy	Verti
59	22	WE DON'T TALK ANY MORE, Cliff Richard	EI
60	NEW	MEMORIES, Public Image Ltd.	Virg
61	67	STRAIGHT LINES, New Musik	GT
62	NEW	SO MUCH TROUBLE IN THE WORLD, Bob Marley	Isla
63	60	TYPICAL GIRLS/I HEARD IT THRU THE GRAPEVINE, Slits	Isla
64	NEW	YOU'VE GOT MY NUMBER, Undertones	Si
65	38	GOTTA GO HOME/EL LUTE, Boney M	Atlantic/Han
66	72	GOOD GIRLS DON'T, The Knack	Capit
67	NEW	BIRD SONG, Lene Lovich	St
68	57	GHOST DANCER, Adrissi Brothers	Scotti Brothe
69	NEW	BABY BLUE, Dusty Springfield	Mercu
70	NEW	FREEDOM'S PRISONER, Steve Harley	E
71	NEW	CAN'T GET ENOUGH OF YOUR LOVE, Darts	Magn
72	59	NO ONE GETS THE PRIZE, Diana Ross	Tamla Moto
73	NEW	BRIGHT SIDE OF THE ROAD, Van Morrison	Mercu
74	NEW	SAD EYES, Robert John	EI
75	50	ANGEL EYES, Roxy Music	Polyd

10

LONDON CALLING
ARMAGEDDON TIME
THE CLASH
CBS
11

After the horrible production sheen that had made their second album sound like a desperate love-letter to American hard-rock audiences, The Clash got their mojo back by aligning themselves with maverick producer Guy Stevens – no doubt at the behest of Mick Jones, an *uber* Mott the Hoople fan, the band which Stevens had been instrumental in putting together and nurturing. 'London Calling' (the title alludes to the tag-line used by announcers on BBC World Service) touched on several issues such as police brutality, drug use and the commercial re-positioning of what, by now, were ex-punk bands… including The Clash themselves but the central and overarching theme of the song was the fear of an impending catastrophic nuclear accident, or a war that would see the rising tide swamping and sinking central London. Played at a confident, mid-paced tempo, there is a swagger and swing to this track that only bands with a fine-tuned musical chemistry can conjure up and the vocal from Joe Strummer contained compassion, along with a sincere, heartfelt quality that seemed to address each individual listener personally.

9

RAPPER'S DELIGHT
RAPPER'S DELIGHT
(LONG VERSION)
SUGARHILL GANG
SUGAR HILL
3

Rap and hip hop did not start here but this was the record that took the phenomenon out of the Bronx and Harlem and presented it to a worldwide audience. Great credit is due to Sylvia Robinson for having the foresight and belief in seeing the art and potential of this street music, and providing a platform in the form of Sugar Hill Records to expose what was happening in this burgeoning scene. Here, in the pre-sampling world, a live band was assembled to play with the three rappers who comprised The Sugarhill Gang and extracts from existing records were then cut into the track; the most notable and recognisable piece – taken without prior consent – was the bass-line from 'Good Times' by Chic, who promptly sued and got a writing credit as a result. Vocally, 'Rapper's Delight' opens with Wonder Mike rapping about hip hop (at the time, an alien phrase to all but a select few); the microphone is then passed between Wonder Mike, Big Bank Hank and Master Gee, and they jive conversationally on cars, girls, clothes and takeaway food that tastes like wood, along with whatever else was preoccupying their minds. The potential to use the form to say something with deeper meaning is not utilised here – that would come soon though via genuine rap icons such as Grandmaster Flash but this record was the one that unlocked the door... there was no denying the fresh, funky vitality of this sound. 'Rapper's Delight' opened the floodgates on the birth of hip hop, just as Bill Haley's 'Rock Around the Clock' had done for rock 'n' roll.

8 (JOINTLY)

DJ
REPETITION
DAVID BOWIE
RCA

29

BOYS KEEP SWINGING
FANTASTIC VOYAGE
DAVID BOWIE
RCA
7

In many ways, the two singles extracted from David Bowie's album *Lodger* were the most pop-based and commercial that he had released since the glam period; they were buoyant and vibrant and had choruses containing simple, ear-wormy catchphrases that made them fabulous pop singles. Of course,

Bowie being Bowie, not everything was as straightforward as it seemed, and both these records were darker and more subversive than was initially perceived. On 'DJ', he looks at the growing cult of celebrity afforded to the person who spins the discs, and notes how they become trapped and destroyed by audience expectation while 'Boys Keep Swinging' takes aim at gender stereotyping, with a celebration of masculine pleasures that is so insincere that we recognise at once the deliberately mischievous send-up.

7

GANGSTERS
THE SELECTOR
THE SPECIALS
TWO TONE
6

The Specials debut single, released on their own – soon to be iconic – 2 Tone label, was explosive from beginning to end. It was yet another insulting and angry song aimed towards Bernie Rhodes, the on/off Clash manager who had also briefly managed The Specials. On a European tour, supporting The Clash, a hotel room was significantly damaged and The Specials, although having no part in the incident, were chosen to be the fall-guys who would take the blame. Their instruments were seized until they paid the required reparations... naturally they were far from happy to be cheated and abused in such a way. 'Gangsters' utilises the rhythm from Prince Buster's ska hit 'Al Capone', but here it is infused with a wired punk energy and a lyric of sarcastic indignation and affronted honour, delivered deadpan (as always!) by Terry Hall, while all around him, presided over by Jerry Dammers, a maelstrom of musical aggression, rages with fierce intent.

6

ARE 'FRIENDS' ELECTRIC?
WE ARE SO FRAGILE
TUBEWAY ARMY
BEGGARS BANQUET
1

Intending to record in conventional punk rock style, Tubeway Army entered the studio where Gary Numan began experimenting with a mini-Moog that had been left lying around; a completely fresh sound and a new way of working quickly emerged, and 'Are "Friends" Electric?' was created. The song is about loneliness and a liaison with an android prostitute, and it is set in a harsh and austere landscape. Clearly influenced lyrically by Philip K. Dick's sci-fi novel *Do Androids Dream of Electric Sheep* and musically by David Bowie's *Low* album, Numan takes these inspirations and discovers – perhaps to his own surprise just as much as anybody else's – that they fit him like a glove. He inhabits this environment as if it is the home he has been seeking all his life… he is not faking it. 'Are "Friends" Electric?' is the sound of a wounded, sensitive soul who has been marginalised and misunderstood, and has at last found his true voice. With its sci-fi trappings there is a distinctly alien quality to this recording that is undeniably beautiful – but what makes it truly outstanding is the beating human heart at its core.

5

ROWCHE RUMBLE
IN MY AREA
THE FALL
STEP FORWARD
DID NOT CHART

Mark E. Smith had seen-off all the other original members of The Fall and assumed complete artistic control; from here on in, The Fall would reflect his personality and uncompromising nature. Of course, that is not to say that the band he assembled were mere passengers – far from it – they were young and held their leader in the highest regard but they were talented and idiosyncratic players in their own right, with a good deal of chemistry evident in their interplay. In addition, they were talented tunesmiths too; here Marc Riley and Craig Scanlon wrote a piece inspired by (and supposed to sound like) 'Shake Appeal' by Iggy and the Stooges. However, the two guitarists found that the sheer raw power that Stooge James Williamson had at his fingertips, was not so easily located; they were a different breed with different sensibilities, so their approximation was a spidery, thinner and much stranger thing. Riley instructed the drummer to play a particularly distinctive pattern, while Yvonne Pawlett cranked up her keyboard and delivered harsh drones, as the ever dependable Steve Hanley anchored the whole thrilling cacophony on bass guitar. On top of this rocking platform, Smith produced a sneering, yelped vocal that brought to mind David Johansen of The New York Dolls. The lyric involves the unlikely story of an incident from Smith's days as a shipping clerk on Salford Docks; he claimed that (because of an administrative error) he came into possession of a large shipment of prescription grade tranquillisers. In the song he asserts his preference for "speed and grass" but sets about dispensing the windfall anyway. The veracity or otherwise of this tale is barely worth consideration, because whether it is true, or just a myth-building falsification, it is a gripping and hugely imaginative example of Smith's narrative gift, aligned to the raw but highly exciting musicality of his new band-mates.

4

EVERYBODY'S HAPPY NOWADAYS
WHY CAN'T I TOUCH IT?
BUZZCOCKS
UNITED ARTISTS
29

This opens with a brilliantly simple guitar riff, cleanly played in early-1960s Shadows style, rather than the conventional 1970s rock sound; it is totally distinctive and provides a musical hook between the rhythmic verses that lyrically echo the central theme from the classic Aldous Huxley novel *Brave New World*. Pete Shelley sings at the top of his register, adding a cynical sweetness to the lyric in which the narrator realises that the whole world is artificial and the population are blind to this fact, controlled as they are by drugs that strip them of emotions and feelings; but this dissenting voice is then countered by the assertion that "Everybody's happy nowadays". At the point of release, this was the most daring and adventurous single that Buzzcocks had issued, and paired as it was with the experimental 'Why Can't I Touch It?' on the B-side, a huge swathe of their audience – who wished for nothing more than "meat and two veg" punk rock – were instantly alienated.

3 (JOINTLY)

DEATH DISCO
NO BIRDS DO SING
P.I.L.
VIRGIN

20

MEMORIES
ANOTHER
P.I.L.
VIRGIN
60

John Lydon, Keith Levine and Jah Wobble continued to innovate and astound, taking chances, taking liberties and constantly pushing the envelope – they were massively influential and rightly regarded as (artistically) the most important act around. Obviously that didn't last... they would fall out and fragment but in 1979 they were a magnificent entity, they released these two amazing, unobvious singles. The first one, 'Death Disco', was mistakenly publicised by the music press with the erroneous title 'Death to Disco', before Lydon corrected their preconceptions, informing them that he loved disco and that some of the most innovative and exciting sounds were to be found in that genre. 'Death Disco' was actually a far darker thing than the press had imagined, as it concerned Lydon's vigil at his recently deceased mother's bedside as cancer slowly killed her. She had requested that John write a disco song for her, and with this track he fulfilled her request, serving up a bass heavy, dissonant funk-shuffle that he voiced in a defiant howl, while Keith Levine borrowed a musical quotation from Tchaikovsky's *Swan Lake* that was woven into the track amidst the malevolently violent guitar noise that he conjured up.

'Memories' addressed the useless nostalgia that Lydon despised; even as he sought to move forward with P.I.L., he was constantly reminded of his previous band. Here he condemns those who live in a phoney sepia-tinted world of cosy reminiscences, as the highly danceable mutant funk-stomp of two very different takes of the track are inter-cut with each other, producing extremely jarring results – a wake-up call perhaps? P.I.L. were making up their own rules as they went along; it was a revolution of sound and attitude.

2

DREAM BABY DREAM
RADIATION
SUICIDE
ISLAND
DID NOT CHART

Suicide had shocked, bewildered and repulsed audiences, many of whom bayed for their blood, and angered them to the point where (in Glasgow) an axe was hurled at them. No matter, they were unbowed and unrepentant and unwilling to travel along a musical cul-de-sac. Their next move was totally unexpected; they released 'Dream Baby Dream', a devastatingly beautiful piece of music born from an earlier Suicide song called 'Keep Your Dreams'; that in itself had been pretty but in its new incarnation it was positively blissful, though the machined rhythm meant it was never in any danger whatsoever of being dismissed as just another charming piece of fluff. The record was produced by Ric Ocasek of the brilliant pop act The Cars; Suicide were his favourite band and he gives them a high-quality sound – lush and magisterial, that conjures up an image of walking through an enchanted forest. As Martin Rev busies himself supplying the music, Alan Vega provides the words and the voice. On the face of things, he appears to be encouraging, cajoling, expressing tenderness and positivity… but perhaps that is an oversimplified and superficial reading of the song because

'Dream Baby Dream' could equally well be a mockery of those who cannot face reality, choosing falsehood instead – a life of dreams, whether happy or sad? So, does the song reflect hope or despair? Within this ambiguity lies part of its greatness, because for all its melodic gorgeousness and smooth surface, it definitely doesn't lack edge, and there remains forever a feeling that, buried not too far beneath the surface, there just might be a very sharp sting in the tail.

1

SHE IS BEYOND GOOD AND EVIL
3:38
THE POP GROUP
RADAR
DID NOT CHART

Sarcastically naming themselves The Pop Group, this band actually defied any attempt at categorization. They were formed by a bunch of Bristolian teens with lively, imaginative and enquiring minds – presumably they also had great record collections and easy access to extensive libraries. Although they appreciated the energy of punk, it was too conventional and restrictive, and so they decided to become a funk band. However, such was the wealth of contrasting influences and ideas that coalesced within this highly original entity, the funk plan did not work out as intended. 'She is Beyond Good and Evil' was the band's first release, and it was absolutely ferocious. Taking its title and theme from philosopher Friedrich Nietzsche's writings on the repressive and artificial construct of morality and its acceptance, vocalist Mark Stewart screamed and whispered his fractured lyrics, adhering to no concept whatsoever of what is or is not acceptable. He delivered with frightening intensity, while his band mates surrounded him with extremely uncompromising music that simply could not be pigeonholed. In less than three-and-a-half minutes the band touch on free jazz, dub reggae, funk and avant garde, without settling down on any one particular style - imagine Captain Beefheart joining forces with Ornette Coleman, Can and Bootsy's Rubber Band... The Pop Group leave orthodoxy in shreds and bleeding profusely. Their audacity and power left me breathless, shifted my perspective and opened up a world of possibilities that have shaped and directed my life ever since.

These images are from The Hamsters gig on the John Peel Road Show at Cavendish House in Manchester on November 4 1980 but they convey where I was by the decade's close!

Pictures courtesy of Reynard Toombs